Valuing Wildlife
Economic and Social Perspectives

About the Book and Editors

As the public's perception of the wildlife resource in North America has changed over the past two decades, controversy over direction in wildlife management has emerged. The wildlife profession is now faced with pressures to allocate resources for diverse, and often conflicting, purposes. As a result, it has become increasingly necessary to document the "value dimension" of wildlife. This book, based on a symposium sponsored by the New York Chapter of The Wildlife Society, is designed to serve as a state-of-the-art guide to the methods of determining the economic and social values of wildlife, the applications for environmental impact assessment and mitigation concepts in wildlife valuation, and strategies in wildlife planning and policy.

The contributors examine the ecological value of wildlife, the aesthetic experience of wildlife, the educational and recreational benefits of wildlife, and the philosophical value of wildlife. Their discussions are balanced by case studies in wildlife management that illustrate how wildlife values are derived and utilized, including, for example, essays on managing private lands for wildlife recreation and on the economies of controlling damage to agriculture caused by wildlife. Finally, the authors offer prophetic insights into future needs in wildlife resource management—in research, in planning and policy making, and in communications and education—that will help wildlife professionals influence rather than merely react to the future.

Daniel J. Decker, a well-known wildlife extension educator and researcher in human dimensions of wildlife management, has authored numerous papers dealing with wildlife resource values. Dr. Decker and his colleagues in the Human Dimensions Research Unit, Department of Natural Resources, Cornell University, have conducted dozens of studies relating to the human dimensions of wildlife utilization and management. His extension responsibilities have led to the publication of over 100 articles, circulars, and information bulletins to further public education on wildlife and wildlife management. Decker received his Ph.D. degree from Cornell University. **Gary R. Goff** is an extension associate with the Department of Natural Resources, Cornell University. His expertise spans the gamut of woodland management concerns, including wildlife management. Among his many extension publications are several dealing with wildlife resource appreciation and management. Goff has been involved with the planning and implementation of several extension and research projects dealing with wildlife values. Through his extension programs he has addressed hundreds of private landowners on the integration of wildlife values into woodland management decisions. Goff received his B.S. degree from Cornell University and his M.S. from SUNY–College of Environmental Science and Forestry at Syracuse, New York.

Cooperators

Support in a variety of forms by the following organizations and agencies made this symposium possible.

- Fish and Wildlife Service, U.S. Department of the Interior
- Renewable Resources Extension Program of Cornell Cooperative Extension, Department of Natural Resources, New York State College of Agriculture and Life Sciences
- State University of New York, College of Environmental Science and Forestry
- New York State Department of Environmental Conservation
- National Wildlife Federation
- Natural Resources and Rural Development Unit, Extension Service, U.S. Department of Agriculture
- Wildlife Management Institute
- The Wildlife Society
- International Association of Fish and Wildlife Agencies
- Soil Conservation Service, U.S. Department of Agriculture, Syracuse, NY, and Washington, DC
- New York Cooperative Fish and Wildlife Research Unit, Fish and Wildlife Service, U.S. Department of the Interior
- Human Dimensions in Wildlife Study Group
- National Park Service, U.S. Department of the Interior
- Ducks Unlimited, Inc.
- Laboratory of Ornithology, Cornell University
- National Audubon Society
- National Institute for Urban Wildlife
- Forest Service, U.S. Department of Agriculture
- Northeast Association of Fish and Wildlife Agencies
- Conservation Education Association
- Division of Wildlife, Bureau of Land Management, U.S. Department of the Interior

Valuing Wildlife
Economic and Social Perspectives

edited by Daniel J. Decker
and Gary R. Goff

Foreword by Robert E. Chambers

Westview Press / Boulder and London

Published in cooperation with The New York Chapter—
The Wildlife Society

Westview Special Studies in Natural Resources and Energy Management

Copyright © 1987 by Westview Press, Inc.

Published in 1987 in the United States of America by Westview Press, Inc.; Frederick A. Praeger, Publisher; 5500 Central Avenue, Boulder, Colorado 80301

Library of Congress Cataloging-in-Publication Data
Valuing wildlife.
  (Westview special studies in natural resources and
energy management)
  "Based on a symposium sponsored by the Wildlife
Society"—P.
  1. Wildlife conservation—Economic aspects—
Congresses.   2. Wildlife conservation—Social aspects—
Congresses.   3. Wildlife management—Economic aspects—
Congresses.   4. Wildlife management—Social aspects—
Congresses.   5. Zoology, Economic—Congresses. 6. Ani-
mals and civilization—Congresses. I. Decker, Daniel J.
II. Goff, Gary R.   III. Wildlife Society.   IV. Series.
QL81.5.V35   1987   333.95′16   86-11002
ISBN 0-8133-7120-1

Printed and bound in the United States of America

∞ The paper used in this publication meets the requirements of the American National Stan-
     dard for Permanence of Paper for Printed Library Materials Z39.48-1984.

10   9   8   7   6   5   4

Contents

vii

Figures

Tables

Foreword

Robert E. Chambers

Just as it was my privilege and great pleasure to welcome symposium attendees on behalf of the New York Chapter of The Wildlife Society to "Economic and Social Values of the Wildlife Resource," so it is my pleasure to introduce the proceedings.

It is particularly appropriate that those in The Wildlife Society be responsible for production of this book since one of the society's stated objectives is "to increase awareness and appreciation of all wildlife values." The idea for the symposium evolved from discussions of our chapter executive committee regarding an appropriate theme for the annual program. The timeliness of the topic, the presence in our membership of several key people active in wrestling with the questions of wildlife values, and a desire to create a program of national significance all led to the convening of the symposium.

The questions and concerns surrounding wildlife values are not new. Many of our pioneer professional leaders—Aldo Leopold, Paul Errington, Ralph King, and Charles Stoddard (to name but a few)—early recognized the variety of social and economic dimensions of the wildlife resource to humankind. They underscored our need to identify and project these values to a society and a world driven by the forces of cash income, profit motive, and a soaring technology, which were eliminating wildlife and its habitat at a prodigious rate through deforestation, intensified agriculture, wetland drainage, development, and pollution. Wildlife was losing because it lacked perceived value to many segments of society and because its value was not projected in terms understood by those in the courtrooms, legislative halls, and the marketplace.

Fortunately, the profession's growing understanding of the need to better define and convey the values of our wildlife resource has been bolstered by the public forces evolving from the environmental movement of the 1960s and 1970s. Legislative mandates such as the Multiple Use Act and Endangered Species Act have clearly underscored the value that society places on wildlife and have demonstrated the potential of noneconomic levers available to those concerned with the machinery of wildlife management. More recent federal decisions to utilize economic values in resource management decision making, as well as the need to derive replacement cost figures for wildlife in court and other legal proceedings, have propelled us to work toward what Charles Stoddard pleaded for in 1951—"a more intensive development of a branch of knowledge devoted to the economics of wildlife management."

As early as 1938, Aldo Leopold stated that "the economic cards are stacked against some of the most important reforms in land use." We hope that through our efforts in this symposium and those that follow we will help restack the deck to ensure a more secure and lasting future for our wildlife resource.

The members of the New York Chapter would like to express their greatest appreciation and highest compliments to the program committee for an outstanding job of assembling a most stimulating and valuable symposium—a landmark in the evolution of wildlife resource management. The response to our requests for assistance has been both extremely gratifying and essential to our confidence and success in presenting this proceedings. To the many cooperators and to all the individual professionals and students who contributed their time, talents, and resources, we extend our deepest gratitude and sincere thanks.

Preface

As society has changed so has the public's perception of the wildlife resource in North America. Conflicts in management direction are inevitable, and documented social and economic values are increasingly necessary if wildlife and other natural resource professionals are to deal successfully with the pressures and concerns levied on natural resources. For these reasons, the New York Chapter of The Wildlife Society sponsored an international symposium for the exchange of ideas and experiences entitled the "Economic and Social Values of the Wildlife Resource."

The symposium provided a forum for wildlife and other natural resource professionals in administration, extension, research, education, and management to discuss this important realm of resource management. Leaders in the field gave presentations outlining state-of-the-art techniques and results. To complement the formal presentations, the symposium included a series of workshops designed to provide hands-on experience for participants.

All natural resource professionals should find this book, based on the symposium papers, a valuable resource for integrating the "value" dimension of resource management into their work. This is an era of public participation in resource management decisions; even those areas traditionally most remote from the management interface are no longer isolated from economic and social considerations. For example, wildlife researchers today must deal with animal welfare concerns advocated so strongly by animal rights groups—concerns that influence both laboratory and field work. This poignant illustration shows how compelling and unavoidable the manifestations of social values can be on all aspects of natural resource management.

Documentation for economic values of natural resources has become increasingly important. Mitigation of the impacts that all forms of development projects may have on natural resources typically requires economic data. Lack of such information impairs decision makers' ability to compare the benefits and costs of proposed projects. The wildlife manager, for instance, must have facts about the economic as well as ecological impacts of water development projects on wildlife habitat or must accept defeat by favorable cost/benefit ratios that do not include the wildlife element. Like it or not, we must recognize that economic data are perceived as concrete indicators of value and can be used persuasively for—or against—the welfare of wildlife resources.

Natural resource professionals who believe that they can sequester themselves and concentrate on biological or ecological study apart from social and economic influences are naive, misled, or both. Social and economic values and the pressures they exert pervade all aspects of natural resource management today. This book provides insights into the origin, dimensions, and implications of economic and social values of wildlife resource management. It provides extensive but not exhaustive coverage of the topic; it is often provocative, if not always definitive. The authors of the individual chapters and the editors of this book hope that it will enhance understanding of the dynamic interplay among economic and social values with wildlife management.

D. J. Decker
G. R. Goff

Acknowledgments

The "Economic and Social Values of the Wildlife Resource" symposium, which served as the basis for this book, fostered better understanding of the economic and social values of wildlife management. Interest in the symposium and this book came from many quarters, and many forms of assistance made this undertaking possible. We will attempt to acknowledge some of these.

The idea for the symposium was originated by the 1985 officers of the New York Chapter—The Wildlife Society, the sponsor of the symposium. Robert Chambers, Robert Inslerman, and Robert Sanford were instrumental in providing logistical support for the planning stages.

The program committee struggled through the difficult task of specifying the topics to be covered at the symposium. Academic and management interests were well represented by John Kelley and Stuart Free, respectively. Gordon Robertson and William Porter, with assistance from students and support staff from SUNY–College of Environmental Science and Forestry, worked diligently on publicity and local arrangements.

Details of manuscript review and last-minute revisions were greatly facilitated by staff members of the Department of Natural Resources, Cornell University, particularly Margie Peech, Claudia Ng, Nancy Connelly, Laura Mattei, and Nancy Bowers.

The most significant contributions were made by the session chairmen and the many authors. Their willingness to share their combined knowledge and insight has made the symposium and this book a truly valuable resource.

Among the list of cooperators are several organizations that provided financial support for the production of this book: USFWS, Office of Extension and Publications; USDA, Extension Service, Natural Resources and Rural Development Unit; Cornell Cooperative Extension, Renewable Resources Extension Program; New York State Department of Environmental Conservation, Bureau of Wildlife; SUNY–College of Environmental Science and Forestry; National Wildlife Federation; USFWS,

New York Cooperative Fish and Wildlife Research Unit; Wildlife Management Institute; The Wildlife Society. The commitment of these agencies and organizations and of all the other cooperators to this endeavor is gratefully acknowledged.

This book is dedicated to the individuals, named and unnamed in this acknowledgment, who contributed their talents to the symposium.

D.J.D.
G.R.G.

Valuing Wildlife

Economic and Social Perspectives

PART ONE

The Values of
the Wildlife Resource

Introduction

Harold W. Steinhoff

Asking significant questions is thought by some to be supremely important—even more vital than providing answers. We shall try in this book, and in this part, to do both. Some questions may help us later measure our progress in answers and provide a challenge for future exploration.

What do we mean by "values"? Each of us has our own concept of the term's meaning clearly in mind, but we cannot really understand what others mean until we have probed their minds. This book will help us do that. Simple words cannot express precise meanings; whole thought patterns must be explored. For example, several chapters touch on the operative value system as shown in the following illustration:

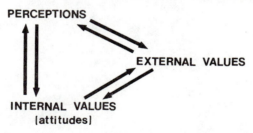

The arrows stand for the word *affect*. And this leads us to a second question.

Is there a universally acceptable and comprehensive conceptual system for organizing our thoughts about values? The many proposed sets of value categories are evidence that many thinkers have tried to define such a system. Even in this part we shall explore the degree to which economic values and social values are mutually exclusive categories while simultaneously looking for evidence that they are merely different viewpoints of the same body of thought. Categories we construct depend upon our experiences and the mind-set of our academic discipline, which our education has produced. Can we, by coming together and sharing our perspectives, arrive at an agreed anatomy for ideas of "value"? In doing so, we may need to find some answers to a third question.

Why do people hold the values they do? Surely the chapters in this book will provide parts of the answer. But we need the help of several disciplines, including at least sociology, psychology, and perhaps endocrinology to explore the constructs further. The principle that knowing "why" is even more important than knowing "what" will surely hold. We still seem only to be at the surface of this exploration; we must go deeper, which will lead us to a fourth general question.

What should our ethical position be with regard to values? As professionals, are we obliged only to support the values of our resource—wildlife in this case? Or should we take the broader view and support all resources or all of humankind's needs and wants? Is our primary objective to *understand* value systems? Is the wildlife administrator to hold one set of values, the wildlife management biologist another, the wildlife researcher another, and the economist still another?

And finally, what can we learn from history? Have the authors of this book taken advantage of the experiences of the past? Will the book be regarded in the future as a significant milestone in the development of the understanding of wildlife values? We think yes. We also think that you will agree upon reading Chapter 1.

Chapter 1

Socioeconomic Values
of the Wildlife Resource:
Are We Really Serious?

Jack H. Berryman

The proceedings based on the symposium, convened by the New York Chapter of The Wildlife Society, will make a very positive contribution to a rather neglected component of wildlife resource management. The International Association of Fish and Wildlife Agencies is pleased to be a cooperator.

I am honored to keynote this symposium, although I am also somewhat apprehensive. Even though I have long been an advocate of economic incentives and directly involved in the social impacts of resource decisions, I have no expertise in the technical aspects of the socioeconomic facets of resource management. The symposium program indicates that the state of the art will be very well covered by some of the most competent workers in both fields.

I do, however, consider myself something of an expert in the problems and issues that confront, frustrate, confound, and sometimes even topple fish and wildlife administrators and threaten the future of our wildlife resources and their sound management. So, I would like to speak from the vantage point of one who knows about the losses and reverses that are being experienced and the role that socioeconomic data play in these issues.

The International Association of Fish and Wildlife Agencies is composed of the fish and wildlife managing agencies of the state, provincial, and federal governments of the U.S., Canada, and Mexico. Because these agencies have legal responsibility for wildlife resources and their habitats, they daily grapple with the thorny problems of management and with their socioeconomic implications.

There is a general consensus among agency administrators that two of the most ominous threats facing wildlife managers are (1) the continuing loss of habitat and (2) the animal rights movement. I would like to pose questions as to whether socioeconomic tools are being used in the solutions to these and other major problems, and if they are not, why not. Do we really have the will to use these tools?

- Are we using the tools we have and are we using them effectively? Are we, in the field of wildlife management, even willing to use and apply sociological and economic data; or are we expending much of our energy in reaching for the next survey, the last decimal, the ultimate refinement?
- How are major resource decisions being made? Are social and economic values being considered in a sophisticated way?
- Is economic and sociological information finding its way into public wildlife education programs and are these reaching the right public?

The search for economic yardsticks has gone on for decades and must continue. There remains the need for economic and sociological data to evaluate energy and other types of development projects, to develop mitigation plans, to support legal actions, to set planning and development priorities, and to make possible negotiations on very complex questions of resource allocation and use. Such data must become part of the decision-making and planning process, along with biological data, engineering feasibility studies, reviews of legislative authority, and so on. Until reliable data are available, fish and wildlife interests and resources will not be a full partner at the bargaining table.

Although we already have a considerable body of socioeconomic information, the question is whether existing information is being used in the solution of the major issues of the day. We know the gross impact of fishing and hunting as a result of the 1980 Survey of Fishing and Hunting, and the 1985 survey is now in preparation. In general terms, we know the economic impact of wildlife depredations caused by various species; we have general information on the value of and public participation in the nonconsumptive uses of wildlife as a result of Shaw and Mangun's 1984 Survey of Nonconsumptive Use of Wildlife in the United States, conducted by the Fish and Wildlife Service. These broad surveys, plus a host of more detailed studies, provide clear, strong, and scientifically valid evidence of the economic importance of and the public interest in wildlife resources and their uses. And that impact and that interest are indeed very significant.

Despite this knowledge—more than we have ever had before—wetlands are being drained and other habitats lost at an alarming rate. And it is painfully clear that public decisions, prompted by the animal rights movement, are disrupting sound, professional wildlife resource management programs. The objective of the animal rights movement is to halt or greatly curtail the killing or harvest of wildlife. Two examples are the prohibition of the leghold trap in New Jersey and the failure to extend the North Pacific Fur Seal Treaty between this country, Canada, Japan, and Russia. There are many other examples but these illustrate the point.

The New Jersey decision, which has halted the use of leghold traps in that state, was made strictly on the basis of popular emotional appeal. The New Jersey fur management program had a sound scientific basis: The fur harvest was economically important. The destruction of the harp seal industry in Canada and the campaign to turn public opinion against fur had a negative impact on the European fur market. It likewise was based on emotional appeal. So, too, has been the threat to Senate action to extend the Fur Seal Convention. Again, the harp and fur seal management programs were soundly based resource management programs—as a matter of fact, classics in successful management—with strong supporting economic data and known and predictable sociological impacts upon several segments of the public. To halt the harvest is a serious management reverse. Because of public decision fueled by emotional appeal, responsible state, provincial, and federal governments have been denied the opportunity to manage these resources for the benefit of all people. There is a loss to the resource, a loss to the public at large, and a severe setback for responsible management. Economic and sociological information just did not play a signficant role in these animal rights decisions or in decisions that result in the loss of wetlands and other critical habitats.

Despite more data supporting the great economic and social values of wildlife resources than ever before, wildlife management is suffering more reverses than ever before. We need to ask ourselves why. Are we using all the tools available in the most effective way possible? It is useful to explore how wildlife professionals look upon the disciplines of economics and sociology and the results of their studies and how the workers in these fields look upon themselves. And, very important, how do the decision makers—the legislators and administrators—look on these disciplines and their workers?

Through the years I have felt that sociology and economics have been considered overly academic disciplines—related but nevertheless removed from the real-world business of wildlife management. And perhaps this is the way that economic and social researchers have looked upon themselves—as contributors and scientists—somewhat removed and aloof from the day-to-day management battles and the politics of resource management. Too often the economists and the sociologists have sequestered themselves by maintaining rather closed clubs and reporting to themselves in their own journals, in their own circles, and as members of their respective associations. There are, of course, some notable exceptions, these are the pioneers, the people who make this kind of symposium possible. And the legislators and administrators seem to have somewhat shared these views. Too often they have failed to see either the need or the usefulness of applying economic and sociological tools to the management regime. Quite simply, the besieged administrator does not need a survey: He knows he is in trouble.

I believe that the members of the wildlife field as a whole—the practicing wildlife researchers and managers—have found it somewhat repugnant to apply the obvious economic values to the uses of wildlife resources. We have documented the values but resisted commercialism of the resource and application of the known economic tools. We have resisted virtually every form of paid hunting. We have only scratched the surface of landowner incentives—easements, tax incentives, land-owner reimbursement—all the while quoting the economic impact of expenditures made for the uses of fish and wildlife; all the while quoting the various opinion polls on public support for various aspects of conservation and a wholesome environment. Taking comfort in the values is not an adequate approach as competition for a fixed resource base increases and the pressures of growing human populations intensify the demand for food and fiber, all within a capitalistic and competitive economic system. Clearly we must bring economic principles to bear in the management of the nation's fish and wildlife resources or they shall continue to be considered as marginal luxury products rather than as a part of the matrix of planning and developing the full uses of our land and water resources.

We managers want fish and wildlife resources to remain a part of the fabric of our total landscape and environment. If this is really our "conservation ethic," then we must undertake research and find ways to make the maintenance of habitat compatible and competitive with other land uses.

This subject was discussed at the 1983 North American Wildlife and Natural Resources Conference in a special session on Emerging Non-Federal Initiatives in Resource Management, chaired by Christopher Leman. At that session, Neave and Goulden (1983:412) reported that the Canadian experience had been "that the success of the manager will depend not so much on budget, but on his ability to influence major financial and land use institutions." And, on the U.S. side, Metzger (1983) observed that success depends as much on economic viability as on land use. Teer et al. (1983) and Smith et al. (1983) made similar observations on the need for economic incentives.

A major impediment to progress is a philosophical and institutional gap between the wildlife biologists and administrators on the one hand and the sociologists and economists on the other. Something of a philosophical gap appears to exist between the economists and the sociologists. These gaps must be bridged if the economic and sociological tools now available and those yet to be developed are ever to be fully integrated and incorporated in the decision-making process. The starting place is probably at the professional working level.

As professional wildlifers, we must overcome our repugnance and reluctance to enter the marketplace. Success in applying socioeconomic tools depends upon our willingness to employ new approaches and every tool, including partnership and cooperation, and upon our ability to influence political, financial and land use institutions at the local, state and federal levels and to make wildlife economically viable. It is to our advantage to take the initiative—not to fight a rearguard action.

The educational programs of wildlife resource agencies and organizations must include understandable information on economics and sociology. Most educational information deals with the wonders of wildlife, its habitats, and its management. But until the public is fully aware of the value of fish and wildlife resources, the economic uses of those resources, and the sociology of its uses, we will continue to lose habitat itself and to lose ground to the advocates of the animal rights movement. Its protectionist line has great popular appeal, and the citizens and their responses to policy makers and legislators influence the future course of events. The animal rightists are doing a more effective job of reaching the public with emotional appeals than we are with legitimate education. It is imperative that the public understands that it is best served by a managed and utilized resource and that there are sound economic and sociological reasons for doing so. The principal tool of the animal rights movement is its knowledge that wild creatures have great appeal. Its members have not bothered to measure the appeal; it does not need to be measured; it exists. (For a very scholarly, educational analysis of the animal rights movement, see Herscovici, *Second Nature— The Animal Rights Controversy,* 1985.)

Wildlife can be a very evocative subject. As a consequence, the sociologist has placed a major emphasis on attitudinal surveys rather than studies on the social impact of decisions. We need to know more about the impact of a decision—not just what people think of the involved animal. Emphasis has been on the welfare of the animal at the expense of the welfare of affected humans. We also need the help of the sociologist and the political scientist to determine how to make rational decisions more acceptable to the public before, not after, the fact.

The future approach should involve the application and uses of socioeconomic tools in the decision and political processes with less emphasis on further surveys and refinement of data. The inclusion of such data and tools as parts of the decision-making process and the development and implementation of management programs would represent a real breakthrough. This approach will require the following steps:

1. We survey what we know, that we more effectively use what we have, and that we carefully prioritize our future work—especially during a period of prolonged budget constraint.
2. We give a high priority to finding ways of bridging the philosophical and institutional gaps between managers and administrators and socioeconomic workers.
3. We concentrate efforts to find ways of bringing economic principles to bear in the decisions affecting the management of fish and wildlife resources.
4. We increase studies and education on the social impact of decisions.
5. We make a planned effort to encourage wildlifers to overcome their repugnance to the use of economic tools.
6. We broaden public educational programs to include socioeconomic coverage.

Success in ensuring sound, balanced decision making and marshaling public support will require the full integration of socioeconomic tools into the management scenario.

In 1957—28 years ago—Pierre Dansereau (1957) pointed out that conservation had undergone four distinct phases: legislative, biological, ecological, and sociological. The scientific approach is not enough because it does not always provide satisfactory answers for the social, political and economic aspects of natural resource utilization. The achievements of scientific management can be realized only within the framework of the accepted sociological structure: fish and wildlife management is now in the sociological phase. I think it is time to give real meaning to the sociological stage. Let us get on with it.

REFERENCES

DANSEREAU, P. 1957. Biogeography, an ecological perspective. Ronald Press Co., New York. 395pp.
HERSCOVICI, A. 1985. Second nature—the animal rights controversy. CBC Enterprises, Montreal. 254pp.
METZGER, P. C. 1983. Public-private partnership for land conservation. Trans. North Am. Wildl. and Nat. Resour. Conf. 48:423–432.
NEAVE, D., AND R. GOULDEN. 1983. Provincial wildlife revenue sources and commitments. Trans. North Am. Wildl. and Nat. Resour. Conf. 48:405–412.

SHAW, W. W., AND W. R. MANGUN. 1984. Nonconsumptive use of wildlife in the United States. U.S. Fish and Wildl. Serv. Resour. Publ. 154, Washington, D.C. 20pp.

SMITH, R. J., J. GOLDSTEIN, AND R. K. DAVIS. 1983. Economic incentives as a conservation strategy for nongame and endangered species of wildlife. Trans. North Am. Wildl. and Nat. Resour. Conf. 48:457–467.

TEER, J. G., G. V. BURGER, AND C. Y. DEKNATEL. 1983. State-supported habitat management and commercial hunting on private lands in the United States. Trans. North Am. Wildl. and Nat. Resour. Conf. 48:445–456.

Chapter 2

Social Values Defined

Perry J. Brown and Michael J. Manfredo

In an ecological sense, all wildlife have value: To birders, all birds have value, but rare birds are more valuable than common birds; to sheep ranchers, coyotes are varmints with a negative value; to mayors of rural communities, elk have market value because they bring hunters who buy gasoline and food. Because of different perspectives, wildlife have either positive or negative value, depending upon human perspective, and the magnitude of value depends upon a plethora of mediating circumstances. Within this context the difficult task of this chapter is to identify and define the social values of wildlife among the many kinds and views of value.

Several researchers have noted a problem in using the term *values* because of the ambiguity of its definition (Shaw and Zube 1980, Steinhoff 1980). In addition to its lay usage, the term has acquired different meanings across and within academic disciplines. Our intent is to specify a social definition for the term and discuss its applicability to the study and management of wildlife.

What do we mean by *value* and what do we value? Steinhoff (1980:11) made a useful distinction in presenting two meanings: "(1) a value . . . is an attitude which results in the value of a thing. (2) The value of a thing is its worth in relation to other things." The distinction here is that there are values about things and values of things. T. Brown (1984) makes the distinction clearer in introducing the notions of "held value" and "assigned value." Held values can be viewed as precepts and ideals held by an individual about something, whereas assigned values can be viewed as the relative importance or worth of something. According to Brown, held values are concepts about objects and assigned values focus on and indicate the worth of these same objects. Held and assigned values are related in that held values regulate preferences that function to assign relative value to objects.

These two kinds of value are operative on several objects of value. Objects of value include ideas, goods, services, behaviors, opportunities for behavior, outcomes of behavior, experiences, and benefits. Ideas are thoughts; goods are merchandise; services are work done for others; behaviors are actions; opportunities are favorable combinations of circumstances for actions or for the realization of outcomes; outcomes are the individual results of behaviors; experiences are combinations of salient outcomes; benefits are outcomes directly tied to goal achievement. Although held and assigned values can be attached to each of these objects, we tend to associate held values more with ideas, behaviors, outcomes, experiences, and benefits and assigned values more with goods, services, and opportunities.

This distinction of held and assigned values is recognized in the social-psychological literature by authors such as Rokeach (1968) and Bem (1970). In this literature, values are described as a particular class of attitudes. Bem (1970:16) stated that "a value is a primitive preference for a positive attitude toward certain end-states of existence (such as equality, salvation, self-fulfillment or freedom) or certain modes of conduct (such as courage, honesty, friendship or chastity)."

Further, Bem (1970) proposed that beliefs (attitudes are defined as evaluative beliefs) are built one upon another and that the human cognitive structure can be viewed as a three-dimensional lattice of beliefs. Higher order attitudes, such as "coyotes are bad," might be traced through a sequence of syllogistic reasoning to basic attitudes (values), such as "security is important to me and my family." The structure of belief might be (1) coyotes are bad because they eat sheep, (2) sheep provide income for me and my family, and (3) income provides security for me and my family. The value of security might also serve as the basis for a host of other higher order attitudes such as "defense spending is good" and "gun control is bad."

A second usage of the term *value* is attained by noting that people differ in the relative importance they place on values. For example, Rokeach (1968) distinguished between civil rights proponents and opponents by the relative importance they placed on the values of freedom and equality. This is the second popular usage of the term *value*, the relative importance of something.

These concepts, held and assigned values, suggest two basic questions for wildlife management: (1) What values form the basis for our attitudes toward wildlife, and (2) what wildlife types and numbers, the settings in which they reside, and the opportunities they provide are most valued by people?

Researchers distinguish a third kind of value in the literature— intrinsic value of objects (Rolston 1983). Intrinsic values are not assigned by humans but rather are inherent in the object or its relationships to other objects. For example, the ecosystemic, or ecological role, value of an object or the organismic value of an object exists apart from human experience. These values are independent of human perception and preference and thus are only dealt with in this chapter when humans incorporate them into their preference realm. We do not explicitly deal with them here because they do not pertain to society and thus are not social.

CATEGORIES OF VALUED OBJECTS

We can approach objects of value in different ways. We can categorize by making a general list of types of objects and refine our list by narrowing our attention to clear and unambiguous objects such as cars or college degrees or deer-hunting opportunities. We can classify objects by their attributes, such as red cars, fast cars, roomy cars, and sleek cars. We can look at different ways that people might behave toward objects, such as adopting or resisting use of new products, promoting radical ideas, or hoarding scarce goods. And we can categorize objects by their function as viewed from different academic disciplines, such as economics, sociology, and biology. This last approach to categorization characterizes our look at values since the symposium sponsor has channeled our attention to social and economic values.

The objects of our attention do not change with this disciplinary look; what changes is the way we view the objects. We essentially put on different colored glasses to see the objects in different light. For example, if we look at them from an economic perspective we might be concerned with their exchange value and thus their prices relative to other objects. If we look at them from a social perspective we might be concerned about their importance in promoting democratization or in fostering personal health.

Economic values, held and especially assigned, pervade the thinking in Western society. They are the values generally associated with production, consumption, and exchange of goods and services. Rolston (1985) offers a view of these values that we accept when he suggests that market prices—those indicators of values that we most often label economic values—are the most subservient values, being overridden by values of individual preference values that themselves are overridden by values of individual good, societal preference, and societal good, all of which are superimposed on the underlying ecosystem.

Following Rolston's argument we illustrate the relationships among social, economic, and intrinsic values in Figure 2.1. There social values (those of or pertaining to society) encompass economic values (those of or pertaining to the production, development, and management of material wealth) and rest upon intrinsic values (those of or pertaining

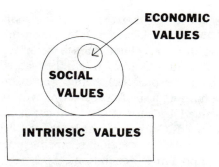

Figure 2.1 Relationships among social, economic, and intrinsic values

to natural processes). The relationships inherent in Figure 2.1 suggest that values other than assigned economic values are enormously important: They are both the source of market values and determinants in making correct decisions for individuals and society. Many of these other values might be difficult to bring into decisions, but that difficulty does not justify ignoring them.

SOCIAL VALUES

Exclusive of economic values we identify four subcategories of social values: cultural, societal, psychological, and physiological. These are social values because they deal directly with the functioning of individuals or societies; they are of or pertaining to society. Each of these subcategories can be subdivided even further.

Cultural values are those held values about the ideas and thoughts that make up a culture. Often they refer to ethics and other predilections that regulate the way societies behave. Within the natural resources arena, for example, a society could develop the idea that "wildlife have standing" and then regulate behavior to adhere to this precept. Also, cultural values regarding either fear or adulation of wildlife are common within different cultures, and for such cultures cultural values are clearly associated with wildlife.

Societal values focus on those held values relating to social relationships among people. Family, social cohesion, and community use values would fit into this subcategory. Examples in the wildlife arena would be values, such as the family togetherness that might be fostered through birding together, the cohesion that might be developed within a group of people working to feed deer during a hard winter, and the community focus and pride that can develop around facilities such as the National Elk Refuge at Jackson Hole, Wyoming.

Psychological values are related to the benefits that one perceives from the object of value. Objects might be valued because they are perceived to enhance personal well-being. For example, wildlife might be valued because hunting leads to satisfaction with one's self-sufficiency. They might be valued because studying them leads to learning more about the natural world. Or they might be valued because knowing that they exist might provide satisfaction regarding one's responsibility to "spaceship earth" and future generations.

Physiological value also may be associated with wildlife if the pursuit of wildlife leads to improving health and functioning of the human body. For example, we might attach value to wildlife because in the pursuit of wildlife, hunters and other recreationists might perceive that they are enhancing their health through exercise, change of pace, and reduction of stress.

Among these subcategories of social values, the psychological values—those having to do with satisfaction of motives or changes in attitude or personality—have been most studied, and a fairly extensive list has been produced of the personal kinds of satisfaction from engagements with wildlife. For example, such authors as More (1973), Potter et al. (1973), Stankey et al. (1973), P. Brown et al. (1977), Hautaluoma and P. Brown (1978), and Hautaluoma et al. (1982) have identified different valued outcomes from use of different wildlife species. Likewise, such authors as Spaulding (1970), Knopf et al. (1973), Driver and Knopf (1976), Kennedy and P. Brown (1976), Driver and Cooksey (1978), and Manfredo et al. (1980, 1984) have identified different valued outcomes associated with fishing.

Only a little study has been devoted to the other subcategories of social value. Still, regarding societal values we find papers such as Orthner's (1976) work on leisure and marital interactions and Sofranko and Nolan's (1972) study of socialization toward participation in hunting and fishing activities; regarding cultural values Kellert's (1980) research on Americans' attitudes stands out; regarding physiological values we have studies such as Wellman's (1979) study of the function of fishing in fostering escape from privacy stress.

We have discussed these various subcategories of social value in terms of held values, although many of the authors cited have transformed such held values into statements of preference and assigned values. For example, the research by Driver and Cooksey (1978) on fishing outcomes used Likert-type psychometric scales to enable rating and ranking the importance of different outcomes.

SOCIAL VALUES AND WILDLIFE MANAGEMENT

To provide a framework for integration of social values into a management context, we can view wildlife management and use in terms of production processes (Fig. 2.2). The model in the figure is an adaptation of the recreation production process models of Driver and Rosenthal (1982) and P. Brown (1984).

The management production of opportunities for use of wildlife involves manipulation of land, labor, and capital (animals being a part of the land component), ensuring the production of animal populations and associated environmental situations in specific areas. Management activities such as planning, allocating, constructing, manipulating vegetation, and regulating users might be involved in this process. Of course, some opportunities for use are produced naturally without human intervention.

An output of these activities is wildlife opportunities in specific quantities and of specific qualities. That is, wildlife of various species and quality are produced in specific quantities in specific settings where they might either be used on-site or harvested and used off-site for a multiplicity of purposes. This production of a variety of wildlife opportunities, using the notions inherent in the recreation opportunity spectrum, has been discussed elsewhere (Brown 1982).

A second production process involves the wildlife user's interacting with these opportunities for wildlife use. Consumers of opportunities for use enter the scene with specific goals, time, financial resources, equipment, skills, and experiences and often in specific social groups (e.g., work and leisure groups). The opportunities to use wildlife that are provided by management are a factor in the production of experiences for these consumers. The users engage in such activities as hunting, photographing, hiking, fishing, and sightseeing in the process of using these opportunities to produce experiences. The immediate results of these activities are individual outcomes, with the set of outcomes that are salient to the user making up the experience (Brown 1983).

A third production process transforms experiences with wildlife into user and societal benefits. Cognitive (e.g., evaluation) and physiological (e.g., chemical change) processes are involved in user transformation of experiences to benefits, and societal (e.g., organization of institutions) processes, often mediated by individual user benefits, are involved in transforming experiences into societal benefits. Between the immediate realized experiences and the production of benefits might be several transformations, since between the first outcome and the ultimate outcome there might be several intermediate outcomes (Lawler 1973).

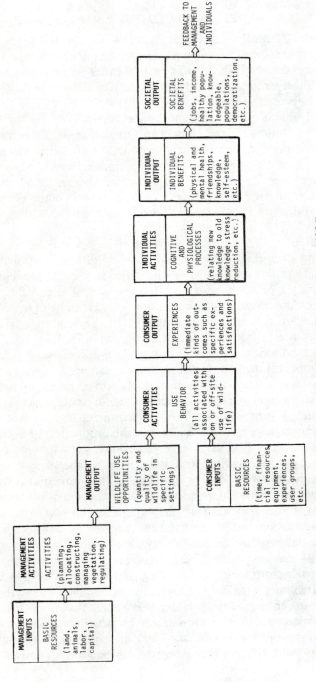

Figure 2.2 Processes for producing wildlife benefits (Adapted from P. Brown 1984)

Not shown in Figure 2.2 are the production of societal benefits directly from management and consumer activities. These can be particularly important in considering economic benefits such as jobs and income, but they are not described here because we discuss only social values.

In terms of our discussion of values of wildlife, held values can relate to any one of the boxes shown in Figure 2.2. Held values will be used to define basic resources and appropriate management activities. They will help define the relevancy of different opportunities to use wildlife and thus whether the outputs of management will be accepted by users. Held values will to some extent regulate user behavior and thus affect the kinds of experiences realized. Held values will be mediating factors in the processing of experiential information and in the transforming of that information into individual and societal benefits. How society views individual benefits and the social systems designed to provide benefits will be regulated by held values too.

Assigned values could be derived for any of the input, activity, and output phases of production shown in Figure 2.2, but more commonly one will focus on the worth of the outputs. For management planning we are often very concerned about the worth of opportunities to use wildlife. A basic question is how much is it worth to provide a particular wildlife opportunity. Another question is whether this worth can be translated into an appropriate price for the opportunity. A third question is how important is one opportunity relative to other opportunities. The consumer also is interested in assigning value to opportunities to use wildlife. The consumer needs to determine the importance of the opportunity relative to his available time, energy, and financial resources.

Some theories of psychology and consumer economics suggest that the consumer's assignment of value to the opportunity depends upon his or her assignment of value to outcomes, experiences, and benefits associated with use (Lancaster 1966, Lawler 1973, Fishbein and Ajzen 1975, Sinden and Worrell 1979). We have already suggested that consumers have held values for outcomes, experiences, and benefits and that in some instances assigned values have been derived regarding outcomes of engagement with wildlife and fish. According to the way we have previously defined social values, most of the values associated with outcomes, experiences, and benefits can be classified as social values, and we can assign worth to these values by using either monetary or other metrics, the selection of metric depending upon the purpose of assigning value.

It would appear then that assigned values regarding wildlife and their use could be useful in wildlife management. They can be used in allocating resources in land use planning, they can be used to establish appropriate prices for access to the resource, they can be used by consumers in deciding whether or not to take advantage of opportunities, and they can be used to estimate the importance of various outcomes and benefits of engagement with wildlife.

The social values that concern us here—cultural, societal, psychological and physiological values—can be both held and assigned. They are revealed when we consider the consumer, individual, and societal outputs of Figure 2.2. That is, they are revealed in the kinds of outcomes and experiences that are realized by users of wildlife and in the kinds of individual and societal benefits obtained from engagement with wildlife. Although the ultimate social benefits of wildlife use are likely limited to a few broad categories such as physical and mental health, education, self-concept development, and employment, there is a vast array of social experiences and specific outcomes that might be valued. Many of these have been revealed in the literature regarding use of wildlife and fish and attest to the fact that people see many social values of wildlife population.

CONCLUSIONS

The many different objects of value in the social experiences and outcomes associated with wildlife and fish and the different levels of value make valuing wildlife for decision making a challenging process. One major problem is that we have very little scientific information regarding the social values of wildlife. What objects are valued in what ways? How are these values developed, how do they change, and how persistent are they? We have some information about values of outcomes, especially psychological outcomes of freshwater fishing and big game hunting, that can be used to draw hypotheses about social benefits of wildlife that might be valued. Apart from this information, however, there is little information about social values of wildlife.

Given that we know very little about specific social values of wildlife, it is difficult to derive meaningful assigned values because we do not know how completely assigned values represent the range of held values. In most cases we do not know if assigned values can be ascribed to many of the objects of value, and consequently we do not know which metrics would be appropriate in deriving assigned values and integrating them into allocation and other planning and management decisions.

The issue of held social values is important in wildlife and other resource planning. It fits directly into goal-setting processes in which it is necessary to decide what we want, those objects we want being those objects for which we have strong held values. Held values, which imply goodness or badness of different objects, may be instrumental in setting priorities. For example, we might need to make choices about financial support given to game, endangered species, nongame wildlife, warm water fish, cold water fish, and marine fish, and knowledge of the held values regarding these objects would reveal priorities of the pertinent actors involved in decision making.

In this context we are concerned that striving toward economic valuation of wildlife and fish is limiting in that the array of relevant held values is not commonly revealed in economic valuation, leaving one to guess for what object assigned values are being derived. And, given the complexity of the relationships among the different levels of social value, from social good values to market price values, it is not at all clear to us that the most relevant social values are necessarily involved in establishing values through market prices.

Our conclusion is that valuation of wildlife is at best rudimentary, and we need to devote a lot more effort toward clarifying the aspects of the wildlife resource that need to be valued and the purposes for such valuation. Since it has been demonstrated previously that cultural, societal, psychological, and physiological values—those values we have described as noneconomic social values—are important to people when they consider wildlife and fish, such social values should be included in future investigations of wildlife values.

REFERENCES

BEM, D. J. 1970. Beliefs, attitudes and human affairs. Brooks/Cole, Belmont, Calif. 114pp.

BROWN, P. J. 1982. Recreation opportunity spectrum with implications for wildlife-oriented recreation. Trans. North Am. Wildl. and Nat. Resour. Conf. 47:705–711.

————. 1983. Defining the recreation experience. Pages 3–12 *in* R. D. Rowe and L. G. Chestnut, eds. Managing air quality and scenic resources at national parks and wilderness areas. Westview Press, Boulder, Colo.

————. 1984. Benefits of outdoor recreation and some ideas for valuing recreation opportunities. Pages 209–220 *in* G. L. Peterson and A. Randall, eds. Valuation of wildland resource benefits. Westview Press, Boulder, Colo.

————, J. E. HAUTALUOMA, AND S. M. MCPHAIL. 1977. Colorado deer hunting experiences. Trans. North Am. Wildl. and Nat. Resour. Conf. 42:216–225.

BROWN, T. C. 1984. The concept of value in resource allocation. Land Econ. 60:231–246.

DRIVER, B. L., AND R. W. COOKSEY. 1978. Preferred psychological outcomes of recreational fishing. Pages 27–40 *in* R. A. Barnhart and T. D. Roelofs, eds. Catch and release fishing as a management tool: a national sport fishing symposium. Humboldt St. Univ., Arcata, Calif.

————, AND R. C. KNOPF. 1976. Temporary escape: one product of sport fisheries management. Fisheries 1:21, 24–29.

_____, AND D. H. ROSENTHAL. 1982. Measuring and improving the effectiveness of public outdoor recreation programs. George Washington Univ., Washington, D.C. 40pp.

FISHBEIN, M., AND I. AJZEN. 1975. Belief, attitude, intention and behavior: an introduction to theory and research. Addison Wesley Publ. Co., Reading, Mass. 578pp.

HAUTALUOMA, J. E., AND P. J. BROWN. 1978. Attributes of the hunting experience: a cluster analytic study. J. Leisure Res. 10:271–287.

_____, _____, AND N. L. BATTLE. 1982. Elk hunter consumer satisfaction patterns. Pages 74–80 *in* Forest and river recreation: research update. Univ. Minnesota Agric. Exp. Stn. Misc. Publ. 18, St. Paul.

KELLERT, S. R. 1980. Contemporary values of wildlife in American society. Pages 31–60 *in* W. W. Shaw and E. H. Zube, eds. Wildlife values. Cent. for Assessment of Non-commodity Nat. Resour. Values, Inst. Ser. Rep. No. 1, Univ. Arizona, Tucson.

KENNEDY, J., AND P. J. BROWN. 1976. Attitudes and behavior of fishermen in Utah's Uinta primitive area. Fisheries 1(6):15–17, 30–31.

KNOPF, R. D., B. L. DRIVER, AND J. R. BASSETT. 1973. Motivations for fishing. Trans. North Am. Wildl. and Nat. Resour. Conf. 38:191–196.

LANCASTER, K. 1966. A new approach to consumer theory. J. Political Econ. 74:132–157.

LAWLER, E. E., III. 1973. Motivation in work organizations. Brooks/Cole, Monterey, Calif. 224pp.

MANFREDO, M. J., P. J. BROWN, AND G. E. HAAS. 1980. Fishermen values in wilderness. Proc. West. Assoc. Fish and Wildl. Agencies Workshop 52:276–297.

_____, C. C. HARRIS, AND P. J. BROWN. 1984. The social values of an urban recreational fishing experience. Pages 156–164 *in* L. J. Allen, ed. Urban fishing symp. proc. Am. Fish. Soc., Bethesda, Md.

MORE, T. A. 1973. Attitudes of Massachusetts hunters. Trans. North Am. Wildl. and Nat. Resour. Conf. 38:230–234.

ORTHNER, D. K. 1976. Patterns of leisure and marital interaction. J. Leisure Res. 8:98–111.

POTTER, D. R., J. C. HENDEE, AND R. N. CLARK. 1973. Hunting satisfaction: game, guns, or nature. Pages 62–71 *in* J. C. Hendee and C. Schoenfeld, eds. Human dimensions in wildlife programs. Wildl. Manage. Inst., Washington, D.C.

ROKEACH, M. 1968. Beliefs, attitudes, and values. Jossey-Bass, San Francisco. 214pp.

ROLSTON, H. III. 1983. Values gone wild. Inquiry 16:181–207.

_____. 1985. Valuing wildlands. Environ. Ethics 7:23–48.

SHAW, W. W., AND E. H. ZUBE, editors. 1980. Wildlife values. Cent. for Assessment of Non-commodity Nat. Resour. Values, Inst. Ser. Rep. No. 1, Univ. Arizona, Tucson. 117pp.

SINDEN, J. A., AND A. C. WORRELL. 1979. Unpriced values: decisions without market prices. John Wiley and Sons, New York. 511pp.

SOFRANKO, A. J., AND M. F. NOLAN. 1972. Early life experiences and adult sports participation. J. Leisure Res. 4:6–18.

SPAULDING, I. A. 1970. Variation of emotional states environmental involvement during occupational activity and sport fishing. Univ. Rhode Island Agric. Exp. Stn. Bull. No. 402, Kingston, R. I. 78pp.

STANKEY, G. H., R. C. LUCAS, AND R. REAM. 1973. Relationships between hunting success and satisfaction. Pages 77–84 *in* J. C. Hendee and C. Schoenfeld, eds. Human dimensions in wildlife programs. Wildl. Manage. Inst., Washington, D.C.

STEINHOFF, H. W. 1980. Analysis of major conceptual systems for understanding and measuring wildlife values. Pages 11–21 *in* W. W. Shaw and E. H. Zube, eds. Wildlife values. Cent. for Assessment of Non-commodity Nat. Resour. Values, Inst. Ser. Rep. No. 1, Univ. Arizona, Tucson.

WELLMAN, J. D. 1979. Recreational response to privacy stress: a validation study. J. Leisure Res. 11:61–73.

Chapter 3

Economic Values Defined

Richard C. Bishop

It is easy to devote too much time to *what* economists are trying to measure and not enough time to *why*. This tends to leave the noneconomist without a broader context within which to view wildlife valuation. Thus, this chapter begins with an explanation of the fundamental economic concepts that underlie wildlife valuation. Once understood, these concepts will help us explore the economist's reasons for defining wildlife values in terms of maximum willingness to pay and minimum compensation demanded. They will also facilitate a systematic survey of all potential wildlife values within a so-called total valuation framework. Furthermore, noneconomists have several suggested alternative value measures that economists often find objectionable, the most notable being recreational expenditures. The fundamental economic concepts introduced at the outset will help clarify economists' reasons for objecting to expenditures as a measure of value. Finally, the fundamental concepts will help show that part of the tension between wildlifers and economists can be traced to a basic difference in their perspectives; wildlifers and economists bring different held values to bear on wildlife issues. Although this is a major barrier to the full integration of economics into wildlife management, I shall argue at the end of the chapter that it is not insurmountable.

The discussion is designed to be understandable to those with little or no training in economics. I have, for example, scrupulously resisted the temptation to introduce graphs and equations. The field of economics ought to contain enough common sense to be communicated without such devices. Better communications between economists and wildlifers is essential to improving the ways that we as a society deal with wildlife conservation and management issues.

FUNDAMENTAL CONCEPTS

Monetary values come under the general heading of assigned values. It is important to recognize, however, that economists, as practitioners of a scholarly discipline, share certain held values. These broader values hold the key to understanding the "why" of monetary valuation.

To begin with, economists usually value wildlife resources from a social, as opposed to a private, viewpoint; that is, they examine issues of public policy from the point of view of society as a whole. From the social perspective, monetary economic values are based on, and derive their meaning from, a branch of economics called welfare economics. Welfare economics does not deal, as the term might imply, with welfare programs for the poor but with the welfare or well-being of all members of society.

Welfare economics always involves the comparison of two or more situations or states of the world. One such state of the world might be the present situation, the situation as it now exists. A welfare economist might ask, for example, if the welfare of society would be improved by increasing the deer population of New York State by a certain amount compared to the current level.

At this point, a fundamental issue arises: How can the well-being of a whole society, say all the citizens of New York State, be conceptualized? How is society's welfare to be defined? Economic theorists decided to define social welfare only in terms of the well-being of individual members of society. Furthermore, the individual member of society is taken as the sole judge of his or her well-being. An increase in New York's deer herd would make an individual better off or worse off only to the extent that he or she personally believed he or she would be better off or worse off. Followed to its full logical implication, this line of reasoning leads to the conclusion that society is clearly better off if—and only if—all members of society believe they are better off or at least not worse off. This is the so-called Pareto criterion of social welfare, named after a nineteenth-century economist, Vilfredo Pareto. Using our deer example, the Pareto criterion states that society would be better off if increasing the herd would make at least one member of society better off and leave no member of societey worse off.

Unfortunately, the Pareto criterion is scarcely ever met: Virtually no action that we as a society take leaves no one worse off. The Pareto criterion makes good logical sense, but it is impractical. Continuing our example, suppose the increased deer herd makes hunters better off by improving hunting success but makes farmers worse off because of crop damage. The Pareto criterion is not met because of the farmers' loss of well-being. The end result of applying the Pareto criterion to all public policy issues would be social paralysis. No change could be justified.

If welfare economics is to be more than an academic curiosity, a compromise in the form of the so-called compensation test is necessary.

We may define as gainers all members of society who believe that they would be made better off by a proposed policy or project. Losers would be all members of society who believe they would be made worse off. The compensation test indicates that a proposal will increase social welfare if the gainers would be able to compensate the losers fully and still be better off. In our deer herd example, the herd increase would make society better off if the hunters could fully compensate the farmers and still be better off. There is no requirement that compensation actually be paid. The compensation test requires only that it be possible for gainers to compensate losers fully.

Whether the issue is wildlife management or a public policy or project in some other area, the compensation test provides the motivation for introducing economic values. All we economists are suggesting is that society may want to think twice about doing things when those who would be made better off could not fully compensate those who would be harmed. For reasons that I will state explicitly, even the most ardent economist would admit that the compensation test alone would not be an adequate basis for sound public decision making. However, in cases that fail the compensation test, would it not make sense to clearly and objectively consider the reasons for going ahead?

Although textbooks full of issues have been ignored in this brief overview,[1] enough has been said to clarify the context within which monetary valuation occurs. Economic value is determined by application of the compensation test. The compensation test in turn forms the theoretical foundation for cost-benefit analysis. Although cost-benefit analyses may not always achieve the ideal in practice, the benefits of a proposed policy or project are defined in theory as the maximum amount that gainers would be willing to pay in compensation to losers. Theoretically, costs are the minimum amount required to compensate all losers fully. Thus, to say that benefits exceed costs is equivalent to saying that the compensation test has been satisfied. Using this conceptual framework, it will now be possible to develop several implications for wildlife economics.

WILDLIFE IN A TOTAL VALUATION FRAMEWORK

Since the compensation test emphasizes society as a whole, the goal must be to measure all the values held by all members of society. This has led economists to seek to develop a total valuation framework. Such a framework is an attempt to cover, within a unified theoretical structure, the full range of possible values that any particular wildlife asset might generate. This section draws heavily on Boyle and Bishop

(1985), in which analytical details are worked out in more formal terms (see also Randall and Stoll, 1983).

The total values that a wildlife asset might generate can be divided into use values and nonuse values. Use values are generated when management decisions affect the enjoyment people get from current use of the wildlife asset. Nonuse values are generated when management decisions affect possibilities for future use or impinge on people's altruistic concerns. The most familiar use values—consumptive use values—generated by hunting, fishing, and trapping. Most economic studies have focused on consumptive values because they form a major category of wildlife benefits and because the members of society receiving consumptive use values are easy to identify. However, it has long been recognized that a second category, the nonconsumptive use values, such as those stemming from wildlife photography and observation, is equally appropriate. A third category of use values—the indirect use values—involves personal enjoyment of the wildlife asset, without the direct contact that characterizes consumptive and nonconsumptive uses. Examples include reading about wildlife in books and magazines and watching wildlife programs on television. Two categories of nonuse values have been distinguished, option prices and existence values. Both categories are relatively new and deserve additional explanation.

The basic idea of option prices is that natural resources including wildlife may generate economic values not only from current use but also from continued availability for future use. As an illustration, suppose that peregrine falcon preservation is being studied. Suppose further that we have an accurate estimate of the willingness of falcon viewers to pay for opportunities to see falcons in 1986. For the time being, assume that we are only interested in the recreational and aesthetic values generated by falcon preservation; genetic resources and scientific values will be considered later. Here the question is whether the 1986 viewing value captures the total recreational value of peregrine falcons for that year. Beginning with Weisbrod (1964), economists have developed arguments to the effect that those who are not going to be 1986 viewers might nevertheless be willing to pay something in 1986 to maintain the option of viewing peregrine falcons in later years, These so-called option prices should, according to this line of reasoning, be added to 1986 viewing values.[2]

Turning to existence values, the argument is that those who do not plan to view peregrine falcons in 1986 or thereafter may still be affected by policies affecting the species. People may be willing to pay something just to know that the falcon will continue to exist in a given area quite apart from any desires to benefit personally from them either now or in the future. Their motivation may be the desire to leave a bequest or to maintain opportunities for others in the current generation to see the bird, sympathy for the birds themselves, or other concerns (Boyle and Bishop 1985). The precise definition of existence values is still a controversial topic (Krutilla 1967, McConnell 1983, Randall and Stoll 1983, Fisher and Raucher 1984), but we can safely conclude that under all proposed definitions of existence values are quite compatible with economic theory and preliminary efforts at estimation are now available including some for wildlife (Brookshire et al. 1983 and Boyle and Bishop 1985). Though there are indications that such values are lower than use values on a per person basis, existence values appear to be widely held and may exceed the values when aggregated over society as a whole, even for popular species such as bald eagles (Boyle and Bishop 1985).

Two additional points are worth noting. First, any given member of society may hold several categories of values simultaneously. To take an extreme but plausible example, a person who is gaining a consumptive use value from current elk hunting may also be an elk viewer, may enjoy television programs about elk, may be willing to pay substantial amounts for options to hunt in the future, and may hold existence values for elk. Second, it must be reemphasized that for all categories within the total valuation framework there are two possible measures of value, willingness to pay and compensation demanded. The appropriate measure in any given case depends on whether the people affected are defined as gainers or losers.

EXPENDITURES AS A MEASURE OF VALUE

Noneconomists sometimes propose to value wildlife using measures other than willingness to pay and compensation demanded; the most commonly proposed measure is recreational expenditures. Valuing wildlife by the amount hunters or other groups spend has strong intuitive appeal. In fact, at first glance, this approach appears to be an application of the willingness-to-pay principle discussed earlier. If, for example, U.S. deer hunters spend $1 billion per year on their sport, they must be willing to pay at least that amount for the opportunity. Or, in the example of increasing New York's deer herd, suppose that the improved chances of success would cause residents to spend $5 million more per year on deer hunting in the state. Why not argue that the benefits are at least $5 million? Hunters would actually pay that amount if the herd increased, so they must be willing to pay at least that.

Measuring how much recreationists spend can be a very useful exercise. Economists themselves often measure expenditures by recreationists in an effort to understand the local economic impacts of hunting, fishing and other wildlife-related activities. In a less formal way, estimated expenditures can give wildlife political clout. To say that deer hunters in my home state of Wisconsin, for example, spend an estimated $100 million annually, as they did in 1980 (U.S. Fish and Wildl. Serv. and U.S. Bur. Census 1982), is an effective way of saying that deer hunting is important to the people of the state and is an important part of the state's economy.

Nevertheless, recreational expenditures are not a satisfactory measure of the economic value of wildlife to society as a whole. The compensation test requires that social values be based either on the maximum willingness to pay or on minimum compensation demanded. Expenditures are already being paid out and are thus not available to compensate losers. Consider again our assumed increase in the New York deer herd that would generate $5 million in hunting expenditures. The $5 million would be required to support the additional hunting and would not be available to compensate farmers. In a similar example, the herd could be reduced, hunting success would decline, and hunting expenditures would fall. The reduced expenditures would not bear any necessary relationship to the amount hunters would require to compensate them for their losses.

It may help to distinguish between gross willingness to pay and net willingness to pay. Gross willingness to pay is defined as the maximum amount that gainers would be willing to pay for a proposed project or policy that would benefit them, including the amounts they actually would pay in increased expenses plus any additional amounts they would willingly pay but will not have to pay. Net willingness to pay is limited to the latter amount, the willingness to pay of gainers over and above what they actually will pay. Only net willingness to pay—or in economics jargon, consumer surplus—is relevant in considering whether the benefits that would accrue to gainers if the project or policy is adopted are sufficient to cover the costs. In the present context, net willingness to pay (consumer surplus) for wildlife and not gross willingness to pay or expenditures is relevant to cost-benefit analysis of wildlife improvements.[3] Parallel arguments apply to measurement of minimum net compensation demanded for the wildlife losses of people like the farmers in our example.

LIMITATIONS OF THE COMPENSATION TEST

Having looked at some applications of welfare concepts to wildlife valuation, let us return for a moment to the compensation test itself. It was introduced as a practical compromise, but the senses in which it is a compromise were not spelled out. Even economists are not totally happy with the compensation test, and their misgivings are a special concern in the wildlife area.

The first limitations relate to the distribution of benefits and costs. The amounts that people are willing to pay and the amounts they demand in compensation depend on their incomes and wealth. Rich persons may be able to pay rather large sums for what, to them, are trivial items or demand large sums to give them up, whereas poor persons cannot pay much even for relative necessities and may sell out cheap. That is, the compensation test may give an unfair advantage to the relatively wealthy. For this reason, economists generally advocate an analysis of who the recipients of benefits will be and who will bear the costs as part of cost-benefit analyses. Most economists would agree that society might justifiably reject proposals that pass the compensation test if the poor would bear significant costs without counterbalancing benefits or the proposal is deemed unfair in other ways.

Fairness is important to wildlife management in the U.S. Our forebears intentionally designed our basic institutions to disseminate hunting and fishing opportunities widely. Wildlife management efforts that fail the compensation test may still be socially justified on the basis of fairness. This is an interesting example of how held values (wide dissemination of hunting and fishing opportunities) may override assigned (monetary) values.

The second limitation relates to endangered species. Conventional cost-benefit concepts are not directly applicable to decisions affecting species survival. The benefits of species preservation occur only as scientific progress and cultural evolution identify which species are valuable to humans and in what ways. Very long time periods must be considered because extinction is irreversible. Since the directions of scientific progress and the evolution of human culture are very difficult to predict in advance, the benefits of preservation are very uncertain and hard to evaluate (Ciriacy-Wantrup 1952). Also potential issues of intergenerational fairness limit the applicability of cost-benefit analysis (Bishop 1978). Thus, economic valuation seems most relevant to wildlife management issues that do not involve possible species extinction, although valuation may still play a subsidiary role in helping decision makers understand the true social costs of avoiding extinction (see Bishop 1980).

TOWARD INTEGRATION
OF WILDLIFE ECONOMICS AND BIOLOGY

What are the prospects for integration of biology and economics in wildlife management? We economists would like to think we have a great deal to offer. Nevertheless, many wildlife professionals are ambivalent about adding economics to their tool kits. In part, they are concerned about the fairness goal: Wide dissemination of access to fish and game is part of our U.S. heritage. Furthermore, economists share the concerns of wildlifers about applying conventional cost-benefit comparisons in cases involving endangered species. Nor do economists and wildlife professionals have any fundamental disagreement about programs to instill Leopold's land ethic in the broader population. Educational programs to foster prowildlife ethics are simply beyond economics. They play no role in our paradigm. Economics takes people as it finds them, and to the extent that such ethics are present, they should express themselves as economic values.

A valid source of tension, however, arises between the two disciplines. Wildlife professionals often hold a strong predilection in favor of wildlife. Wildlife advocacy stems from the basic held values of wildlife management. The economist has no such predilection. In practice, this difference may lead the wildlife professional to view conversion of wildlife habitat to agriculture, for example, as a defeat, whereas the economist may view it as a victory, provided it passes the compensation test. The astute wildlife professional realizes that to embrace economics wholeheartedly would require deemphasizing a deeply held personal commitment. We economists resist adopting such a commitment because it violates our basic held value that things are good or bad only to the extent that individual members of society judge them to be good or bad. Because wildlife has no special place in the economic viewpoint, it must sink or swim in competition with all the other things from which humans derive satisfaction.

This basic difference in held values is the major impediment to integrating biology and economics and cannot be resolved here. As an economist, I can only invite wildlife professionals to consider the advantages of a closer alignment with economics. In public debates over policies and projects affecting wildlife, economic arguments will inevitably arise. That resource developments harmful to wildlife may provide income, jobs, and economic growth carries strong political force. Furthermore, wildlife goals must compete with many other social goals in meager public budgets in which most costs and many benefits are already measured in monetary terms. In the policy arena, those things without a market value are often assumed to have little or no economic value. This is the error that we economists working on wildlife values are trying to correct. By joining us, wildlife professionals do risk defeats in cases in which the economic conclusions run against wildlife, but in instances in which economics favors wildlife, they will gain a powerful tool that will greatly strengthen their cases. Evidence is growing that an economic case can be made for wildlife in many instances. On balance, the integration of economics and wildlife biology would do much to ensure that wildlife gets a fair hearing in the policy arena. It is high time that the economic contributions of wildlife receive full recognition.

Acknowledgments.—Research was supported by the College of Agricultural and Life Sciences, University of Wisconsin–Madison, and the Wisconsin Sea Grant Institute. Helpful comments from Kevin J. Boyle, Robert K. Davis, Daniel J. Decker, Thomas A. Heberlein, and Harold Steinhoff are also gratefully acknowledged.

NOTES

1. More specifically, in the discussion that follows I assume that taxes are nonexistent, full employment prevails, international and interregional trade are irrelevant, all markets are competitive, increasing returns to scale are not a problem, externalities of a Pareto-relevant kind are absent, uncertainty is not an issue, and capital markets operate perfectly. A complete discussion of welfare economics and cost-benefit analysis would deal with these topics. See Just et al. (1982) and Sugden and Williams (1978) for further discussion.

2. The reader will notice that the option prices and not option values are dealt with here. This approach is consistent with current economics jargon by which option value is only one part of option price. See Bishop (1982, 1986) for further discussion. Option price and value concepts must be used with care to avoid double counting benefits, a potential problem first identified by Long (1967).

3. Alternatively, benefits might be defined in terms of gross willingness to pay. Then, however, recreational expenditures would have to be added to costs. Hunting and other forms of wildlife-oriented recreation require goods and services from the marketplace, and the use of these goods and services involves a very real cost to society, which should be subtracted from gross willingness to pay. This leaves net willingness to pay as before.

REFERENCES

Bishop, R. C. 1978. Endangered species and uncertainty: the economics of a safe minimum standard. Am. J. Agric. Econ. 60:10–18.

———. 1980. Endangered species: an economic perspective. Trans. North Am. Wildl. and Nat. Resour. Conf. 45:208–218.

———. 1982. Option value: an exposition and extension. Land Econ. 58:1–15.

———. 1986. Resource valuation under uncertainty: theoretical principles for empirical research. *In* V. K. Smith, ed. Advances in applied microeconomics. JAI Press, Greenwich, Conn. (In press.)

BOYLE, K. J., AND R. C. BISHOP. 1985. The total value of wildlife: a case study involving endangered species. Dep. Agric. Econ., Univ. Wisconsin, Madison. 29pp. (Typescript.)

BROOKSHIRE, D. S., ET AL. 1983. Estimating option prices and existence values for wildlife resources. Land Econ. 59:1–15.

CIRIACY-WANTRUP, S. V. 1952. Resource conservation: economics and policies. Univ. Calif. Press, Berkeley and Los Angeles. 395pp.

FISHER, A., AND R. RAUCHER. 1984. Intrinsic benefits of improved water quality. *In* V. K. Smith and A. D. Witte, eds. Advances in applied microeconomics. Vol. 3. JAI Press, Greenwich, Conn.

JUST, R. E., D. L. HUETH, AND A. SCHMITZ. 1982. Applied welfare economics and public policy. Prentice-Hall, Inc., Englewood Cliffs, N.J. 491pp.

KRUTILLA, J. V. 1967. Conservation reconsidered. Am. Econ. Rev. 57:778–786.

LONG, M. F. 1967. Collective consumption services of individual consumption goods: comment. Q. J. Econ. 81:351–352.

MCCONNELL, K. E. 1983. Existence value and bequest value. Pages 254–265 *in* R. D. Rowe and L. G. Chestnut, eds. Managing air quality of national parks and wilderness areas. Westview Press, Boulder, Colo.

RANDALL, A., AND J. R. STOLL. 1983. Existence value in a total valuation framework. Pages 265–274 *in* R. D. Rowe and L. G. Chestnut, eds. Managing air quality and scenic resources at national parks and wilderness areas. Westview Press, Boulder, Colo.

SUGDEN, R., AND A. WILLIAMS. 1978. The principles of practical cost-benefit analysis. Oxford Univ. Press, Oxford. 275pp.

U.S. FISH AND WILDLIFE SERVICE AND U.S. BUREAU OF THE CENSUS. 1982. 1980 national survey of fishing, hunting, and wildlife-associated recreation: Wisconsin. U.S. Dep. Inter. and U.S. Dep. Commer., U.S. Gov. Print. Off., Washington, D.C.

WEISBROD, B. A. 1964. Collective-consumption services of individual-consumption goods. Q. J. Econ. 78:471–477.

Chapter 4

Evolution of the Valuation of Wildlife

Harold W. Steinhoff, Richard G. Walsh,
Tony J. Peterle, and Joseph M. Petulla

Valuation of wildlife means both appraisal of the values and exploration of the attitudes related to the value. Valuation implies an understanding of the systems that have been proposed to visualize the spectrum of values. The term *value* has two major meanings: an internal one, or an attitude in the mind of a person (which Brown [1984] called a held value), and an external one, or the worth of an object in relation to other objects (Brown's [1984] assigned value). Objects may be concrete objects, events, experiences, or thoughts.

We are primarily concerned with the present status of wildlife valuation in the U.S. and Canada, and we propose to trace certain aspects of the evolution of wildlife valuation. Indications of the evolution come from publications and from laws, which give evidence of the "genetic" composition of valuation thought. One person's thoughts and ideas beget further ideas in the next person who considers the matter. Occasional flashes of insight are the stimuli that produce changes or mutations in the evolution of valuation processes.

We will trace changes and developments of ideas in the following concept areas: (1) development of advocacy for hunting and antihunting attitudes and values, (2) U.S. policies that resulted from attitudes and that stimulated valuation, (3) classification systems for analyzing wildlife values, and (4) methods of measurement of wildlife values. We cannot hope that our discussion will be exhaustive or complete. We have tried to choose representative publications that first presented a new idea or development in each of these lines of thought.

DEVELOPMENT OF ADVOCACY FOR HUNTING AND ANTIHUNTING ATTITUDES AND VALUES

Conflicting views of human-animal relationships have developed over whether human beings are to be considered superior or equal to other animals. In Table 4.1 we present a chronology of the evolution of these two views. In the first view, which started at least as early as the book of Genesis, animals were depicted as primarily for the use of humans, who had dominion over them. Some idealistic and highly ethical thinkers, such as Aldo Leopold (1933), have held this view. Clarke (1958) defended human beings' role as hunters in the natural and necessary functioning of ecosystems. Guthrie (1967) suggested that the inclusion of animals as primary participants in our ethical systems was illogical, pointing out that the action of a wolf's killing a deer is not subject to moral analysis. Most recently, with the rise of the antihunting movement writers such as Shepard (1973) have defended this view as natural and genetically ordained.

The animal rights value system originated at least as early as Hindu thought. Hindus believed that every creature has a soul and that all must be revered. Later thinkers such as Muir (see Appendix A), Schweitzer (1951), and Krutch (1957) advocated a "reverence for life" and called hunting "a damnable pleasure." Recent impetus in the animal rights movement has come from Godlovitch et al. (1972) and Singer (1973), who called prejudice against animals "speciesism." Recent research and writings by Jolly (1985) have provided a new philosophical basis for this view of human-animal relationships. In Appendix A, Petulla gives a detailed discussion of the development of these value systems.

The evolution of attitudes, or at least the analysis of them, has been pursued by many thinkers. Some of them are listed in the third part of Table 4.1. Early studies examined attitudes of the wildlife user (Peterle 1961) or wilderness user (Hendee et al. 1968). White (1969) blamed our mistreatment of resources on the "superiority" attitude of humans. Depth of analysis increased in the 1970s as workers such as Kellert (1974), Shaw (1974), and Driver (1976) probed into the more basic human attitudes related to wildlife. More (1977) investigated the formation of wildlife perceptions. Some interesting recent works (Randall and Stoll 1983, Bishop and Heberlein 1984) have analyzed altruistic attitudes. We seem to be making progress in understanding how attitudes evolved and why people hold the values they do.

U.S. POLICIES THAT RESULT FROM ATTITUDES AND THAT STIMULATED VALUATION

Laws or other governmental policy indications are important evidence of the wildlife values held by large numbers of people (see Table 4.2). Such policy statements not only indicate values that the public holds at the time, but they themselves stimulate the development of methods of measuring the values.

TABLE 4.1
Evolution of Attitudes Relating to Wildlife Values

Advocacy of Attitudes

Superiority of Humans

4000 BC?	Genesis	Man was to have dominion over every living thing.
400 BC	Socrates	Animals are produced and nourished for the sake of man (Petulla, App. A).
1844 AD	Herbert	N.Y. Sportsman's Club founded to protect and preserve game for purposes of hunting (Petulla, App. A).
1929	Leopold	Wrote "American Wildlife Policy" which said that the purpose of wildlife management is to provide benefit for people.
1933	Leopold	"The Conservation Ethic" proposed that ethics be extended to land, but he still advocated hunting.
1957	Anthony	Defended hunting, against Krutch's criticism, as admirable and necessary. He said that hunting was instinctive.
1958	Clarke	Defended hunting as a necessary and desirable part of ecosystem function.
1967	Guthrie	Inclusion of animals as primary participants in our ethical system is illogical. A wolf killing a deer is not subject to moral analysis.
1973	Shepard	"The male of the (human) species is genetically programmed to pursue, attack, and kill for food. To the extent that men do not do so, they are not fully human."

Equality with Humans

1000 BC?	Hindus	Every creature has a soul, all must be revered (Mayhew 1962).
1912 AD	Muir	Said he "never happened upon a trace of evidence that seemed to show that any one animal was ever made for another as much as it was for itself" (Petulla, App. A).
1913	Hornaday	Foe of sport hunting, wrote "30 Years War for Wildlife" (Petulla, App. A).
1951	Schweitzer	Coined the term "reverence for life," but applied human ethics to animals, and approved the righteous killing of predators.
1957	Krutch	Called hunting "A damnable pleasure."
1972	Godlovitch et al.	The case for treating all animals, morally, as humans, and for not using them as food, for pleasure or experimentally.

TABLE 4.1 (Cont.)

Advocacy of Attitudes	

Equality with Humans (Cont.)

1973	Singer	Supported the animal liberation movement and proclaimed that animals were beings with a right to live their own lives. Called prejudice against animals "speciesism."

Analysis of Attitudes

1961	Peterle	Analyzed "The hunter - who is he?"
1968	Hendee et al.	Analyzed values and preferences of wilderness wildlife users. Later suggested a categorization of wildlife values.
1969	White	Blamed the Judaeo-Christian tradition of dominion for our mistreatment of resources, including wildlife (Petulla, App. A).
1969	Erickson	"Attitudes about wildlife and preferences in television programs: A communication study."
1974	Kellert	"From kinship to mastery: A study of American attitudes toward animals."
1974	Shaw	"Meanings of wildlife for Americans: Contemporary attitudes and social trends."
1976	Driver	Analyzed social benefits of outdoor recreation participation, and laid much of the foundation for understanding Kellert's data (D. L. Schweitzer, pers. commun.).
1977	More	Analyzed the formation of wildlife perceptions.
1983	Randall & Stoll	Classified altruism as: interpersonal, intergenerational, and Q-altruism.
1984	Bishop & Heberlein	Defined five categories of altruists.

One of the first such statutes, the Fish and Wildlife Coodination Act of 1946, required that fish and wildlife values be included in the benefit-cost analysis of public water projects. This requirement may have been the stimulus for much of the evolution of valuation in the 1950s. The creation of the Outdoor Recreation Resources Review Commission in 1962 may have had a similar effect.

Publication of what has been popularly called Principles and Standards by the U.S. Water Resources Council in 1962 (with significant revisions in 1964, 1971, 1973, 1979, and 1983) clarified the status of valuation to date and stimulated evolution for the future.

Legislation indicating the influence of the modern environmental movement (which some think began with Rachel Carson's [1962] *Silent Spring*) includes the Endangered Species Preservation Act of 1966 and the National Environmental Policy Act of 1969. Both required consid-

TABLE 4.2
Chronology of Policies Which have Resulted from Attitudes and Stimulated
Measurement of Wildlife Values

1929 American Game Policy	Said wildlife is for people. Greater economic efficiency in wildlife management would be achieved with private ownership, but American tradition won't permit this (Leopold 1929).
1946 Fish and Wildlife Coordination Act	Required federal agencies constructing water projects to consult with appropriate federal and state agencies on measures to prevent harm to fish and wildlife resources.
1962 Outdoor Recreation Resources Review Commission	Made a comprehensive study of all aspects of the status and future possibilities of outdoor recreation, including wildlife use.
1962 U.S. Water Resources Council	Established policies, standards, and procedures for assessing wildlife costs and benefits related to water projects. Revisions in 1964, 1971, 1973, 1979, and 1983 updated their recommendations.
1966 Endangered Species Preservation Act	Protected rare and endangered species. Succeeded by: 1969 Endangered Species Conservation Act, 1973 Endangered Species Act, and 1978 Amendments.
1969 National Environmental Policy Act	Required environmental impact statements.
1971 Goldstein	Federal policies in agriculture have caused farmers to drain prairie potholes, resulting in a significant loss of waterfowl nesting habitat (Davis 1985).
1974 Forest and Rangeland Renewable Resources Planning Act	Required a national review of forest and range resources, including wildlife, on public lands and the formulation of long range plans for management.
1976 National Forest Management Act	Required detailed planning of multiple resource management, including wildlife, by the U.S. Forest Service.
1978 Federal Laboratory Animal Welfare Act	Required that laboratory animals be cared for in a safe, humane, healthful way.
1980 Shabman	Showed that federal tax codes (i.e. policies) encourage conversion of Mississippi bottomland hardwoods (with resultant loss of wildlife habitat) (Davis 1985).
1980 Fish and Wildlife Conservation Act	Grants to states for management of nongame species (U.S. Fish and Wildl. Serv. 1984).

eration of animal values in any proposed environmental change. The Forest Acts of 1974 and 1976 (Table 4.2) showed the need for valuation of wildlife in a way comparable to that for other natural resources. The Federal Laboratory Animal Welfare Act of 1978 seems to be a direct reflection of the rise of thinking supporting animal rights. Davis (1985) has shown through the studies of Goldstein (1971) and Shabman (1980) how fiscal policies of the U.S. government have affected wildlife values, for instance, ducks have been lost in the draining of prairie potholes, and bottomland hardwood wildlife has suffered in the South as a result of timber harvest. The Fish and Wildlife Conservation Act of 1980, which provides for grants to states for the management of nongame species, is recent evidence of evolution of public thought. Attention to nonconsumptive values is increasing.

CLASSIFICATION SYSTEMS FOR ANALYZING WILDLIFE VALUES

The classification of wildlife values has been a recent method of analyzing the whole array of values. An outline of these systems and their development is shown in Table 4.3. The system currently most accepted, especially by economists, is outlined in this section. It is based primarily on the way the animal is "used." The terms and relationships are essentially those proposed by Langford and Cocheba (1978) and further explained and developed by Loomis (1985), Boyle and Bishop (1985), and others.

The types of wildlife values can be classified into two broad categories: option values and exercised values. Option values can be thought of as the willingness to pay a kind of insurance premium to retain the opportunity of possible future use. Exercised values have several sub-categories; the two major ones are direct benefits and indirect benefits. Direct benefits are derived from a user's personal relationship to animals and may take the form of direct consumptive use (using up the animal or intending to) or nonconsumptive use (e.g., viewing the animal in nature or in zoos, photographing it). Indirect exercised values, which arise without the user being in direct contact with the animal, come from such experiences as looking at photographs and films of wildlife or reading about it or benefiting from activities or contributions of animals, such as their use in research. Indirect benefits, sometimes called existence values, are of two forms: bequest (which provide for future generations) and pure existence (which arise merely from the knowledge that animals exist).

Our purpose here is not to describe this system or to define its terms, other chapters in this book will do those things. We should point out

TABLE 4.3
Methods of Classifying Wildlife Values

Currently Most Used Classification System

1978 Langford & Cocheba	Proposed approximately this system.
1985 Loomis	Related this system to Kellert's (1974, 1984).
1985 Boyle & Bishop	Clarified essentially this system.

I. EXERCISED VALUES
  A. Direct Benefits
    1. Direct use
      a. Consumptive use

| 1964 Brown et al. | First used an acceptable economic method to measure this value. |

      b. Nonconsumptive use

1926 McLeod	Estimated value of deer as "creators of aesthetic values."
1968 Myres	Estimated expenditures of the Calgary Bird Club.
1969 Steinhoff	Estimated nonconsumptive values on Kenai National Moose Range.
1984 Stoll & Johnson	Nonconsumptive use values of the Whooping Crane.

    2. Indirect use
      a. Indirect viewing or visualizing
      b. Benefits from activities or contributions of animals, research, etc.

  B. Indirect Benefits (sometimes called Existence Values).

1967 Krutilla	First proposed the existence of these values.
1983 McConnell	Discussed existence and bequest values in national parks and wilderness areas.
1983 Randall & Stoll	Classified types of altruism as related to existence values.
1984 Fisher & Raucher	Existence value of water quality.
1984 Bishop & Heberlein	Defined five categories of altruists as related to existence values.
1984 Walsh et al.	Existence and bequest demands for wilderness.

Endangered Species, a special case

1978 Bishop	"Endangered species and uncertainty: The economics of a safe minimum standard."
1978 Miller	"A simple economic model of endangered species preservation."
1980 Bishop	Recommended tempering efficiency with justice and equity for future generations.
1984 Brown & Goldstein	"A model for valuing endangered species."
1985 Walsh et al.	"Public benefits of programs to protect endangered wildlife in Colorado."

TABLE 4.3 (Cont.)

B. Indirect Benefits (Cont.)
  1. Bequest (especially Krutilla 1967, but also the other references above)
  2. Pure existence (especially Krutilla 1967)

II. OPTION VALUES[a]

1964	Weisbrod	The first and seminal proposer of the idea of option value.
1978	Walsh et al.	Option values related to water quality.
1982	Bishop	Distinguished between demand-side and supply-side option value.
1983	Smith	A conceptual overview of option vlaue.
1983	Brookshire et al.	Related option prices and existence values.

Other Systems of Classification Which Have Been Proposed

I. USES OF WILDLIFE[b]

1947	King	Recreational, aesthetic, educational, biological, social, commercial.
1969	Hendee	Appreciative, consumptive, passive free-play, sociable learning, active-expressive.
1973	Nobe & Steinhoff	Direct user, primary beneficiary, secondary beneficiary, alternative resource user, vicarious user, altruist, environmentalist, option holder.
1974	Shaw	Utility or nuisance, consumptive recreational, aesthetic or existence.
1979	Rolston	Economic, life-support, recreational, scientific, aesthetic, life-intelligibility, plurality-unity, stability-freedom, dialectical-environmental, sacramental.

II. MOTIVES OR ATTITUDES OF WILDLIFE VALUE HOLDERS[b]

1973	More	Display, esthetic, affiliation, pioneering, kill, exploration, challenge.
1974	Hendee	Solitude, companionship, escapism, nature appreciation, outdoor skill, trophy, exercise.
1974	Kellert	Utilitarian, naturalistic, dominionistic, humanistic, ecologistic, moralistic, negativistic, knowledge of animals, scientistic, aesthetic.

III. TYPES OF COMMODITY PURCHASED[b]

| 1974 | Hendee | Back-country hunt, general season party hunt, meat hunt, special skills hunt, fly fish only, cast-drifting, boat-drifting, plunking, etc. |

[a] Option Values might apply to every one of the above categories of Exercised Values.
[b] As a basis for the system.

that even though the system is of fairly recent origin, some of the ideas were proposed as early as 1926 (McLeod).

The decade of the 1960s was a fertile period: Brown et al. (1964) prepared one of the first applications of a technically acceptable valuation method; Weisbrod's (1964) suggestion of option value and Krutilla's (1967) essay on existence values were additional innovations. The special case of endangered species began to receive critical valuation in 1978 with studies by Bishop (1978) and by Miller (1978). Progress is evinced by the depth and variety of studies in the 1980s, including Stoll and Johnson's (1984) development of nonconsumptive use values, Walsh's et al. (1984) application of option, existence, and bequest demands, Brown and Goldstein's (1984) development of a model for evaluating endangered species, and Brookshire's et al. (1983) clarification of option prices and existence values.

People besides economists have proposed other systems of classification. All have helped in visualizing the complete system of existing wildlife values (listed in the second part of Table 4.3). Workers have been primarily concerned with a system based on the uses of wildlife. The earliest of such studies was King's (1947) proposal (Table 4.3), most others were suggested in the 1970s.

Motives or attitudes were the foundation for systems proposed by workers interested in social science, including More (1973), Hendee (1974), and Kellert (1974) (Table 4.3). Hendee (1974) made proposals in all three categories in Table 4.3. One such suggestion was to base the system on the types of commodity (or experience) purchased, such as "meat hunt."

In reality there is only one huge set of wildlife values, which need to be classified in one comprehensive and unified system. But we have not agreed upon what that one system should be. Instead, many arbitrary systems can be applied to this underlying set of values. Selection of the appropriate classification system today depends upon the purpose and the viewpoint of the user.

METHODS OF MEASUREMENT OF WILDLIFE VALUES

The development of attitudes and the conceptualization of values classification systems should result in better methods of measurement. But here, even more than in attitudes, an evolutionary process is evident. One idea gives birth to another, and a flash of new insight produces a whole new species of thought.

Early efforts were directed at using expenditures as an index of the values of wildlife that were the objective of the spending. The earliest U.S. example we found was the study by Gordon (1941) (Table 4.4).

TABLE 4.4
Valuation Methods for Wildlife

EXPENDITURES

1925	Drumaux	An early use of the expenditure method, in Belgium.
1941	Gordon	An early use of the expenditure method, in the United States.
1948	Dambach & Leedy	One of the first uses of expenditure in a state (Ohio).
1955	U.S. Fish & Wildlife Service	"National survey of fishing and hunting."
1950s	Many other references	
1960s	Some references	
1970s	Many references, using the expenditure approach	

TRAVEL COST (TC)

1947	Hotelling	Original seminal idea for using consumer's surplus.
1958	Trice & Wood	Used travel costs to estimate value.
1959	Clawson	First complete development of the method suggested by Hotelling.
1963	Knetsch	Further refined and elaborated the method proposed by Clawson.
1964	Brown et al.	Applied the method to sport fisheries in Oregon.
1965	Scott	Analyzed factors that affect accuracy of the method.
1970s	Many workers	Used the method, with some suggested refinements.
1980s	Many workers	Used the method, with some suggested refinements.

CONTINGENT VALUE (CV)

1964	Davis	First use of the bidding-game technique.
1974	Hammack & Brown	Pointed out significant differences in "willingness" to pay" vs. "willingness to sell."
1985	Knetsch	Convincing analysis of reasons for consistently great differences in "willingness to pay" vs. "willingness to sell."
1985	Walsh et al.	Applied CV to endangered wildlife in Colorado.

HEDONIC

1974	Rosen	An early exposition of the hedonic approach.
1978	Brown, Charbonneau, & Hay	"The value of wildlife estimated by the hedonic approach."
1983	Livengood	Applied to estimating values of hunting.

Studies of statewide expenditures were the typical approach for many years; an early example is the paper by Dambach and Leedy (1948) for Ohio. In 1955 the U.S. Fish and Wildlife Service began a series of national surveys of hunting and fishing. At first these included only attitudes and characteristics of users and their expenditures, but these surveys were improved at five-year intervals since that time. Today some of the most advanced methodological thinking on measurement of wildlife values is included in these surveys. In the 1950s there was a surge of expenditures studies, then fewer in the 1960s and another increase in the 1970s. Today economists regard the expenditures method as having very limited value for most economic purposes.

The travel cost (TC) method (Table 4.4) has become one of the most accepted for wildlife valuation. The germ of the idea was proposed by Hotelling (1947) and first developed by Clawson in his classic paper in 1959. Knetsch (1963), who further refined and applied the principle, is sometimes credited with creating the method. Brown et al. (1964) first applied it to a practical problem, the Oregon sport fishery. A flurry of studies pointed out potential difficulties with the method, and some proposed ways of adjusting results. Scott's (1965) paper was an early analytical example of this approach. Today the TC method is accepted, providing it is fully understood, proper precautions are taken, and it is applied to appropriate cases.

The contingent value (CV) method is currently in greatest favor because of its proven reliability and broadness of application. It was first proposed by Davis (1964), who used this method for studies in Maine forests. Respondents to a questionnaire were asked how much they would pay to have a given experience, object, or privilege. Or they were asked how much they would have to be paid to give up the experience, object, or privilege. Validity of the method was supported by a recent study by Bishop and Heberlein (1984) in which CV estimates of willingness to pay ($28) were compared with actual cash payments ($31) and no significant differences were found in the hypothetical and actual payments for deer hunting in the Sand Hills of Wisconsin. Hammack and Brown (1974) first pointed out the significant differences in "willingness to pay" versus "willingness to sell." Although subsequent studies have shed some light on this problem, Knetsch (1985) has presented a convincing analysis of reasons for consistently great differences in these two willingnesses.

The hedonic (H) method, suggested by Rosen (1974), is similar to the TC method because it compares expenditures of a spectrum of users and assumes other users would pay the amount that the average user (or the biggest spender) would pay, if he or she had to. The method was further developed by Brown et al. (1978) for waterfowl and later by Livengood (1983) as applied to estimating values of hunting.

The repertoire of today's wildlife valuer contains a sizable fund of knowledge about attitudes and methods. We are progressing in the development of classification systems that will permit us to effectively organize such knowledge and methods. We look forward to future mutations and fruitful unions in the evolution of the valuation of wildlife.

Acknowledgments.—D. L. Schweitzer, J. L. Knetsch, J. M. Hughes, J. C. Hendee, F. L. Filion, J. A. Leitch, L. J. Nelson, and P. J. Brown kindly gave us thoughts on key publications and policies in the evolution of the valuation of wildlife or reviewed the manuscript.

REFERENCES

ANTHONY, H. E. 1957. The sportsman or the predator? II. But it's instinctive. Saturday Rev., August 17:9–10, 40.

BISHOP, R. C. 1978. Endangered species and uncertainty: the economics of a safe minimum standard. Am. J. Agric. Econ. 60:10–18.

————. 1980. Endangered species: an economic perspective. Trans. North Am. Wildl. and Nat. Resour. Conf. 45:208–218.

————. 1982. Option value: an exposition and extension. Land Econ. 58(1):1–15.

————, AND T. A. HEBERLEIN. 1984. Contingent valuation methods and ecosystem damages from acid rain. Dep. Agric. Econ. Staff Pap. No. 217, Univ. Wisconsin, Madison.

BOYLE, J., AND R. C. BISHOP. 1985. The total value of wildlife resources: conceptual and empirical issues. *In* Assoc. Environ. and Resour. Econ. Workshop on Recreation Demand Modeling. Boulder, Colo., 17–18 May. 42pp. (In press.)

BROOKSHIRE, S., S. EUBANKS, AND A. RANDALL. 1983. Estimating option prices and existence values for wildlife resources. Land Econ. 59:1–15.

BROWN, G., A. SINGH, AND E. CASTLE. 1964. An economic evaluation of the Oregon salmon and steelhead sport fishery. Oreg. Agric. Exp. Stn. Tech. Bull. 78, Oregon State Univ., Corvallis. 47pp.

BROWN, M., JR., J. CHARBONNEAU, AND M. J. HAY. 1978. The value of wildlife estimated by the hedonic approach. U.S. Fish and Wildl. Serv., Div. Program Plans Working Pap. No. 6, Washington, D.C. 25pp.

————, AND J. H. GOLDSTEIN. 1984. A model for valuing endangered species. J. Environ. Econ. and Manage. 11:303–309.

BROWN, T. C. 1984. The concept of value in resource allocation. Land Econ. 60:231–246.

CARSON, R. 1962. Silent spring. Houghton-Mifflin, Boston. 368pp.

CLARKE, C.H.D. 1958. Autumn thoughts of a hunter. J. Wildl. Manage. 22:420–427.

CLAWSON, M. 1959. Methods of measuring the demand for and value of outdoor recreation. Resour. for the Future Reprint No. 10, Washington, D.C. 36 pp.

DAMBACH, C. A., AND D. L. LEEDY. 1948. A recent evaluation of Ohio's wildlife resources. Trans. North Am. Wildl. and Nat. Resour. Conf. 13:508–520.

DAVIS, R. K. 1964. The value of big game hunting in a private forest. Trans. North Am. Wildl. and Nat. Resour. Conf. 29:393–403.

————. 1985. Research accomplishments and prospects in wildlife economics. Trans. North Am. Wildl. and Nat. Resour. Conf. 50:392–404.

DRIVER, B. L. 1976. Toward a better understanding of the social benefits of outdoor recreation participation. Pages 163–190 *in* Proc. South. States Recreation Resour. Appl. Workshop, U.S. Dep. Agric. For. Serv. Gen. Tech. Rep. SE-9.

DRUMAUX, L. 1925. Forests, hunting, and fishing from the economic viewpoint in Belgium. J. For. 23:670–676.

ERICKSON, D. L. 1969. Attitudes about wildlife and preferences in television programs: a communication study. Ph.D. Thesis, Ohio State Univ., Columbus. 185pp.

FISHER, A., AND R. RAUCHER. 1984. Intrinsic benefits of improved water quality: conceptual and empirical perspectives. *In* V. K. Smith and A. D. Witte, eds. Applied microeconomics. Vol. 3. JAI Press, Greenwich, Conn.

GODLOVITCH, S., R. GODLOVITCH, AND J. HARRIS. 1972. Animals, men and morals: an inquiry into the maltreatment of non-humans. Taplinger Publ. Co., New York. 240pp.

GOLDSTEIN, J. H. 1971. Competition for wetlands in the midwest: an economic analysis. Johns Hopkins Univ. Press, Resour. for the Future, Baltimore. 105pp.

GORDON, S. 1941. A sampling technique for the determination of hunters' activities and the economics thereof. J. Wildl. Manage. 5:260–278.

GUTHRIE, R. D. 1967. The ethical relationship between humans and other organisms. Perspect. in Biol. and Med. 11:52–62.

HAMMACK, J., AND G. M. BROWN, JR. 1974. Waterfowl and wetlands; toward bioeconomic analysis. Johns Hopkins Univ. Press, Resour. for the Future, Baltimore. 95pp.

HENDEE, J. C. 1969. Appreciative versus consumptive uses of wildlife refuges: studies of who gets what and trends in use. Trans. North Am. Wildl. and Nat. Resour. Conf. 34:252–264.

———. 1974. A multiple-satisfaction approach to game management. Wildl. Soc. Bull. 2:104–113.

———, W. R. COTTON, L. D. MARLOW, AND C. F. BROCKMAN. 1968. Wilderness users in the Pacific Northwest: their characteristics, values, and management preferences. Pacific Northwest For. and Range Exp. Stn. Res. Pap. PNW-61, Portland. 91pp.

HOTELLING, H. 1947. Letter cited on page 9 *in* R. A. Prewitt. 1949. The economics of public recreation: an economic study of the monetary evaluation of recreation in the national parks. U.S. Dep. Inter., Natl. Park Serv., Washington, D.C.

JOLLY, A. 1985. The evolution of primate behavior. Macmillan Co., New York. 526pp.

KELLERT, S. R. 1974. From kinship to mastery: a study of American attitudes toward animals. Rep. to U.S. Fish and Wildl. Serv. 216pp.

———. 1984. Assessing wildlife and environmental values in cost-benefit analysis. J. Environ. Manage. 18:355–363.

KING, R. T. 1947. The future of wildlife in forest land use. Trans. North Am. Wildl. Conf. 12:454–467.

KNETSCH, J. L. 1963. Outdoor recreation demands and benefits. Land Econ. 39:387–396.

———. 1985. Values, biases, and entitlements. An. Reg. Sci., July: (in press).

KRUTCH, J. W. 1957. The sportsman or the predator? I. A damnable pleasure. Saturday Rev., August 17:8–10, 39–40.

KRUTILLA, J. V. 1967. Conservation reconsidered. Am. Econ. Rev. 58:777–786.

LANGFORD, W. A., AND D. J. COCHEBA. 1978. The wildlife valuation problem: a critical review of economic approaches. Can. Wildl. Serv. Occas. Pap. No. 37. 35pp.

LEOPOLD, A. 1929. Report of the committee on American wildlife policy. Proc. Am. Game Conf. 16:196–210.

_____. 1933. The conservation ethic. J. For. 31:634–643.

LIVENGOOD, R. 1983. Value of big game from markets for hunting leases: the hedonic approach. Land Econ. 59:287–291.

LOOMIS, J. 1985. Assessing wildlife and environmental values in cost-benefit analysis: the state of the art. Comment. J. Environ. Manage. 19:(in press).

MAYHEW, G. N. 1962. Hindus. Pages 224–225 *in* The worldbook encyclopedia. Vol. 8. Field Enterprises Educ. Corp., Merchandise Mart, Chicago.

MCCONNELL, K. E. 1983. Existence and bequest value. Pages 254–264 *in* R. D. Rowe and L. G. Chestnut, eds. Managing air quality and scenic resources at national parks and wilderness areas. Westview Press, Boulder, Colo.

MCLEOD, K., JR. 1926. Deer in their relation to man and forest. M.S. Thesis, Univ. Calif., Davis. 87pp.

MILLER, J. R. 1978. A simple economic model of endangered species preservation in the United States. J. Environ. Econ. and Manage. 5:292–300.

MORE, T. A. 1973. Attitudes of Massachusetts hunters. Trans. North Am. Wildl. and Nat. Resour. Conf. 38:230–234.

_____. 1977. The formation of wildlife perceptions. Trans. Northeast Fish and Wildl. Conf. 34:81–85.

MYRES, M. T. 1968. A sample survey of the expenditures of naturalists. Can. Audubon, January-February:12–20.

NOBE, K. C., AND H. W. STEINHOFF. 1973. Values of wildlife. Pap. presented at Colo. Gov. Conf. on Wildl. and Environ. Denver, 30 March. 10pp.

OUTDOOR RECREATION RESOURCES REVIEW COMMISSION. 1962. Economic studies of outdoor recreation. U.S. Gov. Print. Off., Washington, D.C. 166pp.

PETERLE, T. J. 1961. The hunter—who is he? Trans. North Am. Wildl. and Nat. Resour. Conf. 26:254–266.

RANDALL, A., AND J. R. STOLL. 1983. Existence value in a total valuation framework. Pages 265–274 *in* R. D. Rowe and L. G. Chestnut, eds., Managing air quality and scenic resources at national parks and wilderness areas. Westview Press, Boulder, Colo.

ROLSTON, H., III. 1979. Values in nature. Colorado State Univ., Fort Collins. 21pp. (Typescript.)

ROSEN, S. 1974. Hedonic prices and implicit markets. J. Pol. Econ. 82:34–55.

SCHWEITZER, A. 1951. The animal world of Albert Schweitzer. Translated and edited by Charles R. Joy. Beacon Press, Boston. 207pp.

SCOTT, A. 1965. The valuation of game resources: some theoretical aspects. Can. Fish. Rep. No. 4:27–50.

SHABMAN, L. A. 1980. Economic incentives for bottomland conversion: the role of public policies and programs. Trans. North Am. Wildl. and Nat. Resour. Conf. 45:402–412.

SHAW, W. W. 1974. Meanings of wildlife for Americans: contemporary attitudes and social trends. Trans. North Am. Wildl. and Nat. Resour. Conf. 39:151–155.

SHEPARD, P. 1973. The tender carnivore and the sacred game. Charles Scribner's Sons, New York. 302pp.

SINGER, P. 1973. Animal liberation. New York Rev. of Books, April 5:17–21.

SMITH, V. 1983. Option value: a conceptual overview. South. Econ. J. 49:654–668.

STEINHOFF, H. W. 1969. Values of wildlife and related recreation on the Kenai National Moose Range. Rep. to Div. Wildl. Res., Bur. Sport Fish and Wildl., U.S. Dep. Inter., Washington, D.C. 33pp.

STOLL, J. R., AND L. A. JOHNSON. 1984. Concepts of value, nonmarket valuation, and the case of the whooping crane. Trans. North Am. Wildl. and Nat. Resour. Conf. 49:382–393.

TRICE, A. M., AND S. E. WOOD. 1958. Measurement of recreational benefits. Land Econ. 34:196–207.

U.S. FISH AND WILDLIFE SERVICE. 1955. National survey of fishing and hunting. U.S. Fish and Wildl. Serv. Circ. 44, Washington, D.C. 50pp.

———. 1984. Summary of the report and recommendations on funding sources to implement the Fish and Wildlife Conservation Act of 1980. U.S. Fish and Wildl. Serv. Biol. Rep. 85(4), Washington, D.C. 54pp.

U.S. WATER RESOURCES COUNCIL. 1962. Policies, standards, and procedures in the formulation, evaluation, and review of plans for use and development of water and related land resources. Sen. Doc. 97, 87th Congr., 2nd sess.

WALSH, R. G., R. BJONBACK, D. H. ROSENTHAL, AND R. A. AIKEN. 1985. Public benefits of programs to protect endangered wildlife in Colorado. *In* Symp. on issues and tech. in manage. of impacted west. wildl. Thorne Ecol. Inst., Glenwood Springs, Colo.

———, D. A. GREENLEE, R. A. YOUNG, J. R. McKEAN, AND A. A. PRATO. 1978. Option values, preservation values, and recreational benefits of improved water quality: a case study of the South Platte River Basin, Colorado. EPA Rep. 600/5-78-001, Dep. Econ., Colorado State Univ., Fort Collins.

———, J. B. LOOMIS, AND R. A. GILLMAN. 1984. Valuing option, existence, and bequest demands for wilderness. Land Econ. 60:14–29.

WEISBROD, A. 1964. Collective-consumption services of individual-consumption goods. Q. J. Econ. 78:471–477.

WHITE. L. 1969. The historical roots of our ecologic crisis. Science 155:1203–1207.

Chapter 5

The Importance of Fish and Wildlife Values to the Profession

Edwin A. Verburg, J. John Charbonneau,
William R. Mangun, and Lynn G. Llewellyn

Fish and wildlife professionals are often asked to evaluate the trade-offs between sport fishing or hunting and other activities engaged in by society. The question is posed this way in the daily decision-making process: "What is this resource worth?" Placing a value on a whole fishery, flyway, or deer herd usually is not the issue. More often the question most relevant to managers is the value of a population increment in the overall resource. Most day-to-day decisions in wildlife resource management involve actions that affect only a small part of a fishery or flyway.

The purpose of this chapter is to address some social values related to fish and wildlife and to explain some basic economic ideas useful to understanding how to value fish and wildlife resources. We will also explore how these ideas fit together to form a methodology that is used most often by fish and wildlife economic advisers to evaluate the economic efficiency of management options and—through that process—to determine the importance of wildlife values.

To understand how we go about evaluating alternatives, we must clearly understand the standard by which alternatives are compared. We judge economic consequences of management actions against how the benefits and costs resulting from each management alternative affect society in general. In other words, we look at the effect on consumer prices, employment levels, and general economic activity for all of society. The distribution of the benefits and costs among various groups is determined after an efficient allocation of resources has been attained. In an increasingly complex society, the application of basic economic reasoning assists decision making for fish and wildlife management problems. The analysis of management alternatives and the description of the social and economic gains and losses in a clear and systematic way will go a long way toward providing improved data for decision making. However, economic analysis will not be able to measure the full extent of all values that play a role in management decisions. The applicability of economics is limited in the measurement of biological, aesthetic, or cultural effects. Relatively few economic analyses that have investigated these and other effects have found it necessary to describe their significance in a manner less amenable to decision making. An interdisciplinary approach to analyses is necessary to bridge the measurement gap in the decision-making process.

SOCIAL VALUES

The importance of social values is less visible than that of economic values; however, in certain instances, social values become extremely critical. An example is the oil spill of February 1976 in the Chesapeake Bay that caused the death of an estimated 30,000 migratory birds. The federal government and the Commonwealth of Virginia filed claims for damage to migratory waterfowl, statutory penalties, and cleanup costs against the Steuart Transportation Company. Steuart filed for summary judgment, maintaining that neither Virginia nor the federal government had the right to sue for the loss of migratory waterfowl, since they did not "own" the birds. Dr. Stephen Kellert, among others, testified for the plaintiffs, who argued that the issue was not one of ownership but the public's right and duty to preserve and protect the public's interests in natural wildlife resources. Steuart's motion was denied, and the company later settled out of court. This case was important not so much because of the size of the settlement (Steuart agreed to pay $115,000 in lieu of recovery for waterfowl damage to a private organization to use for projects to benefit waterfowl) but because the courts recognized the legitimacy of nonmonetary, nonconsumptive wildlife values, the essence of Dr. Kellert's testimony.

Social values have weighed heavily on Fish and Wildlife Service decisions in other instances as well. In 1977, a major grant was awarded to the Yale University School of Forestry and Environmental Studies to conduct the most comprehensive study of U.S. attitudes toward wildlife ever undertaken (Kellert 1979). There is no need to dwell at length on the products of this work; they are well known to conference participants. What is important to recognize is that the study constituted a bold new step for the Fish and Wildlife Service at a time when the wildlife management community was becoming increasingly aware of the changing nature of its constituency.

During summer 1979, economists and behavioral scientists in the Office of Planning and Budget became intensely involved in completing a Secretarial Issue Document on coyote management. Predator control has traditionally been a highly emotional concept, a fact that was quite evident in a content analysis of public comment on the coyote management issue (Llewellyn et al. 1979). Letters from private citizens responding to an environmental impact statement advocated some sweeping changes in predator control policy. Clearly, the Service had good reason to be cautious in its interpretation of the findings, knowing full well that sheer volume of letters may not be indicative of true public opinion. However, results from the Yale University study (Kellert 1979) essentially validated the sentiments expressed in the content analysis. A summary of the data from these two independent efforts became an appendix to the Secretarial Issue Document, and, from what was later pieced together about the decision-making process, the information played a key role in the redirection of policy.

Space does not permit a lengthy discourse on the use of social values in decision making beyond the two examples just cited. Nevertheless, when these variables assume importance in management activities the Fish and Wildlife Service has constantly sought to ensure that assumptions could be empirically verified. For example, rigorous content analysis procedures were used in responding to and implementing recommendations concerning the future of the National Wildlife Refuge System (Peoples et al. 1978). Similar procedures were applied in connection with the reclassification of the eastern timber wolf (Llewellyn 1978). More recently, the Fish and Wildlife Service helped fund and provided technical advice for Dr. Kellert's study, "The Public and the Timber Wolf in Minnesota" (1985). In addition, a 1985 national study of youth and wildlife presents the responses of 3,000 fifth and sixth graders to a questionnaire developed for *My Weekly Reader* (Westervelt and Llewellyn 1986). The results of that study appear to challenge some traditional assumptions about environmental education directed at the nation's youth.

The 1980 National Survey of Fishing, Hunting, and Wildlife-Associated Recreation clearly demonstrated the value of nonconsumptive use of wildlife in the United States in terms of the extent of participation and volume of expenditures. An estimated 93 million Americans 16 years and older participated in some form of nonconsumptive enjoyment of wildlife in 1980, such as observing, identifying, photographing, or feeding wildlife (Shaw and Mangun 1984a). And, the estimated 28 million people who took trips longer than 1 mile for nonconsumptive use spent over $4 billion for food, travel, and lodging (Shaw and Mangun 1984b). These figures demonstrate that nonconsumptive uses of wildlife are pervasive and important aspects of life in the U.S.

Recent concerns over the status of funding for nongame management programs prompted the Fish and Wildlife Service to insert questions into the 1980 national survey to determine societal preferences for funding alternatives (Mangun and Shaw 1984). This information and data collected on expenditures of nonconsumptive users was used subsequently to prepare a report to Congress on recommendations for funding sources to implement the Fish and Wildlife Conservation Act of 1980 (U.S. Fish and Wildl. Serv. 1984).

BASIC ECONOMIC APPROACH

Benefit/cost analysis is the standard economic approach used to describe management alternatives and their implications for society. It can be described best as a way of identifying factors that must be taken into account in making economic decisions. Economists use benefit/cost analysis for resource management decisions when the scope of the problem is large enough to warrant the time and expense involved in a full analysis. Such an analysis is necessary when actions are considered that affect river systems, lakes, or the oceans in such a way as to change the biological characteristics of the system and have a potentially large impact on societal values. Benefit/cost analysis is a systematic method that requires a detailed examination of each option before it is compared with other options. This method seeks to compare the benefits to society with the costs of producing the benefits and to display the results using money as the basis for the comparison. This approach clarifies the choice between options by quantifying as many effects as possible in dollar terms so they can be made additive. A good benefit/cost analysis is an attempt to show all areas in which society benefits and incurs costs as a result of a proposed management action.

NEW ECONOMIC VALUES

A key aspect of benefit/cost analysis that concerns sport fisheries and wildlife management is the derivation of net economic values. The net economic value of a fishing or hunting experience is the economic measure of its worth to participants. This worth is measured as the amount of money sport anglers, for example, would have been willing to pay for the fishing experience over and above their current expenditures for fishing. The measurement of economic worth has been a significant area of effort among economists in the last 10 years; this area is expected to provide most of the improvements in fishery evaluation in the future.

The more sophisticated current approach lets the characteristics of the species of fish and the anglers' behavior toward the fishing opportunity determine value instead of using a simple constant value per day of fishing. Since there is no marketplace to give us a price for a sport fishing experience, we must use other means to derive angler willingness to pay for recreational opportunities. These methods (the travel cost and contingent value models are probably the most widely used) have different attributes and uses that have led to confusion in their interpretation. Without going into great detail (since these models are discussed elsewhere in this book), we would like to point out that technical improvements in these models consist of methods for handling alternative fishing or hunting sites and the quality attributes of the sites. By incorporating this information into the values derived for the recreational experience, the net values become better approximations of what would be expected under actual market conditions.

MARGINAL PRINCIPLE

The logic behind calculating a value for an increment to the fishery or wildlife resource is based on a principle in economics called the marginal principle. Stated simply, the marginal principle means that decisions between alternative courses of action are made by looking at the last increment of the item being valued and assessing its net worth vis-à-vis the last increment of a substitute good. In essence, this means that the economist needs to estimate the benefit of the increment minus the cost of attaining that benefit for each alternative being considered. By comparing the alternatives in this manner a decision maker can be sure of choosing the course of action that brings the largest net benefit to society.

For example, if a fish hatchery is operating at less than full capacity and a management decision is made to add fish production to bring the hatchery to full operating capacity, then the manager has to determine which fish to produce. The alternatives can be evaluated in the following way. Suppose, for example, the hatchery is located near a lake with a large steelhead trout fishery and a smaller, but substantial, lake trout fishery, and there has been a history of management actions taken to help both fisheries. The manager could produce and stock either of these fish in the lake. But which one would produce the most benefits to society?

To meet the capacity of the hatchery, the manager could provide steelhead trout in such quantities as to produce 1,000 recreation days valued at $50 per day and could produce this $50,000 benefit at a production and stocking cost of $5,000. This approach would mean a net value for steelhead trout of $45,000. Alternatively, the manager could decide to produce lake trout. Enough lake trout could be produced to yield 3,000 recreation days valued at $25 per day for a total of $75,000 in benefits. However, the production and stocking cost added up to $4,000, giving a net value of $71,000 for lake trout. The manager in this example should decide to produce lake trout since it contributes a higher net value ($71,000 instead of $45,000) to society.

As this example illustrates, even though a fishery is larger and more valuable in total than another fishery, it does not necessarily follow that adding more increments to the former will make society better off than adding to the latter. In this example we used a simple benefit/cost framework without a time dimension to show that decisions at the margin can be deceiving and do not always follow our expectations. Because a whole fishery is worth more does not mean that additions to it are also more valuable than any alternatives. For simplicity, this example did not take into account any distributional effects, nor did it consider which groups would gain or lose as a result of this action.

In another example, wildlife managers may have to make a decision between increasing the population of deer or increasing that for turkey in a particular forest ecosystem. Even-age forest management involving some clear-cutting tends to favor browsing and edge species such as deer that prefer to feed on new growth within open areas. Turkeys, on the other hand, tend to prefer the more dense hardwood forest habitats.

Suppose that a manager has a forested area approaching or at a climax stage of growth. To increase the number of days for deer hunting opportunities he or she would probably want to have some of the climax forest clear cut to provide opportunities for new growth that would attract and increase the deer population. Analysis of data from a southern state indicates that the additional value to the local economy from a day of hunting was $500 per day for deer and $532 for turkey (D. J. Witter, Mo. Dep. Conserv., per. commun., 1985). Since the manager in this area could provide either opportunity, he or she would have to decide which one would provide the most benefits to society.

If a decision was made to produce 1,000 recreation days of deer hunting valued at $500 per day, this could produce a $500,000 benefit with a clear-cutting cost of $100,000. This would mean a net value for deer of $400,000. The other alternative would be to reintroduce turkeys to the existing area without clear-cutting at a stocking cost of $50,000. At a value of $532 per day, this would produce $532,000 with a net value of $482,000. Other things being equal, the manager should elect to produce turkeys in light of a greater economic benefit to society ($82,000).

ALLOCATION OF CATCH BETWEEN SPORT AND COMMERCIAL FISHERMEN

Another use of economic analysis in fisheries management is in the allocation of catch when a fishery has both sport anglers and commercial fishermen. The same basic economic concepts are used as in determining the net economic value of a fishery—without exception. This time the economist wants to know the change in sport angler net benefits as the total number of fishing trips and catch changes. On the commercial fishery side, the economist is interested in the changes in total revenues and total costs when landings increase and decrease. The number of trips sport anglers and commercial fishermen take during a season is determined by the changes in their net benefits per trip as the number of trips increases. In an unregulated, open access fishery, economic models predict that both sport angling and commercial fishing will take place as long as there are positive net benefits for each group's last trip. This means that sport anglers will stop fishing when their cost of participation equals their expected enjoyment and when costs equal the landings value for commercial fishermen.

If the capacity of the fishery is reduced because of external factors that are reversible with a temporary reduction in landings, then a logical management action would be to reduce the overall landings. How should the reduction be distributed between sport and commercial interests? This management problem is becoming more common in U.S. fisheries. To assist decision makers in reaching an economically efficient solution to this problem, the economist would look at the forces that determine the current level of fishing, the net benefits received by both sport and commercial fishermen. Since a reduction in catch is determined to be biologically necessary for the survival of the fishery, the fishing effort should be reduced in such a way that the greatest reduction is given to the group that loses the least net benefit. Reduction should take place until sport and commercial net benefits are equal at the margin. Following this procedure will keep the total fishing benefits at the highest possible level for society. However, some hardships may be imposed on particular groups within the fishing community. Such cases arise when coastal communities depend to a large extent on fishing to generate income. These social and employment effects would be displayed for the decision maker in the benefit/cost framework and enter the final decision-making process. These effects would augment the pure economic efficiency solution already described and may lead to a distribution of catch that loses some economic efficiency but gains some distributional equity.

DATA NEEDS FOR VALUATION
OF FISH AND WILDLIFE RESOURCES

Managing sport fishery resources in the United States is hampered somewhat by the absence of prices for fishing activities, as are commonly found in some European nations. The fee for a state fishing license is not considered a price in the sense that it is not related to the number of fish caught nor the days fished (with the exception of short-term licenses for nonresidents). Rather the fee is considered an annual contribution to defray the expense of managing fisheries by a government agency. A price is society's way of placing value on the goods it wants to consume. How high the price is depends on how much consumer demand there is for the good and how much of the good can be produced at that price. Society's tastes and preferences are reflected in the prices of all goods. Without prices it is difficult to allocate resources for fishing efficiently because the manager cannot tell where resources would be valued most by society. In particular, fishery managers would like to know the value of a fishing day, the value of a fish caught, the value of increased fish density, and the value of additional access to fishing sites. Similarly, wildlife managers would like to know the value of a hunting day, the value of game bagged, the value of having more game available, and the value of additional access to hunting sites.

It would also be helpful if the economic values were available by the species and geographic site, or mode of fishing or hunting activity. Fishery managers, for example, have long been able to determine the cost of increasing fish density in fresh water and the cost of providing access to fishing sites by adding piers and roadways, but they have not always been able to determine directly if the cost of such projects was worth the expense.

The estimation of a systematic set of economic values is currently being planned for sport fishing and hunting in the U.S. This effort will include the net economic values for days or trips of fishing and hunting. The data base for this analysis will consist of the results of two national surveys. Data from the 1985 National Survey of Fishing, Hunting, and Wildlife-Associated Recreation will be added to the results of the 1980 national survey. The possible inclusion of data from other federal, state, and private collections, such as the Soil Conservation Service, state fish and wildlife agencies, or universities will be considered.

The National Surveys of Fishing, Hunting, and Wildlife-Associated Recreation have been conducted at five-year intervals since 1955. The 1980 survey was conducted by the U.S. Bureau of the Census using personal interviews with anglers and hunters throughout the U.S. In total, over 26,000 anglers and hunters were interviewed and asked to respond to questions about their fishing and hunting activities, including the species sought, the days and trips taken for fishing, and the expenses incurred. A similar survey was conducted in 1986 for these activities that occurred in 1985 and will produce another 31,000 responses. This combined total of 57,000 observations will form the basis for the most comprehensive data base on sport fishing and hunting ever available for analysts and decision makers. The 1985 survey was conducted in early 1986. The potential number of studies that can be accommodated with the data that will be available within the next two years is only limited by the imagination of the analyst.

CURRENT ROLE OF ECONOMICS
IN WILDLIFE MANAGEMENT

Historically, the role of economics in fisheries and wildlife management has been limited to estimating fishing or hunting expenditures and days of fishing by sport anglers and hunting by hunters in order to make comparisons with other consumer expenditures or to show the importance of fisheries and wildlife contributions to local and national economies. Only in the last 25 years has the U.S. Congress asked federal agencies to measure the true net economic value of fish and wildlife programs so that projects proposed during the budget process could be judged for their economic efficiency.

During the last few years, state governments have been looking for net economic value information to facilitate resource allocation decisions within their states. The interest of state governments in the economic value of fish and wildlife resources has intensified the effort at the federal level for more precise methods of calculating fish and wildlife values. This effort in turn has led to increased demand for more and better data. The data base on sport fishing and hunting, which will be available within the next two years from the national surveys, will be used by state agencies facing difficult resource allocation decisions. In 1985, for example, the Western Association of Fish and Wildlife Agencies established a committee to promote the development of net economic values for fish and wildlife. This new interest in economic analysis is directed toward resolving conflicts between fishery and wildlife resources and alternative uses of habitat that reduce or eliminate fish and wildlife populations or fishing and hunting opportunities. The estimation of net economic values for fishing and hunting will bring into focus what society is giving up if it chooses to allow the continued loss of its fishery and wildlife resources. The U.S. Forest Service is also moving ahead with the development of values for wildlife for similar purposes. Some uncertainty will always exist, however, in some of the economic measures developed to reflect society's choices. Estimation techniques and data need to be continually evaluated and improved to contribute effectively in the management of fish and wildlife. Fish and wildlife management is a dynamic process that must respond as new problems emerge if these resources are to survive into the future.

SUMMARY

Natural resource economics has a positive role to play in the evaluation of sport fishing, hunting, and wildlife-related recreation. The application of basic economic approaches such as benefit/cost analysis can help fish and wildlife managers attain an efficient allocation of resources. Benefit/cost analysis is a systematic method that seeks to identify the relevant factors that should be taken into account by a decision maker and the consequences of changes in these factors on society. The measurement of gains and losses among various groups in society is an important factor in benefit/cost analysis. However, methodological approaches need to be developed to incorporate the effect on such intangible factors as aesthetics and cultural values. An interdisciplinary approach to analyses is necessary to bridge the measurement gap in the decision-making process.

A key aspect of benefit/cost analysis of concern in sport fisheries and wildlife management areas is the derivation of net economic values, which has been an important research area among economists during the last 10 years. Significant improvements in sport fishery and wildlife evaluation are expected as a result of improvements in both the methodology and the quantity and quality of data in these activities. The application of net economic value models can assist decision makers with fish and wildlife management problems such as species stocking and management of overexploited stocks. Decisions on the distribution of take reductions by sport and commercial interests for the preservation of a fishery or big game harvests to maintain essential populations can be made with the assistance of net economic value models.

REFERENCES

KELLERT, S. R. 1979. Public attitudes toward critical wildlife and natural habitat issues. U.S. Fish and Wildl. Serv., Phase 1 Rep., Washington, D.C. 138 pp.

———. 1985. The public and the timber wolf in Minnesota. School of For. and Environ. Studies, Yale Univ., New Haven, Conn. 175pp.

LLEWELLYN, L. G. 1978. Who speaks for the timber wolf? Trans. North Am. Wildl. and Nat. Resour. Conf. 43:442–452.

———, A CONROY, L. BALDYGA, S. ATZERT, AND D. ZIMMERMAN. 1979. An analysis of public comment on coyote management alternatives. U.S. Fish and Wildl. Serv., Div. Program Plans Working Pap. No. 14, Washington, D.C. 65 pp.

MANGUN, W. R., AND W. W. SHAW. 1984. Alternative mechanisms for funding nongame wildlife conservation. Public Adm. Rev. 44(5):407–413.

PEOPLES, R., A. HARRIS, AND L. G. LLEWELLYN. 1978. Public reactions to proposed recommendations on management of the National Wildlife Refuge

System. U.S. Fish and Wildl. Serv., Div. Program Plans Working Pap. No. 13, Washington, D.C. 30pp.

SHAW, W. W., AND W. R. MANGUN. 1984*a*. Nonconsumptive use of wildlife in the United States. U.S. Fish and Wildl. Serv. Resour. Publ. 154, Washington, D.C. 20pp.

————, AND ————. 1984*b*. Tourism and nonconsumptive uses of wildlife in the western states. Proc. West. Assoc. Fish and Wildl. Agencies and West. Div. Am. Fish. Soc. 64:171–180.

U.S. FISH AND WILDLIFE SERVICE. 1984. Report and recommendations on funding sources to implement the Fish and Wildlife Conservation Act of 1980. U.S. Fish and Wildl. Serv., Washington, D.C. 203pp.

WESTERVELT, M. O., AND L. G. LLEWELLYN. 1986. Youth and wildlife. U.S. Fish and Wildl. Serv., Div. Program Plans, Washington, D.C. 78pp. (In press.)

PART TWO

Wildlife Resource Values Measurement Assessment

Introduction

Tommy L. Brown

Factual and descriptive information has been collected from hunters, trappers, and anglers on a regular basis for 30 years by the U.S. Fish and Wildlife Service and for at least 50 years in studies by state agency and university researchers. However, most of our progress to date in understanding the values people place on wildlife and wildlife-related activities and in understanding human behavior in relation to wildlife values has taken place within the past 15 years. The chapters constituting this part use historical development, examples, and a theoretical framework to provide an understanding of what we know about the measurement of wildlife resource values.

Economic measures of wildlife values were once used largely as a descriptive index outside any decision-making framework. We measured the millions of dollars of hunter and angler expenditures and tried to argue persuasively that because of the magnitude of expenditures these activities represented some very important values to the people of the state or nation. These expenditures were not sufficient indicators of value, however, because the various developments that threatened wildlife and wildlife habitat also had high economic values to some segments of society. As a result, economists were challenged to conceptualize the various economic values of wildlife, to develop improved measures of wildlife benefits, and to compare these benefits with those of various kinds of development. In Chapter 6 Davis and Lim trace advancements in wildlife valuation methods and provide a case study in which wildlife economic values results are applied as an input to a resource management decision.

A rich body of human dimensions literature has evolved over the past two decades dealing with human behavior in relation to wildlife. These studies on motivations or goals of participation in wildlife recreation, reasons for people's initial involvement in wildlife recreation activities, satisfactions sought or obtained from various wildlife-related experiences, and reasons for discontinuing participation all provide a needed understanding of the basis for the economic values of wildlife as well as social explanations for participation that complement the economic demand models. In Chapter 7 Decker et al. propose a behavioral model of wildlife recreation involvement, which includes the goals of participation, factors that influence participation, and a decision-making structure for continuing or discontinuing participation.

Chapter 6

On Measuring the Economic
Value of Wildlife

Robert K. Davis and Diane Lim

Although there have been significant conflicts throughout history between those favoring wildlife conservation and those promoting economic activity, economists in growing numbers are applying their skills to the analysis of wildlife policy issues and valuation problems. Because economic growth is the antithesis of the conservation of wild nature, wildlife managers adopt a value system and philosophical outlook opposed to that of the business community. Although some may believe economists work exclusively for the goals of economic growth and development, the intellectual endeavors of professional economists are not necessarily dictated by these values. Indeed, the work of economists has provided a powerful argument that our society errs in not having a more active policy toward the preservation of natural assets (Krutilla 1968).

The study of the economics of wildlife is particularly challenging because the production and consumption of wildlife take place outside organized markets. In part because we have chosen to make it so, wildlife is an "extramarket" good. Were we to choose to make wildlife a market resource, its economic value might be more readily apparent but then it would be necessary to deal with the fugitive nature of wildlife. It is difficult, but not impossible, to reconcile a market system based on private property rights with the characteristics of a resource that must be reduced to possession before it can be legally owned. Wildlife policy generally has not fostered or protected markets for wildlife. Most applications of economics to the problem of wildlife valuation have not made use of market values directly observed.

In this chapter, we will review the accomplishments of economics when applied to wildlife. Readers should note that a more complete review and list of references can be found in a recent paper (Davis 1985).

THE HISTORIC ROLE OF BIOLOGISTS
IN WILDLIFE VALUATION

Biologists rather than economists were the first people to show an interest in the economic aspects of wildlife. Fifty years ago Aldo Leopold (1933:391–405) wrote a chapter on game economics and aesthetics in his book *Game Management*. A burst of studies of the economic value of wildlife within states appeared after World War II. Typically based on sample surveys of hunters and fishermen, these efforts estimated the total private expenditures that could be attributed to wildlife within a state and the gross values of raw furs or other wildlife commodities. The first nationwide survey of hunters and fishermen was conducted in 1955 by the U.S. Fish and Wildlife Service and has been repeated each five years since. The imprint of these early studies remains intact; in the national survey and in the minds of wildlife conservationists emphasis continues to be placed on the total expenditures of hunters, fishermen, and other users of wildlife.

Thirty-four years ago wildlife economics was called a neglected tool of management (Stoddard 1951). Even though wildlife economics has not been a neglected research topic for the past 25 years, it may not yet have become a tool of management. To form a basis for answering, I will review briefly the contributions of economists to the valuing of wildlife and then present a case in which the economic values of wildlife could have changed the outcome of a regulatory decision, if they had been applied.

ESTIMATING THE VALUE OF WILDLIFE

Marion Clawson (1959) brought economics to the valuation of outdoor recreation in 1959. By the mid-1960s a sufficient number of economists had worked on the problems of estimating the values of wildlife for a consensus to emerge: The expenditure surveys were missing the point. Use of wildlife has a value to consumers that exceeds their expenditures and is reflected in their willingness to pay more for their recreation. Studies of the problem of valuation must be concerned with estimating the value of the surplus accruing to the consumer. Two basic methods emerged during this period, the travel-cost method (Knetsch 1963) and the survey method (Davis 1964). By 1978 the methods, which had become sufficiently developed and standardized, were adopted as those preferred and sanctioned by the U.S. Water Resources Council for the evaluation of recreation benefits in federal water resources projects.

In a number of studies in the past 10 years, economists have made notable applications of economic methods to valuation problems. Not only have some usable results been obtained, but the work has resulted in refinement and verification of methods. In particular, the continued efforts of the economists in the Fish and Wildlife Service, who have been responsible for designing and analyzing the 1980 and 1985 National Surveys, are hastening the day when we may have regional models using localized values for variables to produce estimates of the values for hunting, fishing, or wildlife watching in a particular state or substate regions.

By their nature methods such as travel cost (TC) and survey or contingent value (CV) are indirect: They are employed without direct observations of consumer evaluations in actual markets. Economists, therefore, have been reluctant to claim that their results are a close approximation of the market. Typically the studies call for further verification of the results.

In a series of experiments in Wisconsin researchers have tested willingness to pay for hunting by actually offering to sell permits to a small sample of hunters. The technique seems to provide a method of directly estimating the price of hunting in controlled settings in which permits are issued through drawings. The results also verify that the TC and CV approaches can produce data reasonably close to those for actual sales (Bishop et al. 1983, 1984).

The usual economic test of consumer interest in an activity such as duck hunting is willingness to pay (WTP) for an additional duck bagged or day of duck hunting. Although most of the applications of the TC and CV methods have concentrated on WTP, many of the situations in which questions of value arise concern the value of hunting opportunities lost to a change in land use. In such cases willingness to sell (WTS) is a more appropriate concept than WTP. Debate continues about whether we should theoretically expect measurable differences between WTP and WTS; however, studies of actual buying and selling of hunting permits have shown that WTS exceeds WTP (Bishop et al. 1983, 1984). Experiments under controlled conditions confirm the difference (Knetsch and Sinden 1984). Although experiment and common sense may agree, WTS may not be measurable by current methods (Kahneman 1984).

Two other concepts borrowed from economics, which are used in wildlife evaluation, are option value and existence or bequest value. The first notion is that users and potential users of a good or service are willing to pay something to retain the prospect or option to use it at some future time. The second notion is that nonusers may be willing to pay something to ensure the continued existence of an asset during their lifetimes or for the benefit of future generations. Researchers argue that most forms of wildlife possess option and/or existence values (Krutilla and Fisher 1975). Experimental attempts to measure option and existence values have indeed been rewarded with positive responses (Brookshire et al. 1978, 1983; Stoll and Johnson 1983). Wilderness values, which include wildlife values, have received more attention in this regard (Walsh et al. 1984). Recent thinking about option values recommends caution about concluding that the value can be consistently measured or that it is necessarily always positive. A total WTP that includes use and option values is the quantity we probably will be measuring for the foreseeable future. There may also be ambiguities in existence values, but such information collected from well-run studies can be useful in making choices that may involve the irreversible destruction of wildlife resources (Brookshire et al. 1983).

The emphasis on estimating a market price should not overshadow the study of the determinants of participation in wildlife sports. Statistical models based on the data from the national surveys could well turn out to have a powerful role in forecasting the future of wildlife sports as economic and social variables change and as supplies respond to habitat losses and management improvements.

THE ECONOMICS OF A BOTTOMLAND HARDWOODS PERMITTING CASE

The payoff to studies in wildlife economics lies in the application of the results to management decisions. Economics is the science of choosing. Managers do not escape the economic realities of scarcity simply by not being economists. We now possess the tools for measuring and comparing wildlife values so that managers can make better use of their resources.

Wildlife managers practicing on public land may have a direct hand in making choices of land uses and management practices. For private land they must understand and moderate the disincentives the landowner may have for wildlife management and habitat preservation. A particular problem involving private bottomland hardwoods is to make wildlife values a part of management decisions (Tomlinson 1985). Perverse incentives in federal agricultural programs have caused farmers in the prairie pothole region to drain more wetlands than would have been drained under the economic conditions of an undistorted market (Goldstein 1971). It is also very likely that the federal tax codes and other public policies encourage the conversion of Mississippi bottomland hardwoods to a greater extent than would an undistorted market (Shabman 1980). The lower Mississippi bottomlands have experienced rapid conversion to agriculture in recent years (MacDonald et al. 1979).

We may believe that many bottomlands used for hardwoods are more valuable as wetlands than in converted uses. Federal and state programs

TABLE 6.1
Willingness to Pay for Hunting in the Bottomland Hardwoods of Louisiana
(in 1980 Dollars Per Man-day)

Cost of Time:[a]	1/4w	1/3w	1/2w	3/4w	w
Big Game Hunting	$63.00	$63.00	$67.00	$71.00	$77.00
Small Game Hunting	$12.00	$14.00	$16.00	$21.00	$27.00
Waterfowl Hunting	$15.00	$15.00	$16.00	$18.00	$21.00

Source: Miller 1984.

[a]Travel cost includes time valued at various fractions of the wage rate
to show sensitivity to this factor.

require permits before certain wetlands can be altered. Although the
powers given to public authorities imply that the economic gains and
losses of an altered wetland will be weighed in the balance, acceptable
procedures for doing so are only now being proposed (Batie and Shabman
1982). When a unique wetland ecotype is threatened with irreversible
disappearance, our abilities to evaluate the economic alternatives meet
the acid test. Though not perfect, the economic methods for wetlands
evaluation are probably good enough to be useful.

We have had the opportunity to test our methods on a recent 404
permitting case. Section 404 of the Clean Water Act requires permitting
by the Army Corps of Engineers (COE) for dredging and filling activities
in wetlands. The U.S. Fish and Wildlife Service (FWS) may review
and comment on 404 permit applications. One of the major problems
facing the FWS in its attempts to protect wetland habitat has been the
lack of quantifiable data to support its position on a given permit.

In 1982 the COE issued Section 404 permits for the agricultural
conversion of the Patten/Boyte/Evans tracts in Catahoula Parish, Louisiana. In its objections to the issuance, the FWS pointed to the hundreds
of hunter-days of big game, small game, and waterfowl hunting that
would be lost on this bottomland hardwoods area if it were converted
to agriculture; however, the FWS was unable to provide an economic
value for these losses. We have employed a regional travel cost model,
using data collected in the 1980 National Survey of Hunting and Fishing,
to produce estimates of the willingness to pay for hunting in the
Mississippi bottomland hardwoods of Louisiana (Table 6.1) (Miller
1984). Because the results are sensitive to the values placed on the
opportunity cost of time, Table 6.1 contains a range of estimates based
on fractions of the wage rate.

Using this information and estimates provided in a COE report of hunter-days on agricultural lands and bottomland hardwoods (U.S. Army, COE 1978), we have determined the value of hunting losses involved in the Patten/Boyte/Evans conversion. The losses are net of the expected values of hunting on the converted land. The estimated annual recreational values are calculated using an opportunity cost of time equal to one-third of the wage rate, a value advocated in a recent work (Cesario 1976). The annual costs and returns of the agricultural conversion were estimated from data in a University of Arkansas study of the economics of converting Mississippi bottomland hardwoods (Herrington and Shulstad 1982). Our analysis uses crop yields based on one-half of the land being flooded at more than a three-year frequency. Because this area is too wet for crop rotation, we assume continuous cropping of soybeans. Proper accounting recognizes the opportunity cost of timber production, also provided by the Arkansas study. Present values of net conversion benefits were calculated using a 20-year horizon discounted at 10% per year for the private opportunity cost of capital.

The net benefits of conversion depend on whether the analysis adopts a private accounting stance or the social perspective. The private decision process is based on the long-term market price that the farmer can expect to receive for the crops produced. Hunting values are considered only to the extent that they are capturable by lease income. An analysis from the social perspective, on the other hand, would recognize the cost of government price support and income programs and would consider the loss of extramarket recreational use values. Although private accounting may reveal that the land operator has an incentive to convert, a social accounting may indicate the reverse.

In accounting for the social gain and losses, we use the U.S. Department of Agriculture (USDA) preliminary market-clearing soybean price (U.S. Dep. Agric. 1985). This market-clearing price strips away the supporting effects of federal agricultural programs. From the perspective of society, this and not the price received by the farmer represents the social value. The result of this analysis is that agricultural conversion yields a net loss to society of $282,298 (Table 6.2). The losses include those to hunting as estimated by the travel cost method but do not account for losses to fishing and other wildlife-oriented recreation. The estimates may be conservative because the estimated values of hunting do not allow for the possibility that the value of hunting would increase as bottomland hardwoods become more scarce. One might also expect WTS to be more appropriate than WTP in this case because the hunters are giving up opportunities, not acquiring them, but as we have seen the state-of-the-art method for estimating WTS cannot yet be used with

TABLE 6.2
Net Social Value of Converting 1,010 Acres of Bottomland Hardwood to Soybeans (1978 Dollars)

Year:	0	1	2	3	4	5-20
A. Yield Per Acre (bushels)[a]	0	27.6	27.6	26.5	26.5	23.0
B. Market-Clearing Price[b]	$4.66	$4.66	$4.66	$4.66	$4.66	$4.66
C. Gross Revenue (AxBx1010)	$0	$129,902	$129,902	$124,725	$124,725	$108,252
D. Conversion/Maintenance Costs[c]	$282,012	$0	$2,495	$1,252	$0	$0
E. Production Cost Per Acre[c]	$0.00	$101.65	$99.38	$83.45	$79.65	$75.86
F. Total Cost (D+(Ex1010))	$282,012	$102,669	$102,865	$85,533	$80,450	$76,619
G. Net Revenue (C-F)	($282,012)	$27,233	$27,037	$39,192	$44,275	$31,633
H. Opportunity Costs (timber, hunting leases)[d]	$0	$15,302	$15,302	$15,302	$15,302	$15,302
I. Value of Recreational Losses[e] (above lease income opp. cost)	$0	$17,090	$17,090	$17,090	$17,090	$17,090
Net Benefit of Conversion (G-(H+I))	($282,012)	($5,159)	($5,355)	$6,800	$11,883	($759)

Present Value of Net Benefit Stream:
(20-year stream discounted at 10% per annum)   ($282,298)

[a] Yield per acre is based on half the tract lying below the 3-year flood elevation with long term yields of 18 bushels per acre and the other half of the tract yielding 28 bushels per acre.

[b] Market-clearing price is a preliminary estimate from the USDA Economic Research Service based on a scenario of no farm price supports.

[c] Source: Herrington and Shulstad 1982.

[d] Opportunity costs of timber production ($9 per acre) are from Herrington and Shulstad 1982. Opportunity costs of hunting ($5 per acre) are from local information.

[e] Social value of recreational losses are computed from Table 6.1 values at 1/3 wage rate. Rates of use are from U.S. Army, COE 1978.

TABLE 6.3
Net Private Value of Converting 1,010 Acres of Bottomland Hardwood to Soybeans (1978 Dollars)

Year:	0	1	2	3	4	5-20
A. Yield Per Acre (bushels)[a]	0	27.6	27.6	26.5	26.5	23.0
B. Long Run Price (per bushel)[b]	$5.51	$5.51	$5.51	$5.51	$5.51	$5.51
C. Gross Revenue (AxBx1010)	$0	$153,597	$153,597	$147,197	$147,197	$127,997
D. Conversion/Maintenance Costs[b]	$282,012	$0	$2,495	$1,252	$0	$0
E. Production Cost Per Acre[b]	$0.00	$101.65	$99.38	$83.45	$79.65	$75.86
F. Total Cost (D+(Ex1010))	$282,012	$102,669	$102,865	$85,533	$80,450	$76,619
G. Net Revenue (C-F)	($282,012)	$50,928	$50,732	$61,664	$66,747	$51,379
H. Opportunity Costs (timber, hunting leases)[c]	$0	$15,302	$15,302	$15,302	$15,302	$15,302
Net Benefit of Conversion (G-H)	($282,012)	$35,626	$35,430	$46,362	$51,445	$36,077

Present Value of Net Benefit Stream:
(20-year stream discounted at 10% per annum) $42,409

[a]Yield per acre is based on half of the tract lying below the 3-year flood elevation with long term yields of 18 bushels per acre and the other half of the tract yielding 28 bushels per acre.

[b]Source: Herrington and Shulstad 1982.

[c]Opportunity costs of timber production ($9 per acre) are from Herrington and Shulstad 1982. Opportunity costs of hunting ($5 per acre) are from local information.

confidence. We can find no grounds for believing the estimates of returns from conversion are equally conservative.

In taking the private accounting stance, a \$12/ha/year value is used as the capturable amount of hunting value in the analysis. The value of the recreational losses above this amount is ignored, and the market price is the relevant one. This analysis results in a present value of conversion of \$42,409 (Table 6.3), which demonstrates the presence of an incentive to convert. This is a return to the operator's labor, management, and risk taking because we have not assigned an opportunity cost to any of these factors.

CONCLUSIONS

In this example a certain degree of success was demonstrated in using state-of-the-art economic methods for valuing the losses in hunting when wetlands are converted. Estimating the social gains and losses clarifies the problem facing the agency that has to choose; in this case the COE faces a regulatory choice. But comparing the social gains and losses with the gains and losses to the private individual points up a dilemma: The permit is detrimental to society but may be beneficial to the private entrepreneur.

Even though FWS reports describe the adverse impacts of dredging and filling in biological terms, they are largely unable to answer the arguments concerning the economic returns that would result from issuance of a permit. As a reward of 25 years of persistence by the economists, we are now able to estimate economic values of wildlife with some confidence and to useful ends. The irony is that when shorn of the relative comfort of ambiguity the choices in such cases become inordinately more difficult.

REFERENCES

Batie, S. S., and L. A. Shabman. 1982. Estimating the economic value of wetlands: principles, methods, and limitations. Coastal Zone Manage. J. 10(3):255–278.

Bishop, R C., T. A. Heberlein, and M. J. Kealy. 1983. Contingent valuation of environmental assets: comparisons with a simulated market. Nat. Resour. J. 23:619–633.

————, ————, M. P. Welsh, and R. M. Baumgartner. 1984. Does contingent valuation work? Results of the sandhill experiment. Joint meet. of the Assoc. of Environ. and Resour. Econ., the Am. Agric. Econ. Assoc., and the Northeast Agric. Econ. Counc. 5–8 August. Cornell Univ., Ithaca, N.Y. 35pp.

BROOKSHIRE, D. S., L. S. EUBANKS, AND A. RANDALL. 1978. Valuing wildlife resources: an experiment. Trans. North Am. Wildl. and Nat. Resour. Conf. 43:302–310.

———, ———, AND ———. 1983. Estimating option prices and existence values for wildlife resources. Land Econ. 59(1):1–15.

CESARIO, F. J. 1976. Value of time in recreation benefit studies. Land Econ. 52:32–41.

CLAWSON, M. 1959. Methods of measuring the demand for and the value of outdoor recreation. Resour. for the Future, Inc., Reprint No. 10, Washington, D.C. 36pp.

DAVIS, R. K. 1964. The value of big game hunting in a private forest. Trans. North Am. Wildl. and Nat. Resour. Conf. 29:393–403.

———. 1985. Research accomplishments in wildlife economics. Trans. North Am. Wildl. and Nat. Resour. Conf. 50:392–404.

GOLDSTEIN, J. H. 1971. Competition for wetlands in the midwest: an economic analysis. Johns Hopkins Univ. Press, Resour. for the Future, Inc., Baltimore. 105pp.

HERRINGTON, B. E., AND R. N. SHULSTAD. 1982. Conversion of delta woodland and pasture to cropland: economic feasibility and implications. Univ. Arkansas Agric. Exp. Stn. Bull. 858. 30pp.

KAHNEMAN, D. 1984. A report to Off. of Policy Analysis, U.S. Environ. Protection Agency in R. Cummings, D. Brookshire, D. Coursi, and W. Schulze, eds. Valuing environmental goods: a state of the art assessment of the contingent value method. Vol. II. U.S. Environ. Protection Agency, Off. Policy Analysis, Washington, D.C.

KNETSCH, J. L. 1963. Outdoor recreation demands and benefits. Land Econ. 39(4):387–396.

———, AND J. A. SINDEN. 1984. Willingness to pay and compensation demanded: experimental evidence of an unexpected disparity in measures of value. Q. J. Econ. 99(3):507–521.

KRUTILLA, J. V. 1968. Balancing extractive industries with wildlife habitat. Trans. North Am. Wildl. and Nat. Resour. Conf. 33:119–130.

———, AND A. C. FISHER. 1975. The economics of natural environments: studies in the valuation of commodity and amenity resources. Johns Hopkins Univ. Press, Resour. for the Future, Inc., Baltimore. 300pp.

LEOPOLD, A. 1933. Game management. Charles Scribner's Sons, New York. 481pp.

MACDONALD, P. O., W. E. FRAYER, AND J. K. CLAUSER. 1979. Documentation, chronology, and future projections of bottomland hardwood habitat loss in the lower Mississippi alluvial plain. A study performed for the Ecol. Serv. Branch, U.S. Fish and Wildl. Serv., Washington, D.C. 133pp.

MILLER, J. R. 1984. The value of fish and wildlife-associated recreation days in the Mississippi bottomland hardwoods area. Univ. Utah, prepared for the U.S. Fish and Wildl. Serv., Div. Program Plans, Washington, D.C. 23pp.

SHABMAN, L. A. 1980. Economic incentives for bottomland conversion: the role of public policies and programs. Trans. North Am. Wildl. and Nat. Resour. Conf. 45:402–412.

STODDARD, C. H. 1951. Wildlife economics—a neglected tool of management. Land Econ. 27:248–249.

STOLL, J. R., AND L. A. JOHNSON. 1983. Concepts of value, nonmarket valuation, and the case of the whooping crane. Trans. North Am. Wildl. and Nat. Resour. Conf. 49:382–393.

TOMLINSON, B. H. 1985. Economic values of wildlife: opportunities and pitfalls. Trans. North Am. Wildl. and Nat. Resour. Conf. 50:262–270.

U.S. ARMY, CORPS OF ENGINEERS. 1978. The Sicily Island area levee project: general design memorandum no. 15, appendix E: environmental analysis. Vicksburg, Miss.

U.S. DEPARTMENT OF AGRICULTURE, ECONOMIC RESEARCH SERVICE. 1985. Proposed changes in procedures for estimating normalized prices for agricultural planning for water and related land resources implementation studies. Washington, D.C.

WALSH, R. G., J. B. LOOMIS, AND R. A. GILLMAN. 1984. Valuing option, existence, and bequest demands for wilderness. Land Econ. 60(1):14–29.

Chapter 7

Theoretical Developments in Assessing Social Values of Wildlife: Toward a Comprehensive Understanding of Wildlife Recreation Involvement

Daniel J. Decker, Tommy L. Brown,
B. L. Driver, and Perry J. Brown

A primary goal of wildlife management is to provide a variety of benefits and satisfactions to people (Wagar 1966). Responsive wildlife management requires an understanding of the public's attitudes about, uses of, and values received from wildlife resources. In addition to knowledge about the characteristics, requirements, and behaviors of wildlife, wildlife managers must also understand the human dimensions of wildlife management (Hendee and Schoenfeld 1973). Although the latter area of inquiry has lagged behind the former (Mattfeld et al. 1984), studies have been made of the values that wildlife play in recreational, aesthetic, educational, and other situations; of the effects of wildlife on people and the satisfactions they derive; and of people's behavior toward wildlife. Researchers have also begun to determine the worth of wildlife within the mix of resources and alternative uses available to people.

Of the several categories of values derived from wildlife, those associated with the various forms of wildlife-related recreation account for most of our knowledge of the social values of wildlife. Although scholarly discussion of social values of wildlife not associated with recreational use has been offered (Meyer 1979, Kellert 1985), most social science investigations to date have focused on recreational use. The purpose of this chapter is to propose a theoretical framework for the comprehensive examination of wildlife recreation involvement. Such a conceptual scaffold is needed to frame studies of the decision processes used by people, from the time interest is first shown in a wildlife recreation activity until that interest is lost. Understanding these processes and the factors influencing them improves understanding of the social values associated with wildlife recreation involvement.

A conceptual framework of human involvement in wildlife recreation is important not only from a research perspective but also from policy and management viewpoints. Wildlife managers have increasingly sought information on the human dimensions of wildlife management as human populations have increased, land use conflicts have intensified, wildlife and other environmental issues have become politicized, budgets have become more austere, and greater attention has been given to agency efficiency and effectiveness. It has become increasingly necessary for managers and administrators to know the attitudes, desires, and preferences of the constituencies of wildlife management programs (Mattfeld et al. 1984) and to adapt agency policies about supply to changes in public demands for wildlife resources (Shaw 1974).

THEORETICAL DEVELOPMENT TO DATE

The literature on the human dimensions of wildlife has had meaningful contributions from researchers with backgrounds in sociology, psychology, economics, and leisure sciences. The primary foci of past studies of human dimensions in wildlife research have been to

1. understand human attitudes and beliefs about wildlife
2. quantify human preferences for wildlife and wildlife-related phenomena
3. quantify in economic and noneconomic terms the values humans assign to various uses of wildlife
4. understand human behavior related to wildlife
5. relate human wildlife-related preferences and behavior to wildlife management issues

The concerns of philosophers and others about humans' ethical/moral responsibilities toward wildlife have made important contributions to our understanding as well.

From the individual studies conducted within these foci, several useful theories have emerged to explain aspects of human behavior in relation to wildlife. Although some of the theories about wildlife recreation have been tested empirically and corroborated by other researchers, this approach has been the exception. Instead, past studies have been characterized by theory offerings left untested or unchallenged by alternative theories, leaving unresolved disparities. This situation calls for a broad theoretical perspective that provides general guidelines about which concepts should be included, how they should be linked, and how they should be studied (Wagner 1984).

In proposing such a framework for the study of wildlife recreation involvement, we will be concerned with four domains of inquiry:

1. the goals and circumstances (e.g., social, economic, and physical) that influence the individual's decision regarding involvement in wildlife recreation
2. the role of wildlife recreation involvement in satisfying individual needs and desires over time
3. social factors influencing the acceptability/desirability of recreational involvement with wildlife
4. the role of wildlife recreation involvement as a social process itself, particularly in relation to family development and peer group identity

The variables or factors within these domains influence humans' valuation of their involvement with wildlife.

A FRAMEWORK FOR WILDLIFE RECREATION INVOLVEMENT

A behavioral framework for wildlife recreation involvement is depicted in Figure 7.1. According to this model, individuals try to reach certain basic goals. Whether involvement in a particular form of wildlife recreation is chosen as a means of fulfilling those goals depends partly on personal beliefs, values, habits, ability, expected consequences of any involvement, and the drive or motivation to meet these basic goals. Involvement in wildlife recreation is also strongly affected by external social influences—expectations of others, commitments to others, social customs, social opportunities, the degree of support from others to participate, and the degree of force exerted by others, all tempered by normative beliefs about these topics.

The goals of the individual in combination with such psychological (internal) and sociological (external) influences largely determine an individual's involvement in any particular form of wildlife recreation. But involvement also has a temporal dimension that includes trying a particular activity, identifying with it, and perhaps adopting it as a primary means of meeting some basic goals. This temporal process is shown at the bottom of Figure 7.1. The process allows for continued involvement as interest in a wildlife recreation activity increases and for adoption if it meets one or more basic needs. It also allows for rejection or dropping out at any stage if the experience is evaluated to be negative or does not meet the desired goals of the individual.

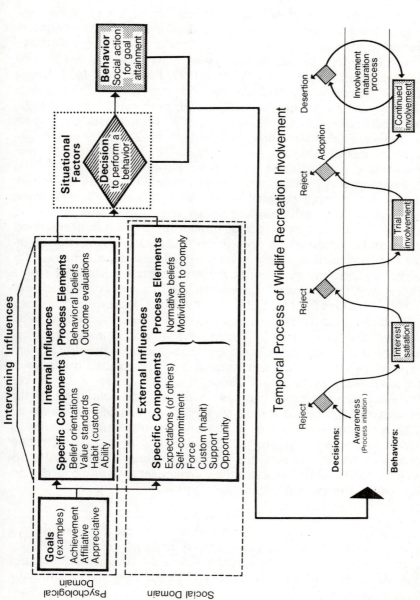

Figure 7.1 Conceptual schematic drawing of social-psychological process determining wildlife recreation behavior

Goals: Antecedents to Wildlife Recreation Involvement

Several studies have identified the specific reasons why people participate in wildlife recreation and the satisfactions derived from outdoor recreation in general (e.g., Hendee 1974, Hendee and Bryan 1978). The specific activity for which such information is most extensive is hunting (e.g., Kennedy 1970, Klessig 1970, More 1973, Potter et al. 1973, Schole et al. 1973, Stankey et al. 1973, Kellert 1976, Brown et al. 1977, Gilbert 1977, Langenau and Mellon-Coyle 1977, Heberlein and Laybourne 1978, Arthur and Wilson 1979, Faunce et al. 1979, Hautaluoma and Brown 1979, Jackson et al. 1981, Applegate and Otto 1982, Decker and Brown 1982, Decker et al. 1984).

Responding to the need for a broader understanding of goals and other antecedents to hunting involvement, Decker et al. (1984) undertook a study using in-depth personal interviews of hunters. The responses, in combination with a thorough literature search, led these authors to conclude that the majority of specific reasons (but not all) for recreational hunting can be combined into three broad categories: affiliative, achievement, and appreciative. These goals had different degrees of saliency for different people and were regarded as more or less important depending upon the situation. Among the previous studies reviewed by Decker et al. (1984), Schole et al. (1973) and Klessig (1970, 1974) presented syntheses that identified these three goal orientations. Furthermore, Kellert (1976, 1980) identified three types of hunters based on reasons for hunting, then characterized the types based on their primary attitudinal orientations, which reflected the achievement and appreciative orientations of the trichotomy proposed by Decker et al. (1984).

For illustrative purposes, we have expanded the definitions of the three goal orientations identified by Decker et al. (1984) to relate to wildlife recreation involvement in general. The resulting trichotomy is an incomplete listing of primary goal orientations for wildlife recreation involvement, but it demonstrates the kind of general conceptual tools being developed to help comprehend the antecedents to wildlife recreation involvement. The expanded definitions follow:

Affiliative—Affiliative-oriented wildlife recreationists become involved in an activity primarily to accompany another person and to enjoy their company or to strengthen/reaffirm the personal relationship between them (during the activity or in planning and recalling the activity experiences).

Achievement—Achievement-oriented wildlife recreationists become involved in an activity primarily to meet some standard of performance. The specific goal could be a hunting harvest for meat or trophy (exhibition) or spotting a given species (discovery) to photograph to add to a life list. Sharing accomplishments may or may not be an important aspect of such involvement.

Appreciative—Appreciative-oriented wildlife recreationists seek from their involvement in an activity primarily the sense of peace, belonging, and familiarity and the resulting stress reduction that they have come to associate with the activity. Just the recollection of experiences can be rewarding.

We recognize that other goals for wildlife recreation participation exist in addition to these three. We also recognize that the three goal orientations could be broken down into more specific categories. (See Knopf [1972] for examples of the motivational determinants of recreation behavior.)

Social-Psychological Determinants of Behavior

Goals spark an individual's behavior, but other intervening influences determine the particular form of that behavior. Two organizations of social-psychological concepts have been incorporated into this portion of our theoretical framework. These are different yet complementary ways to think about determinants of human behavior. In combination they provide a robust and useful approach to understanding the social-psychological antecedents to involvement in wildlife recreation and therefore the social values inherent in such behavior.

The first social-psychological model is that of Ajzen and Fishbein (1980). In their theory of reasoned action, they propose that behavior is determined by a process (Fig. 7.2) having four basic elements:

Behavioral Beliefs—those beliefs that a person has about the desirable and undesirable outcomes of a particular behavior

Outcome Evaluations—a person's assessments of the worth of the consequences associated with a specific behavior

Normative Beliefs—a person's beliefs about whether specific reference individuals or groups think a behavior should or should not be performed

Motivation to Comply—the degree to which a person is motivated to comply with specific referents

According to the theory of reasoned action, these four elements lead to two major considerations in determining behavior. That is, the combination of behavioral beliefs and outcome evaluations results in a person's attitude toward the behavior, whereas the combination of

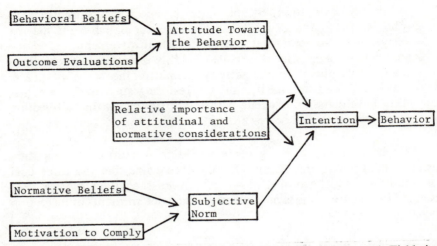

Figure 7.2 Factors determining a person's behavior (Ajzen and Fishbein, *Understanding attitudes and predicting social behavior*, © 1980, p. 100; reprinted by permission of Prentice-Hall, Inc., Englewood Cliffs, New Jersey)

normative beliefs and motivation to comply determines the subjective norm pertaining to the behavior (Fig. 7.2). The attitude toward the behavior and the subjective norm (each having a relative importance weight in the process) determine a person's behavioral intention, a best estimate of probable behavior.

The process elements of Fishbein and Ajzen's conceptualization can be categorized as internally and externally originated influences, according to the distinction shown in Figure 7.3. It is also important to note that Fishbein and Ajzen (1975:9–11) base their proposition on the "notion that attitudes are learned." Similarly, we assert that involvement in a wildlife recreational activity is a learned behavior. Fishbein and Ajzen's conceptual framework of factors influencing an individual's behavior and the model of how these factors interact is useful as a process guide to understanding the general social-psychological complex that influences a particular behavior. However, a more detailed conceptualization can be achieved by integrating a second model of social behavior developed by Reeder (1973).

Reeder (1973) identified 10 significant social-psychological influences on behavior (Fig. 7.4, Table 7.1). They are presented by Reeder as factors influencing decision making for social action (i.e., decisions to perform a behavior). Reeder's model is easily integrated with that of Fishbein and Ajzen, thereby providing more specific concepts that, in combination, constitute the factors used by the latter authors.

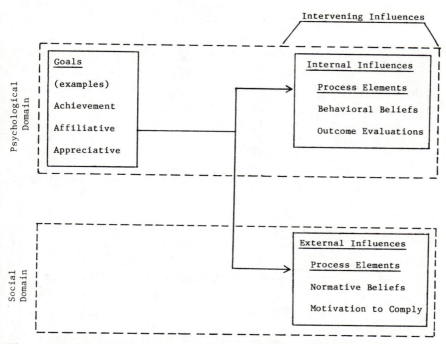

Figure 7.3 Goals and intervening influences (process elements)

Decisions for types of behavior are made in a context with at least three spheres of influence—social-psychological (everything discussed up to now), physical, and physiological. We are concerned especially with individuals' perceptions of physical and physiological factors because such perceptions (which may or may not be consistent with reality) serve as inputs for their decision making. Reeder's model includes such elements—opportunity equates with perceived physical situation (an external influence) and ability equates with perceived physiological situation (an internal influence). Reeder's model also includes the factor goals discussed earlier. The remaining nine factors can be categorized as internally or externally originated intervening influences, and they represent underlying components of the process elements of the Fishbein and Ajzen model. Adding the decision element results in a comprehensive conceptual model of the social-psychological process determining wildlife recreation behavior (Fig. 7.1).

Studies in New York (Decker et al. 1984, Purdy et al. 1985) have shown that factors in Reeder's model vary in saliency to an individual's decisions regarding involvement in one type of wildlife recreation activity—hunting. To a large degree, the factors in Reeder's model cor-

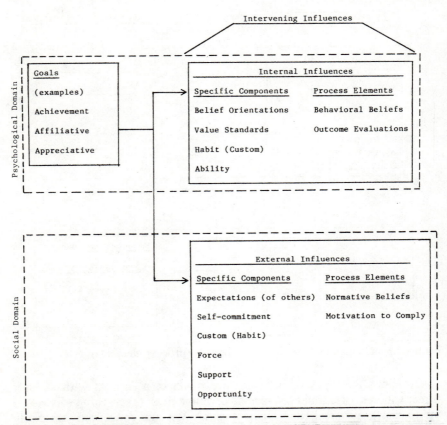

Figure 7.4 Goals of behavior and intervening influences (process elements and specific conceptual components)

respond to the attitudinal and facilitative factors in Driver's (1976) general conceptual model of outdoor recreation involvement. This model, an outgrowth of the Driver and Brown (1975) National Academy of Sciences model, has been a major influence in the development of our understanding of wildlife recreational behavior.

In summary, 9 of Reeder's 10 factors provide added detail about the specific underlying social-psychological elements to a decision to engage in a wildlife recreation activity, whereas the Fishbein and Ajzen model helps us understand how these elements, of both internal and external origin, work together as a process of beliefs–attitudes–behavioral intentions. The entire process is initiated by an individual's goals. To complete this portion of our theoretical framework of recreation participation, we need to explain how an individual develops behavioral beliefs,

TABLE 7.1
Ten Influences of Decision Making for Social Action

1. Goals	Physiological consistency, preservation of self, safety-security, love, belongingness, recognition-esteem, autonomous self satisfying activities, self-actualization and service, N-achievement, knowledge, beauty and esthetics.
2. Belief Orientations	Beliefs about: the existence or non-existence of a referent, the reference category characteristics of a referent, the beliefs and past actions of a referent, the real or potential relationships of a referent to other referents and those things that belong together and those that are independent of each other.
3. Value Standards	Achievement, efficiency, practicality, progress, material comfort, leadership ability, self confidence, understanding, faith in science, belief in democracy, belief in equality, belief in freedom or liberty, belief in God or a Supreme Being, honesty, sexual morality, sobriety, cleanliness, loyalty, keeping of confidence, conformity, ability to get along with others.
4. Habit and Custom	Ways of thinking, ways of dealing with problems, ways of meeting frustrations, cognitions regarding appropriate response for all those situations in which a single response is automatically considered the appropriate one for the situations.
5. Ability	Conceived and perceived capabilities of the actor to cope with the alternatives in the situation, which he may potentially face: rank, power, authority, money, resources, facilities, knowledge, skills, eligibility, manpower, convenience, awareness, size, strength, intelligence, health, endurance, and time.
6. Opportunity	Perceived requirements of the various alternatives in the situation-rank authority, power, money, resources, facilities, knowledge, skills, eligibility, manpower, convenience, awareness, size, strength, intelligence, health, endurance, and time.
7. Expectations Norms	Station expectations, status expectations, position expectations, role expectations, norm expectations, situational expectations, reference category expectations, and self expectations based on cognitions of the relevance of various referents to the actor.

TABLE 7.1 (Cont.)

8. Self- Commitments	Contracts, written agreements, verbal agreements, commitments that go with the acceptance of an office, commitments that are part of group membership, commitments based on actions such as voting, statements of opinions, role playing and commitments deriving from various types of participation.
9. Force	Physical, military, police law, rules, economics, public opinion, threat to livelihood, threat of violence or danger, disability, illness, circumstances, and acts of nature such as floods, hail, drought, etc.
10. Support, Opposition	The amount of help or opposition the actor perceives or conceives others can and will give in relation to actual or potential alternatives: rank, power, authority, money, resources, facilities, knowledge, skills, eligibility, manpower, convenience, awareness, size, strength, health, endurance, time, recognition, guarantee of profit or maximum loss, rationale, goal and value reinforcement, the creation of special supportive climates and conformity.

Source: Reeder 1973.

outcome evaluations, normative beliefs, and motivation to comply, or more specifically, how an individual comes to have particular goals, belief orientations, value standards, and so on. A plausible and entirely congruent explanation lies in social learning theory.

Social Learning Theory: An Explanation for Formation of Values, Beliefs, and Attitudes Relative to Wildlife Recreation Involvement

Social learning theory (Bandura 1977) provides a framework for explaining how people form the values, beliefs, and attitudes that lead to decisions to behave in particular ways. It helps us understand how individuals weigh the social-psychological components of a decision. These evaluative biases are the product of actual and vicarious experience—a social learning process.

In essence, social learning theory states that people learn their goals, values, attitudes, and so on, by doing and watching others and through verbal and written communication. The relevance of social learning theory is evident throughout this chapter. It should be viewed as a source of explanations for the "whys" of the content and evaluative aspect of wildlife recreation involvement.

Of the various types of wildlife recreation, hunting has been studied most extensively from the standpoint of social-psychological antecendents to involvement. The importance of role modeling and social learning to the "development and confirmation of hunting interest" was suggested by Schole et al. (1973:245), among others. More recently, social learning concepts, particularly identification and modeling, were applied to a study of Wisconsin hunters by Jackson (1980). Heberlein (1984) has found the precepts of social learning theory applicable to an explanation of bowhunting behavior. Social learning processes are probably at work for other forms of wildlife recreation as well.

Understanding the Social-Temporal Context of Wildlife Recreation Involvement

We contend that people's involvement in wildlife recreation evolves over time; sometimes adoption of an activity occurs quickly, sometimes it requires many years. Furthermore, an individual's orientation toward the activity may change over time. Thus, we arrive at the temporal portion of the theoretical framework (Fig. 7.1).

Activity Adoption/Rejection. The voluntary adoption of new ideas, practices, or activities by individuals seldom results from a single, pivotal decision. Rather, a series of decisions leading to increasing levels of involvement, similar to that described in the classical innovation-adoption model of Rogers (1962), is the norm for most people. The concept of adoption has been applied to recreation participation previously (e.g., Brandenberg et al. 1982). We have developed an adoption model to help understand and describe the progression of a person's interest and involvement in wildlife recreation (Fig. 7.5). As illustrated, the several stages reflect increasing levels of involvement, from initial awareness of the activity, to gaining interest in it, to actually trying it, and finally to the decision(s) to continue involvement. Recognizing these stages in the theoretical framework is important because it emphasizes that the decision to participate in a wildlife activity is rarely spontaneous; it is the product of a sequence of decisions (as depicted by the diamonds) associated with the increasing levels of involvement leading to the end behavior.

Involvement Maturation. Examination of the notion of a process of involvement in wildlife recreation vis-à-vis the resesarch evidence suggests that continued involvement is neither static nor simply recycling. Rather, considerable evidence indicates that a process of change occurs. Participation can in turn change or develop interests (Brandenberg et

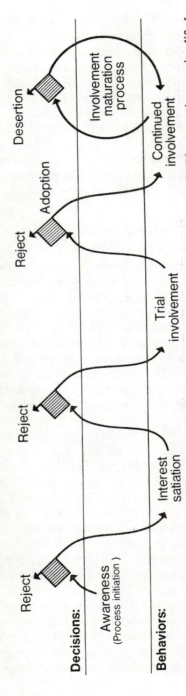

Temporal Process of Wildlife Recreation Involvement

Decisions:

Reject   Reject   Reject   Adoption   Desertion

Awareness
(Process initiation)

Interest
satiation

Trial
involvement

Continued
involvement

Involvement
maturation
process

Behaviors:

Figure 7.5 Stages in the development of an individual's interest and involvement in wildlife recreation: a simplified conceptual model of the process

al. 1982). Hendee et al. (1971) reported a typology of outdoor recreation activity preferences that depicted a change in such preferences associated with increasing age, but they focused on changes among activities rather than changes in involvement within a particular activity category. Among the first researchers to discuss this developmental sequence for an activity were Jackson et al. (1979). They identified five types of general hunting behaviors that they believed were stages in a social-psychological development process (Table 7.2). Although they hypothesized this as a process, our observations indicate that these represent types of behavior that are more likely to be situationally determined, or at least so influenced. If this is indeed a process, regression must be a common occurrence.

Applegate and Otto (1982) have observed that the five stages proposed by Jackson et al. (1979) are somewhat comparable to Kellert's meat, sport, and nature hunters, in that order. This may suggest that Kellert's typology, developed from a cross-sectional or "slice-in-time" study, may be describing the attitudinal structures associated with hunters as they pass through a "sequence of cumulative experience" (Applegate and Otto 1982:22) over time.

Bryan (1979) also hypothesized the existence of a process of involvement with wildlife, as well as other forms of outdoor recreation. He believed that specialization continua existed whereby outdoor recreationists tended to move from activities of low specialization to those requiring higher specialization (Fig. 7.6). He elaborated on two versions of specialization—within categories of activity and between categories of activity (Fig. 7.7). Again, even though the existence of this general trend was supported by various research, regression must be common.

Recent studies by the senior authors also have suggested that a change occurs among some hunters over time (Decker et al. 1984, Purdy et al. 1985). However, rather than describing this process in terms of behaviors, as did Jackson et al. (1979) and Bryan (1979), we believe the change to be on the more basic and general level of goals. Many hunters we studied seemed to shift, at different rates, from primarily affiliative or achievement goal orientations to a primarily appreciative goal orientation. We found no one who began hunting with primarily an appreciative orientation and subsequently developed primarily an achievement or affiliative goal orientation. In fact, none of the hunters we studied became involved in hunting with primarily an appreciative goal, although the possibility exists for such an initial orientation.

Our findings do not conflict with those of the previously mentioned researchers; they merely represent a different and, we believe, more fundamental explanation for the behavioral changes described by others. Our theoretical perspective would lead us to believe that over time the

TABLE 7.2
Stage Descriptions in the Jackson et al. (1979) Hunting
Development Sequence

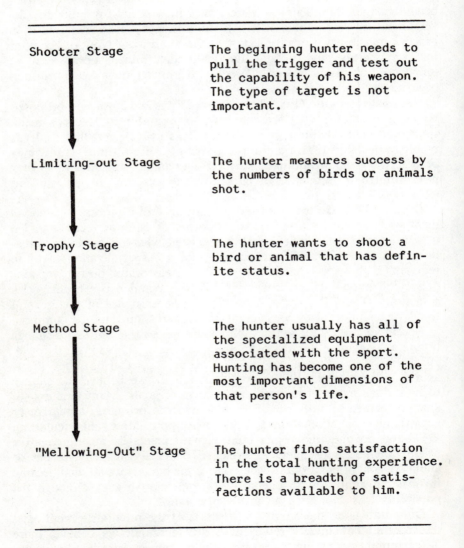

Shooter Stage	The beginning hunter needs to pull the trigger and test out the capability of his weapon. The type of target is not important.
Limiting-out Stage	The hunter measures success by the numbers of birds or animals shot.
Trophy Stage	The hunter wants to shoot a bird or animal that has definite status.
Method Stage	The hunter usually has all of the specialized equipment associated with the sport. Hunting has become one of the most important dimensions of that person's life.
"Mellowing-Out" Stage	The hunter finds satisfaction in the total hunting experience. There is a breadth of satisfactions available to him.

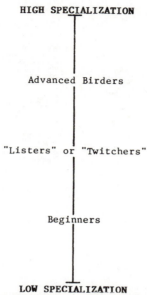

HIGH SPECIALIZATION

Advanced Birders

"Listers" or "Twitchers"

Beginners

LOW SPECIALIZATION

Figure 7.6 Specialization in wildlife recreation (e.g., birdwatching) (Bryan 1979; reprinted by permission)

needs (goals) of many people initially having primarily achievement or affiliative goals for their involvement in hunting, or other wildlife recreation activities, are reduced. Possibly the social values of the activity change as well. Some people undoubtedly leave the activity when this "need reduction" occurs, but others continue for other social-psychological reasons (e.g., habit, expectations, commitment) and with an appreciative-affiliative or appreciative-achievement orientation combination. The stages identified by Jackson et al. and the levels of specialization recognized by Bryan may actually be behavioral indicators of these goal orientation shifts. Thus, our theoretical framework includes an involvement maturation dimension in the continuation-desertion stage of the activity adoption/rejection process described earlier. We expect corresponding changes in the social values of the activity for an individual.

A THEORETICAL FRAMEWORK FOR WILDLIFE RECREATION INVOLVEMENT: SUMMARY

To summarize, we have developed a theoretical framework that we believe can serve as a guide for organizing further thinking and research

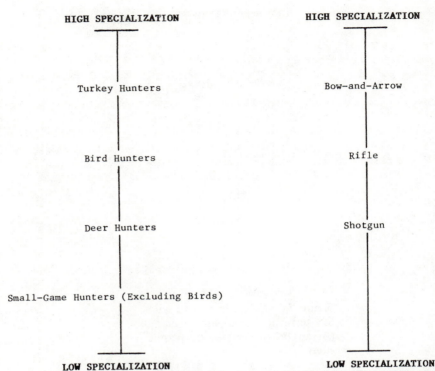

Figure 7.7 Examples of two forms of specialization in hunting—between categories of hunting (left column) and within a category (right column) (Bryan 1979; reprinted by permission)

about the interplay between people and wildlife. If this framework is seriously examined by human dimensions scientists, it may provide a valuable second benefit of providing order to both the existing knowledge base and the results of future studies. To the degree that this framework is either challenged or built upon, that process will continue to clarify the goals and benefits of wildlife recreation involvement, and it will continue the evolution of human dimensions in wildlife management as an emerging applied discipline. Wildlife program managers and administrators will benefit from an improved understanding of the degree to which various forms of wildlife recreation in particular settings meets the needs of recreationists. Ultimately, the wildlife recreationist public itself will benefit because wildlife programs will continue to be improved to offer a more complete "benefits package" for those interested in enjoying the wildlife resource and the social values it provides.

REFERENCES

AJZEN, I., AND M. FISHBEIN. 1980. Understanding attitudes and predicting social behavior. Prentice-Hall, Inc., Englewood Cliffs, N.J. 278 pp.

APPLEGATE, J. E., AND R. A. OTTO. 1982. Characteristics of first-year hunters in New Jersey. N.J. Agric. Exp. Stn. Publ. No. R-12381-(1)-82. 27pp.

ARTHUR, L. M., AND W. R. WILSON. 1979. Assessing demand for wildlife resources: a first step. Wildl. Soc. Bull. 7(1):30–34.

BANDURA, A. 1977. Social learning theory. Prentice-Hall, Inc., Englewood Cliffs, N.J. 247pp.

BRANDENBERG, J., W. GREINER, E. HAMILTON-SMITH, H. SCHOLTEN, R. SENIOR, AND J. WEBB. 1982. A conceptual model of how people adopt recreation activities. Leisure Studies 1:263–276.

BROWN, P. J., J. E. HAUTALUOMA, AND S. M. MCPHAIL. 1977. Colorado deer hunting experiences. Trans. North Am. Wildl. and Nat. Resour. Conf. 42:216–225.

BRYAN, H. 1979. Conflict in the great outdoors. Bur. Public Adm. Sociological Studies No. 4, Univ. Alabama, University. 98pp.

DECKER, D. J., AND T. L. BROWN. 1982. Degree to which participants in the 1978 hunter training course subsequently bought a hunting license. N.Y. Fish and Game J. 29(2):184–188.

————, R. W. PROVENCHER, AND T. L. BROWN. 1984. Antecedents to hunting participation: an exploratory study of the social-psychological determinants of initiation, continuation, and desertion in hunting. Outdoor Recreation Res. Unit Ser. No. 84-6, Dep. Nat. Resour., Cornell Univ., Ithaca, N.Y. 175pp.

DRIVER, B. L. 1976. Toward a better understanding of the social benefits of outdoor recreation participation. Pages 163–189 *in* Proc. South. States Recreation Res. Appl. Workshop. U.S. Dep. Agric., For. Serv. Gen. Tech. Rep. SE-9, Southeast. For. Exp. Stn., Asheville, N.C.

————, AND P. J. BROWN. 1975. A socio-psychological definition of recreation demand, with implications for recreation resource planning. Pages 64–88 *in* Assessing demand for outdoor recreation. Natl. Academy of Sci., Washington, D.C.

FAUNCE, F. R., A. S. KEZIS, AND G. K. WHITE. 1979. Characteristics of Maine's resident and non-resident hunters. Univ. Maine Life Sci. and Agric. Exp. Stn. Bull. 760, Orono. 19pp.

FISHBEIN, M., AND I. AJZEN. 1975. Belief, attitude, initiation, and behavior: an introduction to theory and research. Addison-Wesley Publ. Co., Reading, Mass. 578pp.

GILBERT, A. H. 1977. Vermont hunters: characteristics, attitudes, and levels of participation. Univ. Vermont Agric. Exp. Stn. Misc. Publ. 92, Burlington. 71pp.

HAUTALUOMA, J. E., AND P. J. BROWN. 1979. Attributes of the deer hunting experience: a cluster-analytic study. J. Leisure Res. 10(4):271–287.

HEBERLEIN, T. A. 1984. Hunting behavior and the technique-setting specialist. Pages 149–158 *in* Proc. Mid-West Bow Hunting Conf. LaCrosse, Wis.

———, AND B. LAYBOURNE. 1978. The Wisconsin deer hunter: social characteristics, attitudes, and preferences for proposed hunting season changes. Cent. for Policy Studies Working Pap. No. 10, School Nat. Resour., Coll. Agric. and Life Sci., Univ. Wisconsin, Madison. 96pp.

HENDEE, J. C. 1974. A multiple-satisfaction approach to game management. Wildl. Soc. Bull. 2(3):104–113.

———, AND H. BRYAN. 1978. Social benefits of fish and wildlife conservation. Proc. West. Assoc. Fish and Wildl. Agencies 58:234–254.

———, R. P. GALE, AND W. R. CATTON, JR. 1971. A typology of outdoor recreation activity preferences. J. Environ. Educ. 3(1):28–34.

———, AND C. SCHOENFELD. 1973. Human dimensions in wildlife programs. Mercury Press, Washington, D.C. 193pp.

JACKSON, R. 1980. Models and influences shaping hunter attitudes and behaviors. Proc. 42nd Midwest Fish and Wildl. Conf. St. Paul.

———, R. NORTON, AND R. ANDERSON. 1979. Improving ethical behavior in hunters. Trans. North Am. Wildl. and Nat. Resour. Conf. 44:306–318.

———, ———, AND ———. 1981. The resource manager and the public: an evaluation of historical and current concepts and practices. Trans. North Am. Wildl. and Nat. Resour. Conf. 46:208–221.

KELLERT, S. R. 1976. Attitudes and characteristics of hunters and anti-hunters and related policy suggestions. School For. and Environ. Studies, Yale Univ., New Haven, Conn. 55pp. (Unpubl. manuscript.)

———. 1980. Activities of the American public relating to animals. Fed. Grant No. 14-16-0009-77-056, School For. and Environ. Studies, Yale Univ., New Haven, Conn. 178pp.

———. 1985. Social and perceptual factors in endangered species management. J. Wildl. Manage. 49(2):528–536.

KENNEDY, J. J. 1970. A consumer analysis approach to recreational decisions: deer hunters as a case study. Ph.D. Thesis, Virginia Polytechnic Inst. and State Univ., Blacksburg. 182pp.

KLESSIG, L. L. 1970. Hunting in Wisconsin: initiation, desertion, activity patterns and attitudes as influenced by social class and residence. M.S. Thesis, Univ. Wisconsin, Madison. 152pp.

———. 1974. Hunting: social beginnings and social endings. Pages 57–64 *in* Proc. Hunting: Sport or Sin Conf. Univ. Wisconsin, Stevens Point.

KNOPF, R. C. 1972. Motivational determinants of recreation behavior. M.S. Thesis, Univ. Michigan, Ann Arbor. 146pp.

LANGENAU, E. E., JR., AND P. M. MELLON-COYLE. 1977. Michigan's young hunter. Mich. Dep. Nat. Resour. Wildl. Div. Rep. No. 2800. 54 + xxiv pp.

MATTFELD, G. F., D. J. DECKER, T. L. BROWN, S. L. FREE, AND P. R. SAUER. 1984. Developing human dimensions in New York's wildlife research program. Trans. North Am. Wildl. and Nat. Resour. Conf. 49:54–65.

MEYER, N. 1979. The sinking ark: a new look at the problem of disappearing species. Pergamon Press, Oxford. 305pp.

MORE, T. A. 1973. Attitudes of Massachusetts hunters. Trans. North Am. Wildl. and Nat. Resour. Conf. 38:230–234.

POTTER, D. R., J. C. HENDEE, AND R. N. CLARK. 1973. Hunting satisfaction: game, guns, or nature. Pages 62–71 *in* J. C. Hendee and C. Schoenfeld, eds. Human dimensions in wildlife programs. Mercury Press, Washington, D.C.

PURDY, K. G., D. J. DECKER, AND T. L. BROWN. 1985. New York's 1978 hunter training course participants: the importance of social-psychological influences on participation in hunting from 1978–1984. Hum. Dimensions Res. Unit Ser. No. 85-7, Dep. Nat. Resour., Cornell Univ., Ithaca, N.Y. 127pp.

REEDER, W. W. 1973. Beliefs, disbeliefs and social actions. Cornell Univ. Agric. Exp. Stn. Bull. No. 74, Ithaca, N.Y. 33pp.

ROGERS, M. 1962. Diffusion of innovations. Free Press, New York.

SCHOLE, B. J., F. A. GLOVER, D. D. SJOGREN, AND E. DECKER. 1973. Colorado hunter behavior, attitudes and philosophies. Trans. North Am. Wildl. and Nat. Resour. Conf. 38:242–248.

SHAW, W. W. 1974. Meanings of wildlife for Americans: contemporary attitudes and social trends. Trans. North Am. Wildl. and Nat. Resour. Conf. 39:151–155.

STANKEY, G. H., R. C. LUCAS, AND R. R. REAM. 1973. Relationship between hunting success and satisfaction. Trans. North Am. Wildl. and Nat. Resour. Conf. 38:235–242.

WAGAR, J. A. 1966. Quality in outdoor recreation. Trends 3(3):9–12.

WAGNER, D. G. 1984. The growth of sociological theories. Sage Publ. Inc., Beverly Hills, Calif. 152pp.

PART THREE

Direct Economic Uses
of the Wildlife Resource

Introduction

James E. Miller

Although most wildlife resources are recognized as having some value, most of us, including the authors of this book, would probably agree that land is our fundamental and most valued resource. The future of the wildlife resource depends on proper stewardship of the land today and in the future. These statements provide the proper perspective for examining the direct economic uses of the wildlife resource, particularly as they can be applied to private land management alternatives. This approach does not ignore the fact that these direct economic uses are vital to public land management decision making or that other wildlife values over and above the direct economic ones are significant.

Most of the land in the contiguous United States is privately owned, and its management significantly affects public values. According to recent estimates, approximately two-thirds of our wildlife is produced on private lands, the remainder on public lands. Therefore, the stewardship, or lack thereof, by private landowners or managers affects watersheds, flood plains, wetlands, timber stands, rangelands, wildlife habitats, and other natural resources that provide public benefits. One reason that knowledge of the direct economic uses of the wildlife resource is so important is that the majority of our private landowners and managers have yet to recognize that these wildlife values should be considered in land management decision making. Some of the difficulties in acknowledgment of these values arise because wildlife is owned by the public, and many people are uninformed about the economic benefits derived from the wildlife resource and fail to accept them.

However, landowners and managers in some areas are beginning to realize that access to their lands for wildlife recreational use has an economic value and can be marketed for direct economic returns. Thus improving the quantity and quality of wildlife habitat on these lands can provide more wildlife for recreational use and potentially increase their value. When these facts become evident, some decisions about land stewardship must be made, and if the incentives outweigh the disincentives, the landowner or manager is better equipped to determine future land use.

The assumptions in the preceding paragraph are rather simplistic: In reality land management decision making is significantly more complex and must consider other impacts of changing land use and economies. One of the potential impacts often overlooked in our zeal for encouraging private landowners to manage for wildlife is the economic impact of wildlife damage. It can have significant impacts on the owner or manager's other interests, including wildlife habitats or desired wildlife species. These and many other factors must be included when examining the economic alternatives that impact on wildlife resource values.

The chapters in this part will provide an examination of price and value alternatives for the wildlife resource, wildlife commercialization options on private lands, impacts of fee hunting on land management, the economic values of wildlife habitat mitigation, waterfowl resource values, costs of wildlife production and damage control, and value-added conservation. The authors of these chapters will provide an analysis of how and why this information should benefit natural resources managers and administrators as we plan for the present and future use of these resources. It is imperative that we understand all the values of the wildlife resource and use these in our decision making, which will impact on the future availability and use of all natural resources.

Chapter 8

Price and Value Alternatives for Wildlife

James H. McDivitt

The application of economic concepts to evaluations of wildlife and fisheries management decisions has a limited history in both public and private sectors. If nature provided all the wildlife that humankind could want and they were free for the taking, the economist would judge that wildlife species had no economic value and no costs for their provision could be justified. This is not the case, however: Wildlife are goods with economic value (Loomis et al. 1984). They satisfy the criteria for an economic good by providing at least some members of society with satisfaction and by being insufficient in quantities or abundance to meet all human wants and needs for free.

Why then are economic principles not routinely applied to decisions of wildlife management? A brief look at the basics of benefit/cost analysis may reveal some possible answers. (*Valuation of Wildland Resource Benefits* by Peterson and Randall [1984] provides an excellent background and overview of benefit/cost analysis.) A simplification of benefit/cost analysis is that actions are feasible and appropriate as long as benefits exceed costs. There are three principal issues. First, what do the management actions cost? Second, how are benefits related to costs? Third, what are the benefits worth? Although unimportant to the theory behind benefit/cost analysis, the identification of who bears the cost and who reaps the benefits is important to decision making.

The costs are reasonably unambiguous. If you can describe the actions taken to manage wildlife, you can assign costs to those actions. Wildlife management costs are no more difficult to ascertain than costs for any other resource area. Less obvious are the costs of opportunities foregone because of management actions—for example, instances in which timber cannot be cut and sold if wildlife habitat is provided (Judge et al. 1984). These opportunity costs are difficult to measure for any resource area.

The relationship between inputs (costs) and outputs (benefits) is crucial to the conduct of an economic analysis. If the outputs resulting from actions taken are unknown, then the cause and effect process of production cannot be described. The estimation of probable outputs from actions taken is often uncertain; the intervention of natural events can change anticipated outputs. In reality wildlife management professionals are as knowledgeable concerning needed management actions and expected outcomes as are most other natural resource managers.

The valuation of wildlife benefits causes some significant problems for wildlife evaluations (Peterson and Brown 1985) because it is difficult to determine to whom the benefits accrue and how the values can be captured by producers. In the remainder of this chapter I will discuss alternative perspectives on wildlife values and their impact on economic evaluations of wildlife management.

THE SELLER'S PERSPECTIVE

Before a private producer can sell a good, he or she must own or hold a property right in the good. Since the individual states own the wildlife, a private producer cannot sell wildlife in a traditional market sense. As a result a farmer, rancher, or other landowner produces goods to own and sell, but he or she would logically not produce wildlife except as a by-product. In fact, the production of any wildlife, unless for social benefits, is often a cost because of animal damage to the landowners' crops, livestock, or property for which they receive no benefit.

Although landowners cannot sell wildlife, they can sell access to wildlife for hunting or other wildlife associated recreation. Access is controlled by the right in property to prevent trespass and can be sold as an entrance fee or a lease. The result, for example, may be a market in the right to access hunting sold for a price. The magnitude of the price determines how much the landowner can incur in costs to supply hunting. The price depends on the demand for the particular experience sold and varies depending on a number of factors.

One factor that influences price is the availability of alternative sites to hunt. Unless neighbors likewise restrict access to their land, hunters would simply move to free access areas. When the market area for hunting includes blocks of public land on which no fee is charged, the private landowner would find charging difficult or impossible until congestion or rationing limits use on the free areas. Another factor that will influence price is the uniqueness of the experience. If the charge site has a different product to sell that is more desirable to the consumer, such as greater success rates, the consumer will pay more.

For the seller of access, the price for which a unit of hunting sells determines how many units the seller will provide and whether he or she will increase the supply. If more units can be provided for less than the unit price, the seller would make more money and may rationally decide to increase production. Conversely, if the cost of more units exceeds the price, the producer would hold production constant or decrease production to save costs.

To sell wildlife access, landowners need to ensure a harvestable surplus on a continuing basis of adequate size to provide a production unit of whatever species is being considered (Shult 1984). This means that in some cases large blocks of land are needed to sell access successfully, since animals are confined by an ecological, not legal, boundary. If a landowner needs a production unit of white-tailed deer, the density of deer that the land can support is important. Equally important is the probability that the animals will stay on the landowner's land. To provide a white-tailed buck with a home range of up to 356 ha and movement of up to 11 km the landowner needs quite a piece of real estate, and several bucks would be required to provide a production unit with a harvestable surplus.

Alternatively, the situation may be that the potential seller only provides the production unit with a small portion of the unit's overall requirement, but that portion coincides with the timing of hunting seasons. Examples of small landholdings. adjacent to migratory bird routes or owning water developments are also opportunities to charge fees for access. The ranch containing deer or elk winter range, which happens to be the location of those species during hunting season, is another example in which access fees can be charged without providing all the species' requirements.

Although large holdings tend to create a natural monopoly, greater benefits can be captured by the private landowner if he or she controls access to wildlife during the critical time of harvest. The example of the ranch providing winter range has reversed some of the conventional wisdom for wildlife economic analyses. Not long ago the analysis relevant to the rancher involved the determination of how many feed units for cattle were being consumed by wildlife and the value of that feed to the rancher's cattle. It was economically a rational decision to spend money trying to prevent wildlife use up to the value of feed lost. The impact was that a reduction in wildlife population solved the rancher's problem but was contrary to the hunter's objectives. By selling access to winter range for hunting, the objectives for both the hunter and the rancher may be increased wildlife. The prices received by the landowner for hunting may exceed the value of the feed when used by domestic livestock.

The price that the private producer of wildlife can charge for access rights may change the decision-making economics. However, he or she will only be interested in producing wildlife species when an access market exists. Species not hunted will continue to be unprofitable to produce. Consequently, although private production may be encouraged to provide improved wildlife habitat and increased populations of wildlife, the mix of habitats and species might not be diverse.

For the private landowner, the appropriate measure of value is the price received for access to wildlife resources. This measure of value determines in part the rate of return on the land investment and the profitability of the enterprise. The price and costs of wildlife production compared to the price and costs of alternative products provide the information necessary to decide what and how much to produce.

THE BUYER'S PERSPECTIVE

The consumer has a different perspective concerning the value of wildlife. Rather than trying to generate income like a producer, he or she spends income trying to buy the package of goods and services that will provide the greatest amount of total satisfaction. For opportunities to hunt, the consumer has a certain willingness to pay (WTP) from his or her limited income. The WTP level depends chiefly on the consumer's desires for the product, his or her income, and the availability of other products to use as substitutes.

The consumers' value for wildlife resource opportunities is the consumers' WTP. This value is not necessarily the same as the price. If consumers can find a way to satisfy their desires at a price below the WTP, they have a good deal and gain an economic surplus (WTP minus price). If the consumers cannot find a price at or below the WTP, they will not consume but will prefer a substitute.

The economic procedures (Gum 1985) used to value wildlife most frequently estimate the WTP. Although it is an appropriate measure for the consumer and for federal agencies (U.S. Water Resour. Counc. 1983), it is not the same measure as prices paid. The argument for public program evaluations using WTP is simply that the surplus to consumers is part of the benefits to society as a whole and contributes to the general welfare. To use only price measures is to understate the benefits for projects undertaken in the public interest. How significant the understatement will be depends on a number of variables. Few attempts have been made to estimate the difference. One example (Martin et al. 1974) showed total revenue generated by a nondiscriminatory pricing system would be only 33% of the WTP for big game hunting and 55% for warm water fishing. If prices alone were used for public program evaluation, less costs could be justified and fewer projects undertaken.

The other aspect of value to consumers that is important for public management but of no consideration to private producer is value of nonexclusive use. Hunting requires the right to exclusive use since the animal will be taken or harvested. One person's use of wildlife makes it unavailable to another. This is true for most economic goods. Wildlife has a sizable number of users who observe, photograph, or receive satisfaction from knowing the species does and will survive even if they never see it (Randall and Stoll 1983). Since this value is so dispersed through society and satisfaction comes without any obvious transaction, payments from consumers can come only by gift or taxation. Supply can only be ensured by subsidy or regulation. The market in the traditional sense would have such high costs for information that it would be economically infeasible. Although a market system may fail to identify transactions, extract prices from consumers, or compensate producers, this does not mean no value exists. Even if consumers wished to pay rather than be free riders to whom would they send payment?

THE STATES' PERSPECTIVE

The perspective of the states is also different. They own the wildlife: With that right of property, they can and do sell wildlife. A hunting license conveys to its purchaser the right to take individuals of a particular kind or group of wildlife species. It is a contract with conditions that represents the exchange of legal rights between the purchaser and the states. The states could manage the wildlife resources for the purpose of making the most money possible.

Since the states have a monopoly on wildlife, they could choose pricing schemes to generate far greater income. If price bids were taken on licenses, the bidders would bid near their WTP for the rights the license conveys. Otherwise, they could be prevented from satisfying their desires to hunt. The state could accept bids in decreasing amounts from highest bid down until it sold the number of licenses it wished to manage the animal populations. This situation, like the private landowner case, has a significant bias toward species used for hunting.

Fortunately, the states do not manage wildlife only for economic return. Although it is possible that greater revenue could be generated on hunted species and this might warrant consideration, the states also recognize public goods such as nonconsumptive wildlife and genetic or ecological diversity as appropriate goals. The goal of a public good is to satisfy all users, rather than just one person. Since the demand is not for exclusive use (such as hunting), the animal used as a public good can be seen, counted, or photographed many times. To provide the opportunity once is to provide it many times with no additional cost to the supplier. Reimbursement to the supplier cannot come from a traditionally organized market in the form of prices received. Some states have found that a checkoff on state income tax returns allows consumers with a demand for these resources to act accordingly. However, states with a history of income tax checkoffs have found that people's inclination to participate decreases over time. An action that generates half a million dollars the first year may result in only $50,000 by the sixth year. Since the collection and disbursement of funds and the process of informing the taxpayers have some cost, the long-run viability of such programs is questionable.

THE FEDERAL PERSPECTIVE

The federal perspective is different: Any of the previous discussions may apply, depending on the circumstances (Gum 1985). The federal perspective ranges from the parochial view of the private landowner to an extremely philanthropic view. According to one extreme, if user fees are not collected, then why should the product be offered? The arguments against this view are many. The public trust obligation of government and the public ownership of wildlife with responsibility for provision to all citizens regardless of income or other status are frequently cited. The major arguments are based on the legislation, policies, and commitments to manage for a diversity of species. Conversely, the philanthropic perspective from traditional welfare economics suggests that maximizing consumers' benefits regardless of charge provides the best mix of resources allocated in the public interest.

Pivotal to the federal policy decisions concerning wildlife are the impacts on budget deficits and political beliefs. The probable general statement of policy is likely to be a mixed strategy of user fees for access to hunting with simultaneous emphasis on minimum levels of nonconsumptive species. This strategy seems consistent with the administration's emphasis on user fees while recognizing requirements under legislation like the Endangered Species Act.

The Forest Service, while conducting evaluations of program alternatives under the Resources Planning Act requirements, has found that wildlife values vary depending upon the federal perspective held. The initial analyses used wildlife values that were measures of WTP (Sorg and Loomis 1984). These values could be challenged on the basis of precision and accuracy since they were derived from nonstatistical samples and may not have been representative of the general population. Although these challenges were discussed, the principal reason for changing the values in later analyses was their inability to represent a collectable price or user fee in a competitive market sense. Although emphasis was being placed on selling products traditionally provided for free, discussion continued concerning special initiatives to increase funds and habitats for nongame species.

CONCLUSION

What is the correct or right value for wildlife? The answer depends on our perspective, objectives, and political or economic philosophy; no single value fits all situations. Although price is important to producers and is influenced by other producers' actions, the WTP values better represent value in the sense of public welfare. Of particular concern is the fairness of using money generated by taxation to provide wildlife products. People who favor wildlife and greatly value the benefits wildlife provides tend to favor general taxation to ensure supply and believe all people benefit. An appropriate argument for tax usage is that most people cannot provide a variety of wildlife for themselves. If one is apathetic about wildlife and unaware of receiving any benefits, he or she favors provision exclusively by user fees. The issue becomes largely who pays and who benefits, and the decisions on this issue are political.

REFERENCES

GUM, R. L. 1985. Assessment of wildlife values. Draft pap. prepared for the Nat. Resour. and Environ. Comm. of U.S. Dep. Agric. (In review.)

JUDGE, R. P., R. STRAIT, AND W. F. HYDE. 1984. Economics of endangered species management: the red-cockaded woodpecker. Trans. North Am. Wildl. and Nat. Resour. Conf. 49:375–381.

LOOMIS, J. B., G. L. PETERSON, AND C. F. SORG. 1984. A field guide to wildlife economic analyses. Trans. North Am. Wildl. and Nat. Resour. Conf. 49:315–324.

MARTIN, W. E., R. L. GUM, AND A. H. SMITH. 1974. The demand for and value of hunting, fishing, and general rural outdoor recreation in Arizona. Univ. Arizona Agric. Exp. Stn. Tech. Bull. 211, Tucson. 56pp.

PETERSON, G. L., AND T. C. BROWN. 1985. The economic benefits of recreation: common confusions and informed replies. Proc. Southeast. Recreation Res. Conf. Myrtle Beach, S.C. (In press.)

———, AND A. RANDALL. 1984. Valuation of wildland resource benefits. Westview Press, Boulder, Colo. 258pp.

RANDALL, A., AND J. R. STOLL. 1983. Existence value in a total valuation framework. Pages 265–273 *in* R. Rowe and L. Chestnut, eds. Managing air quality and scenic resources at national parks. Westview Press, Boulder, Colo.

SHULT, M. J. 1984. Wildlife management alternatives for large or small ranches. Pages 347–353 *in* L. D. White and D. Guynn, eds. Proc. Int. Ranchers Roundup. Tex. Agric. Ext. Serv., Texas A&M Univ., Uvalde.

SORG, C. F., AND J. B. LOOMIS. 1984. Empirical estimates of amenity forest values: a comparative review. Rocky Mt. For. and Range Exp. Stn. Gen. Tech. Rep. RM-107, Fort Collins, Colo. 23pp.

U.S. WATER RESOURCES COUNCIL. 1983. Economic and environmental principles and guidelines for water and related land resource implementation studies. U.S. Gov. Print. Off., Washington, D.C. 137pp.

Chapter 9

Fee Hunting Systems and Important Factors in Wildlife Commercialization on Private Lands

Ross "Skip" Shelton

The three types of fee hunting systems used in the South are permit, leasing, and commercial membership enterprises.

PERMIT HUNTING SYSTEMS

Several large industrial timber companies offer permit hunting systems. Although the income producing permit programs have a number of variations, most base their fees on where the individual wants to hunt (in one or more counties or statewide), on whether the individual is 16 years old or older, and on whether the individual is a resident or nonresident. One company charges hunters under 16 $3 per county, whereas those over 16 pay $15 or $20 per county. Nonresidents must pay $30 per county. Residents pay $50 for statewide hunting; nonresidents pay $75. The timber companies place advertisements in various city and county newspapers. Permits can be obtained by mail or from designated agents, brochures explaining the permit programs and illustrating the location of the company's property are then sent to permit purchasers.

Permit hunting programs have been tried on a designated-day basis. A certain number of hunts are set up on designated days by managers in charge. Permits may be bought for individual hunts, or a seasonal permit can be purchased to include all hunts. The cost of daily permits averages $4 to $10, that of seasonal permits averages $15 to $25.

Another variation of the system called the party permit system, applies primarily to deer hunting. For example, a 1,620-ha is reserved for a particular party to hunt on a certain day. The hunting party is allowed to hunt the area by itself. Fees may be assessed in two ways: (1) Each member of the party is charged a certain fee, and a minimum number of hunters is required; or (2) the party is charged a flat fee to hunt the area regardless of the size of the group (e.g., $200 to $400 a day to hunt the 1,620-ha tract of land).

One method used to introduce a permit program on land with low game populations is to post such property against trespass and to initiate conservation practices. Game poaching is reduced, wildlife populations increase, and the public can see that the landowner has gone to obvious expense to improve the hunting. Therefore, when a fee program is introduced, the landowner can better justify the case for charging for hunting privileges. Advantages of the permit programs are that they provide recreation to a larger and more varied group of recreationists and they allow landowners to increase or decrease the number of permits issued in order to increase or decrease the harvest of wildlife. Disadvantages of permit programs include (1) higher administrative, labor, and other operating costs; (2) uncertainty about the amount of revenue that will be received; and (3) possibly less control over the quality of hunters on the property, thereby increasing the chances of conflict with other permit holders and/or neighboring landowners.

Shelton (1969) reported an annual income of $0.17/ha excluding expenses in 1968. Interviews with representatives of several large timber companies revealed that current returns from permit programs averaged about $0.99/ha excluding expenses. One company official said that, on some of the permit areas returning $0.99/ha excluding expenses, he could have leased the area for $1.48 to $5.55/ha with nominal expenses.

HUNTING LEASE SYSTEM

Several companies have reduced or eliminated their permit programs in recent years in favor of leasing, the most popular fee hunting system in the South. Most leases are on a seasonal or annual basis. Most southern property owners lease to clubs, individuals, or counties. Most southern timber companies prefer to lease to local residents rather than to distant urban residents in an effort to create better local public relations and reduce public reaction to income producing programs. The return per hectare from hunting leases has risen from an average of $0.79/ha in 1968 to over $7.41/ha in 1984. The bottomland hardwood areas along the Mississippi River lease for from $5 to $12/ha. One 4,050-ha tract near the Mississippi River recently leased for $25/ha/ year. If this $100,000 a year is capitalized at an investor's accepted rate of 10%, it would immediately increase the purchase value of that particular property by $1 million because of its hunting value alone. Another hunting area in the Mississippi Delta reportedly leased for an up-front payment of $716,000 in 1970. This 10-year lease, with an option to renew for another 10 years, covered only 220 ha and the hunting lease purchase price of the land exceeded the total value of the land several times over (Tomlinson 1985). Several large landowning enterprises indicated that they received higher (up to 300% higher) lease fees for high game density bottomland hardwood areas along major streams as compared to upland sites. Waterfowl leases bring from $10 to $123/ha for choice areas. Many hunting clubs invest large sums of money in road development, culverts, fence building, and patrolling and employ full-time caretakers that benefit landowners. Advantages of leasing programs include (1) better control over land, (2) members' concern over land, (3) cooperation from hunters with work crews, (4) higher game populations, and (5) quality recreation for the maximum number of people the land can support. Other advantages include a minimum of management expenses to the lessor, negotiations with only one person or board of directors over the leasing of the property, and advanced knowledge of the amount of income that will be derived from the leasing program. Disadvantages of leasing programs include that (1) some members of hunting clubs may begin to feel that they own the land and sometimes disagree with or interfere with the owner's land management policies, (2) some clubs may want to build club houses and secure utilities (some landowners express fear of eventual easement problems from these activities), and (3) some clubs may not take in enough members creating public relations problems with those persons without a place to hunt.

COMMERCIAL MEMBERSHIP ENTERPRISES

The commercial membership enterprise system of fee hunting purveys quality recreation to the person willing to pay a relatively high membership fee. The landowner sells or leases the right to hunt and/or fish through an annual membership fee and normally expends considerable time and money in managing the enterprise for the production of wildlife. These memberships generally range from $1,000 to $5,000 per year in the South. Deer, duck, turkey, and quail hunting appear to be the most popular sports associated with commercial membership enterprises. The owners of enterprises normally blend farming and wildlife conservation practices to complement each other. Advantages of the commercial membership enterprises include (1) high income compared with other systems of wildlife management, (2) some preknowledge of potential annual income, and (3) possibility of becoming a complementary part of forestry and/or agricultural operations. Disadvantages of commercial membership enterprises include (1) large capital investment, (2) high administrative and operating expenses, (3) strict location and managerial requirements, and (4) smaller but perhaps more profitable sportsmen market.

LANDOWNER MEMBERSHIPS

A relatively new development in the South does not involve fee income but the outright purchase of timberland by wealthy individuals for hunting purposes. Memberships for one tract were recently advertised at $105,000 each with financing available. A number of these areas have been developed during the past three years with membership prices ranging from $35,000 to $115,000.

LIABILITY CONSIDERATIONS

One problem that landowners fear in making their lands available for hunting and fishing is the prospect of possible lawsuits. The amount of care owed to recreationists partially depends on whether they are trespassers, licensees, or invitees (Prosser 1955). Despite many recently passed liability relief laws, most authorities feel that persons involved in income-producing wildlife programs would be prudent to shift liability risk to insurance companies.

A little known fact is that some landowners require leasing groups to take out liability insurance. Landowners are then named as an additional insured party on the contract for only 10% of the basic policy cost. In some cases this procedure can reduce the cost of a landowner's personal liability insurance because of the double coverage. One timber company manager revealed that his company required each club to carry $300,000 for bodily injury and $50,000 for property damage.

IMPORTANT FACTORS IN COMMERCIAL DEVELOPMENTS FOR WILDLIFE ON PRIVATE LANDS

The following discussion will focus on factors important in commercial utilization of wildlife regardless of geographical boundaries. This discussion should be beneficial for those considering fee hunting systems as well as for those already involved in such endeavors.

Uncertainty

Swank (1981) indicated that public ownership of wildlife to a great extent precludes the flexibility and freedom of choices for managing deer that landowners have with domestic livestock. However, wildlife rules and regulations can be made that will enhance the prospects of commercial wildlife development on private lands. Texas has taken a step forward by allowing ranchers in regulatory counties to enter into a deer management plan with the parks and wildlife department. These plans take into consideration land management and wildlife management objectives of the individual rancher. This is a positive step to reduce uncertainty in program planning for commercial wildlife development. Mississippi, North Carolina, and Louisiana also have flexibility, particularly in their antlerless harvest system. Those landowners that furnish deer harvest data to the Mississippi Department of Wildlife Conservation are allotted antlerless hunting permits based on biological data and given extended seasons in which to remove antlerless deer. These permits have allowed many clubs and landowners to manage quality deer. California is considering going a step further by passing a regulation that allows landowners to submit plans to their resource department and receive more flexibility in harvest regulations plus extended seasons. This would be a step in the right direction for those interested in wildlife development. An extended consistent marketing season plus flexibility in harvest would greatly improve landowners' inventives as well as their prospects of being successful with wildlife enterprises.

Property

Property has been defined as a bundle of rights of control over resources. The only way a landowner has greater interest in or more stable rights to wildlife than anyone else is through the trespass law. Because of the problems associated with protecting land rights, many sportsmen and landowners are reluctant to make wildlife enhancement investments if they are not sure they can reap at least a portion of the rewards of their efforts. Poaching and illegal trespass are serious deterrents to wildlife development on private lands. In a 1981 article in *Outdoor Life,* Georgia Laycock indicated that an incredible 2 million deer and countless moose, elk, ducks, rabbits, and other game species are killed every year by poachers. Poaching does not occur just on public land. Shelton (1969), in a survey of forest landowners owning 11,298,000 ha in the South, indicated that lack of property control was the greatest constraint to these owners preventing the development of wildlife opportunities on their properties.

Landowners cannot be expected to make investments for wildlife enhancement if they cannot reasonably expect to harvest the benefits, either through personal enjoyment, enjoyment of friends, or income gained from recreational enterprises. No farmer will invest in a crop of corn, soybeans, or wheat if no one knows who—the farmer, the neighbor, or someone else—will harvest the crop. For a landowner interested in managing for wildlife recreation, the factors of production may be land, labor, capital, management, and more stable rights to harvest wildlife. Landowners in states that have trespass laws that require written permission before one can hunt generally receive more protection from poaching and trespass. Most states need to increase the amount of fines and penalties for poaching and trespass.

Tenancy

Generally long-term farm leases tend to encourage conservation because the lessee will have time to recover his or her investment in conservation practices. A similar parallel may be made with the length of hunting leases. The majority of hunting leases in the United States appear to be issued on an annual basis: Lewis (1965) found that the majority of hunting leases in Louisiana were issued on an annual basis. Goose and duck hunting areas in Illinois are normally leased on an annual basis (McCurdy and Echelberger 1968). In the early stages of a leasing program, annual leases can be justified, but, after a cooperative landowner-sportsman relationship has been established, longer leases would probably provide both parties with additional benefits. As indicated earlier, many of the older hunting clubs in the South invest substantial sums of money in road building and equipment, fences, firelanes, bridges, law enforcement, and wildlife enhancement projects that benefit the landowner as well as the sportsmen. These investments would not be made if the sportsmen were not assured that they would get the majority of the benefit from their expenditures. Investments in land improvements plus personal fringe benefits certainly increase the rate of return from wildlife on private lands.

Credit

Banks and other lending institutions hesitate to make loans on wildlife recreational enterprises for the following reasons: (1) shortage of data to use in evaluating potential returns on recreational businesses; (2) the feeling that in a recessionary period recreational businesses may not be profitable (the marginal utility of recreation will be lower than that of food, clothing, and so on). In a new region and in new enterprises (e.g., wildlife enterprises) interest rates include a high allowance for uncertainty, and lenders may not reduce these rates as much as is justified when the region or the enterprise and economic conditions become more stable. Methods of appraising wildlife assets have not been fully developed; more studies are needed to learn about the profitability of wildlife recreational enterprises. As more data are presented to lending institutions, which are usually eager to learn about new enterprises, loans to the wildlife recreation business will become more common. Well-managed quality deer herds may in the future receive appraisal very similar to quality cattle herds at this time. This approach should free up credit and loan policies, enabling people to finance operations based on the value of their wildlife assets. Lending institutions do not currently place much value on wildlife assets because of the lack of information on profitability plus the uncertainty of trespass and possible wildlife rules and regulations changes. If regulatory wildlife agencies could expand marketing seasons, permit greater flexibility in harvest for landowners and strictly enforce trespass laws, lending institutions would probably reevaluate their appraisal of wildlife assets.

Taxation

A number of tax benefits can be gained from fee hunting systems. Certain conservation expenses that benefit wildlife can be deducted. Landowners engaged in wildlife recreational enterprises can purchase equipment (tractors, disks) that qualifies for investment credit tax treatment. For example, a $10,000 tractor purchased and assigned for wildlife for the five years or more would mean a $1,000 savings in taxes. This 10% tax savings can also apply in some cases to duck blinds, deer stands, decoys, and so on.

Tax laws have been generous in allowing the fees paid to social, sporting, or athletic clubs to be treated as entertainment facility expense if such expenses have approximate relationship to the taxpayer's business and can be reasonably expected to benefit the business. Landowners interested in income-producing wildlife enterprises should explore possible arrangements with companies, corporations, banks, and such institutions to take advantage of this tax deduction.

SUMMARY

In this chapter I have attempted to outline some of the fee hunting systems in the South and the factors that affect the growth of the wildlife recreation industry. I have shown that a commercial wildlife management system site index is needed for determining the proper program of management on any given tract of land and tailored to the interest, resources, and abilities of the individual landowners. This index might include the following factors: public and community relations, effectiveness of trespass law, enforcement of wildlife and trespass laws, location and amount of manageable land (urban proximity, scattered or contiguous blocks), size and mobility of sportsmen market, educational level of sportsmen, proportion of sportsmen market that is urban or rural, personal and disposal income of sportsmen, size of game population and management requirements of game species, preferred game species of sportsmen, local traditions and hunting procedures, liability risks and laws, tax and insurance considerations, and political and social conditions. Even though many of these factors are not subject to accurate or convenient evaluation, they are useful in choosing the proper program suited to the individual landowner.

With wildlife habitats shrinking at an alarming rate, the number of hunters increasing, and hard evidence that hunters are willing to pay for quality hunting, it is obvious that landowners can derive much more than supplemental income for managing their wildlife resources.

REFERENCES

LAYCOCK, G. 1981. Socking it to poachers. Outdoor Life, January, 54–56.

LEWIS, J. H. 1965. The role of large private forest ownership in outdoor recreation in Louisiana. M.S. Thesis, Louisiana State Univ., Baton Rouge. 144pp.

MCCURDY, D. R., AND H. ECHELBERGER. 1968. The hunting lease in Illinois. J. For. 66(2):124–127.

PROSSER, W. L. 1955. The law of torts. 2nd ed. West Publ. Co., St. Paul. 989pp.

SHELTON, L. R. 1969. Economic aspects of wildlife management programs on large land holdings in the Southeast. M.S. Thesis, Mississippi State Univ., Starkville. 88pp.

SWANK, W. G. 1981. Wildlife laws and their effect on deer management. Pages 361–366 *in* L. D. White and A. L. Hoerman, eds. Proc. 1st Int. Ranchers Roundup. Tex. Agric. Ext. Serv., Texas A&M Univ., Uvalde.

TOMLINSON, B. H. 1985. Economic values of wildlife: opportunities and pitfalls. Trans. North Am. Wildl. and Nat. Resour. Conf. 50:262–270.

Chapter 10

Wildlife Values in Texas

Dwight E. Guynn and Don W. Steinbach

The private land sector has an extremely important role in wildlife management and thus greatly affects the sports of hunting and fishing as well as other recreational pursuits. The magnitude of importance of private land is evidenced by the large amounts of private land in the United States. Horvath (1976) reported that there are 9.2 billion ha of land in the U.S. of which 60% is privately owned. Forty-seven percent of this privately owned land is used by 3 million farmers and ranchers to produce our nation's food and fiber. These privately owned lands in agricultural uses and related forest and range lands provide the greatest opportunity for recreational pursuits and habitat development.

Berryman (1957) reported that 98% of the land in Illinois was in private ownership, 97% in Ohio, 85% in Wisconsin, and 79% in Michigan. In contrast, many states in the Rocky Mountain region have large areas of national forest and of Bureau of Land Management lands. For example, 37% of Colorado is public land. However, this does not mean that private ranches in these western areas are any less important in their influence on wildlife populations and recreational opportunities. For example, public lands in national parks and national forests often encompass portions of major mountain ranges, particularly at higher elevations, and these lands typically make up the big game summer range. However, the critical winter ranges where big game traditionally survive the cold months at lower elevations are often located partially or wholly on private ranches. Thus, private lands in states like Wyoming, Colorado, and Utah are critically important to wildlife populations and wildlife-oriented recreation.

WILDLIFE'S NEGATIVE ASPECTS FOR LANDOWNERS

Wildlife management is necessarily closely tied to land management: "Land use practices determine the quality and quantity of plant life, which in turn determine the animal life, so the landowner is the real wildlife manager" (Anderson 1962:481). "Most rural private land is managed so as to maximize revenue from income-producing crops . . . and not such intangibles as recreational potential, wildlife production, watershed conservation, and scenery" (Stoddard and Day 1969:187). Because many states may hold landowners liable for accidents taking place on their premises, the presence of wildlife habitat can be detrimental to private landowners. "Indeed to the extent the habitat is an attraction to hunters, hikers, bird watchers, or any other category of citizens who frequently trespass in the pursuit of their pleasures, habitat becomes a positive liability" (Gottschalk 1977:240).

The negative aspects of wildlife, such as costs of management, and the negative aspects of the associated recreational pursuits often outweigh the positive benefits such as aesthetics for the landowner with wildlife on private land. Thus, in many cases the private landowner has no incentive to manage for wildlife and often a reason to manage against wildlife.

This situation has been at the root of much of the decline in wildlife habitat so lamented by wildlife biologists. More than 30 years ago Steen stated: "The serious and continuing deterioration in the quantity and quality of fish and wildlife environment is the Waterloo of modern management" (1951:73). Simply put, other land uses outcompeted economically for land that was once prime wildlife habitat.

WILDLIFE AS AN ENTERPRISE ENCOURAGING POSITIVE MANAGEMENT

Incorporating wildlife as an enterprise in the landowner's total land operation provides the framework in which wildlife can compete economically with other agricultural uses of land. This competition in turn provides an economic incentive for increased management of wildlife and its habitat. Ranchers in South Africa sum up the idea of game animals on their ranches and of the selling of safari hunting in a simple phrase referring to animals managed by the ranchers: "If it pays, it stays" (Tomkinson 1984).

Managing wildlife as an enterprise on private land directly benefits wildlife by providing an economic basis for it to compete successfully with other agricultural enterprises. In addition, wildlife can provide an often economically favorable enterprise option to ranchers currently struggling to "hold things together." The more traditional agricultural enterprises are failing to sustain many producers.

CURRENT ECONOMIC SITUATION OF FARMS AND RANCHES

The current situation of farms and ranches was best summarized by Lukas:

Of the nation's 2.2 million farms, says the Agriculture Department, nearly 70,000 were technically insolvent by the start of this year. Another 73,000 had debts equalling 70% to 100% of their assets, meaning insolvency was imminent. A further 222,000 with debts equalling 40% to 70% of their assets, faced severe financial stress. The situation was particularly acute among the nation's 679,000 family-run commercial farms . . . with annual sales of $50,000 to $500,000. Nearly one-third of such farms had significant financial problems. (1985:10)

TAKING ADVANTAGE OF ALL LAND RESOURCES

Farmers and ranchers are feeling the economic squeeze of smaller profits or total lack of profits in traditional agricultural enterprises. To survive today agriculture is changing. Landowners have to broaden their perspective of what can be produced by the land and take advantage of all productive resources. One of these resources is the wildlife present on the land. Landowners who stick to only traditional agricultural enterprises will be squeezed out by more progressive farmers. Only by capitalizing on all productive land resources and nontraditional as well as traditional enterprises can landowners survive in these economically turbulent times.

DIRECT OVERHEAD COSTS AND GROSS MARGIN

A brief look at the economics of several enterprises on a typical Texas ranch will help illustrate a method called gross margin for comparing enterprises. By using this simple gross margin example of economic comparison, the advantages of wildlife enterprise over more traditional agricultural enterprises will become clearer. To begin, we will look at direct costs and overhead costs—what they are in a ranching operation and how ranchers might use these. Overhead costs are the relatively fixed costs that do not change if the production of the ranch is either increased or decreased slightly. For example, if a rancher adds 1 cow to a herd (or 20 cows), the overhead, including land costs and permanent labor, vehicle, or utility costs, does not change. In another example, when running a hunting operation a landowner can add one or five more hunters, but the costs of land, the hunting cabin, and electricity at the cabin—the overhead—remain the same.

In contrast, direct costs vary directly with units of production (e.g., the number of cows owned, number of hunters handled). Examples of direct costs are amounts of vaccine and quantity of supplemental feed for the livestock. These costs increase or decrease with every head of livestock added or deleted from the herd. In a hunting operation, if a

TABLE 10.1
Financial Sheet - Willie Makit Ranch (Gross Margin
Analysis)

	Cattle	Quail	Deer
GROSS INCOME			
Livestock or hunt sales	$20,600	$5,000	$5,000
Sale of deer and quail photos	------	200	500
Drought die-off of stock and wildlife	- 5,000	- 1,000	- 1,000
Total Gross Returns After Drought Losses	$15,600	$4,200	$4,500
DIRECT COSTS			
Purchase feeds	$ 8,000	$ 500	$ 500
Salt and minerals	1,800	0	0
Veterinary and AI	1,500	0	0
Day labor (*Guides)	3,000	1,400*	1,000*
Fuel for vehicles	1,800	75	80
Total Direct Costs Per Enterprise	$16,300	$1,975	$1,580
Gross Margin Per Enterprise	- $ 700	+ $2,225	+ $2,920

- $ 700	Cattle
+ $ 2,225	Quail
+ $ 2,920	Deer
Total Gross Margin Income + $ 4,445	

rancher has guided clients, guide cost would increase or decrease with every hunter added or deleted from the operation. If meals were provided for hunters, then food costs would also be a direct cost item.

The definitions of overhead cost and direct cost can be useful in a ranching operation. Each ranch enterprise should have a financial sheet. The example in Table 10.1 is for a ranch selling cattle, deer (*Odocoileus virginianus*) hunts, and quail (*Colinus virginianus*) hunts. One can compare direct costs to income and see which ranch enterprises are returning the most dollars (without counting overhead); this is referred

TABLE 10.2
Profit/Loss Calculation for Total Ranch Enterprise -
Willie Makit Ranch

OVERHEAD EXPENSES	
Pickup and equipment (feeders, etc.)	$ 4,000
Salaries	6,000
Repair costs	200
Electricity	1,000
Insurance/licenses	400
Blinds (cost/year spread over life of blinds)	1,000
Fencing (cost/year spread over life of fence)	800
Advertising	800
Total Overhead Expense	$14,200

+ $ 4,445 Total Gross Margin Income (from
Table 10.1)
- $14,200 Overhead Expense
- $ 9,755 Loss for Total Ranch Enterprise

to as the gross margin for each enterprise. By adding the gross margin profits and/or losses for all the enterprises together, a total gross margin income is computed. By subtracting the overhead costs from the total gross margin income, one can see if the ranch is actually making a profit (Table 10.2).

GROSS MARGIN CALCULATION

By collecting the gross margin for each enterprise, one can evaluate the economic worthiness of each enterprise and decide to change, continue, or drop that enterprise from the overall ranch operation. The simplified economic analysis for a ranch (presented in Tables 10.1 and 10.2) shows three important things: (1) that deer and quail are returning dollars in the gross margin analysis, (2) that the cattle enterprise is costing more than it is bringing in, and (3) that the total income is not equal to the total costs. This kind of breakdown of finances can show where major financial problems are and can serve as a starting point for solution. In this example, options would be to decrease the livestock costs, get out of the cattle business, and/or increase deer and quail operations so that a ranch profit can be made.

When using the gross margin concept of analyzing ranch enterprises the lack of overhead associated with wildlife enterprises compared to livestock enterprises becomes obvious. Wildlife, which are naturally present on most ranch lands, do not have to be purchased like livestock. Most wildlife enterprises do not require fence construction or maintenance like livestock ones. Vaccinating, branding, roundup, and other expenses associated with livestock are not required for a wildlife enterprise. It is little wonder the wildlife enterprise can exhibit such a high gross margin for the ranch. For many ranches in Texas, income from wildlife has been the only factor keeping ranches solvent during recent years.

WILDLIFE-GENERATED INCOME AS INCENTIVE TO MANAGEMENT

Income to private landowners from wildlife-oriented recreation is significant. Kennamer (1983) reported hunting lease costs for wild turkeys as follows: Alabama—$0.80 to $8 per hectare, Florida—$1.60 to $8 per hectare, Georgia—$2 to $4.80 per hectare, Mississippi—$1.60 to $24 per hectare (average $5.60/hectare), and California—$1.60 to $10 per hectare.

Private landowners in Colorado reported that fees charged for hunting in 1977 provided an income averaging $3.21 per hectare (Guynn 1979). These results are similar to those reported by Teer and Forrest (1968); they stated that the average income to landowners per hectare for deer hunting in central Texas was $2.64 in 1965. In Texas, landowners in much of the state have a tradition of leasing their land for hunting and fishing that dates from the 1930s. Income to Texas ranchers from leasing, hunting, and fishing privileges often exceeds income from the livestock on these same ranches (Teer and Forrest 1968). Based on my experience during the past six years working with ranchers in Texas as an extension wildlife specialist, this seems to be even more the case in recent years than in 1968. Steinbach (unpubl.) found gross income from hunting leases to average $8.05 per hectare in the Edwards Plateau and $11.05 per hectare in the Rio Grande Plains of Texas during 1984. Statewide in Texas, $80 million to $100 million per year is received by Texas landowners from leasing of hunting and fishing privileges (Guynn 1983).

Because of the economic importance of wildlife to Texas ranchers who are managing a wildlife enterprise, a tremendous effort has been made to manage for wildlife on these private lands. Building deer-proof fencing—one example of expenses willfully incurred by landowners—currently costs approximately $10,000 per 1.6 km. In the southwest and south central areas of Texas, approximately 5% (Steinbach, unpubl.) of the ranches utilize deer-proof fencing. Most ranches using this type fence have built an average of 11.2 km of fence (Steinbach, unpubl.) for an average cost of $70,000 each.

Supplemental feed is sometimes viewed by landowners as necessary to achieve wildlife management goals. Several Texas ranches have spent from $12,000 to $30,000 per year for supplemental feed for wildlife. Steinbach (unpubl.) reported that 12% of landowners in South Texas and the Edwards Plateau region of the state provide supplemental feed. Feed cost averages range from $1,500 to $20,000 for landowners, and each landowner spends an average 15 hours annually distributing this feed.

In addition, the practice of hiring professional wildlife biologists on a part- or full-time consulting basis is used to benefit wildlife by 5% of Texas ranches. Also, 21% of Texas landowners in the Edwards Plateau and South Texas region of the state spend an average of 12 hours annually conducting a wildlife census. Of these landowners 46% use helicopter census techniques (primarily for white-tailed deer) at an average annual cost of $845 per landowner (Steinbach, unpubl.).

In addition, 14% of the landowners in this region of Texas keep records on their wildlife (e.g., harvest records) (Steinbach, unpubl.).

In summary, findings in this chapter substantiate Aldo Leopold's (1933:395–400) contention that positive management for wildlife will be undertaken (often at considerable expense) by the private landowners when a monetary incentive is available to that landowner.

REFERENCES

ANDERSON, J. M. 1962. Can biologists break the bottleneck. Trans. North Am. Wildl. and Nat. Resour. Conf. 27:479–484.

BERRYMAN, J. H. 1957. Our growing need: a place to produce and harvest wildlife. J. Wildl. Manage. 21(3):319–323.

GOTTSCHALK, J. S. 1977. Wildlife habitat—the "price-less" resource base. Trans. North Am. Wildl. and Nat. Resour. Conf. 42:237–245.

GUYNN, D. E. 1979. Management of deer hunters on private land in Colorado. Ph.D. Thesis. Colorado State Univ., Fort Collins. 253pp.

———. 1983. Exotic game production and fee hunting in Texas. Pages 285–296 *in* L. Hoerman and L. White, eds. Symp.: Foothills for food and forests. Oregon State Univ., Corvallis.

HORVATH, W. J. 1976. Habitat programs and recreational opportunities on private agricultural lands: opportunities and constraints. Trans. North Am. Wildl. and Nat. Resour. Conf. 41:504–512.

KENNAMER, J. E. 1983. Rio Grande wild turkey management and market potential. Pages 394–400 *in* L. Hoerman and L. White, eds. Symp.: Int. Ranchers Roundup. Tex. Agric. Ext. Serv., Texas A&M Univ., Ulvade.

LEOPOLD, A. 1933. Game management. Charles Scribner's Sons, New York. 481 pp.

LUKAS, J. A. 1985. When a farmer may lose his land. Parade Mag., May 5:10–13.

STEEN, M. O. 1951. Fish and wildlife: which way will we go? Trans. North Am. Wildl. and Nat. Resour. Conf. 16:72–79.

STODDARD, C. H., AND A. M. DAY. 1969. Private lands for public recreation: is there a solution? Trans. North Am. Wildl. and Nat. Resour. Conf. 34:186–196.

TEER, J. G., AND N. K. FORREST. 1968. Bionomic and ethical implications of commercial game harvest programs. Trans. North Am. Wildl. and Nat. Resour. Conf. 33:192–204.

TOMKINSON, A. J. 1984. South African safari methods. Pages 376–380 *in* L. White and D. Guynn, eds. Symp.: Int. Ranchers Roundup. Tex. Agric. Ext. Serv., Texas A&M Univ., Uvalde.

Chapter 11

Mitigation by "Banking" Credits: An Economic Incentive to Compliance

Michael D. Zagata

Resource values may be measured in economic terms, in aesthetic terms, or in ecological terms. Generally, marketplace or commodity values are measured in economic terms and are set through the private sector. Other values are often set and/or protected by government through laws and regulations.

To date, the wildlife profession has focused mainly on government controls to broaden its impact in protecting noncommodity values. This approach has often resulted in placing the private sector, with one criterion for measuring value, at odds with the public sector. All too frequently the results have been polarization and diminished resource protection. Thus, there is a definite need to develop creative approaches to habitat protection that capitalize on marketplace values, that is, the profit motive.

If the public sector is to successfully attract private sector participation in the conservation of public values, it must be willing to incorporate economic considerations into its programs. One way to do this is to offer incentives that will save time and money while still affording protection to resources with public value, such as wetlands. In this chapter I will describe one attempt to accomplish that goal that demonstrates how industry and government can work together in designing a program that will provide both increased habitat protection and an incentive to a permit applicant.

LEGISLATION

The Fish and Wildlife Coordination Act (FWCA) and the Clean Water Act (CWA) provide for the adverse ecological impact of a development project to be mitigated by the developing agency or individual. The Endangered Species Act (ESA), in certain cases, may also provide for impact mitigation. The "banking" concept offers a unique approach to satisfying those mitigation requirements. As an example, Section 404 of the CWA provides protection for the nation's navigable waters (the definition of navigable waters has been interpreted by the courts to include virtually all wetlands). That protection is provided by requiring a permit for dredge and fill operations in navigable waters, including most wetlands.

The Environmental Protection Agency (EPA) is charged with administering the program, and operational responsibility is vested with the U.S. Army Corps of Engineers (COE). The Fish and Wildlife Service (FWS), the National Marine Fisheries Service (NMFS), and state wildlife and fish agencies, under the aegis of the FWCA, have the responsibility to comment on the potential impact of a dredge and fill operation on wildlife habitat. They may recommend approval, denial, and/or certain measures to mitigate adverse impacts.

MITIGATION

Mitigation is a term used to describe actions that are intended to offset adverse impacts of a project on the functional aspects of ecosystems, including wildlife habitat. It may involve requiring the permittee to set aside and/or enhance habitat of a similar type. This is often done by a fee title transfer of land from private to public ownership; the land can then be managed by a state or federal wildlife agency for the benefit of wildlife. The Council on Environmental Quality (1981) provided that the definition for mitigation include

> (a) avoiding the impact altogether by not taking a certain action or parts of an action; (b) minimizing impacts by limiting the degree or magnitude of the action and its implementation; (c) rectifying the impact by repairing, rehabilitating, or restoring the affected environment; (d) reducing or eliminating the impact over time by preservation and maintenance operations during the life of the action; and (e) compensating for the impact by replacing or providing substitute resources or environments. (40 CFR Part 1508.20[a-e])

The FWS (U.S. Fish and Wildl. Serv. 1981) has adopted this definition of mitigation and considers the specific elements to represent the desirable sequence of steps in the mitigation planning process (40 CFR Part 1508.20 [a-e]).

Section 404 of the CWA has been the source of controversy between the regulating agencies and permit applicants, in part because the consideration of the need to mitigate comes at the end, rather than the beginning, of the permit process (mitigation is permitted only after other alternatives have been examined). Thus mitigation is often perceived as an additional source of delay. Because time is money to developers and contractors, this situation often places them, even though they generally desire to comply with the law, in the position of appearing to be callous toward the need to protect wetlands.

Historically, the amount of mitigation required to offset damage has been a qualitative judgment. However, the FWS and others have been developing more quantitative methodologies for making such decisions. One of those methodologies is the Habitat Evaluation Procedures (HEP) (Schamberger and Krohn 1982), which allow one to determine the adverse and positive impacts of a perturbation on a given habitat for one or more species. The unit of measure of HEP is habitat units (HU), a number obtained by multiplying the number of affected acres times the habitat suitability index (HSI) (zero to 1.0) for the affected species.

For example, the HEP process can be used to determine the impact of two theoretical actions on a given wetland of 100 acres with a habitat suitability index of 0.8 (0.0 is the poorest and 1.0 is the best). At time zero 80 habitat units are present (100 $\times$ 0.8). If an action is taken that temporarily destroys 50 acres or reduces the HSI from 0.8 to 0.4 for all 100 acres, then 40 HUs would be lost for some time.

The length of time is dependent upon the duration of the impact and the ecological factors that affect recovery time (moisture, length of growing season, and so on). To offset this loss of 40 HUs, some form of mitigation would be required that would either enhance the habitat, maintain the remaining habitat through management, or replace it with an area of equal habitat value. The intent of the mitigation is to restore the 40 HUs lost to the adverse impact.

The same principle can be applied when the goal is to maintain a habitat type that may be lost through succession or subsidence. Although there may appear to be no net loss or gain of HUs, the management objective was attained. For example, if the rate of wetland subsidence can be reduced from 6% to 4% per year, the wetlands would benefit.

Actions to enhance a habitat would result in that habitat being made more productive than it was at time zero. If the wetland had an HSI of 0.6 today, it would be raised to an HSI greater than 0.6 and then kept at the higher level through maintenance (management).

BANKING OF HABITAT UNITS—
AN OPPORTUNITY FOR INDUSTRY AND WILDLIFE

Because the HEP process can be used to measure gains as well as losses in habitat, it offers us a unique opportunity to expedite the mitigation process by crediting a permittee with HUs gained through

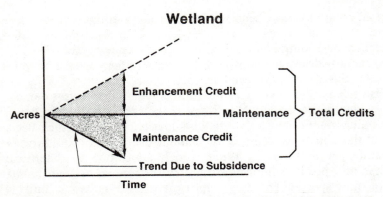

Figure 11.1 Basis for habitat units of credit for a mitigation bank in a coastal marsh undergoing subsidence

a management program. This approach can potentially save permittees money while affording protection and often enhancement for wetland habitats.

The mitigation banking process affords the potential developer an opportunity to cooperate with state and federal regulatory agencies in implementing a management program on land the developer owns or that is set aside for its wildlife values. As a result of this management program, the developer would be given credits in the form of HUs, which would be deposited in a mitigation bank to be partially used at some later date to offset mitigation requirements. Credits could be given for maintenance and/or enhancement programs (Fig. 11.1).

The bank would be established before a permit application and thus would have the effect of placing mitigation up front in the permit process. Current practice places mitigation at the end of the process (Fig. 11.2). Because the bank is established before a permit is applied for, such a program is not under the normal time pressure imposed on the applicant and agencies. Thus, it would provide an opportunity for the agencies and developer to work together in developing a project that is integrated into an overall land management program.

The ecological benefit per dollar of investment (management program) will in many cases be greater with the banking program than with normal mitigation. In general, permit applicants are seeking a permit for a small project (less than 4 ha). It is very expensive, on the basis of the benefit per unit area per dollar spent, to mitigate for these projects. However, the cost per unit area drops markedly when a large project is undertaken, and thus the ecological benefit per dollar spent should increase.

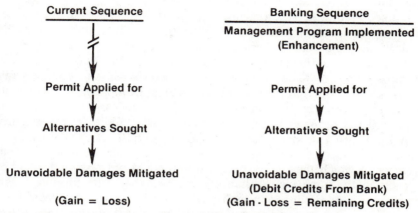

Figure 11.2 Comparison of the current mitigation sequence with the sequence that would occur under a banking program

INCENTIVES TO INDUSTRY

The HUs credited and deposited in the bank can be used by a bankee in numerous ways. They can be used to expedite permits and therefore save money; an applicant with banked credits could use those credits as collateral or as a bond to ensure good faith compliance with a permit stipulation once it is agreed that the impacts are unavoidable. The details of mitigation will be worked out after a permit is granted rather than standing as a hurdle to the issuance of the permit. The applicant could later cash in part of the credits to meet the mitigation requirement or perform some other form of on-site mitigation. The bankee would be spending today's dollars to buy credits to satisfy future mitigation requirements. Assuming that some inflation will occur, this approach will result in a long-term savings to the entity holding the credits.

The bank could allow a lessee to operate on the land of an entity that had a bank. That entity could sell (transfer) credits to the lessee, thus enabling the lessee to fulfill the mitigation requirements while permitting the holder of the credits to recover part of the cost of establishing those credits (HUs). Consider a case in which a company owns land for energy production. It may allow a lessee to come in and drill. That lessee may not get a 404 permit unless he or she can purchase land off the site for mitigation. Drilling could be expedited and/or conducted if the lessee could obtain credits for previous work done in advance of the permit application that would satisfy the mitigation requirement stipulated in the permit.

Banked credits may be bought, sold, or traded. However, the appropriate agency must approve the application as an approved form of mitigation. Major landholders could exchange credits to facilitate operations in frontier areas in which they have no holdings or credits. For example, Company X owns land and has credits in Alaska, and Company Y owns land and has credits in Louisiana. Company Y decides to undertake a project in Alaska but is hampered by the mitigation requirement. Company Y could either buy Alaska credits from Company X or exchange Louisiana credits for Company X's Alaska HUs. The credits could only be applied with concurrence of the appropriate state agencies in which they were generated and could only be used to offset impacts in the same type of habitat in which they were produced. For example, credits produced in hydrologic Unit 5 in Louisiana could only be used to offset impacts in hydrologic Unit 5 in Louisiana no matter who owned them.

One would not need to own land to develop a bank. A management program on public land or on private land set aside for wildlife would generate credits. The entity responsible for funding and/or implementing the program would receive the credits produced. For example, a company could fund a management program on state or federal land or on an Audubon sanctuary and receive mitigation credits in that state and habitat type. The mitigation banking process affords an opportunity to integrate mitigation actions into a land management program and thus internalize mitigation as a cost of doing business. If mitigation is put up front in the mitigation process, it will allow one to plan expenditures and therefore be in a better position to budget money for wetland management. In the past, the level of funding for mitigation was determined by the number of permits applied for and the extent of mitigation per permit. This procedure made it difficult for private land managers to obtain funds for large-scale management projects other than those required for mitigation. The banking process would encourage the implementation of intensive management programs on lands needing to be managed because the funding level required for a given year would be known in advance.

Intensive management can be in the landowner's best interest. For example, in coastal Louisiana, wetlands are being lost at a rate of 10,125 ha per year (Fruge 1982). Indeed, landowners run the risk of losing title to subsurface minerals once the land becomes inundated.

Mitigation banking can foster cooperation between industry and state and federal agencies charged with protecting wetlands. Participants will gain mitigation credits while enhancing their land. For example, the

COE is considering a program to create wetlands from its dredge spoil. If the spoil were placed on wetlands to enhance the wetland, the owner could gain credits and delay subsidence, thereby retaining title to the minerals and obtaining mitigation credits.

Mitigation banking works when it is in both parties' interest. Banking benefits the applicant by the management practices being applied to his or her land and from the banking credits. The public benefits from the increased level of management and protection being afforded the private sector wetlands. The Tenneco LaTerre project discussed later in this chapter is an excellent example.

BENEFITS TO WILDLIFE HABITAT

The incentives for industry to maintain and enhance wetlands to obtain credits will benefit wildlife habitat. The number of credits in the bank reflects the benefit to habitat. Those credits are counted annually and, as long as they exceed one, wildlife benefits. The interest on those credits results in a benefit to wildlife through habitat maintenance/ enhancement. Because of the economies of scale, the large projects used to establish a bank will result in more benefit to wildlife per dollar spent than would the smaller, discrete projects done to satisfy a permit condition. Mitigation banking is an approach that provides a carrot rather than a stick. By encouraging the landowner to undertake management programs well in advance of actions requiring a permit, the public values associated with wetlands will be given increased protection.

PROPOSED ADMINISTRATIVE PROCEDURES

The mitigation banking program can be used to satisfy mitigation requirements under Sec. 404 of the CWA. Its administration is patterned after the banking program implemented by the EPA via the Clean Air Act. However, in the case of mitigation banking the FWS would serve as the banker. An agreement or a contract is needed to stipulate the terms of the banking arrangement and must be agreed to by the banker and bankee. Once the banking conditions are formalized, mitigation credits could be added to or deleted from the bankee's account. The exchange commodity is an HU. The bankee will be given credit for the number of HUs developed or debited for the number of HUs lost as a result of a project's impact. The credits or debits would be made via the HEP process as administered by the FWS or NMFS in consultation with the developer.

TENNECO LATERRE—A PILOT PROJECT

In January 1984 the final signature was applied to a memorandum of agreement (MOA) between Tenneco Oil Exploration and Production (TOE&P) and the FWS, NMFS, Soil Conservation Service (SCS), Louisiana Department of Fish and Wildlife (LDFW), and the Coastal Management Section of the Louisiana Department of Natural Resources (CMS). It contains 18 provisions that spell out how the bank is to be administered and what the responsibilities of the signatories are.

According to the MOA, Tenneco will install and maintain for at least 25 years a system of weirs, dikes, and mud dams to maintain and enhance 2,916 ha of wetlands, 2,025 ha of which are within Tenneco's LaTerre property. There were no immediate plans for development of subsurface minerals within the tract. The expected life of the area without the program is 77 years.

As a result, TOE&P will generate 11.9 million HUs on 2,916 ha (Soileau 1984). Of these, they will receive 8.4 million HUs for the 2,025 ha they own. Thus there will be an initial benefit to the public of 3.5 million HUs.

The total number of expected HUs (8.4 million) was divided by 77 (the expected life of the marsh without the project) resulting in 108,000 average annual habitat units (AAHU) in category 2 wetlands. Tenneco agreed to maintain the project for 25 years, based on the expected life of the management structures. At year 25, the agencies and TOE&P will reevaluate the project. Because of the agencies' need to protect the public's values in perpetuity, they reduced the number of available credits by the fraction 25 over 77. The result was that TOE&P would be allowed to use a total of 35,300 AAHUs over the first 25 years of the bank. If credits are not used in a given year, they are lost (they are not cumulative), and once credits are used they are deducted from each subsequent year (Fig. 11.3).

About 73,500 credits were withheld in each year of the first 25 years (108,733 produced—35,300 available). Thus 1.8 million AAHUs were withheld. If this—the worst case scenario—is assumed and calculations are based on the expectation that Tenneco would abandon the project after year 25, then this withholding can be justified as an effort to mitigate in years 26 through 77 (52 years) for impacts caused in years 1 through 25. Indeed the calculations in Figure 11.4 show this to be true ($52 \times 35,300 = 1.8$ million) (D. M. Soileau, pers. commun.). In fact, there will be about 3.5 million AAHUs available for use in years 26 through 77.

According to the MOA,

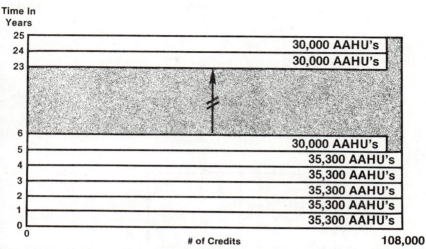

Figure 11.3   Impact on the bank of a project started after five years and requiring 5,300 habitat units for mitigation

Mitigation by debiting available AAHU's from the mitigation bank is appropriate and will be used to offset only unavoidable impacts on fish and wildlife when the applicant can demonstrate to the satisfaction of all parties to the MOA that there are no on-site alternatives which are available and capable of being done after taking into consideration cost, existing technology, and logistics in light of overall project purposes.

Thus, it should appear evident that the program is in no way intended to circumvent the regulatory process. The application of credits was restricted to Louisiana wetlands in hydrologic unit 5, and a penalty is attached to projects in the 5,000-acre management area. The banking approach to mitigation puts mitigation up front in the permit process and thereby reduces the delay historically associated with this facet of the Section 404 permit process.

SUMMARY

We live in an economy influenced by both marketplace forces and government regulation. Because of the noncommodity values often associated with resources with commodity or economic value, the two influences often appear to be at odds. The minerals underlying Louisiana's wetlands have commodity value whereas the wetlands themselves have both commodity and noncommodity values. To develop the mineral resources, a permit that attempts to protect the public values must be

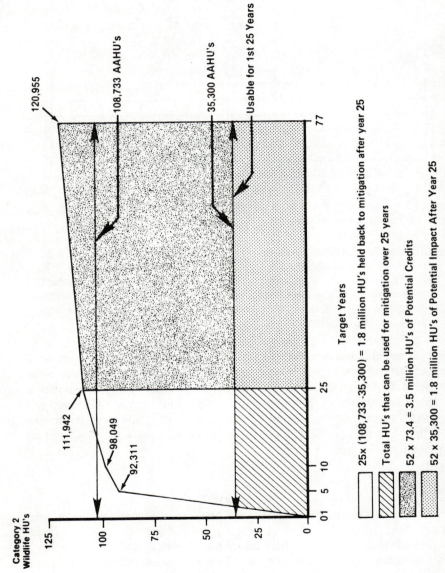

Figure 11.4 Mitigation banking allows for mitigation in perpetuity while meeting immediate mitigation needs via habitat units of credit.

obtained. Mitigation may be a condition of that permit, and, if it is, the applicant may be forced to experience costly delay and the mitigation agreed upon may not be cost effective. The banking program will reduce delay associated with obtaining a permit and allow the bankee to budget for and implement large-scale management programs in cooperation with state and federal fish and wildlife agencies. As a result of this pilot project, Tenneco expects to maintain its property and mineral rights by reducing the rate of subsidence, to bank enough credits to offset the mitigation requirements for more permits than we expect to apply for, and to expedite the permit process by reducing the delay associated with the mitigation process. Based upon the Tenneco pilot project, the process should maintain and/or enhance the wetland base and expedite the conduct of business in wetland areas.

Members of the wildlife profession have the necessary expertise to identify innovative approaches to regulatory compliance from an ecological standpoint. The business community has the necessary economic skills. The two should work together to meld their mutual interests and expertise into creative programs that will benefit both the public and private sector. Only when this cooperation is set up will we have truly effective regulation.

REFERENCES

COUNCIL ON ENVIRONMENTAL QUALITY. 1981. U.S. Fish and Wildlife Service Mitigation Policy. Fed. Register 46:15:7644–7663.

FRUGE, D. W. 1982. Effects of wetland deterioration on the fish and wildlife resources of coastal Louisiana. Pages 99–107 *in* D. F. Boesch, ed. Proc. of the conf. on Coastal erosion and wetland modification in Louisiana: causes, consequences, and options. U.S. Fish and Wildl. Serv., FWS/OBS-82/59.

SCHAMBERGER, M., AND W. B. KROHN. 1982. Status of the habitat evaluation procedures. Trans. North Am. Wildl. and Nat. Resour. Conf. 47:154–164.

SOILEAU, D. M. 1984. Final report on the Tenneco LaTerre Corporation mitigation banking proposal, Terrebonne Parish, Louisiana. U.S. Fish and Wildl. Serv., Lafayette, La. 23pp.

U.S. FISH AND WILDLIFE SERVICE. 1981. U.S. Fish and Wildlife Service Mitigation Policy. Fed. Register 46:15:7644–7663.

Chapter 12

Socio-Duckonomics

David E. Wesley

The wetlands that our waterfowl depend on throughout their life cycle for food, rest, and reproduction are disappearing at an alarming and possibly accelerating pace. Within North Dakota, South Dakota, and Minnesota, which include the major breeding habitat in the U.S., 135,675 ha of prime wetlands were lost in the 10-year period from 1964 to 1974. This loss amounts to 10% of the total area of such habitat that ever existed in these states. Virtually all wetlands of Iowa have been drained since the early 1900s. The same growing demands for agricultural lands exist in Canada, in which 70% of North America's waterfowl are incubated.

The squeeze on our wintering habitat for waterfowl is comparable to what has happened in the nesting areas. A high percentage of the inland wetlands in the U.S., so important to waterfowl, has been converted to productive croplands in the attempt to satisfy the world's growing appetite for more grain and other agricultural products. Of the original 10 million ha of bottomland hardwood wetlands along the Mississippi River system, only 30% remained intact in 1969. The annual loss of such wetlands approached 81,000 ha per year (U.S. Dep. Agric. 1971). The coastal marshlands of the U.S. are also rapidly changing, to the detriment of waterfowl. A recent mapping survey by the U.S. Fish and Wildlife Service showed a loss of fresh marsh in the Louisiana portion of the Mississippi River Deltaic Plain of nearly 202,500 ha between 1956 and 1978. Unfortunately, fresh marsh is the most valuable type of coastal marsh for ducks. Gosselink et al. (1979), who conducted studies of wetland loss in the Chenier Plain Ecosystem of Southwest Louisiana and Southeast Texas, reported losses of similar magnitude.

The various wildland habitat agencies of the state and federal government are making every effort to stay the tide of habitat destruction, but any success must be kept in perspective with our incessant losses. Those who lament the passing of habitat and the birds that frequent it must not accept the threatening requiem. Perhaps a stronghold of overlooked potential for averting inevitable and permanent drought for our ducks lies within the private sector and the capitalist system.

The key to a landowner's involvement with waterfowl in a capitalist society is monetary incentive. Most drainage today is privately financed because the landowners' economics seem to dictate the action. With a cognizance of the basic laws of supply and demand, we can place a price tag on ducks and the time we spend in their pursuit that will provide the farmer with more reason to leave a pothole or marsh than to drain it.

PAYING THE PIPER

There must be something special about four dead teal that occupy a minuscule portion of the bottom of an $8,000 mudboat that zooms through the frigid marsh at midmorning following four hours of intensive hide and seek. Typically, the boat is shared by four or more hunters who have spent $200 to $300 each for a two-day hunt. Their hunt is hosted by a fellow sportsman who has spent an additional $150 to $350 per guest per day for dogs, lodging, gasoline, equipment, food, and drink just to give the guests an opportunity to pursue these peregrinating wildfowl.

The understanding of "socio-duckonomics," as we shall call it, requires some insight into the psychology of the hunter, the habits of the hunted, and the value of the places where the two meet. Numerous economists, such as Clawson (1959), Carey (1965), and Pearse (1968), have tried to evaluate recreational experiences by measuring various direct and indirect value factors associated with the hunting experience. Direct methods usually measure actual expenses, such as travel and equipment costs, and indirect methods, in which a hypothetical valuation is assigned to a willingness to pay or a willingness to accept compensation for giving up a recreational experience.

In an example of the direct cost approach, a survey of 1,882 randomly selected Ducks Unlimited (DU) members was conducted to determine the extent of certain expenditures they encountered in waterfowling. By extrapolating to the full membership, the survey conductors calculated that a conservative, personal investment by these waterfowlers for equipment and supplies alone approached $1 billion. Of this figure, more than $100 million was an annual expense. The survey revealed that 56% of the DU members hunted waterfowl 10 days or more per year and that 43% traveled over 161 km to hunt. No attempt was made to estimate travel, food, lodging, ammunition, and incidental costs. Based on data gathered by the U.S. Fish and Wildlife Service in a 1980 survey, 33,774,000 hunter-days and $500 million are spent annually in pursuit of ducks and geese (U.S. Fish and Wildl. Serv. and U.S. Bur. Census 1982).

The experience of waterfowling is a montage made up of the beauty of sunrise, cupped wings, frosted decoys, attentive retrievers, warm laughter, and hot coffee. The value of such abstract experiences cannot be easily expressed on a printed price tag. Bishop and Heberlein (1979) gained some insight to these extra-market commodities by studying the value placed on early season goose hunting permits for the Horicon Zone of east central Wisconsin. These permits entitled a hunter to take one goose from a defined area during the first two weeks of October 1978. Actual cash offers for a predetermined number of the permits yielded an average value of $63 per permit. Adjusting this figure by using the Consumer Price Index would make these permits worth $102 in today's market. Twelve percent of the hunters indicated that they would not have sold their permit for $200, which was the maximum offer made! In today's dollars, this would equate to $325.

The Environmental Research Group at Georgia State University (Horvath 1974) conducted a similar study and set the dollar value required to induce a waterfowler to give up one day of duck hunting at $67. In today's dollars, this day of duck hunting would command $144. A random sampling of commercial fees charged for duck and goose hunting agrees well with these real and hypothetical values (Table 12.1).

Louisiana has approximately 1,620,000 ha of marsh, and over 202,500 ha of rice were planted in 1984. Most of these lands were leased for duck hunting, thus creating enormous revenues for the state. Fruge and Ruelle (1980) reported that the current supply of waterfowl hunting in one sizable area of Louisiana could accommodate only 78% of the demand. By the year 2000, the percentage of supply to demand would be only 49% and by 2020, only 31%. The demand estimates in his projections were based on use by Louisiana residents only so the total demand would be considerably greater.

It is significant to note that the four-county area in southern Illinois supports 40,000 to 70,000 hunter-days for geese each year, which adds $4 million to $5 million annually to the area's economy.

At the upper end of these lease figures, waterfowling is competing well on a per unit acre basis with the profits that a farmer could expect to derive from clearing the land and renting it for soybean farming. Where bottomlands have already been converted to soybean and rice production, double cropping ducks as a second crop is a natural approach. Such lands have excellent marketability, and the process for preparing such lands for waterfowling is usually simple and relatively inexpensive. With a shrinking supply and a swelling demand, coupled with the

TABLE 12.1
Fees Charged for Duck and/or Goose Hunting on Selected Areas

Location	Arrangements	Fees	Facilities and Other Amenities Provided
SW Louisiana	Daily hunt	$260/day/ hunter	Everything except shells, game cleaning, and gratuities
NE Louisiana	Annual lease	$3,500 to $7,500/ blind	Ten flooded acres, with blind, in rice field or greentree reservoir; no additional services
SW Louisiana	Annual goose lease	$2,500 to $3,000/ blind	Approximately 10 acres in dry rice field; flooding extra
Cameron Parish, Louisiana	Annual lease	$18.75/acre	Four blinds in 640 acres of natural marsh; no additional services
Cameron Parish, Louisiana	Annual lease	$31.25/acre	Four blinds in 640 acres of rice field; no services; lease includes clubhouse
S. Illinois	Daily fee	$50/day/hunter	Goose blind use only
Sacramento Valley, CA	Annual lease	$1,200 to $1,500/ hunter	Duck hunting blind only; 2 persons per blind minimum
N. California, Tule Lake area	Daily fee	$150/person	Primarily goose hunting; guide and over-night accommodations; 2 day, 2 person minimum
N. California	Daily fee	$100/person	No accommodations; guide only; 2 to 5 persons per blind

Source: Personal communication.

current depressed price of crop products, the concept of managing lands for waterfowl has become more feasible. Lessees should go one step further—they should insist that the lessor put some of these funds back into the resource. Landowners are beginning to learn that maintaining the quality of waterfowl habitat, like upholding the quality of croplands, requires care and service. Assistance for such endeavors is available in every state through the Soil Conservation Service, Cooperative Extension Service, or private wildlife consultants. In some cases, progressive-thinking hunters have found that rather than leasing, purchasing these wetlands provides them with excellent hunting and sound investments. This approach would be particularly beneficial when a group of hunter-investors form a partnership and purchase lands with income potential as well as affording recreational opportunities.

BUCKS FOR DUCKS

Can waterfowlers afford to play a role in the marketplace in which lands, particularly wetlands, are bought, sold, and leased? Since their involvement may ultimately determine the fate of the U.S. wintering habitat, can those who love ducks afford not to? According to the 1980 National Survey of Fishing, Hunting, and Wildlife-Associated Recreation (U.S. Fish and Wildl. Serv. and U.S. Bur. Census 1982), over 35% of the respondents made $25,000 or more per year. More than 10% of those responding to this survey reported incomes of over $40,000. In DU's 1984 survey of its own membership, over 53% indicated incomes of over $35,000 per year, and over 32% revealed incomes in excess of $50,000. From these figures, it would appear that waterfowlers have the financial resources to create a recreational demand for wetlands. To save the wetlands and the migrants that frequent them each fall, we must develop a strong willingness to pay for the commodity and let the landowners know it! To some extent, we have already been successful with this approach. In the mid-1960s about 0.93 million ha of waterfowl habitat in the Mississippi Flyway were controlled by private hunting clubs (Ladd 1977). During the same period, the Wildlife Management Institute estimated that waterfowl clubs had preserved a minimum of 1.34 million ha of habitat in the U.S. This figure did not include land from Louisiana, Mississippi, and several other states, since no data were available for those areas. With every shovelful of soil extracted to create a drainage canal or deposited as marsh fill, we remove a little more of our waterfowling opportunity. The "average" American will be impacted most because, like it or not, what remains will be enjoyed by those who can afford it.

The land ethic that Leopold spoke of 40-odd years ago is real, alive, and well among those who place high priorities on being good stewards of the land resource. It is a noble philosophy for all who have a sense of accountability for our natural resources. To the farmer who must face the loan officer of the local bank or Production Credit Association each fall, however, nobility is secondary to paying debts. Dollars in a capitalist system are the universal language. Waterfowl can speak this language if we recognize their tremendous value to the spirit of humankind and place them prominently in the marketplace.

VESTED COMMITMENT

The welfare of waterfowl, as of any commodity, rests with those who have a vested interest in their well-being. To date, those with the most interest have been the hunters. We have now added a new dimension to the economics aspect of this chapter—the "socio" impact. What role does it play? Quite simply, hunters will pay the piper as long as there is a song in his or her anticipation. The stabilized season and bag regulations were much discussed issues during last year's flyway and national waterfowl council meetings. The restrictions that resulted emanated from genuine concerns about the populations of certain species of waterfowl, specifically mallards and pintails. Groups like Ducks Unlimited have been concerned about their well-being for 50 years. Resource managers, however, must be sure that restrictive regulations are not imposed on the hunter just because the gun is perceived as the only factor that could possibly impact duck populations that we, as game managers, can get our hands on. As wildlife biologists, let us be sure that such restrictions on hunters' opportunities will achieve the desired effects. Be aware that with that lost opportunity may well go hunters' interests in maintaining their lease on a marsh or a bottomland slough. Land-clearing and drainage equipment are always waiting in the wings for just such opportunities.

REFERENCES

BISHOP, R. C., AND T. A. HEBERLEIN. 1979. Measuring values of extra market goods; are indirect measures biased? Am. J. Agric. Econ. 61:926–930.

CAREY, O. L. 1965. The economics of recreation: progress and problems. West. Econ. J. 3:172–181.

CLAWSON, M. 1959. Methods of measuring the demand for and value of outdoor recreation. Resour. for the Future, Inc., Reprint No. 10. Washington, D.C. 36pp.

FRUGE, D. W., AND R. RUELLE. 1980. Mississippi and Louisiana estuarine areas. U.S. Fish and Wildl. Serv., Div. of Ecol. Serv., Lafayette, La. 86pp.

GOSSELINK, J. G., C. L. CORDES, AND J. W. PARSON. 1979. An ecological characterization study of the Chenier Plan coastal ecosystem of Louisiana and Texas. U.S. Fish and Wildl. Serv., Off. Biol. Serv. Vols. 78/9–78/11.

HORVATH, J. C. 1974. Economic survey of wildlife recreation. Environ. Res. Group, Georgia State Univ., Atlanta. 76pp.

LADD, W. N. 1977. Waterfowl habitat problems and preservation programs in the Mississippi flyway of the United States. Miss. Waterfowl Flyway Counc., Biloxi. 16pp.

PEARSE, P. H. 1968. A new approach to the evaluation of non-priced recreational resources. Land Econ. 44(1):87–99.

U.S. DEPARTMENT OF AGRICULTURE. 1971. Land use in the southern Mississippi Alluvial Valley, 1950-69. Econ. Res. Serv., Agric. Econ. Rep. 215. 26pp.

U.S. FISH AND WILDLIFE SERVICE AND U.S. BUREAU OF THE CENSUS. 1982. 1980 national survey of fishing, hunting and wildlife-associated recreation. U.S. Dep. Inter. and U.S. Dep. Commer., U.S. Gov. Print. Off., Washington, D.C. 156pp.

Chapter 13

Maryland's Waterfowl Resource: A Best Case Example of Noncommodity Values

Carlo R. Brunori

The value of wildlife to landowners is best measured by the economic return that can be achieved in combination with other land uses. This direct return will be the main measure of how much influence wildlife management has on the land in future years. During the early history of the U.S. the Old World tradition of hunting rights and game belonging to the kings and landed gentry was changed, and these rights were given to the citizens (Brokaw 1978). Although until recently the idea of selling hunting privileges has been held in low esteem, this situation has changed with the growth in the human population and with losses in habitat and free access. Compensation for the landowner has become increasingly common in some areas during the past 25 years (Henderson 1984); the form of compensation has generally changed from donation of goods or services to actual cash payments. This chapter is based on the author's experiences with and observations of such changes in Maryland during the past 21 years. The eastern shore of Maryland on the Del-Mar-Va peninsula is the principal area in which the changes that have brought about the opportunity for high economic return have occurred (see Fig. 13.1).

AREA LAND USE AND CHANGES

The main change in land use has been the shift in agriculture to predominantly field crops. Dairy and other general uses have given way to production of corn, soybean, wheat, and other grain crops. The Del-Mar-Va chicken broiler industry has greatly spurred this change over the past quarter century and with it the change in wildlife populations, especially waterfowl.

The main population change in wildlife has been the increase in Canada geese (*Branta canadensis*) over the past 20 years and in snow

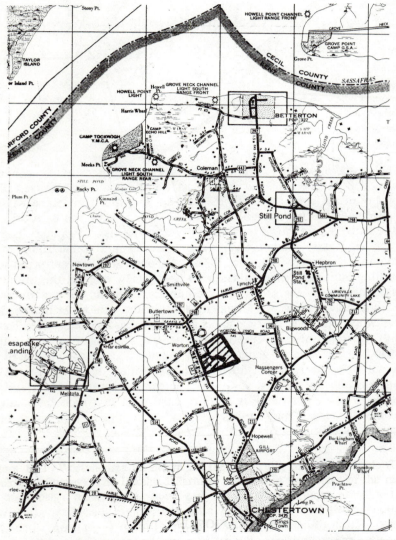

Figure 13.1 Kent County, Md., area. The Lakeland Farm is highlighted in the center of the map.

geese (*Chen hyperborea*) over the past 8 years. The eastern shore area of the Del-Mar-Va peninsula, with its many tidal creeks along the western edge of the Chesapeake Bay and the Atlantic Ocean to the east, has always attracted waterfowl. From the Susquehanna Flats at the mouth of the Susquehanna River in the north to the brackish marshes to the south, water and wetlands have always been abundant (McCormick and Somes 1982). Relatively mild winters have left open water for waterfowl feeding during the winter.

The steady loss of submerged aquatic vegetation (SAV) has been a problem over the past 20 years and has been associated with eutrophication and runoff of harmful pollutants. The duck population has suffered from this loss of aquatic vegetation, but the geese have adapted to the increase in food in the upland fields. The feeding pattern has shifted to the upland crop fields, with the water areas being used mainly for day and night resting.

SITE LOCATION AND DESCRIPTION

This chapter will concentrate on the Kent County–Worton, Maryland, area, where the best-case example is located. As shown in Figure 13.1, Kent County is in the upper eastern shore of Maryland, with water bodies on three sides: the Chesapeake Bay tidal area to the west, the Sassafras River to the north, and the Chester River to the south. The main drainage in the area is provided by Morgan Creek, which drains south to the Chester River (Martin 1953). Morgan Creek, which drains an area of 84.2 sq km, is approximately 16.5 km long, and enters the Chester River at kilometer point 47.7 (Md. State Planning Dep. 1966). This area is in the Coastal Plain physiographic province and was created mainly by the deposits from the Susquehanna River during the glacial periods. The Chesapeake Bay is the drowned valley of the river formed after the last sea-level rise (Vokes 1961).

The soils on the farm at Worton (Fig. 13.2) are composed mainly of the Sassafras and Matapeake series and are good agricultural soils (White 1982). The farm operation centers on corn production with secondary crops of soybean and winter wheat. The example farm is composed of 143.5 ha, with 117.7 ha in crop use; the pond area covers 7.4 ha, and 3.3 ha of Japanese millet are planted along the 0.9-m drawdown area during summer. Approximately 8.2 ha of corn and milo are planted and left standing as winter food for waterfowl. Annual rye grass strips (6m) on each side of the food strips are also planted. Grass strips are left around the pond site as a filter strip; the pond site drains approximately 369 ha of watershed (Fig. 13.3).

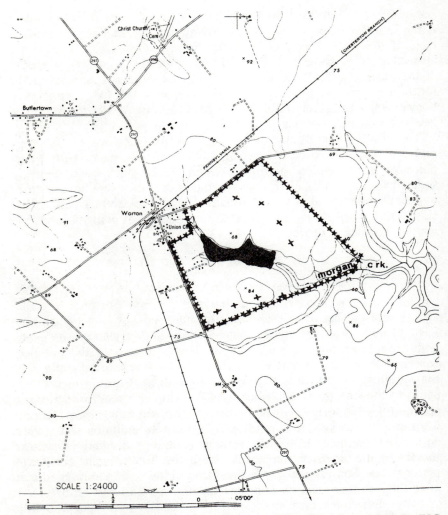

Figure 13.2 Worton area as shown on the Betterton, Md., quadrangle (U.S. Geological Survey). The Lakeland Farm is outlined in the center of the map.

WATERFOWL POPULATIONS

The area in which the farm is located is in the Atlantic Flyway, and the population of Canada geese has increased greatly there over the past 20 years. Because of the influence of Chesapeake Bay to the west, the Chester River to the south, and the Sassafras River to the north, the site is provided with good local flyways for daily movements. Since

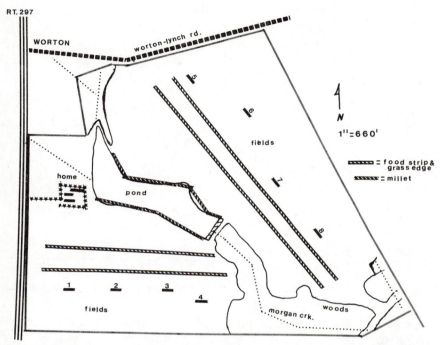

Figure 13.3 Layout of the Lakeland Farm showing the location of the pond, agricultural fields, food strips and grass edge, and eight pit blinds

the early 1960s, the average goose population has increased in Maryland from the 100,000 to 200,000 range to over 500,000 during the last decade (Fig. 13.4). Midwinter survey counts since 1954 highlight the population increase (U.S. Fish and Wildl. Serv. 1984). In 1966, the Canada goose population reached more than 300,000; in 1968 it was more than 400,000, in 1974 it exceeded 500,000; and in 1981 it reached more than 600,000 (for the only year so far). Kent County is the center of the eastern shore population.

The snow goose population has also increased greatly since the 1977 midwinter survey count of 19,800. Before 1977, the snow geese were concentrated on the Atlantic Coast area of Delaware and Maryland. Winter 1977 was severe, and Delaware populations of snow geese began daily feeding movements westward into Maryland near the Delaware border. Kent County and Queen Anne County (adjacent to the south and east) became, and are today, the main areas of concentration in the Chesapeake area. Although the snow goose population has generally grown along the flyway, it has increased greatly in the last five years in Maryland (Fig. 13.4). The 1985 midwinter survey count for Maryland

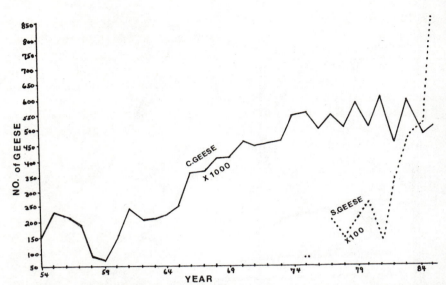

Figure 13.4 Maryland midwinter Canada and snow goose survey counts (U.S. Fish and Wildlife Service 1984)

was 85,300. The Maryland Chesapeake area population is still centered along the eastern portion of the two named counties, but the bird population continues to spread out, and snow geese are considered a bonus trophy bird.

The concentration of these geese populations in Maryland has caused a shortage of birds in lower coastal states (Virginia, North Carolina, South Carolina) that traditionally had much higher populations (Linduska 1964). The combination of available food, open tidal water, and new freshwater pond construction with relatively mild winters has caused the "stop gapping" of the geese. Attempts at using Atlantic flyway regulations to mitigate this problem have met with little success, and I foresee no relief in the immediate future with present conditions.

LAKELAND FARM—DESCRIPTION AND OPERATION

The present farm operation for managed hunting along with agricultural production was begun in 1966 with the construction of the 7.4-ha pond. The pond construction cost $20,000, exclusive of engineering studies furnished by the local Soil Conservation Service (SCS). The pond also serves as a recreation pond for swimming and fishing.

The pond serves as a complete sanctuary once the returning waterfowl begin using the area. During the gunning season, typically begun near the end of October, no one is allowed near the pond, and all gunners in the pit areas (Fig. 13.3) are required to stay behind the standing corn strips and not chase any geese beyond the strip closest to the pond. Over the years this protection has made the sanctuary of the pond a valuable tool in keeping the geese on the farm once they have returned. The birds' movement from the pond is generally in a north-northeast or south-southeast direction.

MANAGED HUNT

The use of waste corn, standing corn, and milo, millet, and grass strips contribute to the managed hunt operation by keeping the birds in the area. However, most of the gunning is "pass shooting": Very little decoying is needed, and the birds are taken as they leave the area over the pits on their usual twice-a-day movements. Hunters are usually transported to the pits in the morning by first light, by J. Elgin and family in a four-wheel-drive pickup truck with cap and seats. Pick-up times or signals are arranged for departures if parties are not staying all day or if they limit out early (they raise a flagged pole). The pits, made of salt-treated lumber, can accommodate up to five persons. Either the tops are covered with cut corn plants or the pits have sliding tops with various camouflage coverings. Hunters are required to sign in for each pit with their names, addresses, and license numbers; they are required to obey all federal and state regulations. "Sky busting," or shooting birds out of range, and shooting at returning geese (usually high) are discouraged. During cold weather, charcoal heaters are set up in the blinds. Cards for bird tagging are provided to identify owners' birds, and cleaning of birds can be arranged at nearby commercial pickers.

The primary bird taken at the farm is the Canada goose. On Lakeland Farms alone the harvest averages 1,600 to 1,800 birds per season. The next in order of kill is the mallard (*Anas platyrhynchos*) of which about 100 birds are taken. A few early season birds taken are the pintail (*Anas acuta*), blue-winged teal (*Anas discors*), green-winged teal (*Anas crecca*), and shoveler (*Spatula clyplata*). Although the snow goose is currently a later season rare trophy bonus, it should appear more frequently in the harvest as its numbers continue to increase in the Bay area. An earlier opener to the duck season would make available to the gunner an estimated 2,000 mallards and 2,500 pintails, plus 500 teal, 500 black duck (*Anas rubripes*), and 50 to 100 shoveler before the birds move south. Canada goose populations average over 10,000 birds during the regular season. In earlier years before additional sanctuary ponds were constructed by other operators, highs on the pond and farm area exceeded

25,000 birds; estimated counts by J. Elgin ranged from 3,000 to 40,000 over the many years of operation.

ECONOMIC RETURNS

The value of hunting to the economy has been demonstrated in the 1980 National Survey of Fishing, Hunting and Wildlife-Associated Recreation, completed in 1982 (U.S. Fish and Wildl. Serv. and U.S. Bur. Census 1982a). Nationwide, 5.3 million hunters made 40 million trips and spent 42.9 million days afield. They spent $56 million primarily for fees and other related expenditures. In Maryland, 183,000 hunters spent $81 million (U.S. Fish and Wildl. Serv. and U.S. Bur. Census 1982b). Migratory bird hunters (67,000) spent $10 million for the sport. In Kent County alone, it is estimated that 3,500 people were employed during the hunting season in occupations related to waterfowl hunting: guiding, building blinds, digging pits, and making decoys (Kent County Comm. 1982). Kent County sells the most hunting licenses of all subdivisions in the state.

At Lakeland Farms, the economic return is based on a two-system leasing use of the property and the eight pits. A lease of a pit site for the entire season (90 days) costs $180/day: Thus $180 \times 90 = \$16,200$. A daily lease for one pit costs $200/day: Thus $200 \times 90 = \$18,000$. The minimum income for one season from eight pits if all were leased for the entire season would be $\$16,200 \times 8 = \$129,600$. The maximum for one season for eight pits if all were leased on a daily basis would be $\$18,000 \times 8 = \$144,000$. In 1985, income was approximately half the daily rate because of unfilled days.

The yearly maintenance costs are $1,000 for pit maintenance, $1,000 for vehicle maintenance, and $500 for gasoline costs. However, on top of these costs J. Elgin pays a high rental fee for the use of the land. The economic return is still very profitable despite the rental and maintenance costs, as evidenced by the high fees commanded to hunt a trophy bird such as the Canada goose. Because many managed farms in the general area are already owned, the landowners do not have to pay a high rental fee that offsets income. The other income from the agricultural operation ties in well with this example of a managed hunt for waterfowl since the land-management operation easily accommodates the two incomes.

GOVERNMENT TECHNICAL ASSISTANCE

The primary technical assistance comes from two agencies: the Maryland Forest Park and Wildlife Service (FP&W) and the Kent

County Soil Conservation District. The FP&W, through the district biologists, regional managers, and species specialists, provides technical assistance relating to forestry and wildlife management and wildlife information to landowners who have specific need for species information and/or management plans (Helinski and Brunori 1981). Trees and shrubs are also provided at cost. The Technical Services Division of the FP&W provides assistance and information on environmental review needs, helping cooperators obtain needed state and federal permits for construction of projects. In its 1984 annual report the Kent County Soil Conservation District staff discussed the Waterfowl Restoration Program and pointed out that almost all new farm ponds participated since the start of the program in 1983, with a pond total of 45 to date. The district provides technical assistance for ponds and erosion control work through the SCS (Kent County Soil Conservation District 1980). The Agricultural Stabilization and Conservation Service (ASCS) also provides funds for the conservation reserve program. The food strips on Lakeland Farms were set aside under this program and used for wildlife conservation purposes.

In 1981, the Maryland legislature passed the Maryland Waterfowl Restoration Program, which gave the landowner a tax incentive for installing waterfowl ponds and habitat areas (Md. For., Park and Wildl. Serv. 1982). A 10-year agreement can be signed if at least 0.4 ha of water is provided with a minimum of 4.1 ha of land in the project. A plan is developed by the FP&W staff and checked yearly. All costs for pond construction, food, and cover development are considered a tax contribution to the State of Maryland and are tax deductible. However, this agreement is not available for areas with commercial hunting operations.

Problems relating to government assistance have centered around the crop depredation of planted farm fields. An overabundance of waterfowl on these fields has been exacerbated by the loss of submerged aquatic vegetation in the traditional tidal feeding areas and the change in agriculture on the uplands to increase production of corn, soybeans, and other grains. Large birds, such as the tundra swans (*Cygnus columbianus*), have moved to the upland fields in the last 25 years and cause crop damage, especially with the large increases in their population. During the past year in the Atlantic Flyway, an experimental, limited gunning season for the tundra swan was tried for the first time. If successful and practical, this approach may be tried in other states, especially in crop damage areas. Also, if pollution control efforts are successful on the Chesapeake Bay drainage in the future, the return of the SAV may reduce the feeding pressure on the upland fields.

CONCLUSIONS

This chapter has focused on the possible economic gains from managing for wildlife, especially a trophy waterfowl species such as the Canada goose. In the right place with the right management, a high return can be realized in conjunction with the normal agricultural land practices. Our wildlife depends on the land and water; our technical expertise to assist the landowner in managing these resources is the key to future wildlife abundance. The wildlife professional must combine the information from different agencies and programs to provide the best incentive for the landowenr. Additional assistance programs like the Waterfowl Restoration Program in Maryland are needed to turn the tide away from past abuses to our wildlife habitat. Aldo Leopold, chairman of the Committee on Game Policy, outlined an appropriate partnership between the landowner and the sportsman:

> Recognize the landowner as the custodian of public game on all private land, protect him from the irresponsible shooter, and compensate him for putting his land in productive condition. Compensate him either publicly or privately, with either cash, service, or protection, for the use of his land and for his labor, on condition that he preserves the game seed and otherwise safeguards the public interest. In short, make game management a partnership enterprise to which the landowner, the sportsman, and the public each contributes appropriate services, and from which each derives appropriate rewards. (1930: n.p.)

Acknowledgments.—This chapter would not have been possible without the help and informtion of James Elgin, manager and operator of Lakeland Farm, Worton, Maryland. His continuous interest in helping the resource has guided his work in agriculture, wildlife, and conservation in general. His information on managed hunting methods, farm layout, crops, bird numbers, and personal finances was vital to presenting this best-case example to help others learn to manage our wildlife resource.

REFERENCES

BROKAW, H. P., editor. 1978. Wildlife and America. Counc. on Environ. Quality, Co-sponsor, U.S. Fish and Wildl. Serv., Natl. Oceanic and Atmos. Adm., Washington, D.C. 532pp.

HELINSKI, R. R., AND C. R. BRUNORI. 1981. Waterfowl habitat improvement. Md. For., Park and Wildl. Serv., Annapolis, Md. 12pp.

HENDERSON, R. F., editor. 1984. Guidelines for increasing wildlife on farms and ranches. Great Plains Agric. Counc.-Wildl. Resour. Comm. and Coop. Ext. Serv., Kansas State Univ., Manhattan. 519pp.

KENT COUNTY COMMISSIONERS. 1982. Kent County, Maryland, an account of the land, the water and the people. Chestertown, Md. 18pp.

KENT COUNTY SOIL CONSERVATION DISTRICT. 1980. Our enduring resources. Board of Superv. of Kent County Soil Conserv. Dist., Chestertown, Md. 14pp.

———. 1984. Annual report. Board of Superv. of Kent County Soil Conserv. Dist., Chestertown, Md. 6pp.

LEOPOLD, A. 1930. Report of the Committee on American Wildlife Policy. *In* Proc. 16th Am. Game Conf. Wildl. Manage. Inst., Washington, D.C. (Unpaged.)

LINDUSKA, J. P., ed. 1964. Waterfowl tomorrow. U.S. Fish and Wildl. Serv., Washington, D.C. 770pp.

MCCORMICK, J., AND H. A. SOMES, JR. 1982. The coastal wetlands of Maryland. Md. Dep. Nat. Resour., Coastal Zone Manage. Program, Annapolis, Md. 241pp.

MARTIN, R.O.R. 1953. Drainage areas in Maryland. U.S. Geol. Surv., Washington, D.C. 37pp.

MARYLAND FOREST, PARK AND WILDLIFE SERVICE. 1982. Maryland waterfowl restoration program. Annapolis, Md. 5pp.

MARYLAND STATE PLANNING DEPARTMENT. 1966. Maryland water supply and demand study. Part I. Vol. 5. Baltimore. 64pp.

U.S. FISH AND WILDLIFE SERVICE. 1984. Mid-winter waterfowl inventory, Region 5, Atlantic Flyway 1954–1984, trend analysis. U.S. Dep. Inter., Newton Corner, Mass. 284pp.

———, AND U.S. BUREAU OF THE CENSUS. 1982a. 1980 national survey of fishing, hunting and wildlife-associated recreation. U.S. Dep. Inter. and U.S. Dep. Commer., U.S. Gov. Print. Off., Washington, D.C. 156pp.

———, AND ———. 1982b. 1980 national survey of fishing, hunting and wildlife-associated recreation. U.S. Dep. Inter. and U.S. Dep. Commer., U.S. Gov. Print. Off., Washington, D.C. 76pp.

VOKES, H. E. 1961. Geography and geology of Maryland. Dep. Geol., Mines and Water Resour. Bull. 19, Baltimore. 243pp.

WHITE, E. A., JR. 1982. Soil survey of Kent County, Maryland. U.S. Dep. Agric., Soil Conserv., Kent County Soil Conserv. Dist., College Park, Md. 125pp.

Chapter 14

Economics of Wildlife Production and Damage Control on Private Lands

Dale A. Wade

During a symposium, "Wildlife Management on Private Lands," held in Milwaukee, Wisconsin, 3–6 May 1981, numerous papers were presented in support of the objective: "to accelerate the application of wildlife management practices on private land." The basis for and purpose of the symposium were summarized as follows: "The collective experience of resource managers, landowners, and concerned conservation organizations, nationwide, must be integrated to refine and implement management schemes for habitat restoration on private lands. Such a coalition is needed to build and maintain the political momentum to change existing programs and to develop and implement new ones" (Dumke et al. 1981:2).

This theme is iterated and reiterated by most of the papers in the proceedings: Much more habitat must be developed and maintained on private land to increase wildlife populations for the public good. Numerous methods and techniques were suggested by symposium participants to encourage landowners to support this objective. Suggested inducements varied from flattery and name-dropping, public recognition and praise to technical advice and support, tax incentives and direct monetary compensation. Other suggestions included new laws and regulations to protect landowners from illegal trespass and liability suits by hunters, bird watchers, and other users, including "slob hunters" and "unwanted crowds whose presence threatens their [landowners'] property and economic well-being." More forceful methods of persuasion also were suggested ranging from gaining control of committees and political offices to influence or dictate decisions and policies, political action to develop coercive laws and regulations, and land use controls to condemnation of private lands "for the public good" and "suing the bastards" (Cutler 1981:350, Strange 1981:364).

As a consequence of these various proposals, many methods for encouraging private landowners to produce more wildlife for the public good were considered during the symposium. However, a review of the proceedings indicates that some methods were not considered: Most presentations failed to offer significant consideration of current wildlife damage problems, which can be expected to increase as wildlife habitat is improved and/or expanded. Nor were suggestions offered to provide relief for such problems. Neither of the two keynote papers mentions wildlife damage as a factor to be expected with habitat increase or improvement. Acknowledgment of wildlife damage was mentioned in 10 of some 45 papers in the proceedings; only 2 of these (Bishop 1981, Ramsey and Shult 1981) provided significant discussion of wildlife damage problems and the perceptions of landowners in this regard.

Thus, from review of these proceedings one might readily conclude that wildlife damage is not really significant and that "those interested in wildlife management," including management agencies, have no great interest in nor responsibility for wildlife damage. Burger and Teer suggested that U.S. wildlife "is owned by both everybody and by nobody [and—as a result] everybody's business is nobody's business and . . . what belongs to everybody belongs to nobody and is, therefore, fair game for anybody" (1981:254).

The content of the proceedings therefore suggests that even though wildlife enhancement has extensive support, wildlife damage control has very little, perhaps because "nobody is responsible for that which is owned by everybody, anybody and nobody." Also of interest is McConnell's comment that "we must realize that, on private lands, wildlife managers must work within the bounds of existing land uses, and respond to the whims of landowners for the most part" (1981:285). His entire discussion of programs to increase wildlife on private lands culminates in an integrated systems management diagram (1981:287) that includes all the physical factors, the primary agencies involved in resource management, and the public but does not include private landowners. This interpretation may well indicate a significant underlying reason for the reactions of landowners, as described by Harmon: "Consumed in this debate, we have neglected to consult with the owner of the resource—the landowner. Without any basis, we have decided that each landowner has a latent sense of moral obligation to provide the public with free wildlife . . . and . . . that . . . landowners . . . have sent clear signals that no program exists to which they can relate" (1981:377).

Ramsey and Shult (1981) reviewed at length principles that they suggested should be applied in educational approaches to wildlife production and management on private lands. Two of these, specifically important to habitat improvement, wildlife management, and damage control, are summarized as follows:

Management programs for wildlife must be integrated with the total land use program as envisioned by the landowner. Economic and/or social costs and benefits of wildlife must be available to facilitate the decision-making process if wildlife is to be considered in the farm-ranch-woodlot scheme.

The wildlife profession must, if education is a viable method of implementing management practices, do a much better job of interpreting costs and benefits of wildlife management practices in terms of value to the landowner. (1981:322)

From review of these proceedings it seems apparent, and unfortunate, that many of the presentations seemed to neglect these principles in the midst of the participants' enthusiasm to increase wildlife production by private landowners. However, this consideration appears to warrant a high priority because social and economic costs of wildlife production to landowners, including wildlife damage, are obviously significant to their management decisions.

Wildlife, as well as other species, cause damage and must be controlled; brief examples of the social and economic costs are presented in Table 14.1. Berryman pointed out in part that

What is forgotten in the frustration and in the heat of debate and the desire and need for effective control programs is that we are talking about virtually every form of wildlife at one time or another. . . .

Successful management protects and enhances. It must also be willing to regulate. . . . Wildlife management must be more than a noble crusade. It must include a willingness to deal with the less attractive side of wildlife management. (1983:4)

Berryman further commented, in regard to suggestions for removal of professional damage control responsibilities from the U.S. Department of Interior, Fish and Wildlife Service, that

One of the best ways to remove the temptation to transfer responsibility from the fish and wildlife agencies is for those state and federal agencies to do a competent, responsible and acceptable job of control . . . regrettably, the Department of the Interior and the Fish and Wildlife Service, along with a number of states, have too often viewed animal damage control as nothing but a political liability—something to be avoided, or at least to be treated with benign neglect.

Despite the limited amount of accurate data on the total costs and benefits of wildlife damage control, numerous examples document cost-benefit ratios in favor of control for both social and economic reasons.

TABLE 14.1
Common Social and Economic Costs of Wildlife in Urban and Rural Settings

Animal Species	Urban Damage	Rural Damage	Hazards
BIRDS			
Starlings	defacing of buildings	damage to crops	carriers of diseases to livestock & people
Blackbirds	sidewalks, shrubbery, etc.	damage to crops	same as above
Pigeons	sidewalks, shrubbery, etc.	damage to crops	same as above
House sparrow	sidewalks, shrubbery, etc.		same as above
Egrets	sidewalks, shrubbery, etc.		
Waterfowl	damage to golf courses, parks and ponds	damage to crops	
Woodpeckers, flickers	damage to buildings, utility poles, etc.	damage to buildings, utility poles, etc.	
RODENTS			
Beaver	damage to trees, shrubs, landscaping, etc.	damage to crops, timber, roads, etc.	Giardiasis in humans
Nutria	same as above	damage to crops, timber, roads, dams & levees	
Muskrats	not common	damage to crops, roads, dams & levees	
Black and Norway rats	damage to buildings, food supplies, shrubs, etc.	damage to buildings & crops, kill poultry	disease transmission to humans and animals

TABLE 14.1 (Cont.)

Animal Species	Urban Damage	Rural Damage	Hazards
House mice	damage to buildings, food supplies, etc.	damage to buildings, food supplies, etc.	contamination of food, disease carriers
CARNIVORES			
Black bear		damage to bee-yards, trees, crops, and livestock	hazards to humans
Grizzly bear		damage to livestock	hazards to humans
Coyotes	nuisance in residential areas	damage to livestock & poultry	occasional hazards to humans
Raccoons	same as above	same as above	hazards of rabies transmission
Skunks	same as above	same as above	same as above

For example, control of dogs, cats, rats, and mice in urban areas is considered important for public health and welfare. Control of rabies in bats, skunks, raccoons, and other species also is considered essential. Likewise, excessive bird populations on or near airports present major hazards to air traffic, and their reduction or removal is believed necessary. Bird roosts in urban and suburban areas are considered a health hazard. Even in rural areas, when human risk is involved, wildlife population control may be implemented. Endemic sylvatic plague in ground squirrels and other rodents often results in population control when the disease occurs in recreational areas or in proximity to residential areas. Moreover, not only social benefits are attached to such control actions; reducing the number of people who require medical treatment because of exposure to injury and disease also results in substantial economic savings.

For example, the total costs caused by one rabid animal in California in May 1980 were estimated to be $105,790. These costs include antirabies prophylaxis at $1,500 per person for 70 people who were exposed, $4,190 for animal vaccinations and veterinary services, and $8,950 for health department and animal control programs (Cent. Disease Control 1981).

The Center for Disease Control estimated that approximately 25,000 persons per year in the United States receive rabies prophylaxis (Cent. Disease Control 1984). Thus the costs and benefits associated with the extensive rabies eruption in raccoons on the East Coast (1,608 raccoons confirmed rabid in 1983 [Beck 1984]) must have been substantial, perhaps the most important economic benefits resulting from reduction of human exposure through educational and control efforts. Various operational control programs have been carried out to protect humans and domestic animals from rabies in coyotes, skunks, bats, and other species. Despite arguments to the contrary, rapid reduction of the carrier populations in rabies outbreaks is effective in reducing exposure of humans and domestic animals (see Cocozza and Alba [1962], Humphrey [1970], Seyler [1974], Glosser [1981]).

Economic cost and benefit data associated with wildlife damage to livestock, farm crops, timber, and other animal or crop production are not commonly available. Data on sheep losses to predators (U.S. Fish and Wildl. Serv. 1979:140–142) indicated that average losses without predator control were 3.2% of ewes and 14.9% of lambs. Comparable loss rates with predator control in effect were 0.3% of ewes and 4.3% of lambs. The U.S. Fish and Wildlife Service (USFWS) report indicated that the difference between the estimated loss levels would be "about 929,000 sheep with a value of $49.5 million" in the 16 western states if predator control were stopped. By using an income multiplier of 2.5, the USFWS suggested that the impact on the overall economy would be $123.75 million. However, in the report the USFWS cautioned that "the limited studies to date are inadequate to indicate the overall effectiveness of the ADC program in reducing predation loss." In a study of predator control to protect sheep and goats in 21 central Texas counties, Pearson and Caroline (1981) estimated that the cost-benefit ratio of the Animal Damage Control (ADC) program was 1:4.5 for 1975 in these counties.

A more recent report on cost-benefit ratios, primarily for predator and rodent control, of the current ADC program in California indicated that a conservative estimate of benefits to producers was 1:6.90 to 1:11.50 and that losses would increase twofold to fourteenfold if the program were deleted. The same report indicated a substantially greater benefit to consumers. Using a multiplier of 2.62, benefits to consumers were calculated to be a minimum of 1:18.09 and a maximum of 1:30.14 under the current ADC program. If the program were deleted, the costs to consumers would be expected to increase twofold to fourteenfold (Berryhill 1984).

Hill (1976), Arner and Dubose (1982), Miller (1983), Woodward (1983), Bullock and Arner (1985), and others have described the increasing costs of beaver damage in the U.S., particularly in the southeast, and the benefits that can accrue from effective damage control. Miller (1972) also described benefits attributed to effective control of muskrats in Arkansas, particularly to rice and fish farmers. Also, beaver control for protection of the endangered Paiute cutthroat trout in California was initiated by the U.S. Forest Service in 1976 (Hunter 1976).

Beaver and nutria damage to trees, shrubs, and landscaping has also become common in urban areas of the southern and eastern U.S. Both species also cause extensive damage to flotation blocks under boat docks and marinas in the South. As a consequence, urban residents have become far more demanding of efforts for damage control.

Cummings and Marsh (1978) described the wildlife damage problems to citrus, particularly by rodents, the benefits derived from control, and the deficiency of control methods for protection of citrus seedlings and trees. Various authors have described damage by a variety of field rodents to agricultural crops and the economic savings resulting from control, including Spencer (n.d.), Passof (1977) U.S. Forest Service (1978), and the South Dakota Department of Agriculture (1981).

Many similar examples exist in regard to bird damage in livestock feedlots, agricultural and ornamental crops, fish hatcheries, and urban areas. Noise from bird roosts, defacement of buildings and sidewalks, and contamination of food and facilities in grain elevators, in food processing plants, and in warehouses are further examples in urban and rural areas.

The lack of effective, practical, and economical wildlife damage control methods has become an important cause for loss of wildlife habitat on private lands. Common examples of loss include the removal of roadside and ditch bank cover in the farming areas of California; this damage is frequently caused by the lack of effective methods to control populations of ground squirrels, meadow mice, starlings, linnets, and other species that utilize such cover. Minimum tillage practices for crop production recommended by some to limit soil erosion, reduce production costs, and improve wildlife habitat carry similar implications; the improved habitat is frequently occupied by rodent species that cause serious damage. Thus, the reactions of many farmers to public requests for more "acres for wildlife" should come as no surprise.

A lack of interest by landowners in wildlife habitat improvement may result from or be coupled with emotional frustration caused by a variety of factors, including

1. economic costs of persistent wildlife damage
2. time, effort, and costs of attempts to prevent or reduce damage
3. lack of effective damage prevention or control methods

4. inability to produce economically some crops because of damage
5. need to shift to alternate or less desirable crops
6. need to alter production practices, such as planting and harvest data
7. inability to utilize land or forage because of wildlife damage
8. laws and regulations perceived as being excessively restrictive on crop production, the use of pesticides, and so on
9. income deficits resulting from high production costs and low returns
10. intensive opposition by environmental and humane interest groups to crop and livestock production practices
11. economic, emotional, and social stress caused by these and other factors

With these factors in mind, adverse reactions to requests (or demands) from "the public" to increase wildlife habitat on private lands should be expected, if compensatory benefits are not provided or perceived. Moreover, the results may include opposition to hunting, posting of lands against hunting and other forms of recreation, and, indeed, opposition to the entire concept of wildlife production.

Two important factors to recognize are that (1) animal species tend to respond to improved habitat by increasing their numbers and the results are not always beneficial to all people; (2) damage caused by wildlife is often described in terms of "average losses." However, average losses in any economic sector do not accurately reflect the impacts on individuals who may suffer no losses or on others whose losses may be catastrophic. Those businesses whose losses are most severe are likely to fail—a statement equally true whether wildlife damage or another disruption is the cause. As a consequence, public interest in and emphasis on wildlife production by private landowners must be coupled with recognition of the economic and other costs that may result (Ramsey and Shult 1981). Without this recognition and appropriate consideration of such costs, landowners are likely to continue to "stay away by the thousands" (Harmon 1981:377).

REFERENCES

ARNER, D. H., AND J. S. DUBOSE. 1982. The impact of beaver on the environment and economics in the Southeastern United States. Trans. Int. Congr. Game Biol. 14:241–247.
BECK, A. M. 1984. An epizootic of rabies. Nat. Hist. 93(7):6–8, 10–11.

BERRYHILL, C. 1984. Letter to Walter W. Stiern, Chairman, Joint Legislative Budget Comm., Sacramento, Calif. and attached rep. to the Legislature re the Calif. Predatory Animal Control Program (21pp), 14 November.

BERRYMAN, J. H. 1983. Wildlife damage control: a current perspective. Pages 3–5 in D. J. Decker, ed. Proc. 1st East. Wildl. Damage Control Conf. Coop. Ext. Serv., Cornell Univ., Ithaca, N.Y.

BISHOP, R. C. 1981. Economic considerations affecting landowner behavior. Pages 73–87 in R. T. Dumke, G. V. Burger, and J. R. March, eds. Wildlife management on private lands. Dep. Nat. Resour., Madison, Wis.

BULLOCK, J. F., AND D. H. ARNER. 1985. Beaver damage to nonimpounded timber in Mississippi. South. J. of Appl. For. 9(3):137–140.

BURGER, G. V., AND J. G. TEER. 1981. Economic and socioeconomic issues influencing wildlife management on private land. Pages 252–278 in R. T. Dumke, G. V. Burger, and J. R. March, eds. Wildlife management on private lands. Dep. Nat. Resour., Madison, Wis.

CENTER FOR DISEASE CONTROL. 1981. The cost of one rabid dog—California. Morbidity and Mortality Weekly Rep. 30(42):527.

———. 1984. Rabies prevention—United States, 1984. Morbidity and Mortality Weekly Rep. 33(28):393–408.

COCOZZA, J., AND A. M. ALBA. 1962. Wildlife control project in Baja California. Public Health Rep. 77(2):147–151.

CUMMINGS, M. W., AND R. E. MARSH. 1978. Vertebrate pests of citrus. Pages 237–273 in The citrus industry. Vol. IV. Div. of Agric. Sci., Univ. Calif., Davis.

CUTLER, M. R. 1981. How to influence USDA programs affecting wildlife: the inside view. Pages 341–351 in R. T. Dumke, G. V. Burger, and J. R. March, eds. Wildlife management on private lands. Dep. Nat. Resour., Madison, Wis.

DUMKE, R. T., G. V. BURGER, AND J. R. MARCH, editors. 1981. Wildlife management on private lands. Dep. Nat. Resour., Madison, Wis. 568pp.

GLOSSER, J. W. 1981. Testimony presented and documents submitted for the Hearing Rec., Denver, Colo., 28 July 1981; Hearing on predator control toxicants, Environ. Protection Agency, Washington, D.C.

HARMON, K. W. 1981. Future actions for management of private land wildlife. Pages 374–382 in R. T. Dumke, G. V. Burger, and J. R. March, eds. Wildlife management on private lands. Dep. Nat. Resour., Madison, Wis.

HILL, E. P. 1976. Control methods for nuisance beaver in the Southeastern United States. Pages 85–98 in C. C. Siebe, ed. Proc. 7th Vertebr. Pest Conf. Univ. Calif., Davis.

HUMPHREY, G. L. 1970. Field control of animal rabies. Pap. presented at the Conf. on Rabies, Tokyo, Japan, 12–14 October. 31pp. and appendices.

HUNTER, H. C. 1976. Letter to Riley Patterson, USFWS, Bakersfield, Calif. with attached Environ. Analysis Rep.: Proposed beaver removal in Cottonwood Creek, U.S. For. Serv., Inyo National Forest, White Mountain Ranger District, Calif., 7 May. 10pp.

MCCONNELL, C. A. 1981. Common threads in successful programs benefiting wildlife on private lands. Pages 279–287 in R. T. Dumke, G. V. Burger, and

J. R. March, eds. Wildlife management on private lands. Dep. Nat. Resour., Madison, Wis.

MILLER, J. E. 1972. Muskrat and beaver control. Pages 35–37 *in* J. R. Schmidt, ed. Proc. Nat. Ext. Wildl. Workshop. Colorado State Univ., Ft. Collins.

————. 1983. Control of beaver damage. Pages 177–183 *in* D. J. Decker, ed. Proc. 1st East. Wildl. Damage Control Conf. Coop. Ext. Serv., Cornell Univ., Ithaca, N.Y.

PASSOF, P. C. 1977. Forest rodent damage and control. For. and Wildl. School, Eureka, Calif. 5pp.

PEARSON, E. W., AND M. CAROLINE. 1981. Predator control in relation to livestock losses in Central Texas. J. Range Manage. 34(6):435–441.

RAMSEY, C. W., AND M. J. SHULT. 1981. Educational approaches to wildlife management on private lands. Pages 318–334 *in* R. T. Dumke, G. V. Burger, and J. R. March, eds. Wildlife management on private lands. Dep. Nat. Resour., Madison, Wis.

SEYLER, K. 1974. Emergency rabid skunk control in Montana. Pages 198–203 *in* W. V. Johnson, ed. Proc. 6th Vertebr. Pest Conf. Univ. Calif., Davis.

SOUTH DAKOTA DEPARTMENT OF AGRICULTURE. 1981. Vertebrate rodent economic loss, South Dakota, 1980. S.D. Crop and Livestock Rep. Serv., Sioux Falls. 4pp.

SPENCER, D. A. (Undated). Biological aspects of the 1957–58 meadow mouse irruption in the Pacific Northwest. Bur. Sport Fish. and Wildl., Denver, Colo. 9pp.

STRANGE, M. 1981. Building a more resourceful agriculture. Pages 357–370 *in* R. T. Dumke, G. V. Burger, and J. R. March, eds. Wildlife management on private lands. Dep. Nat. Resour., Madison, Wis.

U.S. FISH AND WILDLIFE SERVICE. 1979. Final environmental impact statement: mammalian predator damage management for livestock protection in the Western United States. U.S. Dep. Inter., Washington, D.C. 789pp.

U.S. FOREST SERVICE. 1978. Management of prairie dogs on lands administered by the supervisor of the Nebraska National Forest. Final U.S. Dep. Agric. For. Serv. Environ. Statement, U.S. Dep. Agric. For. Serv., Washington, D.C. 99pp.

WOODWARD, D. K. 1983. Beaver management in the Southeastern United States: a review and update. Pages 163–165 *in* D. J. Decker, ed. Proc. 1st East. Wildl. Damage Control Conf. Coop. Ext. Serv., Cornell Univ., Ithaca, N.Y.

Chapter 15

Alligator Management and Value-Added Conservation in Florida

Tommy C. Hines and H. Franklin Percival

Historically alligators have been commercially valuable. They were exploited in Florida as early as the late 1800s (Kersey 1975) and were a significant source of income to many rural Floridians during the early part of the twentieth century. Because of perceived depression in population levels, the legal alligator season was closed in Florida in 1962. However, the skin trade continued almost unabated from 1965 to 1970, and the harvest during that period may have exceeded 140,000 skins (Hines 1979). In 1969 the Lacey Act was amended to prohibit interstate movement of illegal alligator skins, and alligators were afforded additional protection by the Endangered Species Act in 1973. The Lacey Act provided the first real tool for controlling illegal movement of skins. After illegal hunting stopped in the early 1970s, the recovery of the alligator population was rapid, providing clear evidence that alligators were never biologically endangered statewide but probably considerably reduced in local areas (Hines and Woodward 1980).

As the Florida Game and Fresh Water Fish Commission (GFC) initiated a sound alligator management program in the 1970s, it was apparent that this controversial animal had generated a great deal of money, and a large amount of public money had been directed toward ensuring its welfare. But ironically, little if any of these moneys had benefited the alligator or its habitat. Also, there was concern that the good will toward wildlife so evident during the early 1970s was a peak in public opinion and would diminish to some unknown proportion.

EARLY PROGRAM DEVELOPMENT

A public opinion poll conducted by the GFC in 1975 revealed widespread appreciation of the alligators. However, significant numbers of people feared them, and about 50% of those responding favored some type of harvest at least in urban areas (Hines and Schaeffer 1977). In

1975 the GFC received 5,000 to 7,000 complaints annually and expended approximately $250,000 per year in relocating nuisance alligators. Because of that very large commitment, a biologically sound management technique was needed to address the nuisance problem and to relieve some of the financial drain.

During 1976, a project that objectively evaluated three alternate methods of responding to alligator complaints was initiated by the GFC (Hines and Woodward 1980). A statewide program based on the results of this evaluation was begun in 1979. GFC regional offices continued to handle the complaints, but they were assigned to private trappers who took specific alligators designated by a GFC representative. The trappers' remuneration for removing the alligators was 70% of the value of the skin received from state hide auctions and the state retained 30%. In addition, the trapper was permitted to sell the meat.

A research program was begun in 1975 to study life history and population dynamics of alligators. The principle objective of this effort was to develop a population model that would guide GFC research/ management programs and eventually enable establishment of specific harvest quotas. Development of such a model is a long-term and expensive undertaking, and without the revenues generated by the harvest programs it is doubtful that such an objective could be pursued.

VALUE-ADDED CONSERVATION

An integral aspect of Florida's sustained-yield management program has been the concept that a portion of the alligator's commercial value must be used for the conservation of the species. Although this idea has been discussed by several authors (Palmisano et al. 1973, Anon. 1982, Rose 1982), the relationship between commercial exploitation and conservation is still not clear. However, we have demonstrated on a small scale that considerable revenue can be directed back to the state for research and management. During the last two years, the state's share of revenue from nuisance and experimental programs has amounted to $221,767 from 6,586 skins. Since the first nuisance harvest in 1977, 15,892 skins have been sold, yielding the state approximately $532,000.

At some future date, the current contract sale system will be replaced by a more traditional license structure. Although the license will probably generate less money per skin than the present 30% of market price, an expanded harvest will provide increasing amounts of revenue to the GFC. The current Florida alligator management plan explicitly recognizes this idea and specifies that the returns derived by the state from commercial alligator exploitation shall be reverted as a source of funding for continued management of the wild resource. This feedback can be direct (e.g., supporting research or habitat preservation and enhancement) or indirect (e.g., providing landowners with economic incentive to preserve their wetlands).

The Florida Alligator Farmers' Association also shares financially in alligator conservation and provides personnel and equipment in the research on early-age-class ecology. In addition, a spokesperson supported by the organization politically champions wetland conservation and international crocodilian conservation. Several large landowners have expressed interest in alligator ranching and harvest on their wetlands—improving chances for their preservation. In addition, all users—whether commercial hunters, sport hunters, ranchers, or even hide and meat dealers—may develop a vested interest in ensuring that wetland systems are maintained and managed to the benefit of alligators and ultimately of all wetlands wildlife. The allure and novelty of the alligator and its management have attracted considerable journalistic attention, which also exposes the notion of value-added conservation to the general public. We view the value-added concept as expressing the idea that through biologically sound management we can take the harvestable surplus and redirect some of the revenues generated back to the management and conservation of the alligator.

CURRENT RESEARCH AND MANAGEMENT STRATEGIES

The present management philosophy allows a quota-type harvest only under the restrictions that it be experimental and that the impacts of the harvest rate be monitored. Particular projects include two experimental harvest studies: One tests the effects of the harvest of >1.2m animals, and the other investigates the removal of eggs and hatchlings from the wild to be commercially reared (ranching). Although these studies have not provided data that would enable us to set precise harvest quotas, we have gained insight into alligator demography that allows the identification of some harvest strategies.

The Louisiana harvest experience (together with some of our own experimental work in Florida) has demonstrated that biologically and economically sound harvest programs can be developed without complete knowledge of the relevant demographic processes. If pragmatic, safe strategies can be properly implemented, they would offer two major advantages: They can provide some immediate economic payoff, and they can generate useful information in a learn-as-you-go framework.

But what specifically have we learned about safe, economically viable strategies? Foremost, appropriate strategies can vary from place to place, and on-the-ground biological evaluation is necessary to discover the specific harvest opportunities offered by a particular locale. For instance,

·on one of the private landholdings we evaluated, alligators annually produce a number of nests in areas where hatchling survival is exceedingly low. We cannot with confidence tell this landowner that he can harvest, say, 7.5% of his total alligator population, but we can suggest that he take 100% of those eggs or hatchlings that probably will not survive. In a much more impressive example, we might consider the case of the Louisiana harvest. By requiring "fishing" with baited hooks of prescribed height and by allowing harvesting only in the canals, Louisiana has implemented a system that very specifically targets males and quiescent females—the reproductively irrelevant members of the adult population (T. Joanen, pers. commun.). In contrast, sex-specific alligator habitats are not so discretely separable in many parts of Florida, and a set-hook scheme appears demographically more risky than a carefully regulated airboats-and-harpoons strategy that allows the hunted populations to develop wariness. In any case, we have learned that although specific-number harvest models have an appealing generality, feasible harvest strategies generally require on-site evaluation both before and after harvest.

Besides the lesson of site specificity, we have gained other insights into the question of viable strategies. We have learned that although limited, our alligator demographic information is valuable. For example, we have been able to address the question of relative demographic and economic value by size class (Abercrombie et al. 1984), and it appears that one can harvest at least 50 hatchling alligators for the same demographic cost as removing one randomly selected animal approximately 2 m in length (Fig. 15.1).

Similarly, other research areas that will yield relevant management information are worth the cost of investigation. For example, M. Jennings (pers. commun.), Florida Cooperative Fish and Wildlife Research Unit, is studying the technique of targeting demographically "free" nests for commercial harvest. Nests scheduled for removal are generally spotted by aircraft. In most cases spotters can determine several nest characteristics from the air (e.g., amount of shade, distance from nearest open water or shore, nest height, and adult attendance). An evaluation of such characteristics may provide an airborne observer with the tools to determine the probability of nest success or perhaps the sex ratio of hatchlings if certain habitat variables affect incubation temperature (Ferguson and Joanen 1983). Since only a certain percentage of located nests would actually be removed, collectors on the ground might be steered away from the demographically most valuable nests.

We also believe that socioeconomic research can be just as important as more traditional biological investigations in designing appropriate strategies for a safe, valuable harvest. For example, managers aware of

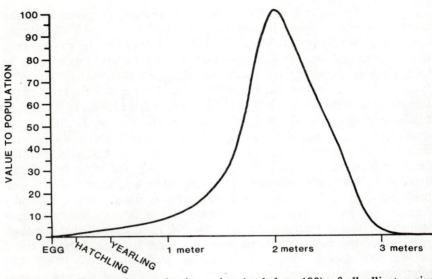

Figure 15.1 Expected reproductive value (scaled to 100) of all alligator size classes to the population (Abercrombie et al. 1986; reprinted by permission)

market conditions may take advantage of demand for specific sizes and direct pressure away from demographically valuable animals. In Florida, a relatively lucrative meat market has been developed. Since large (>3.0m) animals are therefore very valuable, hunter attention is focused away from the middle-size (female-dominated) classes and toward the demographically irrelevant adult males—animals that would be too scarce to target for hunting in the absence of an important meat market (Fig. 15.2).

Market conditions can also direct hunting effort toward demographically inexpensive small-size classes. We have reviewed records of buyers dealing in the illegal trade during the late 1960s, and 1.2m to 1.5m animals consistently made up approximately 60% of the kill (Hines 1979). Plott (pers. commun.) paid premium prices for these sizes to sell to Japanese markets. Thus, the deleterious effects of this illegal trade were probably minimized by the structure of this harvest.

It is still unclear what the eventual economic potential of alligators is either on a statewide basis or to an individual landowner. We hope to clarify this area by entering into cooperative agreements with landowners who allow an experimental alligator harvest on their lands. Some insight may be gained by looking at one of the present cooperators whose first harvest begins this year (1985). Babcock Ranch is a 40,500-

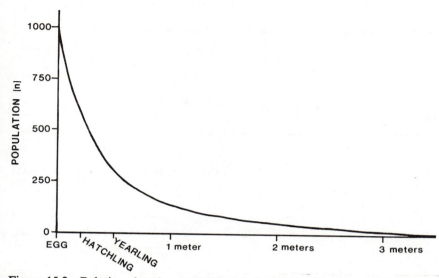

Figure 15.2 Relative abundance of alligator size classes in a population (Abercrombie et al. 1986; reprinted by permission)

ha cattle operation in southwest Florida, east of Fort Myers. The landowners are progressive in wetland management and already place a high value upon the 10,125 ha of wetlands on their property because of water recharge potential. Although they aesthetically value alligators, very large animals on their property probably have been killed because of calf depredation. A planned harvest—considered a modest and demographically safe strategy—includes the collection of eggs and hatchlings from peripheral habitat and the taking of a limited percentage of >3.5m animals. Based on preliminary surveys, we estimate that the area should yield 30 hatchling pods averaging 20 animals per pod worth approximately $12 per hatchling and 50 large animals at $500 per animal for a total of $32,000. Although the cost of taking these animals is unclear, it is important to recognize that these revenues are derived from wetlands that currently provide little if any direct income and from a resource that has in some cases been considered an economic liability.

Further insight may be gained by looking at specific examples of total revenues generated by the GFC's experimental harvest. These harvests have all taken place on public waters and have thus far emphasized 2.1m animals. The north-central Florida study areas, with a combined area of 10,530 ha, have yielded from 271 to 350 alligators (>1.2m) valued at from $63,961 to $97,474 (Table 15.1). The average

TABLE 15.1
Alligator Hide and Meat Yields for the Experimental Harvests on Orange,
Lochloosa, and Newnans Lakes from 1981-84

Year	Total Alligators	Footage of Hides	Gross Value of Hides Sold	Pounds of Meat Sold	Gross Value of Meat Sold	Total Value
1981	350	2283	$ 59,474	8,000	$ 38,000	$ 97,474
1982	379	2709	$ 26,009	10,000	$ 40,000	$ 66,009
1983	277	1926	$ 30,489	8,861	$ 39,874	$ 63,961
1984	271	2101	$ 46,145	12,000	$ 48,000	$ 94,145
Total	1277	9019	$162,117	38,861	$165,874	$321,589
Avg./year	319	2255	$ 40,529	9,715	$ 41,468	$ 80,397

Source: Fla. Game and Fresh Water Fish Comm., Bur. Wildl. Res. 1985.

income per hunter for both meat and skins for the 10- to 12-day hunts has been $4,033. The ranching schemes, which include the harvest of eggs and hatchlings from the wild for rearing in captivity, probably are the best way to maximize biological and economic yield with the least chance of negative impact. Experimental removal at the rate of 50% of the estimated production from Lake Griffin, a 4,860-ha lake in central Florida, has yielded 5,035 hatchlings from 1981 through 1984 (Table 15.2). Abercrombie et al. (1984) estimate that the net value per hatchling of a ranch-raised animal four years from collection is approximately $81, which would result in a total net value for the 5,035 animals of $407,835.

Finally, Florida contains approximately 2.7 million ha of alligator habitat (GFC files, Wildl. Res. Lab.) of varying quality. During the 1965–1971 period, when there were probably more available wetlands, illegal harvest was known to include at least 72,378 alligators (Hines 1979). At today's prices that would generate $10,132,000 for skins and more than $20,000,000 for meat. Analysis of the size structure of the 72,378 hides strongly suggests that the alligator population was probably stable during that period even though some populations were probably under carrying capacity. There is reason to believe that even with some deteriorating quality of wetlands a harvest worth considerably more than that described would be feasible if ranching schemes and other sound management were implemented.

TABLE 15.2
Alligator Nest Production and Collection on Lake Griffin, Florida, 1981-1984

Year	No. Nests Observed From Air(S)	Nesting Success Rate(D)	No. Pods Found - Not Assoc. with Nests(P)	Est. No. of Hidden Nests(P/D)	Total Known Nesting	Total Est. Nesting(N)
1981	53	94.3%	49	52	102	105
1982	58	--	40	40	98	98
1983	114	86.8%	38	44	152	158
1984	81	75.3%	13	17	94	98

Year	Pods Collected	Hatchlings Collected	Clutches Collected	Eggs Incubated	Live Hatchlings From Eggs	Total Hatchlings Produced
1981	52	1303	0	0	--	1303
1982	45	858	0	0	--	858
1983	25	1007	34	1425	998	2005
1984	0	0	32	1273	869	869
					Total	5035

Source: Fla. Game and Fresh Water Fish Comm., Bur. Wildl. Res. 1985.

CONCLUSION

In Florida we have been deeply involved in an alligator research effort for over 10 years. Initially we hoped to construct a population model that would allow us to establish very specific harvest quotas. The GFC has also advocated, as an explicit part of its management philosophy, the diversion of a portion of the alligators' commercial value to resarch, management, and habitat preservation. We believe this aspect to be particularly important because trade in crocodilian products has long been economically important, and little inclination or opportunity has hitherto existed for any revenues to be returned to the natural system.

We still affirm the objective of developing a population model to set harvest quotas, and perhaps ongoing research will in the long term provide data that will enable us to include compensatory response as a function of the population model. Not unlike other efforts to define compensatory mechanisms (Nichols et al. 1984), we have found that such data are difficult and expensive to obtain. Meanwhile, more modest exploitation strategies (developed from our growing knowledge of alligator demography as well as cultural and economic forces) will permit sustained harvest. Our present program recognizes this, and forthcoming research will emphasize the formulation of safe strategies such as hatchling removal, harvest in marginal habitat, and targeting individuals of specific size classes. Such an approach will provide additional biological data as well as revenue for alligator research and management. In principle a license structure is not unlike that charged for furbearer trapping, hunting, and similar pursuits. But because of the higher and more stable value of alligator products the potential for a larger share going to conservation is much greater.

We believe one of the most important aspects of any crocodilian management program should be the use of harvest-derived revenues to support conservation of the exploited species and its habitat. Although the recent harvest of Florida alligators has been limited, over $0.5 million have been returned to the state from alligator programs over the past eight years. These modest revenues have paid additional dividends in terms of public and legislative support for our research and management programs. Research now being conducted on alligator ecology would not have been funded without this emphasis. In other words, we have employed alligator harvest revenue to support the conservation and management of alligator populations. Certainly this approach is desirable from our perspective, but in developing countries in which many of the world's crocodilians are found such revenues may make the difference between a conservation program and no program.

Acknowledgments.—Our studies of the American alligator in Florida have been supported by the Florida Game and Fresh Water Fish Commission, U.S. Fish and Wildlife Service, University of Florida, Wildlife Management Institute and the Florida Alligator Farmers' Association. We acknowledge the assistance, companionship, and criticism of our colleagues, A. R. Woodward, D. David, M. L. Jennings, M. Delany, C. L. Abercrombie, J. D. Nichols and J. D. Ashley.

REFERENCES

ABERCROMBIE, C. L., T. C. HINES, A. WOODWARD, AND H. F. PERCIVAL. 1986. Florida alligator: economics, harvest, and conservation. Presented 7th working meet. Crocodile Specialist Group, October 1984. (In press.)

ANONYMOUS. 1982. National parks policy—conservation of crocodiles in Zimbabwe. Zimbabwe Sci. News 16:214–215.

FERGUSON, M.W.J., AND T. JOANEN. 1983. Temperature dependent sex determination in *Alligator mississippiensis*. J. Zool. 200:143–177.

FLORIDA GAME AND FRESH WATER FISH COMMISSION, BUREAU OF WILDLIFE RESEARCH. 1985. Annual Report. Fla. Game and Fresh Water Fish Comm., Gainesville. 133pp.

HINES, T. C. 1979. The past and present status of the alligator in Florida. Proc. Annu. Conf. Southeast Assoc. Fish and Wildl. Agencies 33:224–232.

―――, AND R. SCHAEFFER. 1977. Public opinion about alligators in Florida. Proc. Annu. Conf. Southeast Assoc. Fish and Wildl. Agencies 31:84–89.

―――, AND A. R. WOODWARD. 1980. Nuisance alligator control in Florida. Wildl. Soc. Bull. 8:234–241.

KERSEY, H. A. 1975. Pelts, plumes and hides. Univ. Florida Presses, Gainesville. 158pp.

NICHOLS, J. D., M. J. CONROY, D. R. ANDERSON, AND K. P. BURNHAM. 1984. Compensatory mortality in waterfowl populations; a review of the evidence and implications for research and management. Trans. North Am. Wildl. and Nat. Resour. Conf. 49:535–554.

PALMISANO, A. W., T. JOANEN, AND L. MCNEASE. 1973. An analysis of Louisiana's 1972 experimental harvest program. Proc. Annu. Conf. Southeast Assoc. Fish and Wildl. Agencies 27:184–206.

ROSE, M. 1982. Crocodile management and husbandry in Papua New Guinea. Proc. 6th Annu. Meet. Int. Union Conserv. Nat. Crocodile Specialist Group. 13pp.

PART FOUR

Wildlife and the Quality of Life

Introduction

Stephen R. Kellert

This part provides some understanding of how wildlife can contribute to human growth and satisfaction, as well as to the well-being of human society. By considering various aesthetic, recreational, educational, ecological, scientific, ethical, and utilitarian wildlife values, the authors reveal that a world made more secure for animals is essentially more attractive, meaningful, and inspiring for people.

Dr. Lee Talbot, internationally recognized scholar and conservationist, initiates this part by delineating the most basic contribution of wildlife to human society—its place in biospheric processes on which all life, including human, depends. More specifically, Dr. Talbot discusses the role of wildlife in a variety of biological support functions, including plant pollination, seed dispersal, and nutrient cycling. In addition, he describes diverse utilitarian benefits to human society stemming from the ecological functions of wildlife including pollution control, human-waste decomposition, soil generation, and predator and pest control.

Professor Holmes Rolston follows with an outstanding and provocative discussion of the aesthetic value of wildlife. Noting the remarkably widespread use of animals as symbols of nature and beauty, Dr. Rolston describes the peculiarly satisfying experience people derive from animals' capacity for moving, for evoking emotional responses, and for stimulating a sense of empathy and kinship. Professor Rolston thus provides us with some understanding of the unique and irreplaceable role of living animals in natural settings as aesthetic and cultural symbols.

The chapter by Dr. Jay Hair, executive vice-president of the National Wildlife Federation, and Dr. Gerri Pomerantz of Cornell University offers considerable information regarding the important role of wildlife in establishing an emotional and intellectual basis for people to understand the natural world. Their work is particularly helpful in identifying the critical contribution of wildlife in childhood education and the various challenges and problems associated with educating children about animals and the environment.

In his chapter Professor William Shaw, chairman of the Wildlife Department of the University of Arizona, offers considerable evidence regarding the scope and importance of wildlife-related recreation in the U.S. today. Even more important, Professor Shaw indicates the unique and special quality of wildlife as an outdoor leisure activity in comparison to other forms of nature-based recreation. Among the distinctive recreational experiences of wildlife that he describes are the special opportunities provided for intellectual stimulation, for the acquisition of skills, for achieving a sense of kinship and responsibility, or for identifying one's cultural and evolutionary roots.

Dr. J. Baird Callicott, professor of philosophy and natural resources at the University of Wisconsin, provocatively offers an understanding of the utilitarian and intrinsic values of wildlife. Professor Callicott's discussion provides insight regarding the spiritual and ethical bases of our relationship with nature, as well as varying moral judgments of human behavior toward animals.

In the final chapter I (as session chairperson) endeavor to contrast these expressions of wildlife's worth with the actual recognition of these values by human society. I provide a somewhat discouraging picture of limited human appreciation and concern, particularly regarding societal recognition of ecological and scientific wildlife values especially toward invertebrate animals. I conclude that our society remains dimly aware of Leopold's hope that wildlife might remind people of the link between themselves and nature inherent in the flow of energies and materials through a biotic pyramid of relationships among waters, soils, plants, and animals. Some comfort is derived, however, in the recognition that the results of this symposium represent an essential step in the creation of this necessary public awareness.

Chapter 16

The Ecological Value of Wildlife to the Well-being of Human Society

Lee M. Talbot

The ecological value of wildlife derives from its role in the ecological processes on which human well-being and, indeed, human survival depend. Most of the other chapters in this book are concerned with the perceived (e.g., aesthetic, ethical, philosophical) and directly realized (e.g., educational, economic, recreational, and other utilitarian) values of wildlife to the well-being of human society. In this chapter I focus on the ecological value of wildlife—its functional role that underlies all other values involved. Consequently, for example, the role of wildlife in maintaining biological diversity is mentioned but not the values of that diversity itself.

In the past the term *wildlife* generally—but not exclusively—was applied to vertebrate species that were the object of hunting or fishing. In the 1960s, with the increasing public interest in environmental matters, concern with wildlife and hence usage of the term broadened to include other vertebrate and invertebrate species (Bertrand and Talbot 1978). *Wildlife* has even been used to refer to wildlife habitat or wild plants in general. In this chapter *wildlife* refers to the full spectrum of wild faunal species, but emphasis is given to the vertebrates that capture most public attention.

ECOLOGICAL PROCESSES

The functioning of the biosphere and hence the maintenance and enhancement of human life depend on countless numbers of plant, animal, and microorganism species interacting in a series of ecological processes. The processes essential to maintaining human life are part of the life support systems, which include the global cycles (e.g., the hydrological cycle and those of carbon, nitrogen, and oxygen) as well as more localized processes such as soil formation and protection, nutrient cycling, and maintenance of critical habitats and stream flow.

These ecological processes are essential for agriculture, forestry, and fisheries and for other endeavors necessary to human life. Ecological processes are also basic to human well-being because they maintain environmental quality by degrading or otherwise removing pollutants and preventing waste accumulation.

THE ROLE OF WILDLIFE

The basic ecological processes involve plants as well as animals. Plants, for example, take up CO_2, but the plants themselves are part of ecosystems that depend on component animals. Most higher plants rely directly on animals (insects, birds, or bats) for pollination and dispersal; many rely on wildlife to protect them from pests; and all rely on invertebrates and microorganisms for nutrient cycling. So even when the key players in the ecological processes appear to be plants, wildlife still usually has a crucial role.

Although birds and mammals are the more conspicuous forms of wildlife, they make up a small part of the biomass of the ecosystems in which they occur. Pimentel (1982) calculated that in the U.S. the average biomass per 0.4 ha of insects and earthworms is about 373 kg, protozoa and algae about 50 kg, bacteria about 560 kg, fungi about 932 kg, and plants about 18,277 kg. In contrast, the biomass figures per 0.4 ha for deer, the largest common wild vertebrate in the U.S., are as follows: Biomass for white-tailed deer in Michigan woodland is about 3 kg; for black-tailed deer in California oak woodland and chaparral it is about 4 kg, and the average mule deer in California and Arizona is about 0.7 kg (Talbot and Talbot 1963a). Even the figures for the most spectacularly abundant wildlife in the world, the mixed plains wildlife in East African savanna, range from about 41 to 58 kg per 0.4 ha (Talbot and Talbot 1963a), which represents only from 10% and 15% of the average for insects and earthworms in the U.S. These latter figures for vertebrates are for specific, selected habitats; they are not overall figures. Consequently, they are much inflated relative to the Pimentel figures, but they serve to emphasize the magnitude of the nonvertebrate component in the ecosystems.

Environmental Quality—Pollution Control

Invertebrates and microorganisms play major roles in most ecological processes. Their roles are particularly evident in the processes that maintain a clean environment and therefore that contribute to a quality environment for humans.

The volume of waste materials annually produced by human activities is staggering. Without the natural processes that degrade, reduce, or remove these from the air, water, and land, the world would be a different place. Data on organic wastes and some fossil fuel combustion products from the U.S. illustrate the point:

1. The human population in the U.S. produces about 118 million t of excreta per year; livestock produces about 1.8 billion t of manure, and in total over 4.5 billion t of organic wastes, about half produced by human activities, are generated each year in the U.S. Since less than 1% of this refuse is burned, virtually all is degraded by microorganisms and invertebrates, earthworms, nematodes, protozoa, bacteria, algae, and fungi (Pimentel 1982).

2. Burning of fossil fuels produces billions of metric tons of air pollution each year, and natural biota act as sinks for some of the key elements involved. Some CO_2 is removed by vegetation; SO_2 is removed by macroscopic plants; carbon monoxide is reduced and oxidized by soil fungi and bacteria; and NO_2 is incorporated into the biological nitrogen cycle. The annual U.S. production of these four pollutants totals around 4.5 billion t (Pimentel 1982).

The invertebrates and microorganisms clearly play major roles in ecological processes. Nevertheless, even the more uncommon forms of vertebrate wildlife have important places in the ecosystems. The larger forms are higher on the trophic levels and often are sensitive indicators of status and trends in the ecosystem. Consequently, the status of wildlife resources provides a good indication of the status of a country's natural resources in general (Talbot 1957).

The larger forms of wildlife play a number of different functional roles in ecological processes, including pollinization, germination, dispersal, biogeochemical transport, soil generation, predation and "pest control," and community and habitat maintenance and manipulation. Through all these functions, they contribute to evolution and maintenance of biological diversity.

Pollination

Many plants require cross pollination to reproduce. In the U.S., 90 crops valued at nearly $4 billion depend upon insect pollination, and 9 additional crops valued at $4.5 billion are significantly benefited by insect pollination (Pimentel 1982). Oil palms provide an example of the importance of insect pollination for a developing country. The oil palm, pollinated in the wild by an African weevil, was introduced to Malaysia as a plantation crop. It required costly, inefficient, labor-intensive hand pollination. In 1980-1981 the weevil was introduced into

Malaysia from its African habitat. It immediately boosted oil palm fruiting by 40% to 60%, an improvement worth about $57 million in badly needed foreign exchange in the first year alone (Syed et al. 1982).

In addition to the cultivated plants, a large number of species of wild flowering ones also depend on insect pollination. Most plants are pollinated by animals. Consequently, insects play an absolutely essential role globally in plant pollination and therefore in a very large number of food chains and ecological processes (Pimentel 1975).

Germination

Some birds (e.g., hummingbirds) and fruit bats pollinate plants. Wildlife, primarily mammals, also assist certain plant seeds to germinate. Some seeds, particularly those with hard fruit cases, must be chewed by an animal and/or passed through a digestive tract before they can germinate. In some cases this relationship is very species specific: A plant relies wholly on a single species of wildlife for its germination and dispersal. For example, the last surviving Tambalacoque trees on the island of Mauritius date from the time when the last dodos were exterminated. It is believed that the dodo ate the tree's hard-shelled seeds, and the passage through the bird was essential for germination. Since the extermination of the dodos no Tambalacoque seeds have germinated.

Dispersal

Often linked to the germination function is the role that animals (birds, fruit bats, other mammals, fish) play in the dispersal of seeds and other propagules of plants. Acorns from oaks are widely dispersed, for example, by the action of California woodpeckers and various squirrels. Many tropical rain forest fruiting trees have their seeds dispersed by fruit-eating bats. Impala in East Africa are a major factor in the germination and dispersal of the seeds of the umbrella acacia.

In another example, the economically important Brazil nut is the basis of an industry worth over $16 million a year from exports to the U.S. alone. Several Euglossine bees visit the flowers and are believed to pollinate the Brazil nut. The male bees attract females before mating after gathering organic compounds from certain species of tree-dwelling orchids, but they depend on other flower species for food. Agoutis, large forest rodents, provide the only known natural mechanism for opening the Brazil nut seed allowing dispersal and germination. Consequently, the ecological processes basic to the Brazil nut industry involve the habitat for the Euglossine bee including nesting and feeding areas, certain orchids and the trees on which they grow, the insects that pollinate the orchids, and the agoutis (R. Goodland, pers. commun.).

Wildlife are agents of biogeochemical transport in other ways also. Seabirds consume very large amounts of marine fishes and transport the resultant guano great distances. One result is the guano industry based on the islands off of Peru.

Soil Processes

Wildlife contribute to plant dispersal and germination by making the soil more suitable for growth. For example, most wild herbivores create disturbed areas in grassland by rolling, pawing, and otherwise creating bare ground. This ground then serves as a suitable habitat for a variety of other plant species to germinate. Vertebrate and invertebrate wildlife also contribute to the soil-building process. Squirrels, gophers, moles, and other tunneling rodents physically plow up large amounts of dirt and transport substantial quantities of plant materials underground from the surface, changing the friability of the soil, adding to the organic matter, and the oxygen content, and the water permeability. Worms, ants, and termites have similar functions, as do some of the larger burrowing mammals such as badgers, foxes, and coyotes in North America.

Nutrient Cycling

All forms of wildlife contribute to the critical ecological process of nutrient recycling. All forms produce excreta, and the chewing by many vertebrates prepares much organic matter for the decomposing action of invertebrates and microorganisms. In these ways the larger forms also contribute to the essential global cycles (e.g., oxygen, carbon and nitrogen).

Community Maintenance

Some of the larger forms of wildlife have such a critical role in maintaining a given community that the system collapses if they are removed. For example, sea otters on the Aleutian Islands are effective predators of the sea urchin. The islands with healthy otter populations have diverse and productive communities in their surrounding waters, with abundant plants and associated animals, whereas the waters surrounding the islands where the otters have been removed are essentially barren. The urchins, freed from otter predation, have destroyed the kelp, and, except for the urchins, little marine life remains (Estes et al. 1978, 1982).

East African elephants and American alligators provide surprisingly parallel examples of key species to community survival. In dry seasons the elephants dig holes in dry river beds to reach shallow subsurface water. The exposed water is then available for the entire faunal community—birds, mammals, and reptiles. During the wet season the alligator digs holes below the normal bottom of the watercourses in its territory. In the dry season these become water holes, again supporting the faunal community. In the absence of either species the community could not survive during dry periods.

Predation

Through predation many species of wildlife depress populations of prey, which if unchecked could alter the ecosystem or cause serious economic damage. A wide variety of insects provide this service (Pimentel 1975), as do birds, mammals, and reptilian predators. The role of some raptors, snakes, and mammalian predators in helping control rodents in the U.S. is well known. A recent study (Smith 1985) identified 17 species of birds, mammals (primarily shrews and mice), and invertebrates (primarily ants and harvestmen) as predators of the gypsy moth in New England.

The relationships between predators and prey are complex, and the traditional generalization that predators maintain stable prey populations has not held up. In some cases, such as for the wildebeest in East Africa, predation may have little if any effect on prey numbers (Talbot and Talbot 1963*b*). However, in other cases predators can significantly depress prey populations or alter the cycles of abundance of the prey, reducing both the peaks and the troughs of prey numbers and extending the period of low populations, with consequent benefit to the vegetation on which the prey feeds (Talbot 1978).

Habitat Management

In some cases because of its ecological role wildlife can be used as a tool for ecological management. For example, current research shows that beavers can be used to stabilize and restore certain degraded habitats. In 1981 a study was initiated to determine whether the recovery of degraded riparian habitats could be effected and accelerated "using beavers rather than the traditional high-cost, high-technology methods" (Apple 1985). The animals were relocated in severely degraded areas within their historic range. The beavers built dams, dispersing the water and the current, stopping erosion, depositing sediment, and raising the water table. The vegetation responded immediately, and within three years fish, birds and other wildlife had moved into the areas (Apple 1985).

CONCLUSIONS

The general public is aware of some ways in which wildlife contribute to human well-being, the roles of wildlife in pollination or predation being obvious examples. But most of the contributions of wildlife simply are not widely recognized or understood. Further, the general public tends to think of wildlife in terms of birds, some mammals, and a few fishes. There is virtually no public recognition of the invertebrate forms that make up most of the world's faunal biomass and play the greatest part in maintenance of ecological processes.

The examples in this chapter have illustrated some, but by no means all, of the ways in which wildlife contributes to the ecological processes that are essential to human survival and well-being. Probably every aspect of human endeavor is in some way affected by wildlife, however indirectly or apparently remotely. As Dasmann (1978:18) observed, "Man depends on wildlife for survival, and wildlife depends equally on man. The two must find means for living together on planet earth or there will be no life on earth. This is the ultimate value of wildlife for man."

REFERENCES

APPLE, L. L. 1985. Riparian habitat restoration and beavers. Pages 489–490 *in* Riparian ecosystems and their management. U.S. Dep. Agric. For. Serv. Gen. Tech. Rep. RM-120. 523pp.

BERTRAND, G. A., AND L. M. TALBOT. 1978. Preface. Pages iii–iv *in* H. P. Brokaw, ed. Wildlife and America. Counc. on Environ. Quality, Washington, D.C.

DASMANN, R. F. 1978. Wildlife and ecosystems. Pages 18–27 *in* H. P. Brokaw, ed. Wildlife and America. Counc. on Environ. Quality, Washington, D.C.

ESTES, J. A., R. JAMIESON, AND E. RHODES. 1982. Activity and prey election of the sea otter (*E. lutris*); influence of population status on community structure. Am. Nat. 120(2):242–258.

———, N. S. SMITH, AND J. F. PALMISANO. 1978. Sea otter predation and community organization in western Aleutian Islands, Alaska. J. Ecol. 59(4):822–833.

PIMENTEL, D., editor. 1975. Insects, science and society. Academic Press, New York. 284pp.

———. 1982. Biological diversity and environmental quality. Pages 44–48 *in* Proc. U.S. Strategy Conf. on Biol. Diversity. Dep. State, Washington, D.C. 126pp.

SMITH, H. R. 1985. Wildlife and the gypsy moth. Wildl. Soc. Bull. 13(12):166–174.

SYED, R. A., I. H. LAW, AND R.H.V. CORLEY. 1982. Insect pollination of oil palm: introduction, establishment, and pollinating efficiency of *Elaeidobius kamerunicus* in Malaysia. Kuala Lumpur Planter 58:547–561.

TALBOT, L. M. 1957. The lions of Gir: wildlife management problems in Asia. Trans. North Am. Wildl. Conf. 22:570–579.

———. 1978. The role of predators in ecosystem management. Pages 307–319 *in* M. W. Holdgate and M. J. Woodman, eds. Conf. Ser. I. Ecology. Vol. 3. Plenum Press, New York and London. 496pp.

———, AND M. H. TALBOT. 1963a. The high biomass of wild ungulates on East African savanna. Trans. North Am. Wildl. and Nat. Resour. Conf. 28:465–476.

———, AND ———. 1963b. The wildebeest in Western Masailand, East Africa. Wildl. Monogr. 12. 88pp.

Chapter 17

Beauty and the Beast:
Aesthetic Experience of Wildlife

Holmes Rolston III

When discussing the social and economic values of wildlife, a first point is that the values fundamentally involved are neither social nor economic. In wild nature there is neither culture nor economy, not in the senses these words carry in human society. Yet wildlife can provide, derivatively, both social and economic values. The puzzle is to analyze how this happens. One answer lies along an aesthetic route, first leaving society and economy to appreciate the wild. Subsequently, the route will bring us back home.

SPONTANEITY: MOTION AND EMOTION

Animals can move. The aesthetic experience of wildlife is one of spontaneous form in motion. In the art museum nothing moves; in the picturesque scene little moves. Wildflowers sway in the breeze, but *they* do not move; they *are moved*. At the cinema, the play, the symphony, there is movement, but for the most part it is programmed so that the audience response is carefully controlled. There is nothing of that kind in the field. The wild life is organic form in locomotion, on the loose, without designs on the human beholder, indifferent to if not desiring to avoid persons. The animal does not care to come near, sit still, stay long, or please. It performs best at dawn or dusk or in the dark. Yet just that wild autonomy moves us aesthetically.

I catch the animal excitement. Here is prolife motion, and for it I gain an admiring respect, even a reverence. Plants are rooted to the spot, and they too move themselves in autotrophic metabolism, slowly, invisibly to my eye. But the animal must eat and not be eaten; its heterotrophic metabolism forces a never-ceasing hunt through the environment, an ever-alert hiding from its predators. If, as a carnivore, its food moves as well as itself, so much greater the excitement. This requires sometimes stealth and sometimes speed. Unlike plants, the animal's resources, though within its habitat, are at a distance and must be sought. Its search is the survival game, with all animal motions closely coupled to it. I take aesthetic delight, as an observer, in animal motion, in reaching to participate in a defended life. In all neural forms, human emotions are attracted by animal bodily motions and drawn through these into animal emotions. I rejoice in the stimulus of spontaneous life.

There is grace in the overtones. In a strange, fortunate mixing of the aesthetic with the pragmatic for which we have no adequate theory, the solving of these problems of motion routinely yields symmetrical dynamics of rhythmic beauty—the gazelle on the run, the eagle in flight, the slithering blacksnake, the streamlined fish, the nimble chipmunk. Even when this grace seems to fail—in the lumbering moose calf or the fledgling fallen from the nest—the aesthetic experience remains. Here is motion in the active, not the passive, voice, clamoring for life. Even the potential for motion, when the animal is motionless, perched, resting, hidden, has as much aesthetic value as does actual motion. Wild lives move themselves, and they move us.

Excitement lies both in surprise and in the anticipated. A principal difference between scenery and wildlife is that the observer knows that the mountain or the cascades will be there, but what about the redtail hawk perched in the cottonwood, the fox running across the meadow, the grouse flushed at the creek? The latter involve probability, improbability, contingency, which add adventurous openness to the scene. The watcher can return to linger over the landscape, but not—with more or less uncertainty—over the bull elk that just stepped from cover. See him now or perhaps not at all. The scenes are frameless; one can stretch or shrink at will what properties of symmetry, form, or color to savor, now or after lunch. But the animal on the run and the bird in flight demand an intense focus: they constrain the observer's appreciation to the moment—catch as catch can—postponing reflection until later.

Time counts, not just space; time brings to the animal freedom in space, and aesthetic experience of that freedom must delight in the spontaneity. Through binoculars, one isolates that redpoll right now—Quick!—picking seed from that dried sunflower, there below the clump of tumbleweed caught in the fence, here on a Nebraska roadside, on this wintry February day. "Did you see him when he turned just before he flew, almost the last of the flock? How the red cap and black chin flashed when the sun broke out! Had we come ten minutes earlier, or later, nothing!"

The creeks and cliffs, the forests and open space, the turns of the trail are on the map, although only sketchily drawn because the map never portrays the particularity of a place. But the wildlife encounters are entirely off the map. They need proper habitat, of course, but habitat is necessary, not sufficient, for encounter. One vacationer had hoped for six days of the Yellowstone trip to see a bear and, on the last day, spied one, only a cub, but a bear nevertheless, feeding in the *Shepherdia* bushes. The traveler never expected the coyote; it walked by the car, just outside, taking the onlooker by such surprise that she could not get the camera from the back seat. We are likely to highlight the surprises, hoped for or not, and to take for granted the certainties of the trip. Even places to which we later return remain haunted with events of the past. "Here, at the mouth of this hollow, a decade ago, I met the bobcat, so intent on chasing the ground squirrel that he almost ran over me. Once upon a time, but no more." And if we do not find wildlife at all? They do not have to be seen; there is a thrill in knowing they are present and hiding.

This immediacy explains why television wildlife programs and wildlife art and photography are poor substitutes for the real thing. The surprise is gone. This explains why zoos do little to preserve wildlife aesthetically. Their motion has been captured; a caged bobcat is aesthetically a bobcat no more. This explains why domestic pets can never be an aesthetic substitute for wild lives. The motion has been tamed; no dog is the equal of a coyote; a thousand housecats are less than a cougar. This explains why the rural landscape offers a different and in this respect poorer pleasure than does the wilderness or the wildlife refuge. Whatever its superiority as a food animal, a cow is never as exciting as a deer. The pariah species, which prosper as parasites and outcastes of civilization, lose their glory. We are disappointed when the bird on the telephone wire is a pigeon and not a kestrel, when the flutter in the bush is an English sparrow, not a warbler.

Now we understand why, contrary to good farming practices, the farmer ought to leave the fencerows overgrown and why, contrary to the economics of agribusiness, there ought be small fields with woodlots and edging. Those habitats enrich the landscape with action. A walk across the fields is twice as exciting if there are rabbits and bobwhites, ten times as exciting with a fox or a great horned owl. Wild lives raise the excitement level; the untrammeled quality of their lives raises the quality of human life.

SENTIENCE: KINDRED AND ALIEN

Not only do wildlife move, but they have eyes. They call. In higher animal life, unlike vegetable life, somebody is there behind the fur and feathers, a center of experience amid the moved excitement. So we move from locomotion to perception, a necessary connection both biologically and aesthetically. With this move comes the appreciation and challenge of kindred and alien life. There is intrusion, intimacy, otherness. The mountains and rivers are *objects,* even the pines and oaks live without sentience; but the squirrels and the antelope are *subjects.* When perceiving an item in the geomorphology or the flora I see an "it." But with the fauna, especially the vertebrate, brained fauna, I meet a "thou." I see them; they also see me. I eavesdrop; they may flee. A hiker may spook a bighorn, but no one can spook a columbine. The aesthetic experience differs because of reciprocity. There is a window into which we can look and from which someone looks out. Wildlife have, so to speak, points of view. There is fire in those eyes.

The window is sometimes clear, sometimes translucent, sometimes opaque. The bear is hungry. The deer is thirsty. The chipmunk scratches an itch; the mallard pair dozes in the sun; the bull elk scans the meadow, becomes uneasy, and edges back toward cover. The jay defends its territory; the plover deceives the predator with its "broken wing," simulates the injury long enough to lead the intruder from its nest, then flies out of sight and detours back. Humans know analogues for these experiences and so share a kinship that cannot arise with aesthetic contemplation of flowers or scenery. But there is never identity, and humans can only imagine what it must be like to be a duck, a chipmunk, an elk, a plover. There is alien subjectivity that stands against human subjectivity, mysterious others with differences both of degree and kind. The natural kinds provide their own categories, which humans appreciate, now at a further level of uncertainty.

But that again adds to, rather than subtracts from, the excitement. Their lives are indeed wild, not only beyond complete human management in their spontaneity but beyond complete human sympathy with their sentience. They have subtleties of cognition and decision that humans do not, as when by echolocation a bat recognizes its own sonar and sees a mosquito with it, in a sky filled with others of its kind. But further, humans have ranges of cognition and decision that bats do not: I can aesthetically enjoy the bats in flight but they cannot enjoy me. This is not a matter of appreciating them by reduction from my own experience to something simpler but of reaching for competence and virtuosity not my own. One form of life seeks to understand another, and this transvaluing brings aesthetic richness and creativity.

In the positing of such kinship, should we say that these aesthetic experiences are not only *of* wildlife but that there are analogues *in* wildlife, at least *kinesthetic* precursors of our *aesthetic* experiences? We may be reluctant to suppose that these beasts know their own beauty. Humans can admire the coyote's lope; the coyote can enjoy a run but perhaps not admire its own dynamic form. Humans admire the pheasant's irridescent color; the coyote sees only a meal, yet one with taste. But these wild lives do know preferences satisfied. Are we to suppose no sensuous delight in the coyote's warming itself in the spring sun, no plaintive loneliness or affection in the howl? The pups play to learn to kill; their games simulate the survival game. But the pups play because they enjoy it—as surely as the dog enjoys chasing the stick that its master has thrown for it to fetch. The animal has no more guarantee of success in its hunt than I have in my hunt for it, and when it succeeds, it knows its own form of delight.

Guided by perception and drawn by desire, the wild animal can enjoy its freedom and pleasures. The frustration of the caged racoon is evidence of that. The peahen delights in the tail of the peacock or else the display would have no survival value. A mockingbird sings to defend its territory in a suburban backyard, but the homeowner who has heard it sing all day and half the night becomes irritated at the song that earlier delighted and wonders at length if the song is not an end in itself, whatever its instrumentality and function. Perhaps a mockingbird even enjoys what it can do with its tail!

The inaccessibility of such subjectivity troubles scientists but augments aesthetic experience. Aesthetic experience runs ahead of cognition. For much of this century psychologists have belittled introspection and inwardness, eliminating these even from human science, much less from animal science. So it is not surprising that science provides limited insight into what these kinesthetic, preaesthetic experiences in animal awareness are like. It is hard to admit as real in the brutes what is hardly admitted as real in humans. Still, a richer science ought to complement aesthetics. Experience is as real as taxonomy, as real as behavior. The ewe who submits to the dominant ram perhaps senses the power in his muscle and horn; that she does is supported by the natural selection theory that requires survival power in his imposing strength. Her appreciation of this is an advantage to her. In her own way, she may catch as much of the "spirit" of the handsome bighorn as does the human admirer. Perhaps the female coyote admires the lope of the handsome male after all, in her own way. How much of this appreciation the ewe and the bitch can bring explicitly into consciousness and how much remains in tacit psychology and behavior are secondary questions; aesthetic experiences in humans too are not less real because they are subliminal.

Perhaps lovers of wildlife have long known what hardnosed, reductionist, behaviorist biologists have chosen to ignore—that there is experience *in* the wild and that experiences *of* the wild catch enough of that kindred yet alien vitality, consciousness, achievement, and joy to treasure its presence. If we could acknowledge the deepest impulses of zoology, these ought to include *anima,* wild spirit (Latin: soul), caught by appropriate human sensitivity to it, and we could let this guide and criticize the human intellectual and empirical experiences of wildlife.

Animals do not, perhaps, make aesthetic judgments, but they have aesthetic sensibilities, perhaps in some less elevated, more affective sense than we formerly counted aesthetic. Animals have no experience of beauty, we may say, though they have the experience of pleasure. But is not a delight in sensuous pleasure, in power, form, and motion aesthetic? What else is the human delight in being bodily outdoors in the spaciousness, the warmth, the sounds, the motions, the smells of a spring morning?

A good deal of argument and even passion has been spent in this century defending sensuous pleasures as a good thing, against a heritage thought too puritan, prudish, too rational, metaphysical, too insistent on the higher pleasures. Even the psychologists, while ignoring experience, have paradoxically defended affect, appetite, desires, and their fulfillment. But if humans value sensuous beauty that they themselves perceive, it seems arbitrary for them to deny feeling and its value in their wild neighbors. What they feel is real and important, and it stretches and enriches the human aesthetic life to contact the animal kinesthetic life. They care, and we should care.

STRUGGLE: IDEAL AND REAL

Behind the motion and sentience is struggle. The animal freedom brings with it the possibility of success and failure in transcending its environment. The scenery cannot fail because nothing is attempted; but living things can be better or worse examples of their kind, they have prime seasons and plain ones, and we have to evaluate achievement. Looking over the herd of elk, we spot the bull with the biggest rack. An adult bald eagle excites us more than an immature one. The big bull does not have more merit than the yearling, but it does have more strength and wisdom of its kind; the adult eagle better exemplifies the glory of its species. Each is a more commanding token of its type. Each has made the ideal real.

The critic will complain against admirers of wildlife that they overlook as much as they see. The bison are shaggy, shedding, and dirty. That hawk has lost several flight feathers; that marmot is diseased and scarred. The elk look like the tag end of a rough winter. A half dozen juvenile eagles starve for every one that reaches maturity. Every wild life is marred by the rips and tears of time and eventually destroyed by them. But none of the losers and seldom even the blemished show up on the covers of *National Wildlife* or in the Audubon guides. Doesn't the aesthetician repair nature before admiring it? Can we pick the quality out of the quantity, praise the rare ideals and discard the rest, which are statistically more real? Benedetto Croce claimed "that nature is beautiful only for him who contemplates her *with the eye of the artist;* . . . that a *natural beauty* which an artist would not *to some extent correct, does not exist*" (1959:99). Oscar Wilde agreed: "My own experience is that the more we study Art, the less we care for Nature. What Art reveals to us is Nature's lack of design, her curious crudities, her extraordinary monotony, her absolutely unfinished condition. Nature has good intentions . . . but she cannot carry them out" (1935:7). Wildlife artists select the accidental best and discard the rest, broken by accidents.

But the matter is not as simple when we couple aesthetics with genetics and evolutionary ecology. The aesthetician sees that ideal toward which a wild life is striving and which is rarely reached in nature. The observer zooms in with a scope on the full-curl ram, or the artist paints warblers ornamented in their breeding prime and perfection. In the language of the geneticists, the artist portrays and the admirer enjoys that phenotype producable by the normal genotype in a congenial environment. Or, borrowing from the computer scientists, the artist executes (and the admirer delights in) the program built into a life, although that ideal has only partly been executed in nature, owing to environmental constraints. Such an ideal is, in a way, still nature's project. In a distinction going back to Aristotle, it is true to the poetry of a thing, though not true to its history, and yet the poetry directs its history (*Poetica* 1947:1451b). The form, though not wholly executed, is as natural as is the matter. Some will insist that all this is not true to the plain facts of nature; others will realize that this is not so much fiction as a way of getting at what one might call a natural essence only partly expressed in any individual existence.

Nor do we aesthetically appreciate only success or the ideal. The admirer of wildlife can enjoy the conflict and resolution in the concrete particular expression of an individual life. The weatherbeaten elk are not ugly, not unless endurance is incompetence; nor is the spike ram displeasing, not unless potential is uninspiring. The warblers in spring are indeed in prime dress, but the warblers in fall plumage are equally fitted to their environment, neither less ideal, less real, nor less beautiful, only requiring more sublety to appreciate, now that the expenditure of energy and motion is not in color and reproduction but in camouflage and survival toward winter. Contrary to Croce and Wilde, none of this is crudity, monotony, unfinished imperfection, to be rectified by the human artist. Rather, if we take the natural kind on its own terms and in its own ecosystem, "intentions" coded in the animal nature are carried out in the struggle for life, and this is heroic and exciting even in its failures. The struggle between ideal and real adds to the aesthetic experience.

The more we know the more there is to see, and the more we see, the more there is to be admired. Now, greater cognitive understanding leads to greater aesthetic sensitivity, and seeing becomes both wisdom and art.

SYMBOL: WILDLIFE IN CULTURE

Aesthetic experience of wildlife begins with what such life is in itself—spontaneous, sentient, struggling. After this, wild lives can become symbols of characteristics we value in our human lives. They carry associations that enrich the cultures we superimpose on landscapes. The bald eagle perches on top of American flagpoles and is portrayed in the seal behind the president, expressing freedom, power, grace, lofty alertness. The British prefer the lion; the Russians the bear. States have chosen their animals: Colorado has selected the bighorn sheep—stately, powerful, nimble, free, loving the hills; Tennessee has chosen the raccoon, Kansas the buffalo, Oregon the beaver. Utah is the beehive state, busy and hardworking. The names of sports teams are often those of animals—the Wolf Pack, Panthers, Falcons, Gators, Razorbacks, Rams. We call our automobiles cougars, skylarks, rabbits. Humans abstract, as in all art, the qualities they wish to express, intensifying (sometimes even imagining) the real to make of it an ideal. We elevate into symbolism something of the competence, the integrity, the character of the wild life.

Nor are these simply symbols of strength, agility, and cleverness. Wild lives as easily becomes images of grace and beauty. They decorate and lighten our homes. We enjoy an Audubon calendar on the kitchen wall, or we pattern the curtains with butterflies, or we steal feathers for fashionable hats. The birds are colorful; they can sing and fly; and we wish that human life were like that too.

Perhaps at times we are not really using any analogues of these wild lives in our human lives. Even so, such creatures add a freshness and a flash to culture for what they are in themselves, regardless of whether humans in culture are metaphorically similar. Still, this flair, beauty, and activity express qualities that penetrate the background of culture. We want a yard with cardinals and squirrels; we want picnics, hikes, vacations where wild lives play around us; we pause to admire the geese overhead in flight or welcome the swallows as they return in spring. We regret that the river through town is polluted and dead; the city is poorer because the fish with their jump and sparkle can be found there no more. Wild lives elevate the quality of human life with the vitality they express; their presence in culture reveals and symbolizes the sensitivity of that culture, even when no particular human virtues correspond to the animal achievements. So the alligator enters the Florida life-style, even though Floridians make no anthropomorphic use of its competence in the swamps.

Wild lives diversify cultures. A culture is more aesthetically appealing if it includes not only artifacts but also fauna and flora. A painting on an executive's office wall is as likely to show a stag or a hunt as the factory or a granddaughter. Wild lives are part of our environmental quality, the most threatened part. Especially in a culture that increasingly tends toward sameness, diversity in wild lives will be something that our grandchildren will be glad we left them or will complain that we took away. Preservation of the grizzly in the Yellowstone ecosystem is a challenge to human integrity because it calls us to discipline ourselves for quality over quantity of human society. Our children will be ashamed if we lose the grizzly, just as we are ashamed for what our fathers did to the passenger pigeon. Americans are proud of the Endangered Species Act; Du Pont employees feel that what the company has done to Delaware is redeemed somewhat with the company's annual $50,000 grants to the Patuxent Wildlife Refuge, which contains some of the few bald eagle nesting sites in the eastern states. What a culture does to its wildlife reveals the character of that culture, as surely as what it does to its blacks, poor, women, handicapped, and powerless.

Wild lives mix with the ethos of a place, when culture is superimposed on nature. In the culture some of the nature that coexists with it shows through. The new, cultured environment is built over the old, spontaneous natural one, and yet the natural world retains enough power to evoke the admiring care of the cultured human world, which values it for its expressive and associative qualities. Wild lives give what our too readily mobile, rootless culture especially needs, an attachment to landscape, locale, habitat, place. We name a street Mockingbird Lane, or we consider a summer home more romantic if it lies in Fox Hollow, and such places are more exciting if they still have mockingbirds and foxes around. Although wildlife has its social values, these values spin off from values intrinsic to the animals themselves because they make symbolic use of them.

After seeing the mating dance of the woodcock, Aldo Leopold concluded, "The woodcock is a living refutation of the theory that the utility of a game bird is to serve as a target, or to pose gracefully on a slice of toast. No one would rather hunt woodcock in October than I, but since learning of the sky dance I find myself calling one or two birds enough. I must be sure that, come April, there will be no dearth of dancers in the sunset sky" (1969:34). Grouse or warblers, buffalo or bear, rabbits or deer—animal lives enrich culture with the age-old dance of life. As much as fine art, theatre, or literture, they are poetry in motion. Our society and economy are surely rich enough that we can afford to keep them; they are not so rich that we can afford to lose them.

REFERENCES

ARISTOTLE. 1947. Poetica. Pages 624–667 in R. McKeon, ed. Introduction to Aristotle. Modern Library, New York.

CROCE, B. 1959. Aesthetic. Vision Press/Peter Owen, London.

LEOPOLD, A. 1969. A sand county almanac. Oxford University Press, New York. 226 pp.

WILDE, O. 1935. The decay of lying. Pages 5–53 in The prose of Oscar Wilde. Albert and Charles Boni, New York.

Chapter 18

The Educational Value of Wildlife

Jay D. Hair and Gerri A. Pomerantz

The awesome beauty and intriguing nature of wildlife have fascinated adults and children throughout the ages. In today's world of mass media, fascination with wildlife remains high, reflected, for example, by the enduring popularity of such television programs as "Wild Kingdom," a hit for the past 30 years, and countless other wildlife documentaries. Even Johnny Carson, the host of such an unscientific program as the "Tonight Show," frequently invites wildlife professionals like Jim Fowler, host of "Wild Kingdom," and Joan Embry of the San Diego Zoo on his late-night program to talk about wild animals.

People enjoy direct experiences with wildlife and, equally important, experience vicarious pleasure from simply knowing that wildlife exists in its natural habitat. The innate attraction of wildlife is invaluable because it provides an entrée to discussion of the natural world. Wildlife is the vehicle that takes youth and adults alike into the broader arena of environmental education.

Many conservation organizations engaged in public education utilize the appealing nature of wildlife to teach messages about resource conservation and environmental protection. For example, although the initial interest for reading magazines such as *National Wildlife* may stem from an interest in animals, the reader is exposed to articles on a wide range of environmental topics like air and water pollution, soil erosion, and toxic wastes.

In regard to the educational value of such activities, two independent studies indicated that young people increased their environmental knowledge after exposure to wildlife magazines. Fortner and Mayer (1983) found that ninth graders who read *National Wildlife* had higher knowledge scores about the marine environment than those who did not read the magazine. Pomerantz (1985) determined that after a three-month exposure to *Ranger Rick,* a children's nature magazine published by the National Wildlife Federation, fifth graders increased their knowledge of animals, plants, and ecological concepts.

Schoenfeld noted that wildlife may well be the most universal symbol for the concept of the environment: "Whatever the total complement of environmental education, wildlife conservation is a key element—a valuable point of entry, a rich source of illustration, a stimulus to action, and an aspect of the ultimate reason for environmentalism" (1978:472). For these and other reasons in this chapter we will expand on the educational value of wildlife to include the broader concepts associated with environmental education. Likewise, even though the value of education for all age groups is well recognized, research clearly indicates the importance that education has on human development during the early years—hence the emphasis placed herein on that important period of life.

ROLE OF ENVIRONMENTAL AND WILDLIFE EDUCATION

As Hawkins and Vinton noted, "The solution to the environmental crisis . . . rests neither with scientists nor with government officials, but with a citizenry educated in environmental problem solving" (1973:7). Lester Brown (1981), in *Building a Sustainable Society,* observed that our future approach to dealing with environmental problems must differ substantially from our present approach. To attain a sustainable society, we will need to recognize limits—to understand that the human population will have to be more or less stable at today's levels; energy will have to be used far more efficiently; and the economy will have to be fueled largely with renewable sources. But we have little hope of reaching a sustainable society unless education helps people understand the fundamental interaction between humans and their environment, including fish and wildlife resources. "The answer for all our national problems, the answer for all the problems of the world, comes to a single word. That word is 'education,'" said former president Lyndon B. Johnson.

Environmental education is similar to the teaching of other scientific subjects: It attempts to help people understand scientific concepts (e.g., ecological principles and the consequences of environmental actions). However, it differs by emphasizing the integration of such environmental knowledge with the development of positive attitudes in an effort to maintain environmental quality. The goal is to transform enlightened environmental attitudes into socially responsible actions (Doran 1977 and references therein, LaHart and Barnes 1978-1979).

Studies have shown that a person's childhood experiences with animals are important factors in the development of adult attitudes toward wildlife (Shaw 1976, Kellert 1976). Many researchers and resource managers believe that an understanding of the underlying reasons for people's attitudes and behaviors toward wildlife would lead to a reduction in the conflicts and misunderstandings among the various users of natural resources (Hendee and Potter 1971, Kellert 1980, Shaw and Zube 1980).

To explain some of these conflicts, Kellert (1980) conducted a national survey of adults' attitudes toward animals. He found the four most common attitudes centered around two themes: human exploitation of animals and human affection for animals. The seeming contradiction in these findings, Kellert suggested, results from the fact that public opinion is split over the right to utilize animals and that some people have strong positive feelings toward animals whereas others have either neutral or negative feelings.

Several studies have examined the relationships of young people's knowledge, attitudes, and behavior regarding wildlife and natural resources (Langenau and Mellon-Coyle 1977; Pomerantz 1977, 1985; Kellert and Westervelt 1983; inter alia). Pomerantz (1977) conducted a statewide study in Michigan of seventh through twelfth graders, comparing the knowledge, attitudes, and behavior of young hunters, nonhunters, and antihunters. Langenau and Mellon-Coyle (1977) in a study of young Michigan hunters employed the questionnaire used by Pomerantz (1977) and additional questions designed for the hunting population. Both studies revealed that young people value wildlife for existential (because wildlife is there) and educational reasons.

In Pomerantz's Michigan study (1977), young people listed areas for watching wildlife, nature centers, and guided nature walks as the things they most desired to increase their contact with wildlife and the natural environment. More than two-thirds of the respondents said they would like to participate in wildlife and environmental education classes and desired more opportunities for such experiences.

A number of researchers (George 1967, LaHart 1978, Baird and Tolman 1982, Kellert 1983) concluded that the outcomes of children's activities and direct experiences with wildlife are as conducive to attitude change as the attainment of knowledge about wildlife, and they suggested that experiential education become an integral part of any wildlife education program. Integration of innovative resource materials by the teacher into the school curriculum, alongside direct wildlife experiences, will help educate youngsters about the environment and give them an appreciation of the natural world.

IMPORTANCE OF ENVIRONMENTAL
AND WILDLIFE EDUCATION IN CHILDHOOD

Because environmental educators are charged with the task of disseminating information in the hope that educated people will make rational decisions, educators need to (1) reach people when formal education has its greatest influence on behavior and (2) use the most effective educational tools. Educational programs appear to have their greatest influence during childhood (Hess and Torney 1967, Cohen and Hollingsworth 1973, Doran et al. 1974, Chemers and Altman 1977, Miller 1975, Moore 1977, More 1977). It has been claimed that the foundations of pre-adult attitudes toward the environment are formed during early childhood (Miller 1975) and that attitudes, preferences, beliefs, and values developed when young will govern behavior throughout adult life (More 1977). The importance of environmental education in childhood was emphasized by Doran et al. (1974), who indicated that people reassess their values during their youth.

In addition to evidence pointing to the early formation of environmental attitudes and of an individual's value system (as outlined in Kohlberg's Theory of Moral Development [Kauchak et al. 1978]), other studies have indicated that early childhood is a crucial time for the development of cognitive abilities for environmental knowledge (Chemers and Altman 1977). Moore (1977:208) said that from about 8 to 12 years of age, "children have their deepest and most extensive relationships with the outdoors," and "interaction with nature on a large scale reaches its highest level of behavioral significance." Much of this relationship is reinforced by reading materials that emphasize a personal relationship between a youngster and an animal. Many of the stories written for very young people give animals human qualities and characteristics.

Although some have argued that this anthropomorphization of animals leads to misconceptions about the natural world, research results have not substantiated this argument. *Ranger Rick* magazine utilizes a story format in some of its articles about animals, and one regular feature anthropomorphizes animals. A study (Pomerantz 1985) comparing *Ranger Rick* subscribers with nonreaders found no evidence that *Ranger Rick* readers had more anthropomorphic viewpoints than did children who did not read the magazine. In fact, *Ranger Rick* subscribers had more realistic perceptions of animal behavior. It appears that using wildlife to teach broader life concepts does not result in the creation of misconceptions about the animal kingdom.

To understand further the development of children's perceptions of the environment, Rejeski (1982) used a Piagetian approach (see Ripple et al. 1982 for discussion of Piaget's stages of cognitive development in children). According to Rejeski, children were not able to acknowledge the effect of human intervention on the environment until ages 9 to 10, and not until ages 13 to 14 did they begin to understand basic ecosystem concepts.

Findings by Kellert and Westervelt (1983) corroborate Rejeski's theory of the stages of development. They show that young children in grades

2 through 5 (ages 7 to 10) were the least informed about animals and the most exploitive. From grades 5 to 8 (ages 10 to 13), children's factual knowledge of animals exhibited a major increase. Children in grades 8 to 11 (ages 13 to 16) became more interested in animals for ecological, moral, and naturalistic reasons.

Research on attitude, value, and cognitive development shows that the middle years, between ages 10 and 13, offer the greatest opportunities for acquiring knowledge and understanding about the environment. Environmental educators need to be cognizant of this result and to emphasize educational programs and activities in this age group that will encourage an individual to assess a situation objectively and develop problem-solving skills to deal with environmental situations.

Today's environmental leaders are living proof of the impact of early exposure to the natural environment. Tanner (1980) completed a study that detailed the early experiences of modern-day environmental leaders. The similarities among all 45 respondents were striking. For example, 35 of the 45 vividly recalled outdoor experiences as a major influencing factor in their choice of professions. Nine others implied the impact of similar experiences, remembering, for instance, their memberships in outdoor-oriented youth groups or school environmental programs.

Of the 35 who pointed to outdoor experiences as an influencing factor, 26 said contact was either "frequent" or "daily." Among these 26, 8 were raised on farms, 7 others came from rural towns, and 2 said they grew up "in the country."

Tanner's study highlights the means by which the ethics of environmental leaders were formed during childhoods more than 30 years ago. Exposure to wildlife and natural habitats was easier to accomplish in rural settings. But educating today's youth, in an era when the majority of children are raised in urban areas, requires educators to bridge the gap between natural and urban environs. More specific plans are needed to teach lasting appreciation and concern for nature to those whose most frequent, and perhaps only, contact with wildlife may occur during a visit to a city park or the zoo.

THE EDUCATIONAL CHALLENGE

Generally, today's environmental education programs are neither implemented uniformly across the nation nor given consistent emphasis. Although public school teachers, for example, use instructional materials from a variety of sources, the majority of materials are still developed by the local teaching staff. Results of a national survey of public elementary and secondary schools (Childress 1978) indicated that inadequate funding and lack of time to develop curricula were perceived as the greatest constraints to the development of environmental education materials.

In many instances, environmental topics are included in social studies programs. However, in the five social studies textbooks used most widely in grades four through six, the treatment of environmental topics is inconsistent, and important management concepts, particularly concerning resource allocation, are rarely discussed (Barnes 1978–1979).

In several instances, private conservation organizations have created curricula that teachers can use to complement their classroom routines. The National Audubon Society, for example, this year premiered "Owl," a nationally syndicated television program focusing on conservation education and supplemented by a monthly teacher's guide. The University of California at Berkeley created OBIS (Outdoor Biology Instructional Strategies) several years ago to supplement environmental education programs in elementary schools; the program is now available from a private publisher. "Living Lightly in the City" was developed as an urban environmental education supplement for elementary and high school students by the Schlitz Audubon Center in Milwaukee, Wisconsin.

In addition, the National Wildlife Federation's conservation education programs include National Wildlife Week, the CLASS (Conservation Learning Activities in Science and Social Studies) project for students in grades six through nine, NatureScope, Wildlife Camp for youngsters ages 9 through 13, and weeklong conservation summits, where family members participate together in a variety of environmental education related activities.

Project WILD (West. Reg. Environ. Educ. Counc. 1983a,b) is an example of an environmental and conservation curriculum guide emphasizing wildlife, whereas Project Learning Tree (Am. For. Inst., Inc. 1977a,b) is a curriculum guide emphasizing forest ecosystems. Both were funded primarily by a consortium of state fish and wildlife agencies and environmental education organizations.

Many state natural resource agencies have made admirable efforts to supplement environmental education in the public schools. Unfortunately, too often curriculum materials are underutilized by classroom teachers because of (1) lack of coordination between natural resource agencies and the public school systems and (2) teachers' lack of confidence in teaching science. It is important to include hands-on techniques for classroom environmental education instruction in future pre-service and in-service training of schoolteachers if we hope to effectively and efficiently transmit information about the natural world to today's children.

In the meantime, however, several undertakings can be initiated by classroom teachers at minimal cost and effort. Fortner and Teates (1980) suggested that teachers make more comprehensive use of films and magazines. They demonstrated, for instance, that television documentaries increased tenth graders' knowledge of the marine environment. In this example wildlife was used as a focal point around which to educate the viewer about the broader concerns of the marine environment.

Pomerantz (1985) found that *Ranger Rick* magazine was not only an effective means of increasing knowledge about wildlife and the natural world but that children who read *Ranger Rick* had more positive conservation attitudes than those who did not subscribe to the magazine. The areas in which *Ranger Rick* subscribers expressed more positive attitudes included energy consumption, water pollution, and overpopulation. Although the greatest number of children indicated that the main reason they read *Ranger Rick* was to learn about animals and that their favorite magazine features were the animal stories, children clearly gained more from the magazine than information about wildlife. The broader educational value of *Ranger Rick* was also shown by the fact that 76% of the subscribers who responded to a national survey indicated that *Ranger Rick* helped them with their schoolwork. The majority (50%) said it helped with science, 29% with reading, and 25% with art.

Direct contact with wildlife and the environment has proved to be an excellent means of increasing children's environmental knowledge (Burrus-Bammel 1978, Collins et al. 1979, Gabel et al. 1980, Crompton and Sellar 1981, Lewis 1981-1982, Olson et al. 1984). Field trips to zoos, nature centers, university facilities, farms, and local parks give children a chance to see, touch, smell, hear, and even taste the things they have discussed in the classroom.

Effective transmittal of knowledge is composed of three elements (1) complete discussion of a topic, (2) illustration of the topic with a field experience whenever possible, and (3) an in-class follow-up discussion after the actual experience. A trip to the zoo by itself may not necessarily increase a fourth grader's knowledge of animals. However, a trip to the zoo combined with teacher-led instruction and an educational program at the zoo would provide a much more meaningful experience (Marshdoyle et al. 1982).

Although implementation of environmental education programs is vitally important, it is not in and of itself sufficient to ensure development of effective programs. Environmental educators and allied researchers also have to evaluate the programs objectively to determine whether they achieve their stated goals (Perdue and Warder 1981, Cohen 1977, Lewis 1981-1982, Bennett 1982, Lucko et al. 1982).

Claims regarding the influence of environmental knowledge on the development of positive environmental attitudes need to be substantiated, and test instruments are being developed for such purposes. Kinsey and Wheatley (1980) studied one such instrument, the Environmental Issues Attitude Defensibility Inventory (EIADI), which was developed to measure the amount of information an individual uses when making a value judgment. They concluded the EIADI has good reliability (.90) and validity. They felt the instrument could be used to help evaluate the effectiveness of cognitive-based environmental courses and to study students' values in relation to their level of moral development.

In addition to studying the link between knowledge and attitude, it is necessary to obtain behavioral measures of environmental education (Hendee 1972). The use of instruments such as the EIADI to study the connection between knowledge and attitudes, combined with behavioral measurements, would greatly enhance the evaluation of environmental education programs. These evaluative methods can objectively demonstrate whether a particular program is effective. Such information will enhance the credibility of the program and increase support for its continued funding.

There is a pressing need for creative environmental education material accessible to teachers and students. The responsibility rests with school boards to make environmental education a more substantial part of the schools' curricula and with state legislators to provide increased funding for environmental programs. These two actions are essential if we hope to develop a more informed and participatory citizenry.

CONCLUSIONS

The ability of wildlife to create interest in and motivation to act on the broader concerns of the environment must not be overlooked. Educators and resource managers should capitalize on this valuable aspect of the wildlife resource by making wildlife education an integral part of their programming efforts.

Schoenfeld aptly stated this educational value of wildlife: "The ultimate purpose of wildlife conservation, then, is more than a concern for wildlife per se. Conserving wildlife demonstrates the totality of our relationships with people and land. The presence of wildlife at harmony with its environment is perhaps the best measure of our success in man-land relations" (1978:483).

Wildlife can teach us more than facts about animals. If wildlife education is taught within the context of a comprehensive environmental education curriculum, it can help us scrutinize our treatment of the environment and force all of us to take responsibility for our actions. We must, therefore, make the fullest use of wildlife education if we hope to impart the tenets of good citizenship and the lasting precepts of good stewardship of our natural resources to the future leaders of our nation and world.

REFERENCES

AMERICAN FOREST INSTITUTE, INC. 1977. Project learning tree: supplementary activity guide for grades K through 6. Am. For. Inst., Inc., Washington, D.C. 210pp.

———. 1977b. Project learning tree: supplementary activity guide for grades 7 through 12. Am. For. Inst., Inc., Washington, D.C. 258pp.

BAIRD, D. D., AND R. R. TOLMAN. 1982. Attitudes of high school students and biology teachers towards animals. Field Mus. Nat. Hist., Div. Mammals, Chicago. (Unpubl. manuscript.)

BARNES, B., R. RIVNER, M. SMITH, AND L. WALN. 1978-1979. Environmental education generalizations in middle-grade social studies series. J. Environ. Educ. 10(2):12–17.

BENNETT, D. B. 1982. Evaluating environmental education in the context of a junior high school state studies program. J. Environ. Educ. 13(4):13–18.

BROWN, L. R. 1981. Building a sustainable society. WorldWatch Inst. Book, Norton and Co., New York. 433pp.

BURRUS-BAMMEL, L. L. 1978. Information's effect on attitude: a longitudinal study. J. Environ. Educ. 9(4):41–50.

CHEMERS, M., AND I. ALTMAN. 1977. Use and perception of the environment: cultural and developmental processes. Pages 43–54 in Children, nature, and the urban environment: proc. of a symposium-fair. U.S. Dep. Agric. For. Serv. Gen. Tech. Rep. NE-30.

CHILDRESS, R. B. 1978. Public school environmental education curricula: a national profile. J. Environ. Educ. 9(3):2–11.

COHEN, M. R. 1977. Using student-determined needs to evaluate environmental education programs. J. Environ. Educ. 8(4):27–30.

———, AND D. K. HOLLINGSWORTH. 1973. Environmental beliefs and educational ability. J. Environ. Educ. 5(2):9–12.

COLLINS, T. A., C. N. HERBKERSMAN, L. A. PHELPS, AND G. W. BARRETT. 1979. Establishing positive attitudes toward energy conservation in intermediate-level children. J. Environ. Educ. 10(2):18–23.

CROMPTON, J. L., AND C. SELLAR. 1981. Do outdoor education experiences contribute to positive development in the affective domain? J. Environ. Educ. 12(4):21–29.

DORAN, R. L. 1977. State of the art for measurement and evaluation of environmental objectives. J. Environ. Educ. 9(1):50–63.

———, R. O. GUERIN, AND A. A. SARNOWSKI, JR. 1974. Assessing students' awareness of environmental problems. J. Environ. Educ. 5(4):14–18.

FORTNER, R. W., AND V. J. MAYER. 1983. Ohio students' knowledge and attitudes about the oceans and Great Lakes. Ohio J. Sci. 85(5):218–224.

_____, AND T. G. TEATES. 1980. Baseline studies for marine education: experiences related to marine knowledge and attitudes. J. Environ. Educ. 11(4):11–19.

GABEL, D., M. KAGAN, AND R. SHERWOOD. 1980. A summary of research in science education—1978. Sci. Educ. 64(4):512–515.

GEORGE, R. W. 1967. A comparative analysis of conservation attitudes where conservation education is a part of the educational experience. Trans. North Am. Wildl. and Nat. Resour. Conf. 31:199–210.

HAWKINS, D. E., AND D. A. VINTON. 1973. The environmental classroom. Prentice-Hall, Inc., Englewood Cliffs, N.J.

HENDEE, J. C. 1972. Challenging the folklore of environmental education. J. Environ. Educ. 3(3):19–23.

_____, AND D. R. POTTER. 1971. Human behavior and wildlife management: needed research. Trans. North Am. Wildl. and Nat. Resour. Conf. 36:383–396.

HESS, R D., AND J. V. TORNEY. 1967. The development of political attitudes in children. Doubleday and Co., New York. 331pp.

KAUCHAK, D., F. KRALL, AND K. HEIMSATH. 1978. The need for education, not indoctrination. J. Environ. Educ. 10(1):19–22.

KELLERT, S. R. 1976. Perceptions of animals in American society. Trans. North Am. Wildl. and Nat. Resour. Conf. 41:533–546.

_____. 1980. American attitudes toward and knowledge of animals: an update. Int. J. of Studies of Anim. Problems 1(2):87–119.

_____. 1983. Attitudes toward animals: age-related development among children. Pap. rep. on S. R. Kellert and M. O. Westervelt's study "Children's attitudes, knowledge, and behaviors toward animals." Gov. Print. Off. Rep. No. 024-010-00641-2. 202pp.

_____, AND M. O. WESTERVELT. 1983. Children's attitudes, knowledge, and behaviors toward animals. Gov. Print. Off. Rep. No. 024-010-00641-2. 202pp.

KINSEY, T. G., AND J. H. WHEATLEY. 1980. An instrument to inventory the defensibility of environmental attitudes. J. Environ. Educ. 12(1):29–35.

LaHART, D. E. 1978. The influence of knowledge on young people's perceptions about wildlife. Final rep. to the Natl. Wildl. Fed., Coll. of Educ., Florida State Univ., Tallahassee.

_____, AND L. W. BARNES. 1978-1979. A holistic scheme for environmental education research. J. Environ. Educ. 10(2):24–29.

LANGENAU, E. E., JR., AND P. M. MELLON-COYLE. 1977. Michigan's young hunter. Mich. Dep. Nat. Resour. Wildl. Div. Rep. No. 2800, Lansing. 78pp.

LEWIS, G. E. 1981-1982. A review of classroom methodologies for environmental education. J. Environ. Educ. 13(2):12–15.

LUCKO, D. J., J. F. DISINGER, AND R. E. ROTH. 1982. Evaluation of environmental education programs at the elementary and secondary school levels. J. Environ. Educ. 13(4):7–12.

MARSHDOYLE, E., M. L. BOWMAN, AND G. W. MULLINS. 1982. Evaluating programmatic use of a community resource: the zoo. J. Environ. Educ. 13(4):19–26.

MILLER, J. D. 1975. The development of pre-adult attitudes toward environmental conservation and pollution. School Sci. and Math. 75:729–737.

MOORE, R. C. 1977. The environmental design of children-nature relations: some strands of applicative theory. Pages 207–214 *in* Children, nature, and the urban environment: proc. of a symposium-fair. U.S. Dep. Agric. For. Serv. Gen. Tech. Rep. NE-30.

MORE, T. A. 1977. An analysis of wildlife in children's stories. Pages 89–94 *in* Children, nature, and the urban environment: proc. of a symposium-fair. U.S. Dep. Agric. For. Serv. Gen. Tech. Rep. NE-30.

OLSON, E. E., M. L. BOWMAN, AND R. E. ROTH. 1984. Interpretation and nonformal environmental education in natural resource management. J. Environ. Educ. 15(4):6–10.

PERDUE, R. R., AND D. S. WARDER. 1981. Environmental education and attitude change. J. Environ. Educ. 12(3):25–28.

POMERANTZ, G. A. 1977. Young people's attitudes toward wildlife. Mich. Dep. Nat. Resour. Wildl. Div. Rep. No. 2781, Lansing. 79pp.

————. 1985. The influence of "Ranger Rick" magazine on children's perceptions of natural resource issues. Ph.D. Thesis, North Carolina State Univ., Raleigh. 261pp.

REJESKI, D. W. 1982. Children look at nature: environmental perception and education. J. Environ. Educ. 13(4):27–40.

RIPPLE, R. E., R. F. BIEHLER, AND G. A. JAQUISH. 1982. Human development. Houghton Mifflin Co., Boston. 673pp.

SCHOENFELD, C. 1978. Environmental education and wildlife conservation. Pages 471–484 *in* H. P. Brokaw, ed. Wildlife and America. Counc. on Environ. Quality, Washington, D.C.

SHAW, W. W. 1974. Sociological and psychological determinants of attitudes toward hunting. Ph.D. Thesis, Univ. Michigan, Ann Arbor. 84pp.

————, AND E. H. ZUBE. 1980. Wildlife values. A workshop on assessment methodologies and information needs. Pages 4–10 *in* W. W. Shaw and E. H. Zube, eds. Wildlife values. Cent. for Assessment of Noncommodity Nat. Resour. Values, Inst. Ser. Rep. No. 1, Univ. Arizona, Tucson.

TANNER, T. 1980. Significant life experiences: a new research area in environmental education. J. Environ. Educ. 11(4):20–25.

WESTERN REGIONAL ENVIRONMENTAL EDUCATION COUNCIL. 1983*a*.. Project WILD: elementary activity guide. West. Reg. Environ. Educ. Counc., Boulder, Colo. 278pp.

————. 1983*b*. Project WILD: secondary activity guide. West. Reg. Environ. Educ. Counc., Boulder, Colo. 288pp.

Chapter 19

The Recreational Benefits of Wildlife to People

William W. Shaw

Although social scientists consistently argue that leisure is a fundamental and important cultural institution, the concept of recreational benefits is always difficult to quantify or even verbalize. In our pragmatic culture, we hold a reverence for work and productivity and tend to neglect the less tangible benefits associated with leisure activities.

However, a substantial body of literature deals with the importance of leisure activities to cultures. Far from being a superfluous diversion, recreation provides essential benefits for individuals and for society (Driver 1976). In general, recreation, unlike work, affords people an opportunity to choose activities that will fulfill and enrich their lives, and people who have these opportunities to choose and enjoy leisure will be happier, healthier, and consequently more productive members of society.

Theoretically, these benefits apply to all leisure activities, with different forms of recreation tending to fulfill different human needs. In terms of natural resource allocation and management, the important issue is understanding the unique or special aspects of wildlife-oriented recreation. In other words, are there benefits from these activities that cannot be provided by other recreational opportunities? The remainder of this chapter addresses the importance of wildlife as a focus for recreation in our culture and the unique attributes of these activities.

PARTICIPATION IN WILDLIFE-ORIENTED RECREATION

One indicator of the importance of a type of recreation is the number of people who participate in the activity. By this measure, wildlife- or nature-oriented recreation can almost be termed a national pastime. Most Americans participate in some form of wildlife-oriented recreation at least occasionally (Table 19.1), and participants include people from nearly all geographic and socio-demographic groups (Shaw and Mangun 1984, U.S. Fish and Wildl. Serv. and U.S. Bur. Census 1982). For some people, this activity involves a casual commitment involving only a few days each year. For many others, however, wildlife-oriented activities are important recreational pursuits, often becoming the focal point of leisure-time activities. We know, for example, that in many families hunting is a very important family tradition, binding one generation to the next. Similarly, participants in nonconsumptive wildlife-oriented activities run the gamut from casual observers to avid enthusiasts. For example, over 55 million people enjoyed or took a special interest in wildlife near their home in 1980, and of these, 32% (18 million) reported doing this on more than 200 days during the year (Shaw et al. 1985) (Table 19.2).

The significance of nature-oriented recreation is further illustrated when participation figures are compared with those for other common leisure pursuits. In terms of numbers of participants, nature-oriented activities rank above such activities as bicycling, boating, tennis, and camping (U.S. Dep. Inter., Heritage Conserv. and Recreation Serv. 1979).

From these participation figures, it is clear that wildlife-oriented activities are important leisure pursuits in our culture. However, expressing this importance as numbers of participants or recreation days seems somehow incomplete for many of us because in addition to the usual recreational benefits (exercise, health, social interaction, and so on), wildlife-oriented recreation seems inextricably intertwined with benefits to environmental health, education, cultural traditions, and ethics.

CATEGORIES OF BENEFITS

The complexity of this issue is reflected in the literature that addresses wildlife values (Steinhoff 1980). Many approaches attempt to treat recreation as a category apart from biological, aesthetic, and educational values using some variation of the system proposed by King (1947). Although intuitively appealing, none of these classification systems adequately addresses the concept of recreational benefits. It is simply not possible to separate the recreational benefits of hunting or bird-watching from issues like knowledge concerning the ecological significance of wildlife and the role of wild animals in creating a stable and healthy ecosystem for humans. These cognitive attributes greatly complicate the task of discussing the benefits of these activities.

TABLE 19.1
Participation in Wildlife-Oriented Recreational
Activities in 1980

Activity	Participants over 15 years old (millions)	Percent of U.S. population
Hunting	17	10
Fishing	42	25
Nonconsumptive Activities	83	49
All Wildlife-oriented Activities	100	59

Source: Shaw and Mangun 1984, and U.S. Fish and Wildl. Serv. and U.S. Bur. Census 1982.

TABLE 19.2
Frequency of Participation in Residential Wildlife
Enjoyment Activities (Took Special Interest in
Wildlife Around Home)

Number of Days in 1980	Participants over 15 years old (millions)	Percent of U.S. population
1-10	11.0	19.7
11-20	6.2	11.0
21-50	8.0	14.3
51-100	6.9	12.4
101-200	5.2	9.4
>200	18.2	32.5
Missing Data	0.4	0.8

Source: Shaw et al. 1984.

THE COGNITIVE ASPECTS
OF WILDLIFE-ORIENTED RECREATION

Although most recreational analyses focus on overt behavior for describing a particular activity, this approach is incomplete and inadequate for many wildlife-oriented activities. For example, people may choose to engage in nature-study activities during their leisure time because they understand the significance of wildlife to maintaining a healthy ecosystem for people (environmental health), they understand the importance of learning how this system works (educational benefits), and they feel a sense of kinship and responsibility for other forms of life (ethics). None of these dimensions is readily apparent to an observer of the participant unless this observation includes an assessment of beliefs and attitudes. However, these cognitive processes are often central elements in a wildlife-oriented recreational experience.

For example, thousands of people visit Cabrillo National Monument in southern California to observe the annual migration of gray whales. The overt behavior of most of the people involved in this activity includes scanning the horizon for a barely discernible glimpse of the back of a whale and perhaps a whisp of vapor as the animal exhales while swimming a mile or more offshore. Nothing about the visual stimuli is particularly aesthetic, and nothing about the actual activity (scanning the horizon) is intrinsically recreational. Nevertheless, the excitement of the participants is obvious, and, for many, sighting a whale becomes a highlight of the trip. Clearly, the essence of this recreational experience lies in the mind of the beholder rather than in any observable behavior. The demand for this form of recreation comes from people's knowledge that the whales are the largest mammals, that they are intelligent, and that their existence has been threatened by human exploitation and from the human interest in learning more about these creatures.

Using a traditional recreational framework for understanding the benefits associated with wildlife has a further limitation because many of these benefits do not involve direct use or observation of the resource. Although the concepts of existence and option values may apply to many forms of recreation, they are especially important for wildlife-oriented recreation. Wildlife often function as symbols for a host of environmental concerns in our culture. As such, people often value their mere existence as much or more than they value direct uses of the resource. In the example of gray whales, much of the excitement associated with knowledge about whales is present at the national monument even when the whales are not migrating. People still flock to the monument because they value the existence of whales and wish to learn about them and to preserve the option for future generations to use and enjoy this wildlife resource.

Because of the importance of these cognitive elements in wildlife-oriented recreational experiences, the benefits of these activities are very difficult to assess and often extend into areas not typically regarded as recreational benefits. Nevertheless, these benefits are extremely important aspects of the human experience. They accrue in the form of mental peace of mind, a sense of security regarding the viability of our own and future human generations, a sense of moral responsibility for protecting the integrity of the biosphere and for providing future generations with maximum options, and a sense of cultural identity derived from recognition of common evolutionary kinships among all people and animals.

SUMMARY AND IMPLICATIONS

In summary, though it is useful to compare wildlife-oriented recreation with other forms of leisure activity, we should recognize that such comparisons have major limitations. In many situations, the experiences associated with these activities are predominantly mental, and these cognitive processes are often more appropriately thought of in terms like education, tradition, and ethics than in the usual terms applied to recreation.

This point has important implications for resource managers concerned with providing social benefits. It is extremely important to look beyond the overt behavior of participants and attempt to understand their experiences. Wildlife managers must recognize that resource management involves more than manipulating the resource. One of our important functions should be to provide opportunities for people to experience and learn about nature. This approach includes not only managing the resource so it is available but also creating situations in which learning about nature takes place. One of the most powerful tools we have for accomplishing this is the provision of information about wildlife and other environmental issues. Accepting this role as communicators is essential if wildlife managers are to be effective in providing the broad range of benefits associated with wildlife-oriented recreation.

REFERENCES

DRIVER, B. L. 1976. Toward a better understanding of the social benefits of outdoor recreation participation. Pages 163–190 *in* Proc. South. States Recreation Res. Appl. Workshop, U.S. Dep. Agric. For. Serv. Gen. Tech. Rep. SE-9.

KING, R. T. 1947. The future of wildlife in forest land use. Trans. North Am. Wildl. Conf. 12:454–467.

SHAW, W. W., AND W. R. MANGUN. 1984. Nonconsumptive use of wildlife in the United States. U.S. Fish and Wildl. Serv. Resour. Publ. 154. 20pp.

——, ——, AND J. R. LYONS. 1985. Residential enjoyment of wildlife resources by Americans. Leisure Sci. 7(3):361–375.

STEINHOFF, H. W. 1980. Analysis of major conceptual systems for understanding and measuring wildlife values. Pages 11–21 *in* W. W. Shaw and E. H. Zube, eds. Wildlife values. Cent. for Assessment of Noncommodity Nat. Resour. Values, Inst. Ser. Rep. No. 1, Univ. Arizona, Tucson.

U.S. DEPARTMENT OF THE INTERIOR, HERITAGE CONSERVATION AND RECREATION SERVICE. 1979. The third nationwide outdoor recreation plan: the assessment. U.S. Dep. Inter., Washington, D.C. 263pp.

U.S. FISH AND WILDLIFE SERVICE AND U.S. BUREAU OF THE CENSUS. 1982. 1980 national survey of fishing, hunting and wildlife-associated recreation. U.S. Dep. Inter. and U.S. Dep. Commer., U.S. Gov. Print. Off., Washington, D.C. 156pp.

Chapter 20

The Philosophical Value of Wildlife

J. Baird Callicott

In "The Land Ethic" of *A Sand County Almanac,* Aldo Leopold wrote: "It is inconceivable to me that an ethical relation to land can exist without love, respect, and admiration for land, and a high regard for its value. By value, I of course mean something far broader than mere economic value; I mean value in the philosophical sense" (1966:261). By land, of course, Leopold (1966:189) also meant something far broader than mere real estate; he meant "all of the things on, over, or in the earth"—which would, and certainly did for Leopold, prominently include wildlife.

We have a fairly clear, if general, idea of the economic value of wildlife. The economic value is the expected answer to the question, What good is it? According to Leopold (1966:190), asking this question about an animal or plant is "the last word in ignorance." But what could the value of wildlife in "the philosophical sense" possibly be?

INSTRUMENTAL AND INTRINSIC VALUE

Philosophers like myself are not accustomed to dealing with value questions in these terms—economic versus philosophical value; rather, philosophers more often oppose instrumental and intrinsic value (Callicott 1986a). The instrumental value of something is its utility as a means to some end. The intrinsic value of something is its inherent worth as an end in itself.

Though nothing is universally accepted in philosophy, in the prevailing traditions of Western moral thought human beings or their states of consciousness (like pleasure or happiness or more recently "preference satisfaction") are generally agreed to be the intrinsically valuable things and everything else to be the instrumentally valuable things (Callicott 1984). Gifford Pinchot is supposed to have said that there are two kinds of beings in this world: people and their resources. This statement perfectly captures the kinds of values recognized in Western philosophy and the places where they reside.

The Biblical proverb, "man does not live by bread alone," reminds us that we human beings have spiritual as well as material needs. And wildlife and nature generally have served as spiritual as well as material resources. Indeed, one major historical conflict in U.S. resource management may be understood as a conflict between the spiritual and material utility of natural resources (Nash 1973). Wild things may be fed, eaten, worn, made into implements, built with, and so on, and/or they may be listened to, watched, studied, worshipped, enjoyed, and so on. In other words, the question "what good is a woodcock?" can be answered equally appropriately by saying that its "sky dance" enchants a spring evening and satisfies a deep need for visual variety, grace, and beauty as by saying that a woodcock may "serve as a target and pose gracefully on a slice of toast" (Leopold 1966:36). Those for whom wildlife and other natural resources satisfy primarily spiritual needs usually regard such uses as "better" or "higher" than material ones (Nash 1973). But my point is that from the prevailing perspective of modern Western philosophy, wildlife and other natural resources remain only instrumentally valuable—whether as a means to satisfy the widest possible range of human spiritual needs or the most narrow range of human material needs.

Economic valuation, ideally conceived, is one clear way—though perhaps not the only or even the best way—to compare and adjudicate conflicts between the different utilities that wildlife and other natural resources represent (Daly 1980). It is ideally possible in economics, though perhaps difficult and uncertain in practice, to compare, say, the real dollar value of redwood trees converted into picnic tables and tomato stakes with the shadow-priced dollar value of uncut redwood trees as objects of beauty, awe, and inspiration.

However, since real-world economics rarely takes into account the dollar value of the nonconsumptive/nonmaterial utilities of trees on the stump, birds on the wing, ungulates on the hoof, soil in conservancy (to say nothing of pollinators, decomposers, nitrogen fixers, and other members of nature's service industry), the nonmaterial utilities of wildlife and other natural resources are usually excluded by the term *economic value*. *Economic value,* in other words, often connotes just material, instrumental value and often not even the full range of that type. Leopold, therefore, could have meant by the term *philosophical value* as opposed to *economic value* the more subtle and spiritual, as opposed to the more immediate and material, kinds of instrumental values of land; but the context indicates that he did not.

In general, Leopold recommended a wholly unprecedented ethical relationship between people and land—a relationship between ends and ends, not ends and means. And more particularly, he mentioned in the same breath with philosophical value, love, respect, admiration, and high regard—attitudes we reserve for intrinsically valuable beings, not for instrumentally valuable things however noble and ethereal their uses. From the higher utilitarian point of view, we may be delighted by the song of a mockingbird, awed by the size and age of a redwood, arrested by the stoop of a Peregrine falcon, overcome by the sight of a grizzly bear, but we can only love and respect a being whose worth transcends the positive experiences it affords us and other human beings.

So by the philosophical value of wildlife, if we may take Aldo Leopold as our guide and inspiration, we should understand what philosophers themselves would more technically call *intrinsic* or *inherent value*. The burden of this chapter may thus be transposed into the following question: How may we ground or justify Leopold's ethical proposition that in addition to the full spectrum of instrumental values, spiritual as well as material, wildlife possesses intrinsic value?

THE CONCEPTUAL FOUNDATIONS OF INTRINSIC VALUE

Animal Liberation

The most visible and vocal contemporary defense of the intrinsic value of wildlife has ironically evolved out of classic utilitarianism (Callicott 1980). According to Jeremy Bentham (1823), founding father of utilitarianism, pleasure is good and pain is evil; and an ethical person should attempt, in choosing courses of action, to maximize the one and minimize the other, no matter whose pain or pleasure may be involved. Utilitarians conventionally limited the impartial weighing of pleasures and pains to human beings. However, though entirely clear even in Bentham's day, the combined evidence of comparative anatomy, physiology, neurology, ethology, and paleontology, now overwhelmingly confirms that many animals—all vertebrates most certainly—are also conscious beings that experience pleasure and pain (Midgely 1983). Hence, by the same principle of impartiality, we ought to give equal consideration to the pleasure and pain of other animals, no less than of other human beings, in choosing our courses of action (Singer 1975).

This grounding of the intrinsic value of some nonhuman animals—sentient animals—is popularly known as animal liberation and has been recently and most notably espoused by Peter Singer (1975). I have been a resolute philosophical opponent of animal liberation as a serviceable environmental ethic because it provides for no discrimination between wild and domestic animals, or between overabundant and rare animals, or between native and exotic animals (Callicott 1980). A Holstein steer, a specimen of an overabundant, domestic, exotic species, is equally sentient and therefore is entitled to as much moral consideration as a Dall ram, a specimen of a rare, wild, indigenous species.

On a deeper level, animal liberation is concerned exclusively with the welfare of individual animals, so much so that should the welfare of individuals conflict with that of a population of them—as is often the case with cervids—animal liberation unhesitatingly gives uncompromising priority to the welfare of individuals, more holistic considerations be damned (Singer 1979).

Most disturbingly, a ruthlessly consistent deduction of the consequences of animal liberation would be a universal predator eradication program as a policy of wildlife management (Callicott 1986*b*)! Why? Because predators obviously inflict pain and death on their prey. If we should stop humans from hunting, as animal liberationists advocate, then by parity of reasoning, we should also stop other animals from hunting. The result, of course, would be an ecological nightmare.

This consideration reveals a moral repugnance for wild nature at the core of animal liberation. Death and often pain are at the heart of nature's economy. To the extent that animal liberation morally condemns pain and death, it is irreconcilably at odds with the ecological facts of wild life. Thus we shall have to look elsewhere for a theory of the intrinsic value of wildlife consistent with the ecological facts of wild life.

Theocentrism

One of wildlife's greatest champions, John Muir, stressed the spiritual utility of wild nature: "Mountain parks and reservations are useful not only as fountains of timber and irrigating rivers but as fountains of life" (1901:1). In a more intimate journal, prepared posthumously for publication by William Frederick Badé, Muir (1916), for the first time that I am aware of in U.S. conservation literature, gave expression to the distinctly philosophical value of wildlife.

Muir's argument for the intrinsic value of wildlife was primarily theological. According to the Bible, God created other forms of life as well as human life, and He declared them all to be "good" (May and Metzger 1966:2). More technically expressed, God created all life forms and either at that time or by a subsequent fiat conferred intrinsic value upon them. In Muir's words, "From the dust of the earth, from the common elementary fund, the Creator has made *Homo sapiens*. From the same material he has made every other creature, however noxious and insignificant to us. . . . They dwell happily . . . unfallen, undepraved, and cared for with the same species of tenderness and love as is bestowed on angels in heaven or saints on earth" (1916:98, 139). In Muir's view this Biblical truth—if it is a truth—constitutes the grounds for "the rights of all the rest of the creation" (1916:98).

Muir's theological theory of the intrinsic value of wildlife provides a conceptual context more congenial to an ecologically informed program of wildlife conservation than does Singer's theory. Its intractably in-dividualistic value orientation is the main problem with the animal liberation ethic, from the viewpoint of wildlife conservation (Callicott 1980). On the other hand, Genesis clearly implies that in His acts of creation God established and conferred value upon species primarily, whereas individual specimens are understood to come and go. Nor is there any overriding obligation placed upon us in Genesis or elsewhere in the Bible to try to prevent animals from experiencing pain (though gratuitous cruelty is proscribed). Hence, Muir's theory of the intrinsic value of wildlife is not in direct conflict (as Singer's is) with the more holistic value orientation of wildlife ecology and management.

The main problem with Muir's theocentric axiology is not that its practical implications are inconsistent with an ecologically informed program of wildlife conservation but that its theoretical premises are inconsistent with the scientific foundations of wildlife ecology and conservation. According to science, wildlife species were not created as we find them today; they evolved into their present form. Nature is regarded as autochthonous and autonomous. To the extent that we believe that science gives us a true understanding of nature, a theocentric grounding of the intrinsic value of wildlife simply rests upon false beliefs about the natural world. This deep theoretical inconsistency is rendered more acute and vitiating when we reflect that our appreciation and respect for wildife are deepened the more science discloses about the origins and interactions of wild things. As Leopold observed, "wild things . . . had little [philosophical] value until . . . science disclosed the drama of where they came from [evolution] and how they live [ecology]" (1966:xvii).

Biophilia

Leopold accordingly grounds the intrinsic value of wild things in evolutionary and ecological biology. A theory of the intrinsic value of wildlife grounded exclusively in a scientific world view seems immediately implausible, however. According to the metaphysical foundations of modern science, the natural world, from atoms to galaxies—including the middle-sized organic world—is value free, value neutral. Values, from a general scientific point of view, are subjective: They originate in consciousness and are projected onto objects. If all consciousness were eradicated, there would be no value anywhere in nature; there would remain only brute facts (Callicott 1985).

Leopold appears to respect this objective-fact/subjective-value dichotomy of modern science (Callicott 1984, 1986). Values remain subjective, consciousness dependent in his land ethic. But a closer scrutiny of human values reveals that, though subjective, all values are not subject oriented, that is, selfish (Callicott 1982, 1984, 1985, 1986a, 1986b). We value ourselves and/or certain of our own experiences, but we are also capable of valuing other things equally with ourselves or even more than ourselves (Callicott 1984, 1985, 1986a, b). In other words, although the value of objective things depends upon some conscious subject valuing them, a conscious subject, at least a human conscious subject, can value them for themselves as well as for what they may do for him or her. Most people, for example, value their children and other loved ones in this way.

For human beings and other social animals, this other-oriented valuational capacity is a product of natural selection. In his second great work Darwin (1871) argued that what he called the "moral sentiments," following David Hume and Adam Smith, were naturally selected as a means to social integration and evolution. In short, social membership increases the inclusive fitness of the individuals of some species. But social membership is impossible without "limitations on freedom of action [in regard to proximate individuals of the same species] in the struggle for existence" (Leopold 1966:238). Among social mammals these requisite limitations have taken the form of other-oriented sentiments—love, respect, admiration, fellow-feeling, sympathy, and high regard. In the final analysis, intrinsic value—the value of something as an end in itself—is a philosophical abstraction from these primitive moral sentiments (Callicott 1985).

Since the moral sentiments and the philosophical value that is ultimately erected upon them originally evolved in conjunction with the evolution of mammalian societies, there is a close correlation among community, perceived social membership, and intrinsic value. In the past only our own clan or tribe and our fellow tribespeople were regarded as ends in themselves, and all other human beings and human groups were treated as mere means (Nash 1977). More recently, for many a sense of community has come to embrace all humankind (Nash 1977). Accordingly, modern humanism affirms the intrinsic value of all human beings regardless of race, creed, or national origin and of all humankind. Aldo Leopold observed that today ecology represents both human beings and wild things as members of "one humming community," the biotic community (Leopold 1966:193). Because we now perceive wild creatures as belonging to this expanded ecological society, we are naturally impelled to extend to the biotic community itself and to wild things as members in good standing the same value—philosophical or intrinsic value— once more restrictively reserved for more narrowly defined classes.

In my opinion, therefore, Aldo Leopold's account of the philosophical value of wildlife is the most persuasive of the three alternatives reviewed here. It best articulates our ecologically informed intuitions about the transutilitarian value of wildlife. It subordinates the value of specimens to populations, species, and biocenoses. And it is based neither on an outmoded moral philosophy (utilitarianism) or on an outmoded theology (Judeo-Christian theism), but squarely on modern science.

REFERENCES

BENTHAM, J. 1823. An introduction to the principles of morals and legislation. Vol. 1. W. Pickering, London. 381 pp.

CALLICOTT, J. B. 1980. Animal liberation: a triangular affair. Environ. Ethics 2(4):311–338.

———. 1982. Hume's is/ought dichotomy and the relation of ecology to Leopold's land ethic. Environ. Ethics 4(2):163–174.

———. 1984. Non-anthropocentric value theory and environmental ethics. Am. Philos. Q. 21(4):299–309.

———. 1985. Intrinsic value, quantum theory, and environmental ethics. Environ. Ethics 7(2):257–275.

———. 1986a. On the intrinsic value of non-human species. Pages 138–172 in B. Norton, ed. The preservation of species. Princeton Univ. Press, Princeton, N.J.

———. 1986b. The search for an environmental ethic. Pages 381–424 in T. Regan, ed. Matters of life and death. 2nd ed. Random House, New York.

DALY, H. 1980. Economics, ecology, ethics. W. H. Freeman and Co., San Francisco. 372pp.

DARWIN, C. 1871. The descent of man and selection in relation to sex. 2nd ed. J. A. Hill and Co., New York. 314pp.

LEOPOLD, A. 1966. A sand county almanac. Ballatine Books, New York. 226pp.

MIDGELY, M. 1983. Animals and why they matter. Univ. Georgia Press, Athens, Ga. 158pp.

MAY, H. G., AND G. M. METZGER, editors. 1966. Genesis. Pages 1–66 in The holy bible: revised standard version containing the old and new testaments. Oxford Univ. Press, New York.

MUIR, J. 1901. Our national parks. Houghton-Mifflin and Co., New York. 370pp.

———. 1916. A thousand mile walk to the gulf. Houghton-Mifflin and Co., New York. 220pp.

NASH, R. 1973. Wilderness and the American mind. Yale Univ. Press, New Haven, Conn. 300pp.

———. 1977. Do rocks have rights? Cent. Mag. 10(6):2–12.

SINGER, P. 1975. Animal liberation: a new ethics for our treatment of animals. New York Rev., New York. 297pp.

———. 1979. Not for humans only. Pages 191–206 *in* K. E. Goodpaster and K. M. Sayer, eds. Ethics and problems of the 21st century. Univ. Notre Dame Press, Notre Dame, Indiana.

Chapter 21

The Contributions of Wildlife to Human Quality of Life

Stephen R. Kellert

Considerable information has been offered to suggest that wildlife is valuable on a variety of economic, social-psychological, and biological grounds. Moreover, despite the complexity of the issue, the question of wildlife's value seems academic at times because life itself would not be possible without the vast energy flows stemming from the interrelation of living matter and ecosystems. Even this most basic wildlife value, however, is beyond the comprehension of all but a few people. Most members of society are strained to feel particular concern for more than a few species or to believe that wildlife is somehow related to human well-being or the quality of life. As a consequence, we often engage in an elaborate game of mental gymnastics, striving to impute enduring monetary, spiritual, or even life-sustaining value to the animal world.

This exercise is certainly important, honing our public relations skills and helping to address the many legislative mandates to incorporate wildlife values in diverse environmental mitigation and trade-off situations (Shaw and Zube 1980). Additionally, considerable evidence has been provided at this symposium indicating that wildlife can demonstrably enhance human aesthetic, biological, recreational, educational, and even spiritual experiences. For example, the contributions of wildlife have been related to a sense of historical tradition and cultural ties or even to enlarging the human capacities for intellectual growth and a sense of spiritual meaning (Leopold 1968, Shepard 1978, Rolston 1981, Kellert 1984, Wilson 1984). Moreover, the economic expressions of this worth have been indicated in patterns of recreational activity, educational programs, agricultural production, pollination, seed dispersal, or even in the decomposition of human waste (Pimentel 1975, Bishop 1981, Myers 1983).

The "fly in the ointment" is the disquieting uncertainty that we may have been preaching largely to the converted. I am not alone in doubting that most of the public remains skeptical and unconvinced of this range of wildlife values. Our strenuous efforts call to mind Shakespeare's admonition, "Me thinks the lady doeth protest too much" (Ribner and Kittredge 1971:1075).

It might be useful to consider briefly how the general public actually values wildlife and its contributions to human society. Recent studies (Kellert 1980*a*, 1985*a,b*) have collectively revealed a degree of appreciation of wildlife among the general public, but it is typically narrow in its emotional and intellectual focus and largely directed at a small component of the animal community. As a shorthand means of describing these perceptions, a typology of attitudes toward animals is used, briefly defined in Table 21.1 (Kellert 1980*b*).

Data on changing attitudes toward wildlife from 1900 to 1975 indicated considerable decline in utilitarian or commodity-oriented valuations of wildlife, as well as in the overall levels of fear, hostility, or indifference to animals (Figs. 21.1 and 21.2). These findings encouragingly suggested that Americans today value wildlife in broader, less competitive, and less negative terms than in the past. On the other hand, this and other studies revealed that negativistic and utilitarian perceptions of wildlife still remain very common, particularly among lower socioeconomic, elderly, rural, and natural-resource-dependent groups (Figs. 21.3 and 21.4). Moreover, more positive and appreciative wildlife attitudes were largely restricted to particular vertebrate species, characterized by cultural familiarity, aesthetic appeal, presumably higher intelligence, and complex sentient capacities. In contrast, ecological and scientific wildlife values were rarely encountered except among a small fraction of the general public.

Further studies of public attitudes toward invertebrate wildlife revealed widespread antipathy and fear of these animals (Table 21.2). More positive perceptions of invertebrates almost exclusively focused on species generally regarded as possessing unusual aesthetic or practical value (e.g., butterflies or bees). On the other hand, feelings of emotional attachment or ethical concern for invertebrate animals were almost never encountered. And even though some scientists (mostly organic, not inorganic, scientists) recognized the ecological and scientific value of invertebrates, the general public rarely acknowledged such life support or basic knowledge functions.

These results collectively suggested that most philosophical, educational, economic, and ecological wildlife values were little recognized or understood by the general public. Additionally, more positive valuations of wildlife were largely directed at phylogenetically higher or culturally important vertebrate species or, in the case of invertebrates, toward those few species possessing unusual aesthetic or utilitarian appeal.

TABLE 21.1
Attitudes Toward Animals

Term	Definition
Naturalistic:	Primary interest and affection for wild-life and the outdoors.
Ecologistic:	Primary concern for the environment as a system, for interrelationships between wildlife species and natural habitats.
Humanistic:	Primary interest and strong affection for individual animals, principally pets. Regarding wildlife, focus on large attractive animals with strong anthropomorphic associations.
Moralistic:	Primary concern for the right and wrong treatment of animals, with strong opposition to exploitation or cruelty toward animals.
Scientistic:	Primary interest in the physical attributes and biological functioning of animals.
Aesthetic:	Primary interest in the artistic and symbolic characteristics of animals.
Utilitarian:	Primary concern for the practical and material value of animals or the animal's habitat.
Dominionistic:	Primary interest in the mastery and control of animals, typically in sporting situations.
Negativistic:	Primary orientation an active avoidance of animals due to dislike or fear.
Neutralistic:	Primary concern is a passive avoidance of animals due to indifference or lack of interest.

<u>Source:</u> Kellert 1980b.

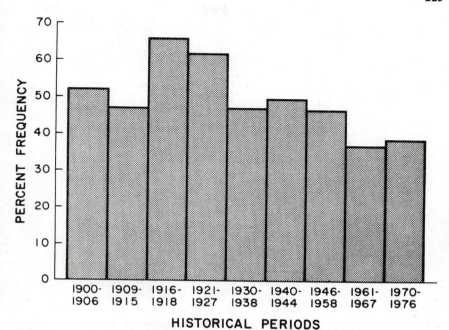

Figure 21.1   Frequency of utilitarian attitude, 1900–1976

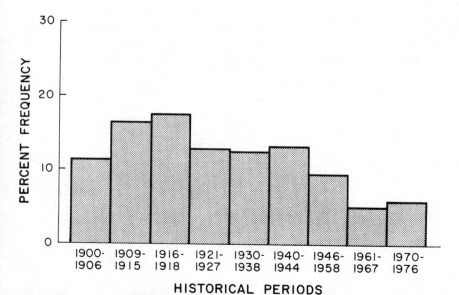

Figure 21.2   Frequency of negativistic attitude, 1900–1976

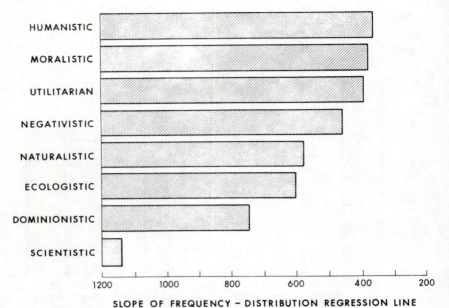

Figure 21.3 Relative frequency of American attitudes toward animals

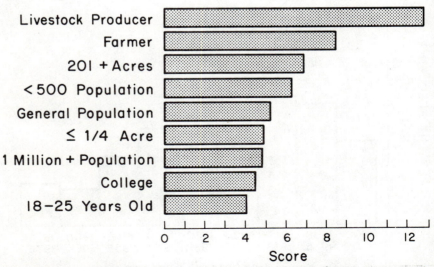

Figure 21.4 Utilitarian scale × selected property-owning and demographic groups

TABLE 21.2
Attitudes toward and Knowledge of Invertebrate Animals
by Major Groups

Attitude/ Knowledge	Standardized Scale Mean Scores				F-value[a]
	General Public	Farmers	Scientists	Members	
Negativistic	.50	.45	.16	.29	17.4
Aesthetic	.40	.41	.69	.51	10.3
Utilitarian	.34	.51	.03	.09	19.1
Naturalistic	.29	.22	.55	.43	13.1
Scientistic	.25	.22	.59	.43	14.9
Moralistic	.22	.19	.44	.38	11.6
Humanistic	.14	.06	.45	.19	23.3
Knowledge	.53	.61	.90	.70	57.6

[a]$p < .0001$.

Source: Unpublished data.

One might be grateful for the limited expression of what can be called humanistic, moralistic, or aesthetic wildlife values. These seemingly appreciative attitudes, however, can cause more, rather than less, difficulties for wildlife and natural habitats. The tragic experience of Hawaii's endemic fauna represents a classic example in which a combination of forces including habitat destruction and exotic animal introductions led to the extinction or endangerment of much of the islands' native wildlife (Banko 1979, Berger 1981, Kellert 1985*c*). This decline was ironically fostered by strong wildlife interests among birders and hunters who often regarded exotic species as a means of enhancing their outdoor recreational interests, as well as by overzealous landscape architects who often contrived tropical gardens consisting exclusively of nonnative plant and animal species. Or, to cite a more contemporary example, we have all too often witnessed the unfortunate consequences of undue public affection or aesthetic attraction for particular species that can result in inordinate concern for baby seals or mute swans but little sympathy for the possible extinction of a Tecopa pupfish or Dismal Swamp shrew.

This lament should not suggest that affection or aesthetic appreciation for animals is regarded as unimportant or regrettable. On the contrary, such attitudes can represent the incipient emergence of what often become more sophisticated ecological and philosophical concerns for wildlife. Nevertheless, most humans have remained aloof from the biological matrix of so-called lower life forms and only recently have begun to question this assumption of superiority, although mostly in expressions of sympathy for the downtrodden or affection for the aesthetically attractive. This process of concern, however, must move beyond feelings of compassion and kindness for selected animals to a conviction that the health and well-being of wildlife and natural habitats are ultimately linked to human well-being and even survival. The results of this symposium mark an important step in the creation of this necessary awareness. Nevertheless, our professional efforts should not delude us from the realization of how far the general public must evolve before the contributions of wildlife to human quality of life are broadly recognized.

The mark of the progress required will be signified when society has recognized that the land is as much a place for nurturing people as it is for growing plants and animals; when it becomes aware that the earth's most important products are not crops or timber or harvestable wildlife but the opportunities provided for human growth and development. This context of stewardship (or what might better be called "studentship") for wildlife can provide human society with a sense of belonging to a community of relationships binding it to all living creatures. In this spirit, an aesthetic appreciation of wildlife will signify a recognition of variety, an awareness of complexity, and a feeling of wonder in a world tending toward homogenization and sameness. The outdoor wildlife experience will mark the opportunity for "recreation" through renewal of our atavistic ties to the land. Or, more philosophically, a sense of spiritual relationship to wildlife will mean the possibility for achieving feelings of personal meaning and historical and cultural connection. The most important incentives for conserving wildlife, in other words, will not be bribes of material enhancement, public spiritedness, or the acceptance of scientific theory but a personal conviction that land managed for wildlife is land ultimately more satisfying, attractive, and enjoyable for people. This level of recognition will signify a stage in which human society has come to appreciate that efforts on behalf of wildlife are really creative ventures on behalf of itself; the true self-interest stemming from a sense of relationship to the nonhuman world.

REFERENCES

BANKO, W. 1979. Historical synthesis of recent endemic Hawaiian birds. Coop. Natl. Parks Resour. Study Unit Rep. 1, Univ. Hawaii, Monoa. 14pp.

BERGER, A. J. 1981. Hawaiian birdlife. Univ. Press Hawaii, Honolulu. 260pp.

BISHOP, R. 1981. Economic considerations affecting land owner behavior. Pages 73–87 *in* R. T. Dumke, G. V. Burger and J. R. March, eds. Wildlife management on private lands. La Crosse Print. Co., Wis.

KELLERT, S. R. 1980a. Public attitudes, knowledge and behaviors toward wildlife and natural habitats. Trans. North Am. Wildl. and Nat. Resour. Conf. 45:111–124.

————. 1980b. Contemporary values of wildlife in American society. Pages 31–60 *in* W. W. Shaw and E. H. Zube, eds. Wildlife values. U.S. For. Serv., Rocky Mt. For. and Range Exp. Stn., Fort Collins, Colo.

————. 1981. Wildlife and the private landowner. Pages 18–35 *in* R. T. Dumke, G. V. Burger, and J. R. March, eds. Wildlife management on private lands. La Crosse Print. Co., Wis.

————. 1983. Affective, evaluative and cognitive perceptions of animals. Pages 241–267 *in* I. Altman and J. F. Wohlwill, eds. Behavior and the natural environment. Plenum Press, New York.

————. 1984. Assessing wildlife and environmental values in cost-benefit analysis. J. Environ. Manage. 18(4):353–363.

————. 1985a. Historical trends in perceptions and uses of animals in 20th century America. Environ. Rev. IX(1):19–33.

————. 1985b. Attitudes toward animals: age-related development among children. J. Environ. Educ. 16(3):29–39.

————. 1985c. Social and perceptual factors in endangered species management. J. Wildl. Manage. 49(2):528–536.

LEOPOLD, A. 1968. A sand county almanac and sketches here and there. Oxford Univ. Press, New York. 226pp.

MYERS, N. 1983. Wealth of wildlife species: storehouse for human welfare. Westview Press, Boulder, Colo. 274pp.

PIMENTEL, D., editor. 1975. Insects, science and society. Academic Press, New York. 284pp.

RIBNER, I., AND G. L. KITTREDGE, editors. 1971. Complete works of Shakespeare. Gynn and Co., Toronto, Canada. 178pp.

ROLSTON, H., III. 1981. Values in nature. Environ. Ethics 3(2):113–128.

SHAW, W. W., AND E. H. ZUBE, editors. 1980. Wildlife values: a workshop on assessment methodologies and information needs. Cent. for Assessment of Noncommodity Nat. Resour. Values, Inst. Ser. Rep. 1, Univ. Arizona, Tucson. 117pp.

SHEPARD, P. 1978. Thinking animals. Viking Press, New York. 274pp.

WILSON, E. O. 1984. Biophilia. Harvard Univ. Press, Cambridge, Mass. 176pp.

PART FIVE

Using Values Information: Practical Applications of Values Knowledge

Introduction

Daniel J. Witter

Wildlife professionals often find themselves face to face with problems whose solutions appear simple. Indeed, an obvious solution often can resolve the problem, although perhaps not to the satisfaction of all parties, and the problem subsides. At other times, wildlife professionals have difficulty identifying and describing all facets of an issue and unexpectedly find themselves at odds with the public and perhaps other resource professionals, unable to agree on the problem much less the solution.

Management of wildlife is complex and involves many social and biological variables. One of the most important aids in sorting the confusing array of management alternatives and arriving at decisions is an understanding of the wildlife values held by the public. Depending on the situation, insights to the worth attached to wildlife by the public can be gained by considering attitudes, motives, preferences, interests, types and frequency of wildlife-related participation, effort and harvest, expenditures, and willingness to pay for and sell experiences—any of the social, psychological, and behavioral indicators that reveal something about the value that a person attaches to a wildlife-related experience. Not only are there many indicators of values but many constituencies that might express these values, most obviously, sportsmen; aesthetic-oriented watchers, photographers, and natural history enthusiasts; private landowners; preservationists and protectionists; other resource professionals; and the general public.

Though an important aid in decision making, public opinion should not dictate wildlife management policy. Resource professionals probably are best equipped to propose strategies for accomplishing specific goals of wildlife conservation. But wildlife decisions involve more than biology and management techniques. The essence of policy formation is the assignment of priorities, which often entails weighing wildlife habitat and population factors in view of management philosophy of an agency's governing board or commission, fiscal constraints, legislative climate, and public values.

The three chapters that follow address the incorporation of public values into resource management decisions. Communication is the underlying theme of these presentations. The authors seek to examine who speaks for the public interest in wildlife-related decisions and how this input occurs.

The definition of wildlife in these papers will include fisheries resources. The worlds of wildlife and fishery management are inextricably linked for purposes of comprehensive resource planning and policy, particularly from the standpoint of resource mitigation.

Three main topics are addressed: (1) environmental impact assessment and mitigation, (2) communication and education, and (3) wildlife planning and policy making.

Chapter 22

Public Interest and Environmental Impact Assessment and Mitigation

Norman P. Stucky, Joseph P. Bachant,
Gary T. Christoff, and William H. Dieffenbach

Although many individuals and organizations during the twentieth century have spoken out on behalf of the nation's natural resources, the age of widespread environmental action by government began in 1969 with the passage of the National Environmental Policy Act. Key federal legislation that followed included the 1972 Clean Water Act and the 1974 Rare and Endangered Species Act.

The Missouri Department of Conservation (MDC) maintains four environmental coordinator positions to assist in the implementation of this legislation. Moreover, the coordinators monitor state and local issues related to MDC's charge to manage Missouri's fish, forests and wildlife. The purpose of this chapter is to examine the role of environmental coordinators in making impact assessments and management recommendations on the basis of environmental law or authority. Moreover, special attention is focused on how the public interest is represented in this decision making process.

One could argue that environmental protection laws in and of themselves reflect the public interest, and, therefore, further citizen involvement in coordination activities is not necessary. Although enacted legislation ideally reflects the voice of the people, all agencies do not interpret or enforce laws with equal vigor; therefore, continued public support and involvement are necessities to ensure effective implementation of environmental laws and regulations. This support is particularly necessary when coordinating with development-minded decision makers who have not accepted the reality that the public wants and is demanding a quality environment. Indeed, nationwide polls repeatedly show that a solid majority of U.S. people strongly supports environmental quality and strict enforcement of existing statutes. This is reassuring in carrying out our charge to protect environmental values and particularly important in carrying out day-to-day coordination on minor projects or short deadlines when it is difficult to obtain public input.

Against this background, four case histories are presented that exemplify our effort to obtain public input and advocate the best public interest in resource management and protection are presented.

CASE 1: MISSOURI RIVER BANK
STABILIZATION AND NAVIGATION PROJECT

The Missouri River, one of the world's largest river systems, flows through the state of Missouri for a distance of approximately 890 km. The fact that 70% of Missouri's people live in the counties bordering the river emphasizes the importance of the river's fish, wildlife, and recreational resources.

In 1912 the U.S. Army, Corps of Engineers (COE) was authorized by Congress to construct a 1.8-m-deep commercial navigation channel on the Missouri River. Congress amended and reauthorized the project in 1945 to provide a 91-m-wide, 2.7-m-deep channel. Throughout the early years of development, little concern was voiced for the serious adverse impact that channelization was having on the river's fish and wildlife. The increasing environmental awareness of the 1960s and early 1970s brought into focus the public resource values that had been and were being lost. In 1974, though the project was nearly completed, a project review was initiated by COE to determine if something could be done on behalf of these resources. It was discovered that the 1958 Fish and Wildlife Coordination Act provided statutory authority to require mitigation of adverse impacts to fish and wildlife habitat. The MDC, through the environmental coordinators, was responsible for assisting COE and the U.S. Department of Interior, Fish and Wildlife Service (FWS) in preparing a Fish and Wildlife Report and recommended mitigation plan. Completed in 1981, the study revealed that approximately 20,250 ha of aquatic riverine habitat, publicly owned according to state statute, had been destroyed and converted to privately owned agricultural cropland. Public interest and values for wildlife habitat had also been impacted as 101,250 ha of bottomland terrestrial habitat were cleared and converted to agricultural cropland. The recommended mitigation plan, at a cost of $48 million, would restore only 3% of the aquatic and 7% of the terrestrial losses. At present, the plan is awaiting congressional action.

Public Interest

Public involvement in this effort was strong at first. Ten years ago, at the outset of the study, the public responded enthusiastically to MDC's and FWS's notice of intent to mitigate fish and wildlife project losses. Public hearings held in communities along the river were well attended, and an organization called the Missouri River Society sprang into being. Other active, vocal groups included the local chapter of the Sierra Club, the Audubon Society, the Conservation Federation of Missouri, and the public at large. The press played a key role in providing editorials and articles that kept the public informed and interest high. However, the legislative process does not move quickly, and, as the years drag on, changes in personnel, issues, and public values may make it difficult to muster again the citizen support necessary to secure congressional authorization and funding.

Practical Insights

1. After the fact mitigation of environmental losses is difficult in that separate authorization and appropriation are required. Even with strong public support, elected officials are not easily convinced of the merits or need for such a project.

2. The general public has little understanding of the legislative process and the time and commitment required to secure a congressional authorization. Without knowledgeable, committed leadership it is difficult to maintain strong public interest and support.

3. A major challenge facing environmental coordinators is the monitoring of the Washington climate to know when Congress is receptive to proposals in support of the environment. Rallying the public pressure at this time to confirm the benefits of the proposal in a legislator's mind can result in major environmental victories.

CASE 2: WITHDRAWAL OF WATER FROM THE JAMES RIVER BY THE CITY OF SPRINGFIELD, MISSOURI

In 1978, Springfield, a rapidly growing city in southwest Missouri, announced plans to supply municipal water by withdrawing water from the James River, a high-quality, free-flowing Ozark stream that supported considerable public use, including fishing, canoeing, and swimming. Because the project involved the placement of fill material in U.S. waters, the Clean Water Act required that an authorizing permit (404) be secured from the COE. As a state agency that reviews such authorization requests, the MDC was provided the opportunity to comment on how public resource values would be impacted by the project. Since the city's proposal appeared capable of severely dewatering the river in times of low flow, our primary concern was to ensure an adequate flow regime to protect the aquatic resources and other instream values of the James River.

A procedure, known as the Instream Flow Incremental Methodology, was used by MDC and FWS to determine how much living space was available in the stream at several flow rates for four representative fish species. It was determined that the proposed withdrawal of 76 million l per day and a minimum flow of 0.24 cu m per second could result in a habitat loss of up to 50% thereby severely degrading public resource values. By again using the Instream Flow Incremental Methodology, an alternative flow regime that would minimize the habitat loss was developed and presented.

Public Interest

A draft environmental impact statement was prepared by COE that identified the significant adverse impact the project would have on environmental and recreational resources in the James River. The trade-offs between the proposed project and alternatives therefore become public knowledge. As part of the review process, COE held a public meeting. A highly informed, vocal public expressing concern for resource values in the James River and scientifically established alternatives combined to convince the reluctant city utility that an alternate plan should be adopted. Negotiations began that led to the utility's restudying the project feasibility in light of the recommended alternate flow regime. A binding agreement was reached that protected instream values of the James River and still allowed the utility to proceed with an expanded water supply system.

Practical Insights

1. Professional credibility is critical in communicating with project developers, regulatory agencies, and a concerned public.

2. An educated, informed, participating public is important in communicating the best public interest to decision makers, such as COE and city fathers.

CASE 3: HARRY S. TRUMAN DAM AND RESERVOIR

The 22,275-ha Harry S. Truman Dam and Reservoir (HST) is located in west central Missouri on the Osage River. Completed by the COE in 1979, the primary project purposes are flood control and hydropower.

Public Interest

From the outset, HST was the focus of public debate and controversy. In a 1973 lawsuit, environmental interests unsuccessfully attempted to stop construction and avoid anticipated severe impacts on fish, wildlife, and forest resources of high public value. Faulty design and early operational problems resulted in numerous fish kills, which served to keep the project in the public limelight. As the project completion date neared, a draft environmental impact statement was released that revealed that the hydropower and pumpback operation could have serious adverse impacts on fish and wildlife resources and recreational use on Lake of the Ozarks, a 22,275-ha privately owned reservoir with extensive recreation and real estate development, immediately downstream of HST. Fears generated by the report were realized in 1982 when a three-hour test of two pumps killed over 746 kg of fish. Simple mathematics revealed that planned pumpback operation for one year could destroy up to one-fifth of the estimated fish population in Lake of the Ozarks. In response to extensive media coverage, a new public outcry arose for making the project a "good citizen." Operation of the project without protection of the downstream fishery was not acceptable.

As the state agency responsible for Missouri's fishery resources, MDC assisted in producing factual information and interpreting data and reports for attentive publics. Emotions ran high as an educated citizenry pressured elected officials to protect their interests. The hundreds of phone calls, stacks of letters, and numerous meetings, plus general citizen foment in the region, led to a meeting between the governor and the division engineer responsible for the project. The ultimate result was the formation of the Harry S. Truman Coordination Team, a group with representatives from the COE, state and federal agencies, elected officials, power companies, and private citizens groups.

The coordination team was charged with seeking a compromise that would minimize adverse impacts to downstream resources and still permit some level of hydropower generation. Although the ultimate operation of the project is still in question, the planned hydropower pumpback operation appears to have been eliminated and other project modifications may be in the offing.

Practical Insights

1. Factual information on impacts to fish and wildlife resources can play the crucial role in stimulating public action.
2. The media can be effectively used to heighten public awareness and concern when important resource values are at stake.

3. Negotiation and compromise are two essential ingredients in any coordination process. When communication between opponents and proponents ceases, problem resolution is difficult if not impossible.

4. The roles played by federal and state agencies in impact assessment and mitigation can change depending on circumstances and issues. For example, a federal water resource agency and a state fish and wildlife agency normally might be allies in attempting to mitigate resource losses. In another instance, like HST, these same state and federal agencies might be at odds over identifying and rectifying problems.

5. Elected officials, the voice of the people, play an important role in applying the necessary pressure for conflict resolution.

CASE 4: MERAMEC PARK LAKE

The Meramec River is a high-quality, free-flowing Ozark stream located in east central Missouri. Its close proximity to the St. Louis urban area makes it highly favored as a canoeing and float-fishing stream. In 1966, Congress approved a COE plan to construct five major reservoirs in the Meramec River Basin. Flood control, recreation, and water supply were among the major benefits promised the public. Meramec Park Lake, the largest of the proposed reservoirs at 12,600 surface acres, would only be a one-hour drive from St. Louis.

Public Interest

Federal and state resource agencies joined with a small segment of the public early in the project in lamenting the loss of a natural river and its abundant fish and wildlife resources. This proclamation of concern, however, was all but drowned out by prodevelopment interests. Project lands were acquired and a visitor center constructed; the lake seemed as good as built.

Then came federal legislation of the late 1960s and 1970s, such as the National Environmental Policy Act and the Endangered Species Act, which required a full accounting of the environmental impact of major federal construction projects. Preparation of a draft environmental impact statement by COE stimulated the FWS to quantify resource impacts for their Coordination Act Report. Using a habitat evaluation procedure developed by the FWS and MDC, impacts of the reservoir construction project were identified and weighed. The rich, diverse, natural environment that would be impacted was found to be difficult, if not impossible, to replace. Offsetting losses to terrestrial habitat alone would require the acquisition of many more acres of habitat than were contained in the entire project.

The report sent shock waves through the public and decision makers alike. Through several years of debate, it was becoming clear that public interest in the project was changing. The Fish and Wildlife Report fed the fires of concern and changed the minds of many people previously neutral on the project. An aroused public demanded a second say on the merits of the project.

Ultimately, the state legislature acted to determine the will of the people through a referendum in the 10 eastern Missouri counties that would be most directly affected by the project. The fate of unique environmental resources was the principal issue at stake. When the polls closed, the message communicated by a majority of the people was that the effort to build the dam should be terminated. Soon thereafter, Congress moved to deauthorize the dam and set up a means to protect the river environment. Most of the land acquired for the reservoir project is to be sold back to private citizens. A modest amount was added to existing state parks and wildlife areas to protect further the public interest and the river.

Practical Insights

1. This 15-year issue is a clear illustration that public values either change or can be changed with better information. As environmental coordinators, we have a responsibility to be sensitive to these changes or to situations in which changes might be made. As brokers of environmental information, we need to be absolutely sure of our facts.

2. Putting a price tag or yardstick on environmental resources is extremely difficult. New and innovative ways to evaluate and quantify resource values made a difference in the Meramec case. However, a keener insight to environmental conditions and a more sophisticated public demand that we constantly improve our evaluation skills.

3. Effective communication with the public and elected officials is critically important in resource issue resolution. In the Meramec case, our desire and effort was to remain emotionally neutral in the issue which helped maintain our credibility with both proponents and opponents.

CONCLUDING REMARKS

Several common characteristics of public involvement are apparent to some extent in each of these case studies.

Time

Projects impacting natural resources often are lengthy efforts extending over decades from the inception of the idea to completion. The slow pace at which matters proceed sometimes lulls interested government agencies and the public into complacency. To avoid this, it is essential that the public be involved at the early stages of project planning and stay involved if benefits and costs are to be evaluted and mitigated.

Mitigation of Missouri River habitat losses may never be a reality because massive modification of the channel preceded by many decades public expression of concern. In contrast, citizen involvement in Harry S. Truman and Meramec Reservoirs focused on threatening aspects of the projects and decisively changed the course of events, despite the fact that both projects were well along in their development schedules. Early public involvement in project planning, like that in the James River dewatering proposal, results in the best representation of public values in resource decisions.

Information

Just as it is critical that the public be involved at an early stage of project consideration, so is it important that the citizenry be kept informed. Resource values, impacts, and trade-offs must be spelled out in clearly understandable terms. Timely, accurate, and reliable information builds credibility with the public. An informed, educated public is indispensable in defining issues and resolving conflicts.

Scale of Involvement

Decision makers are particularly sensitive to the sheer number of citizens expressing concern and the range of interests represented by these citizens. We like to imagine that in a democracy, the voices of a few are heard in the decision-making process. Although this indeed may be the case, experience has shown that the more voices raised in support of a common cause, the more likely they are to be heard. Similarly, as the range of interests becomes more diverse, the likelihood of the citizenry being heard increases. An important exception is "political muscle." For example, it is remarkable how strong the single voice of a local garden club can suddenly become when one letter from the governor joins it in expressing concern over the fate of a rare orchid.

In the final analysis, environmental coordination is something of an art. Each case or incident is different, and there is no systematic process or "cookbook" to which one can refer. The art of assessment and mitigation blends laws and regulations, resource values, and public interest to yield a resource management strategy conserving our natural environment while serving society.

Chapter 23

The Role of Values
and Valuing in Wildlife
Communication and Education

R. Ben Peyton and Daniel J. Decker

Communication and education (C&E) programs are important aspects of wildlife management. Such programs, in a variety of forms, are conducted by state and federal wildlife management agencies, state cooperative extension services, and private wildlife conservation organizations. These C&E programs perform a difficult role in bringing public involvement to decision making and in influencing public perception of and behavior toward wildlife resources and their management. The traditional focus of these C&E efforts has been to raise informational levels of the public (Hendee 1972, Witter and Sheriff 1983). The basic assumption of many C&E programs has been that an informed individual will make the right (desired) decisions and follow the appropriate behavior—an assumption based on the theory of cognitive consistency. Indeed, considerable evidence indicates that people do tend to behave in a manner consistent with what they know (that is, cognitive structure) (Heberlein and Black 1981).

Nevertheless, behaviors of wildlife resource users do not always seem consistent with their knowledge. Jackson et al. (1979) found waterfowl violators were more likely than nonviolators to belong to Ducks Unlimited and to read technical magazines for information about hunting skills. One could assume these violators had at least equal—if not more—opportunity to be exposed to information about waterfowl regulations, penalties, and needs as nonviolators. In another study of 82 anglers who reported they had eaten fish from contaminated waterways in southeast Michigan, 71 admitted they had read some sort of advisory warning against consumption (G. Rodabaugh, Ph.D. candidate, Mich. St. Univ., pers. commun.).

We are not suggesting that efforts to inform wildlife resource users are ineffective. Rather, we want to illustrate the need to improve our C&E effectiveness by identifying and addressing a wider range of factors that influence wildlife resource users' behavior. Many of the factors that require more attention in C&E programs relate to the values and valuing processes that are components of public attitudes and often play key roles in creating wildlife issues. The purpose of this chapter is to operationalize this values component further and to emphasize the need for professionals to develop effective means of incorporating this dimension in wildlife C&E programs.

The term *values* is defined here as those standards held by an individual that influence perceptions of fact and are used to guide choice and action. (See Brown [1984] for a more detailed discussion of held and assigned values.) Beliefs differ from values in that the word *beliefs* refers to what the individual perceives to be knowledge (fact) (e.g., the belief that clear-cutting improves white-tailed deer habitat). However, values will influence how beliefs are formed, and beliefs influence how values are prioritized. The formation of attitudes involves a number of valuing processes, including identifying pertinent values and beliefs relative to an issue, establishing priorities of relevant values, and evaluating consequences for those value priorities. The resulting perceptions may be simple or extremely complex, stable or unstable, but they largely determine attitudes about the issue. A more detailed discussion of the attitude formation process and its implications for C&E programs has been presented by Langenau and Peyton (1982).

Knowledge of values and beliefs held by segments of the public can help make C&E attempts to influence behaviors more effective. For example, a study of waterfowl hunters in Florida showed that hunters opposed to steel shot placed higher value priority on satisfactions associated with shooting skills and bagging game than on enhancing habitat quality for game and nongame species. They also held erroneous beliefs regarding the severity of the lead-poisoning problem and the effectiveness of steel shot as a solution (Myers 1985). C&E efforts to increase voluntary use of steel shot based on an appeal to ecologistic values (Kellert 1978) would have little influence on that group of Florida hunters.

C&E roles in helping to resolve wildlife issues (e.g., controversial management plans) are difficult, and the needs for incorporating values dimensions are complex. Peyton (1985) has proposed that most issues are created by conflicts in public values and that C&E efforts must analyze the issue and respond to public value as well as to public belief and science/technology components. Certainly, effective communication of information to public segments before and during the period of their attitude formation about an issue can be an important factor in the outcome of most such issues. However, equally important dimensions are how thoroughly public segments are aware of their own priorities

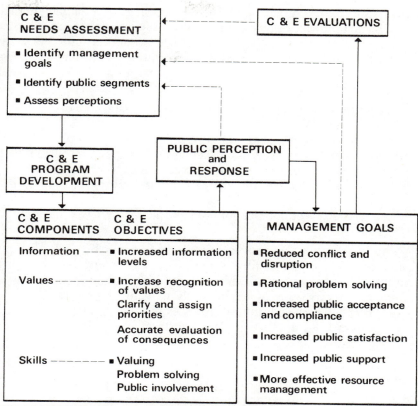

Figure 23.1 The role of values and valuing in wildlife communication and education

and the extent to which they have identified their values, evaluated consequences, and set priorities for those values (Fig. 23.1). Individuals or groups often polarize on one value without considering consequences to other values. This happens frequently when resource issues are allowed to become disruptive and public groups defend their positions rather than work toward joint solutions. For this and other reasons C&E efforts can be more effective at earlier stages of resource controversies. It is incumbent upon wildlife agencies to foresee controversial issues and take a proactive approach, via C&E, to minimize the probability of conflicts between public segments or between a public group and the agency.

As shown in Figure 23.1 in addition to the current state of held-value priorities, agencies must consider the valuing processes. Citizens must be skilled in values processes and problem solving if resource

managers are to accommodate the growing demand for public participation in management, resolve the many issues involving ethical conflicts
between users, and refine the role of ethics in guiding user behavior
toward wildlife resources. Skills involved in valuing and problem solving
include the abilities to

1. recognize all affected values in a resource issue
2. clarify and assign value priorities
3. empathize with differing value positions
4. differentiate the roles of public beliefs and values in resource issues
5. accurately evaluate the potential consequences of actions
6. accept the limitations of science—and its utility—in making decisions
7. use available communication and problem-solving pathways

We recognize that this task is difficult and cannot be performed by
all members of the public. Identifying public values and incorporating
them into C&E design may be easier to do than finding C&E strategies
to promote effective use of public skills in valuing processes. In the
rest of this chapter we will discuss instances in which values and valuing
processes have been applied to C&E efforts and will illustrate further
needs for these strategies.

ASSESSING HELD VALUES FOR C&E
AND RESOURCE MANAGEMENT

Mattfeld et al. (1984) have reviewed several projects funded by the
New York Department of Environmental Conservation (DEC) that have
assessed held values of public segments and have used these measures
to develop management plans and to improve communication efforts.
Several of these projects involved an instrument developed and standardized by Purdy et al. (1984), which allows groups to be typed
according to the importance each group places on three value dimensions
of wildlife species. The instrument uses measures of attitudes regarding
(1) economic/extractive use beliefs, (2) noneconomic/nonextractive use
beliefs, and (3) wildlife damage tolerance beliefs (Decker 1985). The
survey instrument was used to

1. analyze attitudes of landowners towards black bears (Purdy et al.
   1984) and beavers (Purdy et al. 1985)
2. determine differences in held values between resource managers
   and public groups (Purdy et al. 1983)

3. identify taxpayers who made voluntary contributions to a wildlife tax check-off program (Brown et al. 1986)
4. understand the values held by leaders of organizations having an interest in deer management (Smolka and Decker 1985)
5. examine the values characteristics of suburban residents toward deer in their community (Decker and Gavin 1985)

In other studies in upstate New York, researchers measured values of several groups (e.g., opinion leaders, landowners) concerning illegal deer kill. Findings that target groups already disapproved of illegal deer kill caused the DEC to change earlier plans for a C&E program to shift attitudes against deer poaching. Efforts were instead directed toward providing opportunities for area residents to take action against illegal activities.

Kellert (1978) developed a typology of nine attitude domains held toward animals. The evaluative component of each attitude domain suggests that they are reflecting key values. Kellert's findings for the general public, hunters, antihunters, and other groups have implications for C&E efforts.

For example, Kellert's findings that antihunting is primarily motivated by moralistic and humanistic values (concern for individual animal rights and welfare) rather than by the ecological value of species indicate that ecological defenses of hunting would have little influence on people holding strong antihunter attitudes. However, a much larger group of nonhunters does not reject hunting or management but has concerns reflecting a broad set of values relating to hunter behavior (Rohlfing 1978, Shaw 1981). C&E programs should recognize these values and provide pertinent information to allow an evaluation of hunting by nonhunters. Because many of these values relate to hunter behavior, C&E should also make hunters aware of the legitimacy of nonhunter concerns and the consequences of inappropriate hunter behaviors. Hunters who destroy property, trespass, and so on may not have placed high priority on the values of hunting jeopardized by their behavior.

Some traditional conceptualizations of wildlife and wildlife users need rethinking in view of recent studies of wildlife values. The utility of one common dichotomy of wildlife users—consumptive versus non-consumptive—has come under considerable scrutiny. These classifications have traditionally been associated with stereotyped values. However, Connelly et al. (1985) have shown that consumptive and nonconsumptive wildlife users are often the same individuals. Classifying a person exclusively into one class has led to the equivalent of perceptual and programmatic blinders for wildlife managers. Again, without ignoring the benefits of identifying public segments, we must strive to understand people's full range of values relative to wildlife or we cannot hope to serve the public's interests.

An additional, important aspect of the values dimension in wildlife management involves the unanticipated influence that management or C&E programs may have on public values. Brown et al. (1984) found that landowners who spend much time on their property and those who are more actively involved in the use of the forest and wildlife resources on their property posted at significantly higher rates than those who were not actively involved in resource use or improvement. Brown et al. (1984) raised the question of whether state and federal C&E programs to encourage landowners to engage in wildlife habitat enhancement are producing the unforeseen by-product of closure of recreational access to private lands, a situation that has been the focus of many agency C&E programs with the aim of increasing public access. Put another way, have C&E programs designed to influence one set of landowner values (stewardship of wildlife resources) inadvertently influenced a related set of values (protection or private use of those resources because of personal investment) that generally is not considered in the public's best interest in many areas of the country? This dilemma points out the great importance of thoroughly analyzing the values dimensions and impacts of a C&E program in relation to other C&E programs or management goals.

THE ROLE OF VALUING SKILLS IN RESOURCE C&E

Training procedures in values education are being implemented in formal disciplines such as environmental education for public school children (Superka et al. 1976, Caduto 1983). Formal education offers some guidelines for C&E efforts aimed toward preparing children for a role in managing and using natural resources. As a part of their citizen hotline program (Report All Poaching, R.A.P.), the Michigan Department of Natural Resources funded the development of a values education program for use in middle schools based on several of the values education strategies available (Peyton and Dudderar 1982).

Central to the curriculum design was the theory proposed by Kohlberg (1976) that individuals pass through several moral reasoning stages. Educational activities can be designed to assist the development of children through these stages (Iozzi 1980, Rest 1974). The objectives of the program were to develop students' valuing skills and provide an opportunity for students to consider their own values concerning poaching and reporting poaching activities, as well as to increase student awareness of the R.A.P. program and teach skills for observing and reporting violations. The unit was not developed to indoctrinate students with antipoaching values; it was designed to allow students to investigate freely and openly the values, morals, and consequences involved in the poaching issue. This skill-oriented approach is consistent with the recommendation by educators (e.g., Iozzi 1980) that students should be prepared with skills for solving future problems rather than being indoctrinated with values and answers with limited stability and usefulness.

Jackson and Moe (1985) have suggested that values education also be applied to hunter education programs to increase ethical behavior of hunters. They criticized traditional approaches and called for the use of values strategies that involve students in the necessary valuing processes. Further, since many of the value decisions facing adult hunters may be beyond the moral reasoning capabilities of young hunters, they recommended lifelong hunter education programs to broaden hunter understanding and capability to make ethical choices. The writers also identified the need to train hunter education instructors with these same skills if the strategies are to be implemented effectively.

The need for problem-solving and valuing skill training for adults participating in resource management appears to receive little attention. One approach to resolving value conflicts, which holds promise for resource issues that have not yet become disruptive, has been used by the Oregon Fish and Wildlife Department. Oregon wildlife biologists became concerned with harvest demands on Oregon elk herds. Further, hunter density and distribution were beginning to create hunter conflicts. Before developing a management plan, managers involved elk hunters in a process both to educate the hunter and to gain input concerning hunter preferences and concerns (Eastman 1984).

The process involved a series of local workshops conducted with the interactive method (Doyle and Straus 1976). Hunters attending the public meeting (up to 500 in some regions) were assigned to small groups (20 to 30) and given several tasks to complete, including identifying and setting priorities for concerns that should be reflected in the agency's management plan. Each small group was led by a trained facilitator who kept the group focused on tasks and prevented a vociferous few from dominating the discussions.

A number of conditions were essential to the success of the procedure:

1. Information was provided by the agency before the workshops in the form of news releases and brochures that described the hunter situation, elk herd dynamics, and potential future problems.
2. The agency restricted its role during the meeting to avoid dominating the flow of ideas.

3. The public involvement process was initiated before the issues became critical. Participants were concerned but open to new perspectives.
4. Facilitators and recorders were available who had been well trained to perform their tasks.

The workshops were not formally evaluated, but a number of outcomes were observed (C. Hamilton, Oreg. Dep. Fish and Wildl., pers. commun.). Participants provided managers with needed information on concerns and preferences. More important, participants shared perspectives and had an opportunity to consider alternative views in the value-fair environment provided. Hunters better understood the complexities of management decisions facing the agency. Finally, both the agency and the public developed new perspectives, skills, and rapport that should make future interactions more successful. Whether the resulting management plans are better supported by Oregon elk hunters remains to be discovered as the agency process continues.

Although Oregon managers perceived that their workshops offered real successes, workshops held by the U.S. Forest Service were no more successful in helping the Forest Service reach consensus with workshop attenders than did other involvement techniques (Twight and Carroll 1983). Both those who attended workshops and nonattenders held distorted views of the Forest Service position on the issue and doubted whether their views would be considered by the agency in making the final decision. The Forest Service may have had poor results because of an advanced stage of the land use issue, previous credibility problems, and/or the workshop technique used. However, just holding workshops clearly does not necessarily reduce conflict between participants.

Cooperative extension also has an active adult education program in which wildlife values education is a significant element. Of particular importance is education to increase the integration of wildlife values in land use decisions and management. In some instances, cooperative extension may be able to work more effectively with a particular audience than a state wildlife management agency. Cooperative or coordinated C&E efforts between cooperative extension and wildlife management agencies are common, especially when issues involve landowner groups, such as the posting/access and hunter behavior issue and wildlife habitat enhancement on private lands.

One example of a cooperative extension program that incorporated an assessment of values and used valuing processes involved forest management workshops held for Michigan landowners (G. Dudderar, ext. specialist, Mich. St. Univ., pers. commun.). Early workshops, which emphasized use of tree harvest to generate income and offset costs of land ownership, resulted in disappointment by participants because income contributed so little toward actual costs of owning forest land. A survey of Michigan landowners revealed that they held a range of values for owning forest lands. Although income was rated high as a reason for ownership, several noneconomic values were rated even higher, including personal satisfaction of ownership, place for escape from routine, and aesthetic appreciation. The workshop was redesigned to encourage participants to evaluate forest management practices with a range of noneconomic values as a part of the decision-making process.

VALUES TRAINING FOR RESOURCE MANAGERS

For C&E efforts to deal with values dimensions to be successful, additional attention must be given to values and valuing skills of resource managers. Evidence exists that managers may not be adequately prepared to understand value conflicts and implement valuing skills in working with publics (Purdy et al. 1983, Peyton and Langenau 1985). Henning (1980) has discussed the lack of values training for environmental professionals and summarized very well the role of such training in enhancing public participation.

> Value awareness training [of environmental professionals] could greatly enhance public participation, particularly if the public is clearly and nontechnically informed of value judgements by personnel. Too often, public participation becomes a farce with the agency position based on a given value premise which is fortified and backed with technical data and expert opinion. Inservice in public participation often involved techniques and methods on how to plan, handle, and assess it with little attention to value aspects and judgements which are and should be available to the public. Value awareness training could provide perspectives and analysis on agency operations for identifying and bringing public value judgements to the attention of the public. (1980:7)

Although training needs must be better defined for specific situations, generally it appears that many resource managers are in need of training that (1) broadens awareness of their own values and of public values, (2) increases their skills in using the valuing processes, and (3) makes them skilled in finding ways of incorporating this dimension into the management process.

CONCLUSION

In this chapter our initial intent was to review a number of projects that had first assessed public values in a wildlife issue, and then designed, implemented, and evaluated a C&E program based on the assessment. If such complete efforts exist, they are difficult to find in wildlife management literature. Many investigations identified public values, beliefs, and/or attitudes, but application of these results to C&E program design was not reported. There apparently is a need for an increased effort to utilize values information in C&E programs and to report formal evaluations of the strategies. The need is especially critical to develop and evaluate means of facilitating public valuing processes and choices, given the increasing demand for public participation to resolve value laden wildlife issues.

Acknowledgments.—A contribution of Michigan Agriculture Experiment Station (journal number 11808), New York Federal Aid to Wildlife Restoration Project:W-146-R and Cornell Agricultural Experiment Station Hatch Project 147407.

REFERENCES

BROWN, T. C. 1984. The concept of value in resource allocation. Land Econ. 60(3):230–246.

BROWN, T. L., D. J. DECKER, AND J. W. KELLEY. 1984. Access to private lands for hunting in New York: 1963–1980. Wildl. Soc. Bull. 12:344–349.

———, N. A. CONNELLY, AND D. J. DECKER. 1986. First-year results of New York's "Return a Gift to Wildlife" tax checkoff. Wildl. Soc. Bull. (In press.)

CADUTO, M. 1983. A review of environmental values education. J. Environ. Educ. 14(3):11–21.

CONNELLY, N. A., D. J. DECKER, AND T. L. BROWN. 1985. New opportunities with a familiar audience: where esthetics and harvest overlap. Wildl. Soc. Bull. 13:399–403.

DECKER, D. J. 1985. Agency image: a key to successful natural resource management. Trans. Northeast Fish and Wildl. Conf. 41:(in press).

———, AND T. A. GAVIN. 1985. Public tolerance of a suburban deer herd: implications for control. *In* Proc. 2nd East. Wildl. Damage Control Conf., Raleigh, N.C. (In press.)

DOYLE, M., AND STRAUS, D. 1976. How to make meetings work. Jove Publ., Inc., New York. 298pp.

EASTMAN, D. L. 1984. What do elk hunters want? Oreg. Wildl. 39(8):3–6.

HEBERLEIN, T. A., AND J. S. BLACK. 1981. Cognitive consistency and environmental action. Environ. and Behav. 13(6):717–734.

HENDEE, J. C. 1972. Challenging the folklore of environmental education. J. Environ. Educ. 3:19–23.

HENNING, D. H. 1980. In-service training for environmental personnel: a critical analysis with innovations. J. Environ. Educ. 11(4):4–10.

IOZZI, L. A. 1980. Evaluation of "Preparing for Tommorow's World"—science/ technology/society for grades 7–12: methodology and results. Pages 341–361 *in* A. B. Sacks, L. L. Burrus-Bammel, C. B. Davis, and L. A. Iozzi, eds.

Current issues VI: the yearbook of environmental education and environmental studies. ERIC/SMEAC, Columbus, Ohio.

JACKSON, R. M., AND H. E. MOE. 1985. The future for outdoor training. Trans. North Am. Wildl. and Nat. Resour. Conf. 50:121–130.

———, R. NORTON, AND R. ANDERSON. 1979. Improving ethical behavior in hunters. Trans. North Am. Wildl. and Nat. Resour. Conf. 44:307–318.

KELLERT, S. R. 1978. Attitudes and characteristics of hunters and anti-hunters. Trans. North Am. Wildl. and Nat. Resour. Conf. 43:412–423.

KOHLBERG, L. 1976. Moral stages and moralization: the cognitive-development approach. Pages 31–53 *in* T. Lickona, ed. Moral development and behavior: theory, research and social issues. Holt, Rhinehart and Winston, New York.

LANGENAU, E. E., JR., AND R. B. PEYTON. 1982. Policy implications of human dimensions research for wildlife information and education programs. Trans. Northeast Sect. Wildl. Soc. 39:119–135.

MATTFELD, G. F., D. J. DECKER, T. L. BROWN, S. L. FREE, AND P. R. SAUER. 1984. Developing human dimensions in New York's wildlife research program. Trans. North Am. Wildl. and Nat. Resour. Conf. 49:54–65.

MYERS, C. G. 1985. Factors influencing waterfowl hunter attitude and behavior toward steel shot. M.S. Thesis, Dep. Fish. and Wildl., Michigan State Univ., East Lansing. 105pp.

PEYTON, R. B. 1985. A typology of natural resource issues with implications for resource management and education. Mich. Acad. XVII(1):49–58.

———, AND G. DUDDERAR. 1982. To R.A.P. or not to R.A.P.: a values education curriculum for middle school. Law Enforcement Div., Mich. Dep. Nat. Resour., East Lansing. 83pp.

———, AND E. E. LANGENAU, JR. 1985. A comparison of attitudes of BLM biologists and the general public toward animals. Wildl. Soc. Bull. 13:117–120.

PURDY, K. G., D. J. DECKER, AND T. L. BROWN. 1983. Identifying the attitudinal basis for "Bureau of Wildlife/Wildlife Interest Group" perceptual disparity in wildlife values attributes. Pittman-Robertson Proj. W-146-R-9, Dep. Nat. Resour., N.Y.S. Coll. Agric. and Life Sci., Cornell Univ., Ithaca, N.Y. 55pp.

———, ———, AND ———. 1984. Standardizing basic wildlife attitudes and values data acquisition methods. Pittman-Robertson Proj. W-146-R-8, Dep. Nat. Resour., N.Y.S. Coll. Agric. and Life Sci., Cornell Univ., Ithaca, N.Y. 30pp.

———, ———, R. A. MALECKI, AND J. C. PROUD. 1985. Landowner tolerance of beavers: implications for damage management and control. *In* Proc. 2nd East. Wildl. Damage Control Conf. Raleigh, N.C. (In press.)

REST, J. R. 1974. Developmental psychology as a guide to value education: a review of Kohlbergian programs. Rev. Educ. Res. 44:241–259.

ROHLFING, A. H. 1978. Hunter conduct and public attitudes. Trans. North Am. Wildl. and Nat. Resour. Conf. 43:404–411.

SHAW, W. W. 1981. Wildlife interest groups and wildlife management agencies. Proc. Int. Assoc. Fish and Wildl. Agencies 70:39–40.

SMOLKA, R. A., JR., AND D. J. DECKER. 1985. Identifying interest groups' issue positions and designing communication strategies for deer management in New York. Trans. Northeast Fish and Wildl. Conf. 41:(in press).

SUPERKA, D. P., C. AHRENS, J. E. HEDSTROM, L. J. FORD, AND P. L. JOHNSON. 1976. Values education sourcebook. Social Sci. Educ. Consortium and ERIC/ Clearinghouse for Social Studies/Social Sci. Educ., Boulder, Colo. 259pp.

TWIGHT, B. W., AND M. S. CARROLL. 1983. Workshops in public involvement: do they help find common ground? J. For. 81:732–735.

WITTER, D. J., AND S. L. SHERIFF. 1983. Obtaining constituent feedback: implications for conservation programs. Trans. North Am. Wildl. and Nat. Resour. Conf. 48:118–124.

Chapter 24

Wildlife Policy
and Monitoring Public Values

Daniel J. Witter and Steven L. Sheriff

Wildlife policy ultimately is determined by the board, commission, director, or legislature at whose discretion the staff of a state or federal resource agency serves. At these highest administrative levels decisions are made to buy habitat, hire personnel, set seasons, set bag limits, construct lakes and river accesses, reestablish wildlife populations—any of a multitude of decisions that must be made regarding allocation of scarce public resources for wildlife and fisheries management.

The wildlife professional usually initiates and develops the plans that appear as agenda items on which top administration must act. Professionals who can influence the ways public interests are represented in policies range in level from the wildlife division chief, who manages a multifaceted program involving millions of dollars; to the assistant manager of a wildlife area, who might recommend where wildlife food plots are located, thus influencing distribution of wildlife and accessibility of animals to area users; to the conservation agent or officer, who, as the enforcer of many agency policies, can generate either public support or disdain by his conduct, attitude, and even appearance.

Formulation and evaluation of wildlife policy should be seen as an ongoing process, not as, "well, that's that." Most seasoned wildlife professionals recognize that the process involves (1) collection of resource information measuring population status and habitat quality and (2) assessment of public expectations through phone calls, letters, meetings, and social research. Both demand continuous monitoring of responses to the policy by wildlife and by the public.

The three case studies that follow summarize the continuing efforts of the Missouri Department of Conservation to monitor public values for wildlife and to use the information in formulating and evaluating policy and programs. One case study examines formulation of a conservation education program. Two case studies of policy evaluation are presented, one examining the values of private landowners involved in a technical assistance program and the other examining the interests of users of a state wildlife management area.

CASE 1: EARLY CHILDHOOD EDUCATOR SURVEY

Formulating wildlife policy is rarely easy. However, for many of the decisions on which resource professionals must take action—regulations, habitat management—past experience aids in policy formulation. Moreover, social research directed at the traditional constituency of sportsmen gives additional clues for policy development (e.g., Porath et al. 1980, Hicks et al. 1983). Wildlife professionals today, however, are being asked to go beyond familiar areas of policy formulation and provide innovative services appealing to new or broader constituencies. Following is an example of this approach, involving social research directed at a new clientele.

Background

The dramatic increase in mothers working outside the home has produced a demand for formal, professionally staffed programs of care and training for preschool aged children. The staff of the Department of Conservation believes that the foundations for understanding resource issues as an adult must be laid at the earliest possible age. The education section of the department recognized that preschools were a new place in which to communicate the conservation message. But would preschool teachers welcome the message? And in what forms would they find the message most useful? To gain a better understanding of the conservation education materials and services appropriate for children in early education programs, the education section surveyed 1,008 educators serving youngsters three to five years of age.

Selected Results

Sixty percent of the early childhood educators perceived that parents viewed the primary purpose of preschool programs as "teaching"; 37% thought parents viewed the programs as a "combination of child care and teaching"; and only 3% of the respondents said parents viewed their programs as "primarily child care."

Teaching conservation or nature awareness to young children was considered "extremely important" to 65% and "moderately important" to 31%. Regular lesson plans, suggestions for conservation activities, pictures of wildlife, posters, and story books were the materials that educators thought would be most useful in helping to teach conservation.

Management Implications

Based on the results of the study, as well as the experience of educators of the Department of Conservation, a four-part program entitled Conservation Seeds was developed for the preschool level to be implemented in 1984. The materials for the program are (1) a loose-leaf activities booklet; (2) seasonal posters/pictures designed to highlight selected human activities and land uses; (3) pictures of wildlife and types of wildlife habitat; and (4) early childhood education request sheet, currently listing 30 items available to educators.

CASE 2: PAWS PARTICIPANT SURVEY

Evaluation of wildlife policy involves determining if the programs and services are meeting intended objectives. The following case study reviews an evaluation of a program implemented by the Department of Conservation to encourage private landowners to provide for wildlife.

Background

The loss of wildlife habitat on private lands throughout Missouri continues at an alarming rate. Forest conversion and intensive land use primarily have been responsible for the deterioration in both quantity and quality of habitat on private lands.

Following a severe winter in 1960, the department recognized that wildlife on private lands needed special attention. A program designed to promote wildlife management on private lands was directed by the department's conservation agents. Additional harsh winters dealt Missouri's wildlife another severe blow in 1977 and 1978. During that period, some citizens and the department again recognized that additional effort was needed to maintain and improve wildlife habitat statewide. A program called Planning Ahead for Wildlife Survival (PAWS) was developed in early 1979 and supplied interested landowners with food plot seed and wildlife cover bundles.

The program grew quickly, requiring substantial staff time. For example, in 1982, conservation agents contacted roughly 12,000 people about the PAWS program; 4,505 of these, or slightly more than one-third, requested and were given planting materials as part of their involvement. Although these went to cooperators free of charge, they cost the department $35,000 for seeds, $16,500 for trees and shrubs, and roughly $316,000 for operations and personnel.

A comprehensive survey of the program participants was conducted in 1982 to monitor the effectiveness of PAWS (Purdy 1983). The 4,505 cooperators who received planting materials constituted the sampling frame, from which 764 individuals were selected for interviews. The study consisted of three parts: (1) a personal interview with the PAWS cooperator; (2) an on-site tour of PAWS plantings and evultion of their effect on wildlife habitat using a wildlife habitat appraisal guide for bobwhite quail; and (3) a mail survey of conservation agents ($N=148$) who were responsible for the field mechanics of PAWS to determine their appraisal of program effectiveness.

Selected Results

Wildlife considerations play an important part in the land-management decisions of PAWS cooperators receiving planting materials; 39% managed their lands primarily for "wildlife/recreation." Practically all hunt, fish, and observe wildlife. Most participate in these activities on their lands. Only 23% deny public access to their land for any wildlife activity.

Nearly all cooperators feel the program is worthwhile; indeed, many believe they are having considerable effect on improving wildlife habitat. Conservation agents also see the program as worthwhile, particularly with respect to its public relations value. Agents perceive the program as having some effect on habitat, but not to the extent cooperators believe.

Evaluations of the vitality of PAWS materials planted in 1982 suggested that about one-quarter of the food plots, trees, and shrubs did not survive planting. Attempts to quantify habitat improvement associated with planting materials suggested that the plantings improved the habitats in which they are immediately located, though much of the habitat in which the materials were placed rated at least "good" before being planted.

Management Implications

PAWS program was initiated with three major objectives. The first was to create a public awareness of wildlife habitat loss on private lands. Results of the study showed that generating public awareness of wildlife habitat loss was the least successful element of the PAWS programs according to those in the best position to judge, the conservation agents administering the program. Agents observed that, after the media blitz at the start of the program, publicity regarding PAWS diminished substantially, with the brunt of program promotion falling on them.

The second objective was to develop and maintain a working relationship with private landowners. Indications of the evaluation were that PAWS is a useful program of continuing education that improves communication and strengthens relations with private landowners interested in wildlife management. The PAWS program gives agents opportunity to contact and to annually recontact landowners who have expressed interest in doing some wildlife management. Moreover, the group has proved helpful in alerting agents to wildlife violations and in providing assessments of wildlife populations. Additionally, as a satisfied constituency, the group represents a good potential source of political support.

The third objective was to provide advice, assistance, and materials to carry out a planned wildlife program that would improve wildlife habitat on private lands. The study revealed that improvement to habitat on cooperators' lands is occurring because of the planting materials program. The degree and extent of improvement remain points for continuing professional discussion, as do assertions about specific responses of wildlife populations to the presence of food plants and tree/shrub plantings.

PAWS continues today as an agency program, and 6,000 cooperators received planting materials in 1984. The program is being monitored every other year by a mail survey distributed to a sample of cooperators.

CASE 3: DEER RIDGE PUBLIC USE SURVEY

Evaluation of programs need not be directed at special initiatives and new or targeted constituencies. Indeed, evaluation of long-standing programs aimed at traditional clienteles remains an important part of the process of wildlife policy development. During the evaluation the wildlife professional can determine if specific program objectives are being met, as well as gain new insights or confirm old ideas about public values for wildlife. Following is a summary of a public use survey involving visitors to a wildlife management area owned and managed by the Missouri Department of Conservation.

Background

Participation data are the most basic indicators of the worth attached to wildlife by the public. Though not synonymous with demand as defined by economists, public use information represents a direct message from outdoor participants to wildlife administrators about the importance of wildlife. In turn, wildlife administrators use participation data to answer questions of accountability; most notable, What types of benefits are being produced with resources expended?

A related but more difficult question is how much dollar benefit is being produced, and for whom. Gross expenditures by participants provide insights into the economic activity associated with wildlife participation but do not show the worth or market value of a wildlife-related experience. Market values for wildlife generally are lacking because many public suppliers of outdoor recreation (federal and state governments) and private suppliers (private landowners) make wildlife opportunities available at no cost to participants. Consumer surplus estimates are substitutes for market values of wildlife experiences; though conceptually appealing, and despite encouraging advances in communicating the concept and methodologies (e.g., Weithman and Haas 1980, Feltus and Langenau 1984), consumer surplus in wildlife planning remains more theory than practice.

Several sources of participation data exist. The 1980 and 1985 National Surveys of Fishing, Hunting and Wildlife-Associated Recreation (U.S. Fish and Wildl. Serv. and U.S. Bur. Census 1982, U.S. Dep. Inter., 1984) represent unprecedented efforts by the U.S. Fish and Wildlife Service to provide state agencies with reliable data about participation and expenditures. Many states collect effort and harvest information, and all states have some indication of participation through permit sales.

Particularly costly and difficult to estimate are site-specific figures for public wildlife areas. This information is especially important to the Missouri Department of Conservation, which since 1977 has been involved in an accelerated land acquisition and capital improvements program funded largely by a one-eighth percent sales tax approved by the state's voters and earmarked for conservation programs. The department now owns or operates over 293,625 ha of land available for a wide variety of harvest and aesthetic activities. Over 81,000 ha of the total have been acquired using the special funding, with an additional 40,500 ha targeted.

How many persons use the public areas? For what activities? From where are they coming? These are simple questions but ones that can help the agency monitor public involvement in outdoor opportunities. To help answer questions of public use a pilot study was undertaken on the 1,788-ha Deer Ridge Wildlife Management Area in Northeastern Missouri (Sheriff and Giessman 1984). Deer, turkey, and squirrel hunting is available on the site, as is fishing in a 19-ha lake. Primitive camp sites and picnic tables are within walking distance of the lake. Rifle and trap ranges also are located on this area, and a wide variety of activities take place there, such as horseback riding, hiking, arrowhead collecting, and cross-country skiing. The area has no resident staff, but the district wildlife biologist and county conservation agent regularly inspect the area.

Four study tasks were identified: (1) determination of the types of activities in which visitors engaged and estimate the number of participants, (2) determination of types and numbers of wildlife harvested,

(3) description of selected demographic characteristics of visitors, and (4) evaluation of the data collection techniques.

Selected Results

The study was conducted from 1 October 1983 to 2 March 1984 as a pilot project. Personal interviews were conducted with 1,574 visitors to the area, representing 707 parties that were stopped as they exited the area on 111 sample periods.

Most visitors to the area were male (87%). A majority (51%) were 25 to 44 years old, with 21% older and 29% younger. Miles traveled one way to Deer Ridge averaged 130 (standard error = 2.6, range = 0.5 to 1,900). Based on zip code information, 57% of the visitors originated in the St. Louis area, about a three-hour drive from the area.

Estimates of the numbers of participants in activities during the five-month period revealed that the three most popular were camping (2,987), deer hunting (1,423), and sightseeing (1,136). Estimates of wildlife harvested during this period were 121 rabbits, 79 squirrels, and 6 quail. Deer hunters harvested 78 deer, and fall turkey hunters took 3 adult hens.

Management Implications

The principal application of public use data is provision of greater detail for a situation about which a wildlife professional has a reasonably accurate understanding based on past experience and training. The data are searched for clues to how wildlife programs can be more effective. Occasionally, however, empirical oddities emerge.

Perhaps most surprising in the Deer Ridge survey were the estimates of wildlife harvested on the area through the fall hunting seasons, particularly the small number of quail harvested. Deer Ridge was recognized in the past for providing good quail hunting. More recently, however, the area has acquired a reputation as an excellent camping and deer hunting site (confirmed by participation and harvest). Perhaps the low estimate for quail harvest is attributable to a shortcoming in the sampling procedure. Just as likely, however, the survey revealed a shift in public use, which was correctly perceived by department staff prior to the study.

More generally, fall hunting seasons at Deer Ridge apparently do not result in large harvests of rabbits and squirrels. In fact, the low numbers of animals harvested hardly support the "blood-bath" image sometimes portrayed for public wildlife areas open to the "ravages" of the general citizenry. This finding supports the desire of the department that conservation lands be used but not degraded and represent "gems" of outdoor opportunity, not "junk."

The study confirmed that a substantial amount of visitation is accounted for by St. Louis residents. Services and areas appealing to urbanites are particularly important to the department because the vote in favor of the conservation sales tax would not have carried had not residents of St. Louis, Kansas City, and Springfield so overwhelmingly endorsed the proposal (Brohn 1977).

The fact that most visitors were male was not surprising, in light of the fall season and associated hunting activities. The department, however, would like to provide recreational opportunities appealing to families, including women and children, not only to a fraternity. Heavy area use for fishing, aesthetics, and camping thought to occur through spring and summer would present a more diverse picture of users. To provide a complete profile of use and users through a year, the Deer Ridge Public Use Survey was resumed in August 1984 and conducted through August 1985. The field techniques of data collection, which were adapted from an unequal probability sampling method (Fleener 1972), were deemed satisfactory for the one-year study and likely will be used in the future to collect public use data on other wildlife areas.

CONCLUSION

Incorporation of public values into wildlife policy is a never-ending process of monitoring public participation and expectations and then blending this information with biological data, fiscal constraints, legislative climate, legal limits of agency action, and management philosophy of the agency's governing board. This process sounds like one that is complex and lengthy and involves many characters; and so it can be, particularly with wildlife issues that pit special interest groups against one another.

But more often than not, in the work-a-day world the difficult process of formulating and evaluating wildlife policy falls on the shoulders of a few. A wildlife professional sits at a desk, his or her head propped in a hand, eyes focused on data about a particular wildlife population and perhaps some information about how many people are participants in an activity and what their management preferences are. After a time, the wildlife professional concludes, "Based on this information, I think this is what we should do. I'll propose it to the Wildlife Commission." And on commission meeting day, the board can accept the recommendation, reject it, modify it, or postpone action. Matters then are made final by the board's vote—final, that is, until the next letter, phone call, or study in which the public says, "What we *really* want is. . . ." And the policy-making process continues.

REFERENCES

BROHN, A. 1977. Missouri's design for conservation. Proc. Annu. Int. Assoc. Fish and Wildl. Agencies 67:64–67.

FELTUS, D. G., AND E. E. LANGENAU, JR. 1984. Optimization of firearm deer hunting and timber values in northern lower Michigan. Wildl. Soc. Bull. 12(1):6–12.

FLEENER, G. C. 1972. Recreational use of Gasconade River. Mo. Dep. Conserv., Dingell-Johnson Proj. F-1-R-30, Study S-21, Final Rep. 53pp.

HICKS, C. E., L. C. BELUSZ, D. J. WITTER, AND P. S. HAVERLAND. 1983. Application of angler attitudes and motives to management strategies at Missouri's trout parks. Fisheries 8(5):2–7.

PORATH, W. R., S. L. SHERIFF, D. J. WITTER, AND O. TORGERSON. 1980. Deer hunters: a traditional constituency in a time of change. Proc. Annu. Int. Assoc. Fish and Wildl. Agencies 70:41–53.

PURDY, K. G. 1983. Planning ahead for wildlife survival (PAWS) planting materials evaluation. Mo. Dep. Conserv., Wildl. Div., Jefferson City. 73pp.

SHERIFF, S. L., AND N. GIESSMAN. 1984. Deer Ridge public use pilot study, 1983-84. Mo. Dep. Conserv. 88pp. (Mimeo.)

U.S. DEPARTMENT OF THE INTERIOR. 1984. Proc. Midwest Reg. Tech. Comm.: Planning for the 1985 national survey of wildlife-associated recreation. St. Louis, 13–14 June. (Unpubl.)

U.S. FISH AND WILDLIFE SERVICE AND U.S. BUREAU OF THE CENSUS. 1982. 1980 national survey of fishing, hunting, and wildlife-associated recreation. U.S. Dep. Inter. and U.S. Dep. Commer., U.S. Gov. Print. Off., Washington, D.C. 156pp.

WEITHMAN, A. S., AND M. A. HAAS. 1980. Effects of varying levels of dissolved oxygen on the trout fishery in Lake Taneycomo, Missouri. Mo. Dep. Conserv., Fish and Wildl. Res. Cent., Columbia. 148pp.

PART SIX

Wildlife Resource Value Needs

Introduction

James E. Applegate

An international symposium assembles informed and concerned individuals for a focused consideration of a topic. At minimum, the symposium performs a valuable service by providing a historical summary of past achievements. If the timing of the symposium is correct, there is a rich contribution from those who describe present activity. If the symposium is to have significance in the continuing evolution of the subject, some of the participants must provide grist for the mill of speculation on future problems and opportunities.

This final part looks to the future of economic and social values of wildlife. Four of the presenters have been asked to provide us with guidance—to consider where we *should* be going. Economist Donald Cocheba defines specific needs if economic theory and wildlife biology are to be integrated into a holistic approach to wildlife management decision making. His suggestions for fostering this cross-disciplinary approach provide much food for thought. Although policy analyst and researcher James Lyons identifies some specific gaps in information, such as the understanding of characteristics of subsets of recreational clienteles and the definition of dimensions of satisfaction in recreational experiences, he suggests that it may be more important to apply what we have already learned from past research. Communications specialist James Fazio provides some original research data—the opinions of wildlife professionals on what wildlife values need to be communicated—and suggests that we need to know our publics better, to plan our communications strategies better, and to prepare our future professionals as better communicators. Wildlife administrator Herbert Doig projects a need for better methods of quantifying wildlife values and better integration of human behavior knowledge with biological knowledge. He sees a lack of skills in the human behavior area among practicing and future managers as the principal impediment to such an integration.

And finally, we have given Edward Langenau, Jr., carte blanche to speculate on future values of wildlife to society. He identifies parameters (economic prosperity, age structure, urbanization) that have been related to wildlife values in the past, reviews projections for future changes in these parameters, and infers possible changes in society's wildlife values in coming decades.

Will Rogers told us that prediction can be difficult, especially in dealing with the future. Our authors may not be correct in all their prognostications, but they have certainly provided a rich and provocative collection of thoughts on our theme.

Chapter 25

Opportunities for Improving Wildlife Management: An Economist's View

Donald J. Cocheba

The question for humans has never been, Are we going to manipulate nature in an attempt to improve our own well-being? We have always been a part of nature, and we have always manipulated nature with the intent of sustaining ourselves and improving our lot. The relevant question is, For what purposes and to what extent are we going to manipulate nature?

Objective analyses that yield defensible answers to the second question require a multidisciplinary approach. In the realm of wildlife management, there is universal agreement that knowledge of wildlife biology and ecology is necessary for making good decisions. Information about the benefits and costs associated with alternative courses of action is also essential for making defensible wildlife management decisions. Although a significant number of wildlife managers and biologists still do not agree with the latter point, this has not kept the cold calculus of economics from wedging its way into wildlife management. Furthermore, economic arguments can be used to speak positively on behalf of wild creatures and those who value them. And, an increasing number of wildlife biologists and economists are convinced that the interests of the two disciplines overlap and that they can benefit from working with each other.

Thus, in an attempt to enhance cooperative efforts to improve wildlife management, I describe certain economic concepts and specify how, in general, they can be used as a framework for a multidisciplinary approach to wildlife managment. More specifically, I examine the relationship between biological data and the costs of alternative courses of action, define and list the sources of wildlife values, specify three valuation method requirements, assess our ability to value wildlife quantitatively, and make recommendations for improving wildlife management. My emphasis is on conceptual issues rather than the technical details of quantification.

THE ULTIMATE GOAL OF WILDLIFE MANAGEMENT

In the U.S., legislation and administrative practices dictate that publicly owned entities such as wildlife be managed in the public interest. This means that the ultimate goal of wildlife management activities should be to maximize the net benefits that members of society derive from the existence and use of wildlife.

Among other things, economics examines resource management decisions from the perspective of society as a whole. Economic theory is designed to look beyond the entities called wild animals and beyond the preferences of a few individuals or certain organizations to determine whether society as a whole would be made better off or worse off by a particular course of action. (Bishop, in Chapter 3 of this book, expands on this topic.) Thus, the ultimate goal of wildlife management and the orientation of economics coincide.

GENERAL TYPES OF WILDLIFE MANAGEMENT INFORMATION: BENEFITS AND COSTS

Maximization of society's satisfaction from the existence and use of wildlife requires determination of the optimum size and composition of wildlife populations. In fact, this can be considered the most basic wildlife management decision of all: It encompasses related habitat acquisition, control, and management decisions as well as harvesting and other species management decisions.

In agreement with the ultimate goal of wildlife management, two broad types of information are required for determining the optimum size and composition of wildlife populations: costs and benefits. If the benefits of a proposed change exceed the costs, the change should be implemented; if they do not, the change should not be made. As a concept, cost-benefit analysis is a simple common-sense idea, but to apply it is a challenge fraught with a variety of practical problems.

For clarification, consider this analogy. In managing a cow-calf operation, a rancher must decide how much land, water, fertilizer, machinery, labor, and other production inputs to use for producing calves. Knowledge of the physiological dimensions of production is necessary but not a sufficient basis for management decisions. To complete the cost information, costs of production inputs are required. On the benefits side, the market prices of various sizes and grades of calves are necessary. With both benefits and costs quantified the number and types of calves that should be produced can be determined.

In conceptualizing the problem, no significant difference exists between this management task and that faced by the manager of a wildlife agency; however, functionally there are at least five differences:

1. As compared to ranch managers, wildlife managers usually have less direct control over the physiological aspects of the production process.
2. Rather than managing a single species for a single purpose, wildlife (agency) managers are charged with simultaneously managing several species for multiple uses.
3. Instead of market prices as the indicators of value, wildlife managers must usually rely upon research generated nonmarket estimates of value.
4. Instead of having the relatively simple goal of maximizing an individual's or a family unit's welfare function, wildlife managers face the task of trying to maximize the net benefits that society derives from the existence and use of wildlife.
5. Because of political and institutional constraints, wildlife managers have less freedom and flexibility to make decisions than do their counterparts who manage privately owned businesses.

However, these differences should not be permitted to obscure the critical and fundamental point made earlier: Rational and objective wildlife management decisions require both physiological and economic information.

COST INFORMATION

Costs are technically the foregone benefits of the next best alternative use of the resources in question. Specifying the relevant cost functions requires knowledge of the physiological aspects of maintaining wildlife populations at various levels. Economists call this type of information a production function. Combining production functions with data on the cost of the required production inputs (productive resources) is necessary for generating cost functions.

Production and Cost Functions

When making species-specific wildlife management decisions, production function and production cost information is unequivocally as important as wildlife value estimates. Nevertheless, with few exceptions economists, biometricians, and wildlife management specialists have all ignored this topic. (Hammack and Brown's work [1974] is an exception.)

A detailed discussion is beyond the scope of this chapter, but several general and overlapping comments about production and cost functions are warranted.

1. A review of wildlife management texts, wildlife research periodicals, and resource economics literature suggests that biologists and economists have not made a serious attempt to communicate with each other on the topics of production-function or cost-function research. (The fisheries management literature does, to a limited extent, address this issue.)

2. The production and cost theories of economics are a good foundation to build upon. However, to be useful for wildlife management, the single time period models of the typical microeconomic theory text must be expanded to account for continuous changes over time.

3. What wildlife biologists refer to as population dynamics is not the same as the production-function concept of economics. The two concepts come closest to agreement when population size is chosen as the dependent variable of a single equation model. Since a production function is simply an input-output relationship, economists would specify categories of production inputs as the independent variables. If, for example, time is designated as the single independent variable of a sigmoid population dynamics model, the very relationships that economists consider important are obscured. In research applications several variations of the basic sigmoid model have been used, but the resulting information usually cannot be directly inserted into the decision-making models of economics. Conversely, certain population simulation models offer an excellent basis for integrating wildlife biology and economics, particularly those that attempt to explain and predict changes in population numbers over time by modeling the relationships among environment variables, animal physiology, animal behavior, and human activities. (An example and further discussion of this topic follow the next comment.)

4. Within the discipline of wildlife management there is a need for some integrating mechanism or concept. Wildlife management texts cover topics such as wildlife conservation, animal behavior, and population ecology without ever combining them into a holistic model that can be used for making management decisions. Wildlife research efforts exhibit the same lack of an overall decision-making focus. The production and cost theories of economics along with cost-benefit analysis could be used as the conceptual basis for integrating some of the disparate areas of wildlife biology into a more holistic approach to wildlife management.

A Wildlife Management Example

An example should help clarify the preceding points. For brevity, an extremely simplified hypothetical extension of Medin and Anderson's mule deer population model will be used. (For a useful summary of their work, see Robinson and Bolen 1984:43.) Based on a rough interpolation, assume that a harvest rate of 675 females and 1,000 males per year yields a stable total population of 11,000 deer over time. Next, add to the model a variable called supplemental winter feed. Furthermore, suppose that inserting a certain positive value for supplemental feed into the simulation model produces this result: Twenty-five additional females and 60 males could be harvested each year without altering the total population level. This is the type of production impact information needed for deciding whether a given supplemental feeding program should be implemented.

The next step in the analysis is to determine the cost (technically, the opportunity cost) of the feeding program. Assume it would be $5,000 per year. This figure should then be compared to the value of the additional deer produced by the program. (The question of how to value wildlife is discussed later.) If the value of the additional deer was $7,000 per year, the supplemental feeding program should obviously be implemented.

This, however, is not the end of the analysis. Economic theory (and common sense) dictates that the program be expanded until the additional costs are equal to the additional benefits. (If, initially, the costs exceed the benefits, the program should be contracted until the additional costs and benefits are equal.) In this example, one should go back to the population simulation model and start the analysis over by inserting a larger numerical value for supplemental feed. Increasing the size of the supplemental feed program would obviously increase its cost. Simultaneously, the associated benefits would decline. Thus, repeating the process with larger and larger numerical values for supplemental feed would eventually reveal the point at which the additional costs are equal to the additional benefits, and the correct level of supplemental feeding could be determined.

In summary, the basic cost-benefit analysis is not difficult to understand because it is nothing more than formalized common sense. The computer programming and mathematics required to expand the Medin and Anderson model to functionality are relatively simple. The greatest research challenges lie in specifying and quantifying the necessary population models and in estimating the related wildlife benefits. Nevertheless, both biological science and economics offer sophisticated and useful concepts for addressing the details of these tasks.

WILDLIFE BENEFITS: VALUING WILDLIFE

Economics has a long and rich history of grappling with the question: What is value and how can it be measured? It would take an entire book to detail that history and explain what we have learned about the topic. All I will attempt here is to explain, from the standpoint of economics, what value is and how the profession attempts to measure it.

A Broad Perspective

In general, economists have agreed that the value of an item is what a buyer is willing to pay for it or what a seller is willing to accept in exchange for it. When buyers and sellers freely exchange goods and services in unencumbered markets, this value is revealed. When things are not exchanged in markets, as is the case with most wildlife-related goods and services, alternative ways of measuring value must be found.

The consumer's surplus concept, with its assertion that money can be a satisfactory cardinal index of satisfaction or utility, is the economists' theoretical framework for developing approaches to quantifying wildlife values. Since money is the medium of exchange in our society, it should come as no surprise that it is the chosen yardstick. And though it is not a perfect unit of measure, no functional alternative has been found. Furthermore, there is general agreement that, of the various ways consumer's surplus can be measured, two are appropriate for measuring the value of wildlife: willingness to pay (Hicksian compensating valuation) and willingness to accept (Hicksian equivalent variation). The technical details have been discussed by others (Currie et al. 1971, Willig 1976, Hammack and Brown 1974). The concept is mentioned here simply to make it explicit that the ensuing discussion is based on consumer's surplus theory as an acceptable framework for measuring the value of wildlife.

Valuing a Site

As stated earlier, the value of wild animals per se is required for making species-specific wildlife management decisions. However, another extremely important type of decision requires a different but related kind of information. When making choices about how entire geographic areas should be used, an estimate of the total value of the goods and services produced by that site (or set of resources) is required.

For example, a corporation requests permission to develop a given area of federal land for a ski resort. The site is currently undeveloped and excellent deer habitat. Obviously, the question is which alternative will produce the largest stream of net benefits (over time) for society. It would be useful to know the value of the deer produced by the site's resources because, by itself, the value of the deer lost as a result of development may exceed the net benefits that could be generated by the ski resort. If this were the case, the decision could be made on the basis of knowing only the value of the deer and the value of the proposed alternative. Unfortunately, most comparisons are not this simple. The value of the deer is clearly not the only benefit that can be attributed to the site, and the correct choice is not likely to be so clear cut that the other sources of value can be ignored. In cases like this, a measure of the total net benefits attributable to the site is required.

Conceptually, the total value of a given site can be determined either by estimating the value of each component separately and then summing these values or by directly estimating the value of the site as a composite unit. When a site value is required, the latter is usually the best approach. Directly valuing sites is simpler, and specific defensible techniques, including the contingent valuation and travel cost methods, are available for doing so. In turn, valuing a site as a composite unit is likely to be less costly and, in most cases, less controversial than valuing wildlife populations.

The preceding qualification justifies splitting the discussion into two components: wildlife (population) valuation and site valuation. The subsequent discussion will focus on wildlife valuation.

Human Activities and Sources of Wildlife Value

The following list is offered as a starting point for identifying sources of wildlife values. Among other things, it should help researchers avoid double counting benefits. The issue of double counting is important because even a cursory examination of wildlife management texts and outdoor recreation literature reveals numerous examples of authors' listing sources of wildlife values that clearly overlap. (For example, see Brown's discussion, "Kinds of Benefits from Outdoor Recreation" [1984:214–215].) Each of the categories has in one way or another been discussed elsewhere—some in considerable detail. The flow chart presented in Figure 25.1 shows the relationship between human activities and the specified categories of value.

Recreational Hunting. Hunting is the act of pursuing wildlife with the intention of killing the quarry; if the primary purpose is recreational enjoyment, it is recreational hunting.

Commercial Hunting. Commercial hunting is hunting for the purpose of selling animal products to others. Illegal as well as legal commercial hunting is a source of wildlife benefits.

Meat Hunting. If the purpose of hunting is exclusively to provide one's family, or others, with meat and no remuneration is involved, it is meat hunting.

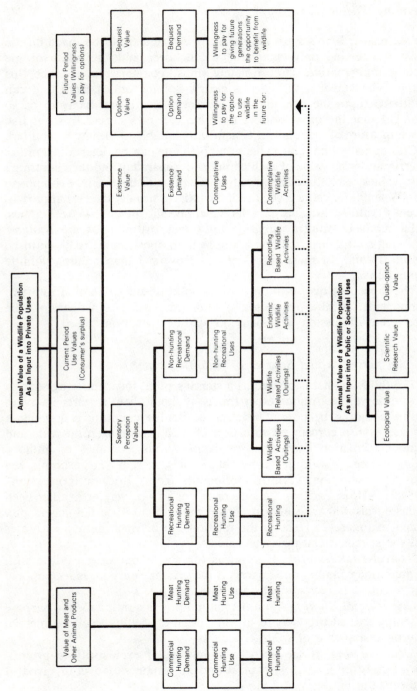

Figure 25.1 Summary of sources of wildlife value

Nonhunting Activities. Nonhunting uses of wildlife include outings, the primary purpose of which is to study, to observe, and/or to photograph wildlife. These activities are classified as wildlife-based activities. In other cases, rather than being the central focus of the recreation activity, wildlife may be one of a number of ingredients that together make up the activity. Examples of these activities include hiking, camping, canoeing, picnicking, and driving for pleasure. These activities are considered wildlife-related activities. A third group is composed of activities that are not outings in the same sense that wildlife-based and wildlife-related activities are outings. Watching wildlife at backyard feeding stations and observing wildlife from one's yard are examples of this type of activity. All wildlife-based or wildlife-related activities engaged in within the immediate vicinity of a participant's permanent residence are classified as endemic wildlife activities. A fourth category, labeled recording-based wildlife activities, includes watching wildlife films on television or at a movie theater, listening to recordings of bird songs, and participating in activities like wildlife painting and carving.

Existence Value. Each of the sources of wildlife benefits discussed so far emanate from sensory perception activities. That is, they all involve relating to wildlife through combinations of impressions received through the senses of sight, hearing, taste, smell, and/or touch. However, just knowing that wild animals exist and contemplating their existence may also give a person satisfaction. Contemplation attributable to the existence of a wildlife species and occurring in the absence of sensory contact with that species is called a contemplative wildlife activity; thus defined, it does not overlap with the previously defined wildlife activity categories.

Option Value. Option value differs from the preceding sources of benefits in a fundamental way. Those benefits can all be classified use values, that is, values resulting from effective demands for current period uses of wildlife species in some sort of activity. (In this context, current period is the year for which the value estimates are made.) Option value is not a use value but an additional source of benefits related to future time periods. More specifically, when future availability of wildlife is in doubt and/or future demand for use of a widlife species is uncertain, option value is likely to be positive. Option value can be viewed as a risk-aversion premium individuals are willing to pay for retaining an option for future use of a species. (For elaborations see Bishop 1982 and Freeman 1984.)

Bequest Value. Bequest value can be defined as the willingness to pay for ensuring that future generations will have the opportunity to benefit from the existence of a species. As this definition implies, bequest value can be considered an intergenerational option value, but Freeman

(1979) treated it as part of existence value and Krutilla (1967) considered it a separate category of value. Thus a more precise definition and the proper role of bequest value vis-à-vis existence and option values are yet to be determined.

Ecological Value. To the extent that it is not accounted for in the preference functions of individuals, the contribution that wild animals make to the viability of the earth's ecosystem should be considered a societal benefit (ecological value).

Scientific Research Value. To the extent that the benefits of the associated scientific research are not incorporated into the value of products used by individuals, the value of wildlife as an input into research processes should be considered a societal benefit (scientific research value).

Quasi-Option Value. The value of wildlife as genetic material for future research or as a future source of useful chemical compounds are additional sources of value. Arrow and Fisher (1974) called the value of preserving options, given the expectation of growth in knowledge, quasi-option value. (For additional comments on the topic, see Randall and Peterson 1984:29.) This type of option value is likely to be most important in cases in which the decremental change being considered will result in species extinction.

Terminology to Avoid

There are two reasons why the terms *consumptive use* and *nonconsumptive use* have not been employed here. First, although they are usually called nonconsumptive uses, bird watching, camping, hiking, and so on can be consumptive in the sense that they result in the destruction of habitat and/or disrupt the natural reproductive cycles of animals. Second, there are nonconsumptive aspects of hunting. For example, sighting game but not taking a shot and taking a shot that does not damage the quarry are nonconsumptive aspects of hunting. For casual discussions, these two points can be ignored, but they are important when defining how wildlife benefits should be aggregated. When specifying sources of wildlife value, the use of the terms *consumptive* and *nonconsumptive* should be avoided.

VALUATION METHODOLOGY: AN APPRAISAL

This section specifies three requirements that wildlife valuation methods must meet, identifies two methods that can fulfill these requirements, and appraises, in a general way, our ability to value wildlife. It is not a detailed critique of valuation methodology. And some of what I have to say is unquestionably esoteric. Therefore, those not familiar with the valuation methodology literature may find portions of this section difficult to understand but bear with me because you should be able to glean some useful information.

Valuation Method Requirements

The basic problem faced in attempting to value wildlife is easy to understand but difficult to solve. Species-specific management decisions require estimates of the value of wild animals per se, but the individuals who provide the necessary data for valuation attempts can be expected to think in terms of the value of activities rather than the value of the animals that help to produce the activities. Conceptually and empirically, the problem becomes one of separating the value of wildlife from the value of the other inputs used to produce wildlife benefits.

In addition, the value estimates must permit the derivation of additional or marginal benefits, and some way must be found to separate private-good from collective-good benefits. When a person consumes a particular good in such a way that no one else can consume the same good, it is conventionally called a pure private good. Pure collective goods are those that can be consumed by one individual without diminishing the quantity available to others. (For discussions of the private good–collective good aspects of wildlife valuation, see Cocheba and Langford 1978, Miller and Menz 1979, Brookshire et al. 1980.)

In summary, if the goal of wildlife valuation is to provide information for making species-specific management decisions, ways must be found (1) to isolate the value of wildlife from the value of the other ingredients which are combined to produce wildlife related activities; (2) to derive estimates of marginal net benefits; and, (3) to separate private-good benefits from collective-good benefits.

Meeting the Requirements

These three requirements can be met by both the hedonic and the contingent valuation methods, and considerable progress has been made in our ability to value wildlife. Nevertheless, there are still no published attempts to estimate all value components of a wildlife population. As dramatic as this may at first seem, it is not surprising. It is still a challenging task just to estimate the value emanating from a single source. One problem is that an approach that works for valuing a particular component may not be effective for valuing other components (Cocheba and Langford 1981). A related problem is that existing valuation methods probably cannot be used to quantify every type of value listed earlier.

Thus, our ability to value wildlife is severely constrained. When no market-generated data are available, either of two types of information must be attainable. The first type is actually a combination of two categories of data. One is an estimate of consumer's surplus (willingness to pay or willingness to accept) associated with a given activity (or population level). This measure of consumer's surplus is the dependent variable in a regression analysis. The other includes the quantity and/ or quality variables to be used as the independent variables in the regression analysis. For example, in a waterfowl hunting model, these variables could be number of birds bagged and number of days hunted, respectively. This implies use of the Hammack and Brown (1974) approach to valuing wildlife. In using it, being able to collect accurate estimates of one or more independent variables is crucial.

The other alternative for valuing wildlife is to ask respondents directly to isolate the value of wildlife from the other inputs that produce the activity or experience in question. For example, if you want to estimate the value of deer to hikers, you have to ask respondents to estimate how much value sighting a certain number of additional deer would add to the value of a given hiking experience. Recreationists, however, do not usually think about their activities in these terms, and they may not be able to provide the necessary information.

Nevertheless, there are ways to circumvent this problem. First, valuing certain components of the experience may be possible. That is, since costs are incurred that are specific to the hunting activity, ways have been found to isolate significant portions of the value of hunted species. Second, people do contribute to causes (usually through conservation organizations) that are designed to help maintain or increase the size of wildlife populations. Thus, the idea of thinking about changes in wildlife populations in dollar terms may not be totally alien to them. In the case of endangered species this idea, plus relatively greater knowledge about the species and its plight, may make a valuation attempt feasible.

Third, researchers are likely to develop new and imaginative approaches to valuing nonmarket goods and services. Improving our ability to lead respondents' thought processes that result in defensible value estimates is one way to proceed. Another is to encourage wildlife agencies to use more auction processes for allocating limited supplies of recreation opportunities. Technically, what a person is willing to pay for a right to hunt is not the same thing as the value of an animal in the stock, but wildlife agencies can and have generated some useful value information by auctioning hunting rights.

This all leads to one simple hypothesis. There is an inverse correlation between the relative importance of wildlife in producing recreation activities and the probability of being able to isolate the associated wildlife values.

A Peripheral Thought

As the foregoing implies, to estimate the value of wildlife one does not need to know anything about people's moral beliefs, their attitudes, or their motivations. For an analogy, you need not know why people use automobiles as they do to determine what they will pay for a car. However, knowing more about human motivation and behavior may be of some use in improving valuation methodology and enhancing quantitative estimates.

IMPROVING WILDLIFE MANAGEMENT: TWO APPROACHES

From an economist's perspective, there are at least two general ways to proceed with attempts to improve wildlife management. They are consistent with the previously specified conceptual framework and recognize the realities of the wildlife management job environment. First, no matter how desirable it is to compare the costs and benefits of an action and then consider the income distribution effects of that action before making a public decision, most decisions are not made objectively on the basis of facts alone. Furthermore, certain decisions will be forced on wildlife managers. When they are, there still may be opportunities to proceed rationally, and cost effectiveness may be the best goal to pursue. This simply means doing what has to be done for the lowest cost possible.

Second, in the foreseeable future, most widlife management decisions will probably continue to be made without wildlife value estimates that pertain to the particular situation of interest. When this is the case, using a cost-benefit simulation model in conjunction with a sensitivity analysis may be the best approach. If defensible estimates of wildlife value are available from other studies, they could be inserted into simulation models as a point of departure; then higher and lower value estimates could be used to carry out the sensitivity analysis. In the absence of value estimates from other studies, administrators and/or researchers may have to use their judgments to specify the wildlife values for the sensitivity analysis. Constructing the simulation model would not be a simple task. Ideally, it would necessitate describing both human behavior and the population dynamics of the species in question. Although population models and information from studies of recreation behavior may be useful, some heroic assumptions may be required for constructing the simulation model. Obviously this is a separate topic of considerable complexity, but it deserves more attention than it has been given to date.

SUMMARY AND RECOMMENDATIONS

Making objective and defensible wildlife management decisions requires combining appropriate information with an acceptable decision-making criterion. Thus, among other things, it is necessary to agree upon some ultimate goal of wildlife management. Because legislation and administrative practice dictate that publicly owned entities such as wildlife be managed in the public interest, the logical goal for wildlife management is to maximize the net benefits that society derives from the existence and use of wildlife. This, in turn, necessitates comparing the societal benefits of proposed courses of action with the societal costs of those actions.

Biological research that uses simulation models to explain and predict population changes over time is the most useful foundation for generating the necessary cost information. Since a knowledge of wildlife biology is indispensable for population studies, wildlife biologists should have the primary responsibility for doing this research; economists should probably take the lead in using the population data to generate cost information. Although not discussed here, these endeavors should not ignore what can be learned from fisheries management experiences and associated research. In any case, the ultimate objective should be to generate information that can be directly inserted into decision-making models.

This approach leads to a related but more fundamental conclusion: The wide variety of topics addressed by wildlife biologists have not been integrated into a holistic decision-making framework. It seems only reasonable that professionals who claim to be managers be concerned about this deficiency. Economic concepts could be used as the basis for integrating some of the disparate areas of wildlife biology into a more holistic approach to wildlife management.

The most detailed section of this chapter deals with the benefits side of the analysis, specifically the identification and definition of sources of wildlife value. An attempt was made to list and define sources of value in a way that avoids overlapping categories and using different names for the same sources of value. The overall goals were to eliminate confusion that arises from the narrowness that accompanies professional specialization and to provide a basis for further refinements.

Conceptually and empirically, the greatest challenge in valuing wildlife is to separate the value of wildlife from the value of the other ingredients that produce wildlife related activities. Both the hedonic method and contingent valuation technique are capable of isolating the value of wildlife. However, no one has conclusively demonstrated that it is possible to estimate the value of wildlife in nonhunting uses such as camping, hiking, watching wildlife at backyard feeding stations, and so on. Consequently, it has not been possible to quantify all sources of value emanating from a given wildlife population. Therefore, in making species-specific wildlife management decisions, the greatest potential for economics to help improve decision-making lies in game species management. To the extent that nongame species management requires information on the value of habitat, economics can also be useful. Our ability to value sites is at least as good as our ability to value wildlife in hunting uses.

Recognizing types of data that are not appropriate for species-specific decisions is as important as knowing the limits of current valuation methodology. Participation rates for various recreation activities tell us little, if anything, about the value of wildlife. Recreation-day values are not measures of wildlife value either. And, though expenditures on recreation activities, employment numbers, income figures, tax revenues, and changes in gross regional products may be useful in debating wildlife management issues in public forums, these measures should be seen for what they are—noncommensurate and overlapping estimates of economic impacts that do not measure the value of a wildlife population.

In the foreseeable future, most wildlife management decisions will probably continue to be made without the use of wildlife value estimates. The challenge to find new ways to value wildlife and improve existing techniques is as great as ever. But we need not wait for better value estimates to improve wildlife management. A restructured physiological data base in conjunction with simulation models and sensitivity analyses offer significant potential for improving our ability to make objective and defensible wildlife management decisions.

REFERENCES

ARROW, K., AND A. C. FISHER. 1974. Environmental preservation, uncertainty and irreversibility. Q. J. Econ. 55:313–319.

BISHOP, R. C. 1982. Option value: an exposition and extension. Land Econ. 58:1–15.

BROOKSHIRE, D. S., A. RANDALL, AND J. R. STOLL. 1980. Valuing increments and decrements in natural resource service flows. Am. J. Agric. Econ. 62:478–488.

BROWN, P. J. 1984. Benefits of outdoor recreation and some ideas for valuing recreation opportunities. Pages 209–220 *in* G. L. Peterson and A. Randall, eds. Valuation of wildland resource benefits. Westview Press, Boulder, Colo.

COCHEBA, D. J., AND W. A. LANGFORD. 1978. Wildlife valuation: the collective good aspect of hunting. Land Econ. 54:490–504.

———, AND ———. 1981. Direct willingness-to-pay questions: an analysis of their use for quantitatively valuing wildlife. J. Leisure Res. 13:311–321.

CURRIE, J. M., J. A. MURRAY, AND A. SCHMITZ. 1971. The concept of economic surplus and its use in economic analysis. Econ. J. 81:741–799.

FREEMAN, A. M., III. 1979. The benefits of environmental improvement. Johns Hopkins Univ. Press, Baltimore. 272pp.

———. 1984. The sign and size of option value. Land Econ. 60:1–13.

HAMMACK, J., AND G. M. BROWN, JR. 1974. Waterfowl and wetlands: toward bioeconomic analysis. Resour. for the Future, Inc., Washington, D.C. 95pp.

KRUTILLA, J. V. 1967. Conservation reconsidered. Am. Econ. Rev. 57:777–786.

MILLER, J. R. AND F. C. MENZ. 1979. Some economic considerations for wildlife preservations. South. Econ. J. 45:718–728.

RANDALL, A., AND G. L. PETERSON. 1984. The valuation of wildland benefits: an overview. Pages 1–52 *in* G. L. Peterson and A. Randall, eds. Valuation of wildland resource benefits. Westview Press, Boulder, Colo.

ROBINSON, W. W., AND E. G. BOLEN. 1984. Wildlife ecology and management. Macmillan Publ. Co., New York, N.Y. 478pp.

WILLIG, R. D. 1976. Consumer's surplus without apology. Am. Econ. Rev. 66:589–597.

Chapter 26

Basic and Applied Social Research Needs in Wildlife Management

James R. Lyons

Social research in wildlife management—or human dimensions research—is becoming an integral part of many state fish and wildlife agency programs for clear-cut reasons. First, fish and wildlife agencies are public agencies. Their mission includes maintaining fish and wildlife and their habitats to ensure their continued existence for the benefit and enjoyment of the public. To do so, agencies must determine what people want from their fish and wildlife resources. Second, people affect fish and wildlife, necessitating rules to regulate wildlife users and the effects of human activities on wildlife habitat. Third, wildlife affects people. Wildlife can add value to a residential setting and increase the quality of a recreational experience. Of course, wildlife can also damage agricultural crops, kill livestock, and harm people and their property. Fourth, the values that people place on fish and wildlife and their habitats can have a significant effect on the ways in which they are managed. These values—social, cultural, and economic—greatly influence management priorities and objectives. Finally, people are ultimately responsible for identifying fish and wildlife management needs, setting management priorities, and implementing management programs.

Recognition of the importance of the human element in fish and wildlife management was probably best expressed two decades ago by John Gottschalk, director of the Bureau of Sport Fisheries and Wildlife (predecessor to the U.S. Fish and Wildlife Service):

> The problems besetting wildlife conservation in 1966 are reasonably clear and have scarcely changed in fundamentals in recent decades. . . . We need habitats. . . . We need access. . . . We need know-how. . . . And we need public support. . . . Obviously public support is what is required to get more healthy habitat, and access to it, and scientific know-how. . . . Fish and wildlife will share the benefit when we have the facts to justify a larger role. To get the facts we need increased research—and I don't mean life history or population dynamic studies—as valuable as

they are for management purposes. We need to know our *customer* better. We need to study the markets—beyond the usual consumptive public. Who is our public—and what do they really want—and what are they willing to pay? We need to know! (1966:359–361)

The need for information on the human factor in wildlife management has grown since 1966 as the result of social changes in the United States and changes in the wildlife-related recreational interests of Americans. Some of these changes include (1) increasing rates of participation in fishing while participation in hunting, as a percentage of the adult population, remains relatively stable; (2) high rates of U.S. participation in nonconsumptive forms of wildlife-related recreation; (3) impending declines in public funding for fish and wildlife management; (4) greater involvement of the governed in government; (5) increased individual initiatives intended to solve resource management problems; and (6) growing recognition of the economic values of fish and wildlife and their habitats.

Overall, these trends serve to justify increased fish and wildlife agency research into the social aspects of wildlife management. Clearly they suggest that wildlife agencies must do a better job of defining their mission and identifying the clientele they serve. The interests and attitudes of the public regarding wildlife and their perceptions of fish and wildlife management agencies will have an even greater effect on agency programs in the future. Wildlife officials must become more cognizant of what their clients want and more objective in determining how well they are meeting these desires. Most important, agency officials must be able and willing to assess the value of their wildlife management efforts and make hard choices in setting priorities and making management decisions. Agencies must be innovative in seeking solutions to management problems, especially in identifying means to support agency programs. In addition, public fish and wildlife agencies must capitalize on private initiatives to manage, protect, and promote wildlife for profit by using the concepts of private enterprise that can be applied to public programs. Wildlife agencies must consider sharing resource management responsibility with the private sector where it is effective, and even contemplate turning some management responsibilities over to the private sector where it can function more efficiently.

BASIC SOCIAL RESEARCH NEEDS

As a result of these trends, the research that will be needed is no different from the research that John Gottschalk recommended two decades ago: We need to know who our public is, what they want, and what they are willing to pay.

Who Is Our Public?

Numerous studies have characterized hunters and fishermen. The most comprehensive of these is the series of national fishing and hunting surveys conducted by the U.S. Fish and Wildlife Service, which have permitted researchers to create demographic profiles of sportsmen nationwide (U.S. Fish and Wildl. Serv. and U.S. Bur. Census 1982). The national fishing and hunting surveys have also been extremely valuable in assessing overall participation trends. However, very few studies have sought to understand the factors that affect participation trends and, most important, what role management can play in influencing these trends.

Studies by Klessig (1972), Applegate (1977), and Langenau and Mellon (1980) yielded information on hunter initiation, participation, and desertion in Wisconsin, New Jersey, and Michigan, respectively. However, until recently, little was known regarding the factors that may influence trends in hunter participation nationwide. A recent study by Applegate et al. (1984) has shed some additional light on the dynamics of the sport hunting population; it notes that urbanization is "of equal or greater importance to the future of hunting than changes in variables that wildlife biologists can affect."

Additional information is needed to determine the characteristics of important segments or subgroups of the hunting and fishing population in order to find out how to effectively and efficiently serve them (Bryan 1979). Certain subgroups of the sportsmen population warranting special study include young sportsmen, those residing in urban areas, and older sportsmen.

Unlike studies of fishermen and hunters, profiles of nonconsumptive or appreciative wildlife users are limited. Forty-nine percent of the U.S. population 16 years of age and older participated in nonconsumptive activities in 1980 (U.S. Fish and Wildl. Serv. and U.S. Bur. Census 1982). A recent study by Shaw and Mangun (1984) described, for the first time, the characteristics and behaviors of nonconsumptive users nationwide. However, many questions remain to be answered regarding nonconsumptive wildlife users and uses: What are the major groups of nonconsumptive wildlife users—their activities, participation rates, and sociodemographic characteristics? What types of wildlife habitats, and settings are most often enjoyed by nonconsumptive users? What are the relationships between nonconsumptive and consumptive users of wildlife resources? What can wildlife managers do to provide benefits associated with nonconsumptive wildlife-related recreation?

Little is known about the views of those Americans who do not enjoy wildlife-related recreation—approximately 41% of the population (U.S. Fish and Wildl. Serv. and U.S. Bur. Census 1982). Studies by Kellert (1979, 1980) and Kellert and Berry (1980) have provided some insight into the attitudes, knowledge, and behaviors of the general public toward wildlife, but much more remains to be learned about those who exhibit little or no interest in wildlife. Given the size of this potential group of wildlife customers, investments in understanding their interests and needs could produce substantial benefits.

What Does the Public Want?

Generating satisfied customers is as important to wildlife management as it is to a private business. However, the factors that contribute to a satisfying day of fishing or a fulfilling hunt are not nearly as well understood as consumer preferences for things like perfume, chewing gum, or toothpaste.

The utility of hunter success and days afield, the traditional measures of wildlife management program effectiveness, and indices of experience quality have been questioned repeatedly. In fact, the debate continues regarding the factors associated with hunting and fishing satisfaction, the forces that motivate people to participate in these sports, and the use of this information by the fish and wildlife manager.

In recent years, the relationship between hunting success (Stankey et al. 1973), user congestion (Miller et al. 1977), and hunter satisfaction has been studied in an effort to better define a quality fishing and hunting experience. Kellert (1978, 1980) generated a typology of hunters: utilitarian meat hunters who were motivated by the value of the kill and viewed hunting as a harvesting activity; doministic/sport hunters who valued hunting for the opportunity it afforded for competition and display of shooting or hunting skills; and nature hunters whose principal motivation was the opportunity for contact with wild animals and a participatory role in nature. Knopf et al. (1973) found similar differences among the motivations for sport fishing. Basic research into the development and metamorphosis of sportsmen's motivations has also provided some insights into how levels of sporting experiences affect perceptions of fishing or hunting quality (Bryan 1979 and Jackson et al. 1979).

Some studies have attempted to assess the relationship between wildlife resources (i.e., supply) and participation in wildlife-related recreation. Miller and Hay (1981) described the relationship between acres of habitat and participation in waterfowl hunting. Similarly, Miller (1980) used measures of elk hunting opportunity to generate a model to predict hunter participation in Washington.

For nonconsumptive wildlife users, information on expectations and participant motivations remains extremely limited. With the exception of studies by Hay and McConnell (1979) and Applegate et al. (1982), few studies have been conducted to determine the relationship between participation in nonconsumptive wildlife-related recreation and experience characteristics or quality. Clearly this research subject needs further investigation.

As public demand for recreational uses of fish and wildlife grows, managers must determine how to best meet user needs with increasing limits on biological and fiscal resources. Since reductions in the quality of fishing, hunting, and other wildlife-related experiences are likely to result in fewer participants, wildlife managers must be cognizant of the quality of the products they offer. Research should focus on defining recreation quality for major wildlife user groups. When possible, the relationships between participation, experience quality, and those site characteristics that can be managed, such as crowding, hunter success, and access, should be quantified and used to guide management decisions. More important, these variables should serve as new indices of management effectiveness rather than the success ratios and days afield measures that are now used.

With regard to the general public, social research should focus on how the public perceives fish and wildlife resources, how these perceptions develop, and what can be done to promote an informed opinion of wildlife and wildlife management. Research of this nature can help fish and wildlife agencies to understand how to cope with or affect public attitudes.

A great deal of basic research has been conducted to determine the attitudes of Americans toward wildlife and their habitats. Pioneering research by Kellert (1978, 1979, 1980) and Kellert and Berry (1980), has provided a framework for characterizing individual attitudes toward wildlife and understanding the sociodemographic characteristics associated with these attitudes. Studies by Applegate (1973, 1977, 1984a) and others have focused on attitudes toward specific issues such as hunting.

A number of basic studies have also sought to determine how the public's attitudes toward wildlife evolve (e.g., More 1977, Pomerantz 1977, and Kellert and Westervelt 1982). The significance of these studies for guiding outdoor education programs is substantial. However, to this point, their use has been limited.

What Is the Public Willing to Pay?

Without public support for fish and wildlife and their habitats, the most altruistic and best intended actions of fish and wildlife management professionals have little value. An understanding of fish and wildlife values is essential to setting and justifying management and program priorities and finding the funds to pay for them.

There can be little question that the demand for values information has increased tremendously during the 1980s. As public wildlife management funds have become more dear, understanding the cost-effectiveness of investments—both public and private—has become more important. Preference is given to those investments that can demonstrate a positive and preferably quantifiable return. Additionally, in an effort to develop quantitative frameworks to aid in making complex management decisions, many public agencies have created elaborate, data-hungry planning systems. To compete on an equal basis with other potential investments (e.g., timber), some measurement of fish and wildlife values must be created. More often than not, this measure is in dollars and cents.

Although a number of techniques have been devised to estimate the value of fish and wildlife resources, much controversy surrounds the accuracy, validity, and applicability of the values generated. Substantial, additional investments in basic economic research in fish and wildlife management are warranted given the growing importance of fish and wildlife values in resource planning and decision making. Among the areas in need of further research are the following:

1. recreation values for consumptive and nonconsumptive wildlife-related recreation
2. studies of the comparability of economic values generated using different valuation techniques in order to validate methodologies and understand their limitations
3. recreation values for activities related to particular fish and wildlife species
4. the relationship between environmental variables such as fish and game abundance, user density, user satisfaction, and the value of recreational experiences
5. the economic benefits of fish and wildlife-oriented recreation to local, state, and regional economies
6. the value to the landowner of leasing hunting rights.

APPLIED SOCIAL RESEARCH NEEDS

Social research has been applied in various ways to investigate fish and wildlife management issues. However, in many areas, applications of the findings of basic research are limited. Considering previously discussed trends, wildlife management agencies will find it increasingly important to apply basic human dimensions research to setting management goals and priorities and evaluating the effectiveness of existing or proposed programs. In addition, basic research into the interests and attitudes of wildlife users should be applied to a larger degree to identifying new means and sources of funding for wildlife management programs. Finally, as new management problems arise, managers must recognize the utility of social research in resolving them. The opportunities to use social research in this manner are greater than any applications that have been exhibited thus far.

Program Evaluation and Development

Applied research is needed to promote and improve public outdoor education programs. Studies by Pomerantz (1977), Kellert and Westervelt (1982), and others have been helpful in understanding how public attitudes toward wildlife and the environment evolve and have aided in developing educational materials (e.g. Project Wild and Project Learning Tree) and publications (e.g., *Ranger Rick*) for children. However, the utility and effectiveness of these teaching materials and publications could be improved by using applied social research.

Similarly, social research could be used more effectively to guide land management planning decisions simply by applying what has already been learned about the value of wildlife resources. For example, with increasing frequency, developers in the Southwest and in other parts of the nation are capitalizing on the value of wildlife to promote their developments. What better way to promote habitat protection than to use current knowledge regarding the economic and social values of wildlife to convince developers that it is in their best economic interest to protect and promote wildlife in their projects? Applied research will be needed to make this happen.

Financing Fish and Wildlife Management

There is growing recognition of the need to expand the base of financial support for wildlife management to maintain the level and quality of current programs and to expand services to address increasing interest in nongame species and nonconsumptive wildlife-related recreation. Current mechanisms of generating wildlife program funds are not adequate for supporting the broad range of fish and wildlife management programs needed or for distributing the costs of wildlife conservation fairly among all those who benefit.

By applying the known facts about present and potential wildlife users, new sources of wildlife program financing may be identified. Many states have launched new programs to generate additional funds to support fish and wildlife management activities or specific programs like nongame and endangered species. Until recently, however, only minimal effort has been expended to determine the effectiveness of these new revenue-generating programs. Applegate (1984*b*) conducted a study of contributors to New Jersey's tax check-off program and determined that the sociodemographic profile of contributors varied little from that of fish and wildlife management's traditional supporters. His study also looked into the manner in which contributors to the tax check-off became aware of the program and determined that an expensive multimedia campaign to market the program might not be a wise investment. Research to identify new sources of program support and to evaluate the strengths and weaknesses of current funding sources will become increasingly valuable.

Given the trend toward private, entrepreneurial approaches to management problems, private investment could play a prominent role in wildlife management's future. Applied social research is needed to assess the feasibility of using this concept for managing wildlife resources. This research should focus on opportunities for promoting private investments in fish and wildlife habitat protection, providing incentives for habitat enhancement, and developing public-private partnerships, where possible, to enhance public agencies' ability to achieve management goals.

Special Management Issues

Applied social research can have immediate utility in addressing pressing management issues. Since the human element is often a key part of these problems, applied research can serve to identify the human factors that may create or exacerbate a problem and help to resolve them. Three examples of issues demanding immediate attention are ensuring access for hunting on private lands in the east, mitigating the effects of recreational use of fragile ecosystems and wilderness areas, and identifying the social and economic factors that promote tropical deforestation in Latin and South America.

SUMMARY

This paper is not intended to provide an all inclusive summary of what has been done to address the human dimension of fish and wildlife management or a complete list of the needed research. Although I have chosen to limit the focus of this discussion to the social research needs of fish and wildlife management agencies, the reader should bear in mind that the breadth and utility of human dimensions research are much greater than these.

At a minimum, a fish and wildlife agency's social research program should (1) identify the agency's customers, as well as those who might develop an interest in fish and wildlife; (2) determine what the agency's current and potential customers want; and (3) determine the values that these individuals place on fish and wildlife and their habitats. The information generated should be used to identify management objectives, establish program priorities, and evaluate the agency's ability to satisfy customer needs. In addition, a great deal more needs to be known about the values of fish and wildlife if they are to compete on an equal footing with other resources whose values can be measured in the marketplace. Most important, however, is the need to apply the information that has already been gleaned from social research to address fish and wildlife management issues.

Changes in American culture and in the manner in which Americans use and enjoy fish and wildlife resources will necessitate changes in the way that fish and wildlife agencies operate. Since people will cause these changes and people—wildlife management professionals—must respond to them, social research must be one tool used by the agencies to respond. Social research techniques, applied to current or anticipated fish and wildlife management issues, can help an agency to define the issues better and to identify alternative solutions. However, social research alone cannot solve fish and wildlife management problems.

The value of the human dimensions field is that it provides for cross-fertilization between the biological and social sciences to strengthen the ability of each to address fish and wildlife management issues. If, in fact, resource management problems are "people problems," then the union of these disciplines will hold the key to effectively resolving future management conflicts and promoting sound conservation.

REFERENCES

APPLEGATE, J. E. 1973. Some factors associated with attitudes toward deer hunting in New Jersey residents. Trans. North Am. Wildl. and Nat. Resour. Conf. 38:267–273.

———. 1977. Dynamics of the New Jersey hunter population. Trans. North Am. Wildl. and Nat. Resour. Conf. 42:103–116.

———. 1984a. Attitudes toward deer hunting in New Jersey: 1972–1982. Wildl. Soc. Bull. 12:19–22.

———. 1984b. Nongame tax check-off programs: a survey of New Jersey residents following the first year of contributions. Wildl. Soc. Bull. 12:122–128.

———, J. R. LYONS, AND P. J. PLAGE. 1984. Dynamic aspects of the sport hunting population. Analysis of the 1980 national survey of fishing, hunting, and wildlife-associated recreation. U.S. Fish and Wildl. Serv. Rep. No. 2, Washington, D.C. 151pp.

———, R. A. OTTO, AND J. A. BUTTITTA. 1982. A cluster analysis of appreciative wildlife users. Wildl. Soc. Bull. 10:65–70.

BRYAN, H. 1979. Conflict in the great outdoors. Univ. Alabama Sociological Studies No. 4, University. 98pp.

GOTTSCHALK, J. S. 1966. Potential effects of land and water conservation fund on wildlife. Trans. North Am. Wildl. and Nat. Resour. Conf. 31:359–365.

HAY, M. J., AND K. E. MCCONNELL. 1979. An analysis of participation in nonconsumptive wildlife recreation. Land Econ. 55(4):460–471.

JACKSON, R., R. NORTON, AND R. ANDERSON. 1979. Improving ethical behavior in hunters. Trans. North Am. Wildl. and Nat. Resour. Conf. 44:306–318.

KELLERT, S. R. 1978. Attitudes and characteristics of hunters and anti-hunters. Trans. North Am. Wildl. and Nat. Resour. Conf. 43:412–423.

———. 1979. Public attitudes toward critical wildlife and natural habitat issues. U.S. Fish and Wildl. Serv. Phase I Rep., Washington, D.C. 138pp.

———. 1980. Activities of the American public relating to animals. U.S. Fish and Wildl. Serv. Phase II Rep., Washington, D.C., 178pp.

———, AND J. BERRY. 1980. Knowledge, affection, and basic attitudes towards animals in American society. U.S. Fish and Wildl. Serv. Phase III Rep., Washington, D.C. 162pp.

———, AND M. O. WESTERVELT. 1982. Children's attitudes, knowledge and behaviors toward animals. U.S. Fish and Wildl. Serv. Phase V Rep., Washington, D.C. 202pp.

KLESSIG, L., AND J. B. HALE. 1972. A profile of Wisconsin hunters. Wis. Dep. Nat. Resour. Tech. Bull. No. 60. 24pp.

KNOPF, R. C., B. L. DRIVER, AND J. B. BASSETT. 1973. Motivation for fishing. Trans. North Am. Wildl. and Nat. Resour. Conf. 38:28–41.

LANGENAU, E. E., JR., AND P. M. MELLON. 1980. Characteristics and behaviors of Michigan 12- to 18-year old hunters. J. Wildl. Manage. 44(1):69–78.

MILLER, J. R. 1980. The effect of intercounty differences in game availability on hunter participation. U.S. Fish and Wildl. Serv., Div. Program Plans, Working Pap. No. 12, Washington, D.C.

———, AND M. J. HAY. 1981. Determinants of hunter participation: duck hunting in the Mississippi flyway. Am. J. Agri. Econ. 63(4):677–684.

MILLER, R. R., A. A. PRATO, AND R. A. YOUNG. 1977. Congestion, success and the value of Colorado hunting experiences. Trans. North Am. Wildl. and Nat. Resour. Conf. 42:129–136.

MORE, T. A. 1977. The formation of wildlife perceptions. Trans. Northeast Sect. Wildl. Soc. 34:81–85.

POMERANTZ, G. A. 1977. Young people's attitudes toward wildlife. Mich. Dep. Nat. Resour. Wildl. Div. Rep. No. 2781, Lansing. 79pp.

SHAW, W. W., AND W. R. MANGUN. 1984. Nonconsumptive use of wildlife in the United States. U.S. Fish and Wildl. Serv. Resour. Publ. 154, Washington, D.C. 20pp.

STANKEY, H., R. C. LUCAS, AND R. R. REAM. 1973. Relationship between hunting success and satisfaction. Trans. North Am. Wildl. and Nat. Resour. Conf. 38:235–242.

U.S. FISH AND WILDLIFE SERVICE AND U.S. BUREAU OF THE CENSUS. 1982. 1980 national survey of fishing, hunting, and wildlife-associated recreation. U.S. Dep. Inter. and U.S. Dep. Commer., U.S. Gov. Print. Off., Washington, D.C. 156pp.

Chapter 27

Priority Needs for Communication of Wildlife Values

James R. Fazio

Wildlife values have been examined exhaustively during the course of this book, so it was benevolent of the organizers to allow concluding chapters to express what can only be termed opinion. When we speak of almost any kind of "needs," there is little likelihood for agreement. When we speak of the need to communicate values, it is virtually impossible. In fact, both a distinguished colleague in the Department of Philosophy at the University of Idaho and the social scientists in our Department of Wildland Recreation Management offered the opinion that I was crazy to accept this assignment.

These same colleagues questioned my sanity when I accepted a previous invitation to address the topic of park ethics at a conference of scholars in the humanities. I survived that by cynically questioning the ethics of everyone from park users and managers to our elected officials in Idaho. The audience loved it. But in my current assignment, I feel safer taking a different approach. Rather than impose my own values and argue that the world will be well served if we communicate these, I have gone to a cross-section of professionals in the field of wildlife. Using this panel, I have tried to determine what we collectively value and believe should be the focus of our attention if we can use communication to benefit the wildlife resource.

WHAT NEEDS TO BE COMMUNICATED?

My sample was a randomly selected group of 75 people listed in The Wildlife Society's *1984 Membership Directory and Certification Registry*. Only regular and life members were selected, thereby excluding those in the student, retired, and honorary categories. Using the Delphi technique (Delbecq et al. 1975), modified because of the deadlines on this chapter, I sent two questionnaires in sequence to the participants.

The first questionnaire included a premise taken directly from the purpose statement in the flier used to publicize this symposium. My intent was to help all respondents have the same frame of reference when thinking about a question they were then asked to answer. The premise was that "future conflicts for wildlife management direction are inevitable and documented social and economic values are increasingly necessary if the wildlife profession is to deal successfully with the pressures and concerns levied on the wildlife resource." Next, each person was asked to make a list that addressed the following question: "To help the wildlife profession deal successfully with 'the pressures and concerns levied on the wildlife resource,' what would you suggest are *the most important wildlife resource values that need to be communicated to 'the public'?*"

Three people refused to participate, 6 did not meet the deadline, and 37 did not respond, but 29 of the 75 sampled professionals responded with suggestions, generating a list of 108 items. Of these, 8 items were eliminated, because although I was liberal in accepting all statements that reflected what we might consider a "value," I chose to exclude a few inappropriate or unclear items. All others were used or combined because they expressed similar values in different wording. This yielded 28 value statements.

A second questionnaire was mailed to the original 75 (less the 3 refusees) who were then asked to help rank the 28 value statements by using a 5-point unipolar scale next to each item. The five descriptors on the scale ranged from "extremely important" to "less important." This time, 59 people responded, or 79% of our original sample. Their ranking of the statements is shown in Table 27.1.

OTHER NEEDS FOR SUCCESSFUL COMMUNICATION

The topics and prioritization suggested by my sample of wildlife professionals are cursory because of the time available, but I hope they will help answer the question about *what* needs to be communicated if we are to deal successfully with the pressures levied on the wildlife resource. Unfortunately, the greater question becomes *how* can we successfully communicate these values. This challenge is more difficult.

The answer lies in somehow coming to grips with three things that seem to continually plague all the natural resource management professions. First, we must understand the publics we serve. I am not suggesting we need to always agree with our publics or lie down and accept their dictates because they are our masters and most of us are the public's servants. But we *must* hear them and understand them if there is any hope of communicating effectively with them, to say nothing of somehow

TABLE 27.1
Ranked Summary of Wildlife Value Statements from Sample of The Wildlife
Society Members

Rank by Mean	Value Statement	Mean[a]
1	Protection of habitat	4.74
2	Inter-relatedness of all wildlife species: wildlife as part of the total ecosystem; All species are important; diversity	4.43
3	Biological barometer of indicator concept- A reflection of the overall health of our environment	4.27
4	Aesthetics: enrichment of life; quality of life	4.16
5	Wildlife is a renewable resource if managed	4.10
6	Professionals should manage the resource, not politicians or industry; professionals should be recognized as experts	4.04
7	Future generations have a right to enjoy wildlife; good land and water use yields useable wildlife; pollution-free environment; clean air, water, etc.	4.02 4.02 4.02
8	Protect endangered species	3.97
9	Financial support needed for wildlife management and research	3.92
10	Human population's negative effects on wildlife	3.79
11	Nonconsumptive opportunities: being able to see wildlife, enjoyment of feeding, photographing, etc.	3.73
12	Economic value of wildlife	3.51
13	National heritage; wildlife has a right to exist	3.40 3.40
14	Hunting as a management tool	3.34
15	Fellow citizens have a right to enjoy wildlife	3.29
16	Restoration of native vegetation	3.26
17	Recreational value in general	3.24
18	Gene pool for "new" genetic material	3.10
19	Preserve all we can now because we don't know enough yet to make the right decisions	2.98
20	Public input to influence management decisions	2.97
21	Potential of learning new things, such as medicinal uses	2.79
22	Wildlife as a biological control agent	2.64
23	Wildlife helps humans develop a sense of caring and responsibility	2.47
24	Use of wildlife populations to model and understand human populations	2.26
25	Food value for humans	1.92

[a]Based on unipolar scale of 1 (less important) to 5 (extremely important). N = 58 in most cases; range of 56 to 59.

being persuasive enough to change values or even instill values where none has yet formed. So I am concerned when the value statement regarding communication to increase the quantity or quality of public input ranks 20 out of 25 in our study. But look what is ranked number 6: the classic statement that *we* are the experts, so let *us* manage the resource! Despite the lip service given to public involvement, I wonder how many of us harbor secret desires for the public to just go play with its home computers or watch its football games and leave us alone to manage the wildlife and forests? A prerequisite to communication is to purge this attitude completely from ourselves and our professional ranks. Then it behooves us to look for ways to *improve* public involvement and to get better in touch with what our publics are thinking and why. Only then can we hope to modify satisfactorily our own input to the process of public education or interpersonal persuasion.

Second, we need to plan for communication. Some of us detest the very word because it brings forth images of hefty forest plans or environmental impact statements. But the planning I am referring to is so simple I sometimes scratch it out on a napkin at coffee break or on a scrap of paper. Whether we are trying to convince local developers to protect urban wildlife habitat or we are facing a power struggle in the office, four simple considerations can help increase our chances for successful communication. Although my assignment was not to discuss specific techniques, I will at least present the four-step plan that I believe needs to be as much a part of a wildlife professional's methods as taking browse measurements or collecting age and sex data. Planning for effective communication needs to include

1. Fact finding

What are the facts as we know them?

Who is involved, how, and where do they stand on the issue? How much do they know of the facts, what do they believe and how firmly? What are the values of these people?

How many publics can I define to deal with differently?

2. Goals and objectives

Is it perfectly clear what needs to be accomplished and in what time frame?

Can I express what I need to achieve in terms of behavioral or learner-oriented objectives?

3. Communication   What channels or techniques will
                          work best with each public or key
                          individual, given my budget and time
                          frame?

                          What is the best timing for my
                          communication, and in what order
                          should publics be contacted or
                          techniques applied?

4. Evaluation/   How will I know if I have been
   monitoring   successful, and how can I monitor this
                          over time?

Nothing is earthshaking about this method of planning to meet communication needs. However, when this method is brought out of the subconsciousness and made part of deliberate, pen-and-paper planning, it is the single best technique for helping us do a better job whether communicating about values or setting up an information center during a forest fire or lost person situation.

Third, we must teach wildlife managers *how* to communicate. The skill of effective communication comes no more by accident or birthright than the understanding of population dynamics. Certainly some people have more talent than others for public speaking or writing, but in our age of supersophisticated communication, I am talking about fields of knowledge that are complex and dynamic, yet essential to being effective.

Specifically, I see the need for an understanding of society, at least a minimal acquaintance with psychology, and certainly a working knowledge of modern public relations and communication methods. We can meet these needs by ensuring that students are exposed to the appropriate subjects as they earn their degrees and their entrance tickets into the ranks of professionals. The Wildlife Society spelled out this need in its recommendations for a minimal educational program. Along with all mathematics, biology, and other sciences, the society recommends 9 semester hours in humanities and social sciences, 12 hours in communications, and 6 hours in policy-related subjects. The lack of formal communication training has been lamented in the forestry profession for years (Fazio 1983), and my friend and mentor, the late Douglas L. Gilbert, spent much of his career trying to overcome this problem in the wildlife profession. I think we are making headway, as The Wildlife Society's standards attest, but progress is slow.

To check on the responsiveness of our wildlife curricula to this widely expressed need, I conducted another ministudy while preparing this

TABLE 27.2
Credit Distribution Related to the Human Dimension of
Wildlife Management in a Sample of Wildlife Curricula

School[a]	Coursework Category Requirements[b] (semester hours recommended by TWS)		
	Humanities/ Social Sciences[c] (9)	Communication[d] (12)	Policy[e] (6)
1	4	12	0
2	4	4	0
3	21	9	3
4	24	9	0
5	6	9	3
6	26	12	0
7	24	9	0
8	24	12	3
	$\overline{x} = 16.6$	$\overline{x} = 9.5$	$\overline{x} = 1.1$

[a]Three schools did not respond and information from 8 schools was insufficient for use in this analysis.

[b]Courses reflect those required of all students in the wildlife major. Not included are seminars or courses within options.

[c]Economics, Sociology, Psychology, Political Science, Government, History, Literature.

[d]English Composition, Technical Writing, Journalism, Mass Media, Public Speaking, Public Relations.

[e]Policy/Administration, Law, Law Enforcement, Land Use Planning.

paper. I made a 20% random selection from The Wildlife Society's list of 93 schools with wildlife management curricula and wrote to them requesting a catalog and information. I used this material to compare the curricula to The Wildlife Society's recommendations (Table 27.2).

I suspect that several years ago the table would have had low numbers in all categories. Now, of the three categories, it is clearly lopsided in favor of the humanities and social sciences. This emphasis, I believe, results from the recent rush on U.S. campuses to ensure a general education for all students, a swing of the pendulum back to required courses and away from self-designed or purely technical curricula. Although this change is constructive because it helps students to better understand society, the old weaknesses in communication skills are still obvious. Of the credit hours shown in the communication category, the great majority were in basic English composition and speech. Although these subjects are needed, they are not the kind of applied communication courses that would move wildlife professionals into the arena of modern communication. In reviewing the schools in my sample, I saw only one that required a journalism course and only two that required all wildlife students to have a public relations course. Few courses are offered in the policy category—courses that emphasize a synthesizing of knowledge about resources, people, and communication. The profile in Table 27.2 is like a building with a good foundation, weak walls, and no roof. The need to make wildlife students as effective in communication as they are knowledgeable in the biological aspects of their discipline is still not filled. If my small sample is indicative, our universities have yet to meet this challenge adequately.

CONCLUSION

I have intentionally said little about communicating wildlife values per se. Changing people's values is an extremely difficult challenge, and for those who are interested I recommend Milton Rokeach's (1973) *The Nature of Human Values,* in which he describes one of the few cases in which positive changes in values toward the environment have been documented in an experimental situation. My contention is that value modification will take care of itself if we focus on what *is* within our reach—more effective dissemination of pertinent information, better public education, especially of the young (with such programs as Project Wild), and, when necessary, persuasive argumentation. To do this, we need to know our publics better, we need to plan our strategies better, and we need to prepare our new professionals better through improved curricula structures.

I am optimistic that if we meet these needs we *can* communicate effectively about the things we value in the wildlife professions—the protection of habitat, the interrelatedness of all life, and seriousness of those signs in nature that predict the future health and quality of our environment. One reason for my optimism is that I believe people will respond positively to our efforts. As Kellert (1980) pointed out from his nationwide studies, there is already fairly widespread, if somewhat unsophisticated, support for conservation. Moreover, he found that although only a small percentage of our population has a strong ecological concern, it happily is found among the people who are usually the agents of change—the young and educated, particularly those living in the western U.S.

There are definite signs that we may be starting a swing back toward environmental values. I am intrigued with the historical undulations in public interest toward the environment as demonstrated by high points in the turn-of-the-century Nature Study movement, the depression-generated interest in conservation education, and most recently in the Earth Day period. During most of this decade environmental interest has been at a low level, at least relative to other issues and interests. However, Lester W. Milbrath (1984) of SUNY's Environmental Studies Center in Buffalo suggested that a vanguard is forming to contest socially and politically the present norms that place utilitarian values above all else. He has data to show that even the general public is aware of our environmental problems and is willing to support fairly drastic action to solve them. Interest is also renewed in an aspect that resembles Leopold's land ethic but that is now called "deep ecology"—a reflection of those personal moods, values, and aesthetic and philosophical convictions that serve no necessarily utilitarian nor rational end (Tobias 1985). Support for deep ecology, the "green movement," and even a neo–Earth Day could well sweep across the land like a tidal wave in response to the Reagan policy or triggered by some unpredicted event.

If a marketing specialist saw all these factors working in favor of recognition and consumption of a new product, he or she would be optimistic. To the wildlife profession, these would be clear signs that if we really believe values need to be communicated, we would work to overcome our deficiencies as communicators and help manage change rather than be managed by it.

REFERENCES

DELBECQ, A. L., A. H. VAN DE VEN, AND D. H. GUSTAFSON. 1975. Group techniques for program planning: a guide to nominal group and Delphi processes. Scott, Foresman and Co., Glenview, Ill. 174pp.

FAZIO, J. R. 1983. Fulfilling the needs of forestry students in developing communication skills. Pages 599–602 *in* Proc. Soc. Am. For. Natl. Convention. Soc. Am. For., Washington, D.C.

KELLERT, S. R. 1980. Contemporary values of wildlife in American society. Pages 31–60 *in* W. W. Shaw and E. H. Zube, eds. Wildlife values. Cent. for

Assessment of Noncommodity Nat. Resour. Values, Inst. Ser. Rep. No. 1, Univ. Arizona, Tucson.

MILBRATH, L. W. 1984. Environmentalists—vanguard for a new society. State Univ. New York Press, Albany, N.Y. 180pp.

ROKEACH, M. 1973. The nature of human values. Free Press, New York. 438pp.

TOBIAS, M. 1985. Deep ecology. Avant Books, San Diego, Calif. 296pp.

Chapter 28

Applying Wildlife Values Information in Management Planning and Policy Making

Herbert E. Doig

Historically, wildlife program managers and decision makers have had little available information on wildlife values to guide or temper program decisions. Most public input came from sportsmen, and, although there was general recognition of interest in wildlife from others in the public sector, little emphasis was placed on species that were not defined as game.

During the early 1960s when water resource planning was in its heyday, wildlife managers were asked to place values on wildlife that could be quantified and factored into benefit-cost analyses being undertaken to justify major capital water projects. At that time wildlife professionals strongly resisted getting caught up in the numbers game, and most rejected the concept as unrepresentative of true resource worth. They were right, of course, but the rationale for drawing that conclusion was based more upon a defensive posture than scientific logic.

Much progress has been made in the last two decades, and efforts to define wildlife values have greatly increased in size and sophistication. There is a broader recognition of the myriad values placed on wildlife by all segments of society and a constantly expanding knowledge base that enhances understanding of these values. However, recognition of the accomplishments in this aspect of wildlife science should not signal satisfaction that the task is done but rather should provide the incentive for a new commitment to the next phase in the use of wildlife values information—effective application of new-found knowledge.

The principal thrusts in the use of values information by management planners and decision makers are in impact analysis and budget justification. Being able to speak the language of fiscal analysts and economists has made these professionals more comfortable as they compete for tight money. Such efforts are primarily defensive, and more often than not they are attempts to justify decisions that have already been made. The first area of definable needs, therefore, is in the application of the knowledge and technology currently available.

Professionals in management-planning and policy-making roles should use values information to gain more credibility with those who speak only in terms of values. Recognition of the broader spectrum of interests in wildlife will convince others that wildlife managers no longer dabble in their favorite hobby but rather have a firm grasp of the complex nature of a resource that has captured the interest and imagination of all segments of society. Understanding of value systems also provides a common denominator for comparison of cost/benefit relationships that provide the basis for decisions on tough issues.

Policy makers need to integrate wildlife values information with biological considerations early in the formulation of priority decisions and policy judgments. Just as the carrying capacity of habitats for wildlife dictates species occurrence and abundance, value systems determine public tolerance for these parameters. Social priorities and land uses in most instances have far more impact on wildlife management decision making than do biological processes. Consideration of one in the absence of others constitutes incomplete analysis and faulty management.

Resource managers must apply values information to demonstrate the importance of wildlife to local economies and the growth of private enterprise. In this way wildlife programs and the benefits they provide can compete effectively with other values in society. The importance of wetlands, for example, can take priority over residential development or commercial exploitation, and alternatives less destructive of wildlife values can be forced upon uncompromising advocates.

Wildlife values information is also needed in developing the basis for new wildlife program revenue sources and giving insight into the people's willingness to support selected programs. Administrators too often fail to research their market before embarking upon new initiatives or planning promotional schemes designed to return substantial financial benefits. We have all found ourselves overcome with the excitement of new initiatives and have failed to gain public support for an idea not because of a faulty concept but because we did not take the time to measure adequately public preferences and desires.

As wildlife constituencies diversify and special interest groups evolve, resource managers must rely on values information to understand better the purposes of these people and communicate with them. It is ineffectual to discuss population management with people whose interests are oriented toward total protection or complete elimination of a species. Such understanding will also temper focused policy and lead to multispecies program goals rather than single-species management. Conversely, the wildlife manager can more effectively use this knowledge to mold public attitudes toward broad and varied resource uses.

Wildlife values information offers new opportunity for support for environmental cleanup efforts and improvement of environmental quality. By demonstrating the relationship between wildlife enjoyment and the quality of life objectives of people, public support for bold environmental initiatives can be generated. Most environmental quality goals are not based upon the improvement of the sterile physical and chemical base but rather on the enhanced biological communities that result. Enhanced desirable species in ecological "balance" cannot be achieved by esoteric logic but rather through the expressed commitment of people. Integration of information by resource managers is a necessary element of this legally mandated goal.

When decisions are made favoring actions that will be costly to wildlife, the extent of mitigation will frequently be determined by the importance of the values lost. Wildlife values information is needed to document the importance of such losses and impress upon ultimate decision makers that documented costs must be offset by compensatory enhancement.

Last, wildlife values information is needed to guide public and private investment in business enterprises based upon wildlife uses. Before committing financial resources to the development of such businesses as shooting preserves, nature centers, raw fur dealing or processing, and paid hunting, market analysis on user interest and potential clients is advisable. Even minimal involvement in financial schemes such as wood duck or bluebird box construction and sale will benefit from examination of wildlife values analysis.

Examples of the ways wildlife values information is needed for routine decision making by biologists, administrators, and the using public are many, but information and application needs are only part of the picture. The scenario is complete only when key people use the information, and research findings are made available to them. It is of little importance that wildlife value assessments have been scientifically crafted and properly carried out if the information is not used. Nor is it necessarily appropriate to blame administrators and managers for failing to take advantage of available information. The plain truth is that many do not know how to include such knowledge effectively in decision making.

A beginning must be made, and special emphasis must be placed on preparing new students so that they integrate wildlife value determinations as they apply their new-found ecological knowledge. Educators need to refocus college curricula to give a higher priority to social values as students become technically prepared to practice their profession. Most of us have learned that wildlife management to a large extent is people management, and yet we have not been trained to factor such influences into program development.

Senior administrators must also be trained to take advantage of wildlife values information in program planning and policy making. Many know the knowledge is there but simply do not know how to use it. One important need is the development of techniques for training practicing professionals in a work atmosphere that already pressures them to do more for less. It is unrealistic to expect employers to give significant release time for employees to return to school for additional training. There must be a different way.

Scientists need to develop simplified techniques for interpretation of wildlife values information. Professionals have a difficult time comprehending and integrating the ecological relationships in the biological community even when they manage for single-species abundance. Superimposing social value systems on top of pressures to manage the total ecosystem may be too much for most to comprehend. We must explore modeling and process development as ways to equip today's decision maker and tomorrow's manager with the tools to understand these complex issues.

This transition will not be easy. Inertia to retain the old ways and suspicion and fear of new technologies will inhibit individual career growth. When selecting new managers and administrators we must favor those who can grasp the "big picture" and can include all parameters, social and biological, in future program development and policy formulation. Some very good scientists will never make the grade, but the tough decision must be made.

The burden of ensuring that wildlife values are integral to program and policy development does not rest with the researchers and teachers alone. Top administrators are critically needed to create mechanisms and processes that require consideration of values information. Planning and program development systems must include evaluation of wildlife values as new programs evolve and priorities are set. Environmental assessment processes must also have these kinds of considerations built in.

As the bank of values information grows and professionals become more expert in its use, managers and administrators may assume the image of tough and efficient advocates, well prepared to do battle in any arena. They may be viewed as unfeeling and without empathy, responding to the desires of the general public, not the wildlife profession. They may be opportunistic and ruthless in their quest for truth and equity for the true values of wildlife resources. We may have created a monster quite different from the creature we perceive today. Coping with that is tomorrow's challenge.

Chapter 29

Anticipating Wildlife Values of Tomorrow

Edward E. Langenau, Jr.

Economic and social values of wildlife vary with time and by species. Despite the wide variation in wildlife values, the literature has described some social factors that are highly correlated with the economic and social importance of wildlife to Americans. These factors include economic prosperity (Langenau 1982), sex and age structure of citizens (Kellert 1980), urbanization (Applegate et al. 1984), knowledge about wildlife (Dahlgren et al. 1977), relationship between human population density and wildlife abundance (Shaw 1974), cultural history of society (Dasmann 1984), and the degree of participation in wildlife-oriented recreation (Kellert 1978).

Forecasters have predicted the ways in which some of these social factors may change in the future. In particular, they have suggested that economic prosperity will continue until the twenty-first century (Flanagan 1983), the mean age of Americans will increase (U.S. Bur. Census 1982), and urbanization will continue (Engels and Forstall 1985). These changing dynamics of U.S. society may offer a clue for understanding the future values of wildlife. The purpose of this chapter is to clarify the relationship between wildlife values and a few of these social trends. Future values of wildlife, which might be associated with these changes in social factors, will then be forecasted.

ECONOMIC PROSPERITY

Exploitation of natural resources normally results in a boom and bust economy. These cycles of economic prosperity can in turn affect the social values within a culture. Periods of economic prosperity in the U.S. have been associated with resource abuse, followed by public outrage, environmental legislation, and subsequent recession. Economic hardship has resulted in reduced concern with environmental values, thereby permitting another cycle of resource abuse and economic pros-

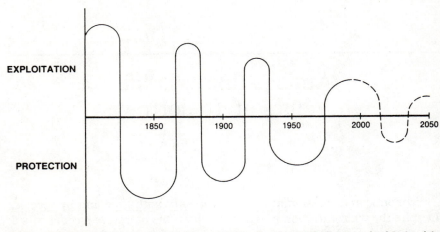

Figure 29.1 Cycles of economic prosperity in the U.S. have coincided with those characterized by exploitation of natural resources, followed by preservationistic legislation, and then economic recession. Environmental concerns have then been relaxed, thereby permitting another cycle of resource exploitation.

perity (Langenau 1982). The specific timing of these cycles (Fig. 29.1) may offer some indication of future trends.

The first of these cycles occurred during an economic boom in the 1810s. This prosperity permitted a period of social reform in the 1840s, denoted as the era of "Jacksonian democracy," when there were movements to abolish slavery, provide voting rights for women, and promote other social reforms. This movement was followed by an economic recession and then another round of prosperity in the 1880s. Prosperity during this period was related to high grading of timber throughout much of the U.S., overgrazing of western range, and excessive mineral development. This prosperity was followed by an intensive period of reform, characterized by the Lacey Act of 1900, which finally halted market hunting. Federal legislation during the administration of T. R. Roosevelt and many notable efforts at the state level began to lose support in the late 1910s as another round of economic prosperity occurred in the 1920s, followed by the Great Depression in 1929. The postdepression years produced some major conservation milestones, such as the publication of Leopold's book on game management in 1933 and the Pittman-Robertson Act of 1937.

There was a surprising stability of both prosperity and attitudes toward the environment between the postdepression years and the late 1960s. Despite our sense that several boom and bust periods occurred between 1930 and 1970, no period of economic hardship approached the severity of the depression years. Similarly, although we may feel that economic prosperity after World War II and during the Vietnam War had a substantial impact on land, water, and vegetation, none of these periods produced the level of economic vitality or resource abuse characteristic of the 1880s or 1920s.

A major period of conservation reform occurred in the late 1960s and early 1970s. As before, the conservation legislation was only part of a larger movement of reform that concerned the Vietnam War, civil rights, government regulation, rights of women, and other social issues. The depression in 1973 halted much of the emphasis on natural resource management. New important government programs were postponed with the argument that environmental regulation was creating unemployment and encouraging a distorted balance of trade. Student enrollments in natural resource classes decreased throughout the nation. Environmental concessions were made to industry as a way of protecting jobs and encouraging economic development.

The current period of economic expansion is expected to continue until 1995 (Flanagan 1983). At that time, 52% of the families are projected to have incomes of $30,000 or more, and 23% will have incomes of $50,000 or more. The current period of economic prosperity (1981–1995) is likely to be followed by political activity to protect natural resources. We might expect renewed interest in conservation issues at the same time as movements develop for social causes, such as children's rights, tax reform, and economic, as well as social, equality.

AGE STRUCTURE

Several studies have shown age differences in environmental values, as discussed by Heberlein (1972). For example, in a survey of visitor attitudes toward oil and gas development in a backcountry forest in Michigan, Langenau et al. (1984) found that younger visitors had preservationistic values whereas older visitors more often approved of oil and gas development (Fig. 29.2).

Preservationistic values might become moderated as individuals mature and become more tolerant. Although this shift seems possible, most studies show a surprising degree of stability for environmental values (e.g., Langenau et al. 1977). Thus, it is more likely that the correlations between different ages and different values result from the respondents' different experiences in early adulthood. Many of these early experiences may have reflected economic and social conditions of the times. For instance, members of the 65 and older age group in Figure 29.2 were born before 1916 and were adolescents during the Great Depression. Not surprisingly the attitudes of this age group were less preservationistic

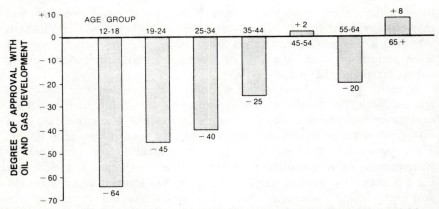

Figure 29.2 Degree of approval with oil and gas development of a Michigan backcountry forest. The attitude measure was computed by subtracting the percentage of respondents that disapproved of oil and gas development from the percentage that approved.

than those of the 35 to 44 year-olds, who were adolescents during the years of prosperity after World War II.

If we assume that values are relatively stable products of historical events that occur during formative years, then we would be able to project the values of future citizens. For instance, current (1981) 12 to 18 year-olds with strong preservationistic values (Fig. 29.2) will be 41 to 47 years of age in 2010 and 66 to 72 years in 2035. If a period of economic prosperity does continue until 1995, then the people who will be 12 to 18 years old in 2010 might be expected to have a preservationistic orientation that favors existence and aesthetic values over utilitarian values of wildlife. In contrast, individuals who were young adults during the recent recession (those who will be 55 to 64 years old in 2010) would be less preservationistic and more likely to be in influential social positions. This difference perhaps creates the tension between the use and the protection of natural resources. Such conflicts between generations are often initiated by youth. The tensions are dissipated when an older age group accepts the criticisms offered by a younger one and institutes changes to improve social conditions. Thus, the 12 to 48 year-olds may form an alliance with the retired baby boomers (those who will be 65 years or more in 2010) to produce another major conservation movement that may peak in 2035, as those people who were adolescents of the early 1970s gain political influence and then retire.

The future age structure of U.S. citizens might also influence rates of participation in wildlife-oriented recreation, which may in turn have

TABLE 29.1
Predicted Numbers of Hunters and Nonconsumptive Wildlife Recreationists in the Year 2000

Age Class	U.S. Population Expected in 2000[a] (thousands)	Estimated Percentage[b] and Numbers of Participants in Nonconsumptive Wildlife-Associated Activities		Estimated Percentage[c] and Numbers of Hunters	
		%	N (thousands)	%	N (thousands)
16-17	7,751	46	3,565	15	1,163
18-24	22,551	50	11,276	14	3,157
25-34	36,387	63	22,924	13	4,730
35-44	43,718	60	25,231	12	5,246
45-54	37,094	53	19,660	9	3,338
55-64	23,779	52	12,365	7	1,665
>64	35,036	47	16,467	3	1,051
Totals	206,316	55	112,488	10	20,350

[a]Source: U.S. Census Bureau 1982.
[b]Source: Shaw and Mangun 1984.
[c]Source: USDI, Fish and Wildl. Serv. and USDC Bur. Census 1982.

both direct and indirect impacts on wildlife values. Population projections made by the U.S. Census Bureau (1982) were used to determine the amount of participation in wildlife-oriented recreation that might be anticipated for the year 2000 (Table 29.1). The percentage of Americans that hunted by age class in 1980 (U.S. Fish and Wildl. Serv. and U.S. Bur. Census 1982) was multiplied by the expected number of individuals in each age class anticipated in the year 2000. Similar projections were made for the expected number of individuals that might become involved in nonconsumptive wildlife-associated recreation from 1980 participation data provided by Shaw and Mangun (1984). Results showed that non-consumptive wildlife use will probably increase at a faster rate (20.6%) than hunting (16.7%) between 1980 and 2000. Wildlife-oriented recreation is expected to increase at a slower rate than that of the general population (21.4% increase). Nevertheless, an additional 2,906,000 hunters and 19,238,000 nonconsumptive users can be expected by 2000, relative to 1980 levels of participation. Although these estimates are crude, they offer some support to the thesis that human-wildlife encounters will increase in the future and possibly lead to increased awareness, use, and appreciation of wildlife.

URBANIZATION

Rural individuals tend to be more knowledgeable than urban residents about wildlife (Dahlgren et al. 1977). Rural individuals are also more utilitarian in their perceptions of wildlife (Kellert 1984) and more apt to hunt and participate in nonconsumptive wildlife recreation than are their urban counterparts (Applegate et al. 1984). Rural people may have a more accurate perception of wildlife because they are more likely to encounter animals and wildlife-oriented recreationists than are urban individuals. Human-wildlife encounters for urban residents may occur under artificial conditions that might reinforce erroneous beliefs about wildlife. Human-wildlife encounters for rural residents may expose people to a more realistic perception of wildlife, even if some of these experiences are negative, as in the case of animal damage and nuisance encounters.

Projections about the future residence of Americans are much less precise than predictions on future age structure. Patterns of migration to and from metropolitan areas have shown reversals. Also, patterns of urbanization have differed by region within the U.S. In general, there was a strong rural-to-urban migration of people after World War II. From 1940 to 1960, a net average of about 1 million people left farms and rural towns each year. The farm population of the southern U.S. dropped 40% during one decade (1950s). In the 1960s there was a rural exodus from the Great Plains, western corn belt, southern coal fields, and the southern Coastal Plain. Nonmetropolitan counties lost an average of 300,000 people per year from migration to cities in the 1960s. During the early 1970s, this trend was reversed. For the first time in the twentieth century, the number of people in rural areas grew more rapidly than in metropolitan areas. From 1970 to 1973, nonmetropolitan areas gained 4.2% in population, and metropolitan areas gained 2.9% (Beale 1975).

In 1979, evidence began to reveal that the new pattern did not represent a permanent change in migration patterns (Engels and Healy 1979). Richter (1983) found that the more rapid growth of rural counties softened toward the end of the 1970s. The most recent study (Engels and Forstall 1985) confirmed the conclusion that another reversal has occurred. The number of people in metropolitan areas increased faster (4.5% increase) between 1980 and 1984 than did the population of nonmetropolitan areas (3.4% increase). This growth differential, however, has varied by region of the country (Table 29.2).

Despite the confusion about metropolitan and urban patterns of population growth, some factors that have affected the distribution of people seem clear: Manufacturing centers in the U.S. have been decentralized, there has been a growth of retirement and rural recreational activity, and much of the metropolitan growth has taken place in

TABLE 29.2
Percentage Increase in Population of Metropolitan and Nonmetropolitan Counties by Region Within the United States, 1980-84

Region	Metropolitan	Non-Metropolitan
Northeast	1.6%	2.4%
Midwest	0.9%	1.0%
South	8.7%	4.8%
West	8.7%	8.8%
Totals	4.5%	3.4%

Source: Adapted from Engles and Forstall 1985.

suburban areas (Beale 1975). These factors have resulted in a short-range impact of increased wildlife-human encounters as people continue to move into suburban areas. Large amounts of crop damage might be expected from deer, cranes, and geese. Residential problems will probably develop with nuisance bear, raccoon, coyote, and beaver. A significant private industry probably will develop for wildlife damage control. At the same time, the symbolic value of wildlife will probably become more important. Species of interest will perhaps include those that do not tolerate human activity, such as bobcat, or those that symbolize a wilderness lost to technology and artificiality, such as moose. Public sentiment may favor the maintenance of wildlife populations in zoos, parks, wildlife preserves, and public forests. Management technology may also expand to include genetic engineering, disease control, artificial feeding, selective harvest, intensive habitat management, and modification of social behavior. The degree of artificiality in management will probably become a public issue.

The movement of urban Americans to suburban settings has some long-range implications. People raised in urban settings who then migrate to nonmetropolitan areas are less likely to hunt, more likely to post land, and more likely to have protectionistic values than are individuals raised in rural settings (Pomerantz 1977). However, their children are likely to hunt and to appreciate nonconsumptive values of wildlife. When these individuals mature, they may add to the renewed conservation movement forecasted to occur in the 2030s.

MITIGATION

The wildlife profession has an opportunity to influence wildlife values of the future, even though some changes will result from inevitable social trends. The following recommendations might be considered:

1. Wildlife interests might as well accommodate the current goal of economic growth. Wildlife populations currently underutilized should be identified and marketed. Species with expanding habitats should be identified so that current opportunities can be developed and needs for animal damage control can be specified.

2. The wildlife profession might get ready for a renewed conservation movement. Wildlife populations expected to experience reduction in habitat or future overutilization should be identified for future plans to protect and regulate those species.

3. Wildlife professionals need to work with suburban species and clients. Leopold in a discussion about the social significance of wildlife management wrote, "The game manager manipulates animals and vegetation to produce a game crop. This, however, is only a superficial indication of his social significance. What he really labors for, is to bring about a new attitude towards the land" (1933:420). This notion—that the product of wildlife management is an educational experience to further the evolution of a more environmentally responsible culture—is difficult to apply. It is easier to conclude that social engineering is the work of politics and that the product of wildlife management is habitat, species diversity, population surplus, recreation, or economic impact. Values that biologists promote for ecosystems (such as diversification and conservation) need to be applied to improve the human habitat and the quality of human life.

Acknowledgments.—R. B. Peyton, P. D. Friedrich, and E. C. Carlson provided valuable comments on early drafts of the manuscript. Editing by session chairman, J. E. Applegate, was appreciated. J. M. Wickham typed the manuscript, and G. F. Lehman drafted the figures. Information on projected residence of Americans was provided by L. S. Rosen. This chapter is a contribution of Federal Aid in Wildlife Restoration, Michigan Pittman-Robertson Project W-127-R.

REFERENCES

APPLEGATE, J. E., J. R. LYONS, AND P. J. PLAGE. 1984. Dynamic aspects of the sport hunting population: an analysis based on the 1980 national survey of fishing, hunting, and wildlife-associated recreation. U.S. Fish and Wildl. Serv. Rep. No. 2, Washington, D.C. 151pp.

BEALE, C. L. 1975. The revival of population growth in nonmetropolitan America. U.S. Dep. Agric. Econ. Res. Serv. Rep. No. 605, Washington, D.C. 15pp.

DAHLGREN, R. B., A. WYWIALOWSKI, T. A. BULBOLZ, AND V. L. WRIGHT. 1977. Influence of knowledge of wildlife management principles and behavior and attitudes toward resource issues. Trans. North Am. Wildl. and Nat. Resour. Conf. 42:146–155.

DASMANN, R. F. 1984. Environmental conservation. John Wiley and Sons, New York. 486pp.

ENGELS, R. A., AND R. L. FORSTALL. 1985. Tracking the nonmetropolitan population turnaround to 1984. Pap. presented at the Annu. Meet. Population Assoc. Am., Boston. 22pp. (Unpubl.)

――――, AND M. K. HEALY. 1979. Rural renaissance reconsidered. Am. Demographics 1(5):16–19.

FLANAGAN, J. M. 1983. Demographic forecasts: income trends, 1980–1995. Am. Demographics 5(5):50–51.

HEBERLEIN, T. A. 1972. The land ethic realized: some social psychological explanations of changing environmental attitudes. J. Soc. Issues 28:79–87.

KELLERT, S. R. 1978. Attitudes and characteristics of hunters and anti-hunters. Trans. North Am. Wildl. and Nat. Resour. Conf. 43:412–423.

――――. 1980. Americans' attitudes and knowledge of animals. Trans. North Am. Wildl. and Nat. Resour. Conf. 45:649–664.

――――. 1984. Urban American perceptions of animals and the natural environment. Urban Ecol. 8:209–228.

LANGENAU, E. E., JR. 1982. Bureaucracy and wildlife: a historical overview. Int. J. for the Study of Anim. Problems 3:140–157.

――――, G. C. JAMSEN, AND R. L. LEVINE. 1977. The stability of attitudes towards clearcutting among landowners in Roscommon County, Michigan. For. Sci. 23:437–444.

――――, R. B. PEYTON, J. M. WICKHAM, E. W. CAVENEY, AND D. W. JOHNSTON. 1984. Attitudes towards oil and gas development among forest recreationists. J. Leisure Res. 16:161–177.

LEOPOLD, A. 1933. Game management. Charles Scribner's Sons, New York. 481pp.

POMERANTZ, G. A. 1977. Young people's attitudes toward wildlife. Mich. Dep. Nat. Resour. Wildl. Div. Rep. No. 2781, Lansing. 79pp.

RICHTER, K. 1983. Nonmetropolitan growth in the late 1970s: the end of the turnaround? Pap. presented at the Annu. Meet. Population Assoc. Am., Pittsburg. 22pp. (Unpubl.)

SHAW, W. W. 1974. Meanings of wildlife for Americans: contemporary attitudes and social trends. Trans. North Am. Wildl. and Nat. Resour. Conf. 39:151–155.

――――, AND W. R. MANGUN. 1984. Nonconsumptive use of wildlife in the United States. U.S. Fish and Wildl. Serv. Resour. Publ. No. 154, Washington, D.C. 20pp.

U.S. BUREAU OF THE CENSUS. 1982. Projections of the population of the United States: 1982 to 2050. P-25, No. 922 (GPO#003-001-91418-2), U.S. Gov. Print. Off., Washington, D.C. 118pp.

U.S. FISH AND WILDLIFE SERVICE AND U.S. BUREAU OF THE CENSUS. 1982. 1980 national survey of fishing, hunting, and wildlife-associated recreation. U.S. Dep. Inter. and U.S. Dep. Commer., U.S. Gov. Print. Off., Washington, D.C. 156pp.

Chapter 30

Proceedings Summary: Where Do We Go from Here?

John C. Hendee

Surely I will be rewarded in the happy hunting ground for reading advance drafts of so many chapters on economic and social values of wildlife. After emerging dazed and incoherent from that task, it took me several days of hunting and watching reruns of Marlin Perkins and Jacques Cousteau to recover. Ultimately, I felt like the fat-farm survivor binging on sweets as reward for such discipline. Perhaps I am half facetious in such claims, but I do admit to being overdosed as well as impressed with the rigor and diversity of chapters in this book. Let me provide you, the reader, with an overview.

TRAVELOGUE OF THE CHAPTERS

Part One chapters challenge the wildlife profession to consider seriously the social and economic value of wildlife, to define social and economic values of wildlife, to trace the development of wildlife valuation, and to identify the importance of fish and wildlife values. It also includes a delightful treatise relating the evolution of wildlife values to larger questions about relationships between humans and animals.

Chapter 1

Jack Berryman, executive vice president of the International Association of Fish and Wildlife Agencies, begins with "Socioeconomic Values of the Wildlife Resource: Are We Really Serious?" An admitted novice in socioeconomic methods, Berryman is an expert in the problems and issues faced in wildlife conservation. He reports a consensus among agency administrators that the two most ominous threats confronting wildlife managers are the continuing loss of habitat and the animal rights movement. Thus, his question to the conference is whether socioeconomic tools are being used in solutions to these problems. If not, why not? I suspect those questions made lots of us squirm. But it is fair to ask whether we really are focusing socioeconomic data and methods on the major issues of the day. And Berryman goes on to say that, because wildlife management is suffering more reverses than ever before, we need to use every available tool as effectively as possible. And he draws a bead on economic and social researchers when stating they seem "somewhat removed and aloof from the day-to-day management battles and the politics of resource management . . . [in] closed clubs and reporting to themselves in their own journals, in their own circles." What more provocative challenge do we need?

Chapter 2

Perry Brown and Mike Manfredo define social values as including held values—concepts about objects—and assigned values—an indication of the worth of those objects. These concepts, held and assigned values, engender two basic questions: What basic values form our attitudes toward wildlife? What wildlife types and numbers, settings and opportunities are most valued by people? But our value system is not that simple; the authors go on to define intrinsic values—those inherent in the object or its relationship to others; economic values—those associated with production, consumption and exchange of goods and services; social values—those pertaining to society and divisible into four subcategories of cultural, societal, psychological, and physiological values. Although some information is available about value outcomes from fish and wildlife use, the authors point out that economic valuation techniques are limiting. Since underlying held values are usually unknown, one is left wondering for what underlying objects assigned values are being derived.

Chapter 3

Rich Bishop bases economic values on the compensation test indicating that benefits exceed costs or that it would be possible for gainers to compensate losers completely. There is increasing recognition that the list of gainers and losers in wildlife studies should include users of nonconsumptive, option and existence values besides traditional hunting and fishing users. Most interesting, Bishop points out that monetary values are assigned values, but that different held values among economists and wildlifers are an impediment to full integration of wildlife economics and wildlife biology. Economists take people and things as they find them, whereas wildlifers hold a strong predilection toward wildlife. Wildlife professionals do risk defeat over economics in the policy arena, where economic conclusions may run against wildlife, but they gain a powerful tool when results favor wildlife—as some studies do.

Chapter 4

Harold Steinhoff, Richard Walsh, Tony Peterle, and Joseph Petulla trace the evolution of the valuation of wildlife with excellent tabular chronologies of literature and events pertinent to attitudes toward wildlife and of legislation and policies. They also categorize methods of classifying wildlife values with a chronology of authors contributing noteworthy advances. These chronologies document the evolutionary process and reveal how ideas and insights have emerged, developed, and followed each other sequentially. One wonders where this dynamic process will lead next.

Chapter 5

Verburg, Charbonneau, Mangun, and Llewellyn of the U.S. Fish and Wildlife Service study the evaluation of trade-offs between sport fishing and hunting and other activities of society. In their chapter they emphasize that the key questions usually focus on a small part of the total resource and concern the value of an increased or decreased wildlife population increment. They then describe benefit/cost analysis and its need to rely on surrogate measures of willingness to pay such as travel cost and contingent value models, net economic values, and the marginal principle. They illustrate the benefit/cost framework and the marginal principle with examples of two hypothetical fisheries decisions—whether to build additional steelhead versus lake trout capacity in a lake, and allocation of catch between commercial and sport fishermen. The authors support economic analyses but argue for improved methods to account for intangibles. Presumably, scientists will continue to improve methods while the national surveys of fishing, hunting, and wildlife-associated recreation will continue to derive participation and cost data. The frameworks for data collection and analysis are in place, but much more study is needed, especially at state and local levels where wildlife programs and their social and economic impacts are felt first and foremost.

As a corollary to Part One, Joseph Petulla offers a lucid essay, "The Evolution of Wildlife Values: A Historical Footnote" (Appendix A). Here, Petulla reminds us about the held values underlying wildlife uses, which embrace a dominion-over-nature view of humankind often blamed on Judeo-Christian traditions but in fact traceable to pre-Christian Greek philosophers. Of greater practical importance is the evolution of new views (that reflect held values in conflict with traditional ones) such as antihunting, animal liberation, opposition to the use of laboratory test animals, or growing opposition to factory farming of chickens, cattle, or pigs. Petulla reminds us that held values are concepts about objects and assigned values merely express their worth. If held values are radically different then assigned values may be worthless.

Chapter 6

Part Two on Wildlife Resource Values Measurement Assessment features two chapters. In the first, Robert Davis and Diane Lim review historical methods for estimating the value of wildlife. They point out that economists are reluctant to claim that their results are a close approximation of the market because the most common methods—travel cost (TC) and survey or contingent value methods (CVM)—are indirect and are employed because market evaluations cannot be observed directly. The recent Wisconsin experiments testing hunters' willingness to pay (WTP) verify that the TC and CVM approaches can produce results reasonably close to actual sales. Two other ideas, option and existence values, have yielded positive results in recent studies and may soon be incorporated in WTP studies. The authors note that economists disapprove of gross expenditure studies, though they are the first evidence to be marshaled in support of wildlife (e.g., expenditures for birdseed, binoculars). Concluding their chapter is a state-of-the-art wetlands valuation example on an Army Corps of Engineers dredge permit.

Chapter 7

In Chapter 7 Dan Decker, Tommy Brown, Bev Driver, and Perry Brown present a theoretical framework to serve as a guide to organizing accumulated knowledge and further thinking and research about wildlife recreation from a social-value perspective. The framework has four major unit theories dealing with (1) goals—the individual's goals to be reached or met by wildlife recreation participation and categorized into three orientations, achievement, affiliative, and appreciative; (2) social psychological influences on behavior—including behavioral beliefs, outcome evaluations, normative beliefs, and motivations to comply; (3) activity adoption/rejection—a modification of the classical adoption and diffusion of innovations model; and (4) involvement maturation—a concept accounting for the growth of involvement in a wildlife recreation activity through sequential stages of interest, intensity, or specialization. This theoretical framework, which incorporates the methods and results from a wide spectrum of previous studies, may be one of the book's greatest contributions to the fields of wildlife and recreation.

Chapter 8

Part Three includes eight chapters on the direct economic uses of wildlife. In Chapter 8, Jim McDivitt of the Forest Service policy analysis staff provides a nice explanation of economic concepts applied to wildlife and fisheries management. It contains straightforward and wildlife-related explanations of benefit/cost analysis, opportunity costs, discounting, present net value, equity, welfare maximization, consumer surplus, economic efficiency, and joint production. That the subject is not that straightforward is also explained. For example, the Forest Service has found that wildlife values depend on the perspective, objectives, and political and economic philosophy. And no single value fits all situations. On public lands the issue becomes one of who pays and who benefits. Thus, the subsequent chapters in this book describing the many values of wildlife are extremely relevant.

Chapter 9

Skip Shelton's chapter, "Fee Hunting Systems and Important Factors in Wildlife Commercialization on Private Lands," provides a wealth of information. Fee systems are defined and illustrative values reported for permit, lease, commercial membership enterprises, and landowner memberships. Liability considerations are described for trespassers, licensees and invitees. Among the important factors discussed are uncertainty introduced by potentially changing wildlife regulations (including a real-life example from Colorado), property values, tenancy, credit, and taxation. Although the chapter is rich in examples, the discriminating reader will note that only three of eight references cited are less than 13 years old—perhaps supporting the author's call for more studies on the profitability of wildlife recreational enterprises. One of the chapter's greatest contributions is the call for development of a commercial wildlife management system site index.

Chapter 10

Dwight Guynn and Don Steinbach point out that the landowners are the real wildlife managers because they control land use, which has a decisive influence on habitat and thus on wildlife populations. In most cases on private land, wildlife is a by-product of crop production and may even be classified as a cost because of trespass, liability, and the nuisance of hunters. But in some places wildlife can pay. Their gross margin example for a Texas ranch shows that deer and quail are returning dollars at the margin, whereas cattle are not, because of typically lower fixed costs for wildlife management. With farmers suffering economic hardship, taking advantage of all land resources makes sense, and wildlife benefit where it pays. In Texas $80 million to $100 million per year are received by landowners from leasing hunting and fishing privileges.

Chapter 11

Michael Zagata of Tenneco Oil says that for the public sector to attract private sector participation in conservation of public values it should offer incentives to habitat protection based on market values and profit motives. He then describes such an approach to mitigation of project impacts through Habitat Evaluation Procedures (HEP) that determine adverse or positive impacts in Habitat Units (HU), a number obtained by multiplying the number of affected acres by the Habitat Suitability Index (HSI) of 0 to 1.0 for the affected species. Impacts and/or enhancement of habitat through management can thus be calculated, and a developer can incur HU credits or deficits to be deposited in a mitigation bank and applied at a later date to offset mitigation requirements. The existence of such a bank would place mitigation up front in the development permit process and help expedite approval. The concept is just that simple. Really! However, application of the concept is more complicated as illustrated by the Tenneco Oil Exploration and Production example in coastal Louisiana. Some of the possible uses of the HU bank may be more controversial; for example would we really want major land holders to sell or exchange HU credits? Should HU credits in Louisiana be transferred to Alaska? The HEP-mitigation bank idea forces us to consider such policies. Zagata describes an innovative approach to regulatory compliance from an ecological standpoint.

Chapter 12

I had mixed reactions to David Wesley's chapter on socio-duckonomics because I am an avid duck hunter, and obviously he is too. We have lost a lot of habitat, and hunters are responsible for protecting and restoring much nesting and wintering habitat. I agree with David that the key to a landowner's involvement with waterfowl is monetary incentive. So in principle I think the chapter's theme is good. But I disagree with his statement that it is typical to find four hunters in a boat "who have spent $200 to $300 each for a two-day hunt. Their hunt hosted by a fellow sportsman who has spent an additional $150 to $350 per guest per day for dogs, lodging, gasoline, equipment, food, and drink." I object to having extreme values cited ($3,500 to $7,500 annual lease fees per blind in Louisiana) as if they were typical. No doubt the data are accurate, but are they typical for waterfowl hunters in general? So, while applauding what economic incentives are doing to restore habitat, I hope enough farmers *do* double crop for ducks to bring the price within range of more typical hunters than the Ducks Unlimited members cited in this chapter—53% making over $35,000 per year and 32% over $50,000. This example proves the need for solid data on who the "typical" hunters are.

Chapter 13

Carlo Brunori provides a best case example of the value of wildlife to a landowner in his description of combined land use for agriculture and goose hunting on a farm at Worton on the Del-Mar-Va peninsula on the eastern shore of Maryland. Managed hunting for pass shooting of geese yields a harvest of 1,600 to 1,800 birds per season with leases of eight pits bringing $180 per day for a season-long 90-day lease or $200 per day for daily leases. The resulting maximum potential returns thus equal $129,600 to $144,000 for full use of the pits, which is added to other income for agricultural use. Obviously, the right location and right management are required for such a high return, and it also depends on careful management of surrounding habitat and conditions on public land and waters by public agencies. But with good management and coordination, those are big values for wildlife!

Chapter 14

Dale Wade argues in his chapter, "Economics of Wildlife Production and Damage Control on Private Lands," that the interest in wildlife production by private landowners must be coupled with recognition of the possible economic costs. Reviewing all chapters from the 1981 symposium on wildlife management on private lands, he emphasizes that, in their zeal to promote and accelerate wildlife management on private land, they make brief mention of wildlife damage in only 10 of the 45 chapters. Only 2 of the chapters provided signficant discussion. Wade's summary table of the kinds of urban and rural damage and hazards by 18 species of birds, rodents, and carnivores also makes a useful contribution. He has an important message, which has become very meaningful to me as the new dean of a forestry, wildlife and range sciences college, that is, that people take damage to forests and livestock very seriously and that since the stockmen's solutions are not acceptable we need some of our own.

Chapter 15

Tommy Hines and Frank Percival tell an interesting and inspiring story about Florida's alligator management program. Thirty percent of the revenues from state auctions of hides from nuisance harvests (a total of $221,767 in the past two years) is invested in research and management of the wild alligator resource. Equally valuable are research data from the program on alligator demographics that, combined with other studies, are contributing to a population model to help establish specific harvest quotas. The revenues from selected harvest of alligators are providing the research information essential to saving habitat and successful alligator ranching that will ensure a future for the species.

Chapter 16

Part Four addresses widlife and the quality of life in six chapters by leading figures in their field of emphasis. Lee Talbot's chapter, "The Ecological Value of Wildlife to the Well-being of Human Society," is outstanding. It provides a concise statement of how the functioning of the biosphere and hence the maintenance and enhancement of human life depend on uncounted numbers and species of plants, animals, and microorganisms interacting in a series of ecological processes. These processes are part of the life support systems, and Talbot provides good examples of how wildlife are involved in processes of soil formation and protection, nutrient cycling, maintenance of environmental quality through degrading or otherwise removing pollutants and preventing waste accumulation, pollination, germination, dispersal of seeds and other propagules, biogeochemical transport, community maintenance, predation, and habitat management.

Talbot explains that, although birds and wildlife are the more conspicuous forms of wildlife, they make up a small part of all biomass. For example, in the U.S. average biomass per 0.4 ha of insects and earthworms is about 373 kg, protozoa and algae about 50 kg, bacteria about 560 kg, fungi about 932 kg, plants about 18,277 kg, white-tailed deer in Michigan about 3 kg, black-tailed deer in California oak woodland and chaparral about 4 kg, and mixed plains wildlife in east African savanna about 41 to 58 kg. Talbot concludes with a quote from Dasman about the interdependence of wildlife and people and how we must cohabit the earth with wildlife or there will be no life on earth—that is the ultimate value of wildlife for humankind.

Chapter 17

Holmes Rolston III provides an outstanding essay ("Beauty and the Beast") on how natural wildlife is perceived and used and on how it enriches human life aesthetically. This unusual chapter is especially rich in wildlife examples. The framework for aesthetic experience of wildlife includes the following relationships:

1. Wild animals are seen as sources of spontaneous movement, excitement, surprise, uncertainty—qualities never replicated in zoos.
2. Wild animals have sentience, both kindred and alien—there is somebody behind the fur and feathers, a center of experience, decision and movement guided by perception and desire—qualities that in human perception help us leave society and culture and see life at its roots.
3. Behind the motion and sentience there is struggle; ideal and real as wild animals in their freedom face success or failure in transcending their environment. What we see as beauty may have only survival value to the animal and we tend to focus on the best and most pleasing and sublime while ignoring the weatherbeaten, which reflect the struggle in nature.
4. Finally, we draw symbols from wildlife of characteristics we value and attach them to such things as automobiles (cougars and rabbits), sports teams (falcons and bears) and streets (Mockingbird Lane) in an attempt to capture the competence, integrity, and character of wildlife. These symbolic uses diversify our culture, but most important they give us an attachment to landscape, locale, habitat, and place.

Chapter 18

A basic theme of the chapter on the educational value of wildlife by Jay Hair and Gerri Pomerantz is that wildlife is the vehicle that takes youth and adults alike into the broader arena of environmental education. For example, even though readers are initially interested in magazines such as *National Wildlife* because of animals, they are exposed to a wide range of environmental topics like air and water pollution, soil erosion, and toxic wastes. As revealed in several summarized studies, a child's early exposure to wildlife and the environment fosters his or her subsequent environmental interest and concern as an adult. Pomerantz's study of the impact of *Ranger Rick* revealed that, although the largest number of children read to learn about animals, the magazine also helped them with their schoolwork, and they had more positive attitudes about energy consumption, water pollution, and overpopulation.

The chapter concludes by urging educators and resource managers to capitalize on the value of wildlife in creating interest and motivation to act on the broader concerns of the environment. Part of an appropriate quotation from Schoenfeld sums it up: "The presence of wildlife at harmony with its environment is perhaps the best measure of our success in man-land relations."

Chapter 19

Bill Shaw's chapter on the recreational benefits of wildlife ties wildlife recreation to traditional recreation frameworks and benefits and also to unique values associated with cognitive aspects of such experiences. For example, a view is becoming accepted that rather than being superfluous diversion, recreation fulfills and enriches lives, leading to happier, healthier, and more productive members of society. Most Americans participate in some form of wildlife-oriented recreation at least occasionally, ranging from casual commitment a few days a year to intense and frequent participation serving as the focal point of leisure time activities. Participation includes 10% of the population in hunting, 25% in fishing, 49% in nonconsumptive wildlife recreation, and 59% in all forms of wildlife-oriented recreation—100 million people over 15 years old. Wildlife-oriented recreation is special because of the cognitive processes associated with these experiences, such as the symbolic and informational content of watching whales off the coast of southern California in a certain phase of their migration as the world's largest but endangered mammal. Shaw's ultimate message is that resource managers need to look beyond the overt behavior of participants to understand the experience. When they do they will find special meanings and thus benefits from wildlife-oriented recreation—and these meanings and benefits might be increased through provision of more information about wildlife.

Chapter 20

J. Baird Callicott writes on the philosophical value of wildlife, focusing on Aldo Leopold's ethical proposition that wildlife has intrinsic as well as instrumental value. The exploration is limited to Leopold's "evolutionary and ecological biology" and perspectives from the animal liberation/rights movement (a moral view found to be at odds with ecological facts of wildlife) and John Muir's "spiritual utility" view of wild nature (a theological orientation found inconsistent with the scientific foundations of conservation). A key argument rests on Leopold's ecological view that even seemingly worthless species are integrated members of the biotic community and contribute to its stability.

Chapter 21

Steve Kellert's chapter, "The Contributions of Wildlife to Human Quality of Life," provides a brief review of the author's highly regarded research on Americans' attitudes toward animals; the conclusions are directed more at policy and philosophical concerns. Kellert notes that, although the general U.S. public has a degree of appreciation of wildlife, it is typically narrow in intellectual and emotional focus and largely directed at a small component of the animal community. Some evidence exists that there has been a decline in utilitarian and commodity-oriented valuations of wildlife, as well as in overall levels of fear, hostility, and indifference, but some negative and utilitarian perceptions persist among lower socioeconomic, elderly, rural, and natural-resource–dependent groups. But Kellert's findings suggest that most philosophical, educational, economic, and ecological wildlife values—some of the values highlighted at this conference—are little recognized or understood by the general public. He warns that the general public has far to go before the contributions of wildlife to the human quality of life will be sufficiently recognized. Nevertheless, Kellert's conclusion reflects the commitment of most wildlifers that "land managed for wildlife is land ultimately more satisfying, attractive, and enjoyable for people."

Chapter 22

Part Five includes three chapters related to practical applications of values knowledge. In the first, Stucky, Bachant, Christoff, and Dieffenbach, all of the Missouri Department of Conservation (MDC), describe the important role of MDC environmental coordinators and review four case studies in which public input reduced or mitigated impacts on environmental values including habitat. Although the authors might have presented a more direct connection to wildlife value methodologies in this chapter, the implication is clear that such values and methodologies are vital to environmental assessment.

Chapter 23

Ben Peyton and Dan Decker, in "The Role of Values and Valuing in Wildlife Communication and Education," emphasize the need to address a wider range of factors that influence user behavior—including values and value-forming processes that are often a key to wildlife issues. Knowing public values can help in developing strategy to resolve issues, but more important they may be addressed by communication and education in the earliest stages before conflicts are aggravated.

Chapter 24

Dan Witter and Steven Sheriff, in "Wildlife Policy and Monitoring Public Values," present three case studies in which surveys of public values in Missouri are used in formulating and evaluating policy and programs. They point out that the incorporation of public values into wildlife policy is a never-ending process of monitoring public participation and expectations for use with other factors in the policy process.

Chapter 25

Part Six includes five chapters on wildlife resource value needs. Donald Cocheba presents an economist's view in "Opportunities for Improving Wildlife Management." His key is a defensible goal for wildlife management—one that looks beyond the wildlife or the preferences of a few individuals and organizations to the net benefits that members of society derive from the existence of wildlife. This approach requires determining the optimum size and composition of wildlife populations, the costs of producing such populations, and some index of the values and benefits derived from such wildlife production. Wildlife management in Cocheba's economic perspective requires a focus on these production functions with research and management information aimed at and shaped for decision-making models. Although most wildlifers might think this perspective oversimplifies things, Cocheba believes such an economic approach can help integrate disparate areas of wildlife biology into a more holistic approach to wildlife management. He goes on to explain more specific economic concepts and how they apply (with qualification) to wildlife management, for example, consumer surplus, marginal value, net benefit, double counting of benefits, types of values and benefits, and so on. This is a back-to-the-basics look at wildlife economics, and the ultimate implication is the need for better information on all aspects of wildlife production, including values, in order to make objectively defensible wildlife management decisions.

Chapter 26

Although Jim Lyons, in "Basic and Applied Social Research Needs in Wildlife Management," says that he does not intend to provide an all-inclusive summary of research on human dimensions of wildlife or a complete list of what is needed, he gives us a lot. Of great interest and value are his statements of why such information is important.

The social, cultural, and economic values that the public places on wildlife determine their interactions with wildlife. A responsive fish and wildlife agency must incorporate the values held by the public into management priorities and objectives. Public interest in wildlife is increasing, and people are ultimately responsible for identifying fish and wildlife management needs, setting priorities, and directing program development.

Although Lyons provides a good review of major studies, his challenging questions hold the key to future research. Who is our public? What does the public want and how do those wants develop? What is the public willing to pay and what is the value of wildlife? He points out how research findings can be applied to important issues such as evaluation of program effectiveness, insurance of access for hunting, determination of effects of recreation on fish and wildlife, and financing of fish and wildlife management. He concludes that a major value of such human dimensions research is that it provides cross-fertilization between the biological and social sciences, which will strengthen them both. Resource management problems are people problems, and the union of social and biological disciplines holds the key to resolving conflicts and promoting conservation.

Chapter 27

Jim Fazio, in "Priority Needs for Communication of Wildlife Values," offers a welcome change of pace with expert opinion backed by some data specifically collected for this effort. Using a modified Delphi technique on a sample of The Wildlife Society members, he asked what they thought were the most important wildlife values to be communicated to the public—and 25 items resulted. Rather than dwell on these findings, Fazio focuses on how we might be more successful in communicating them. His back-to-basics look needs immediate emphasis. To quote him:

> My contention is that value modification will take care of itself if we focus on what *is* within our reach—more effective dissemination of pertinent information, better public education, especially of the young (with such programs as Project Wild), and when necessary, persuasive argumentation. To do this, we need to know our public better, we need to plan our strategies better, and we need to prepare our new professionals better through improved curricula structures.

On the subject of curricula, Fazio offers specific data from a sample survey of The Wildlife Society's list of 93 colleges and universities with curricula related to wildlife management. Although they used to be neglected, humanities and social sciences appear to be excessively emphasized, however, the weakness in communication skills continues. Fazio likens our situation to a building with a good foundation but weak walls and no roof. He urges us to make our incoming professionals as good in communications as they are in biology, social science, and humanities. If we really believe that wildlife values should be communicated, then we must work to overcome our deficiencies as communicators and get on with the job. This chapter begs for action based on what we know now. The advice is sound!

Chapter 28

In Chapter 28 Herbert Doig details the many uses for information on wildlife values and some important challenges in implementing them.

Wildlife managers have traditionally resisted playing the numbers (values) game since most rejected such a concept as unrepresentative of true resource worth. The posture was defensive. During the past two decades, however, estimates of values have been used in fiscal analysis (1) to argue for a bigger share of tight money, (2) to gain credibility in policy debates, (3) to demonstrate importance of wildlife to local economies, (4) to develop new sources of funding, (5) to understand evolving and diversifying wildlife interest groups, (6) to support environmental analysis and mitigation, and (7) to guide public and private enterprises. But often values information is poorly developed or poorly used by managers who do not know how to use it effectively. We have not been trained to factor such influences into program development, and we have had little time to learn in a work atmosphere that pressures managers to do more for less. We need simplified techniques for interpretation of wildlife values information. The transition will not be easy and will require selection of new managers who can understand the big picture and who are capable of including all parameters, social and biological, in program development policy formation.

Chapter 29

Appropriately, the final chapter by Ed Langenau is entitled "Anticipating Wildlife Values of Tomorrow." Drawing on the assumption that dominant shifts in social values are associated with cycles in economic prosperity—and coincide with shifts in attitudes about natural resources—Langenau predicts renewed interest in political activity to protect natural resources in about 1995 when the current period of economic prosperity is predicted to end. Another assumption is that the attitudes of citizens toward the environment are shaped by their historical experience during the prosperity cycle. Citizens shaped during periods of economic prosperity are more likely to favor existence and aesthetic values. Other trends predicted include an aging of the population and shifts in population to rural locations with attendant increases in wildlife impacts.

POSTMORTEM

This impressive book will be the benchmark for economic and social valuation of wildlife for several years. Nearly every perspective has been covered with a few notable omissions: A chapter on subsistence values of fish and wildlife, a topic of special and growing concern in Alaska, would have been a useful contribution; the political value of wildlife in mobilizing environmental action might have been better covered.

This country owes much to the efforts of environmental organizations whose central focus revolves around wildlife—Audubon and National Wildlife Federation being the most prominent examples. Urban wildlife may also have been slighted, and I think fish were not included as prominently as they deserve.

While acknowledging these oversights of emphasis and application, it is important to recognize the most important value of the book—the establishment of analytical and methodological frameworks for looking at socioeconomic values of wildlife. Clearly we have made progress in the use of economics as an analytical tool for wildlife policy and decision making. Just as clearly, we have a long way to go in reconciling the differences in held values between economists and wildlife biologists. Although the book includes several chapters by economists addressing ways in which economics applies to wildlife, perhaps we also need more of the reverse. Ultimately we must make more progress in integrating social and biological perspectives. Perhaps some lessons from physics on mixing oil and water would be useful. But we often do not realize the great progress toward integration being made because so much more is obviously needed.

FOCUS FOR THE FUTURE

Where do we go from here in our attempts to further advance our understanding and use of economic and social values of wildlife? First, we need to see social and economic information integrated more thoroughly into wildlife management. The Wildlife Society has made a start by recognizing human dimensions in its categories of interest for members. Fish and wildlife conferences now acknowledge human dimensions by conducting sessions on the topic and including such papers at other sessions. Our esteemed leaders never fail to mention their importance when outlining wildlife management challenges. But we have a long ways to go to work the perspective and human dimensions knowledge into the fabric of the wildlife management profession—curricula, job descriptions, textbooks, media presentations, and management programs.

Second, it is time for greater recognition of human dimensions funding for wildlife research. How else can we make the needed progress—because we are still at infant levels of understanding compared to our biologist colleagues. Third, our decision making needs to routinely reflect social and economic values. Popular writing about wildlife is replete with values and people's appreciation of wildlife. We need to see how such values are routinely applied in decision making—because they usually are. But we need methods and much better application of our research-based knowledge.

Finally—and this has been said several times in this book—we need to reconcile the differences in held values and assumptions that keep economists and other social scientists apart from biologists. We need to have perspective, understanding, and tolerance, and we need to listen. We also need new methodology, new information, and analytical perspective. These chapters and this conference offer a timely dose of all these things.

The Evolution of Wildlife Values: A Historical Footnote

Joseph M. Petulla

The evolution of valuing wildlife gives rise to interesting questions because it is connected to so many current social issues. How can we understand the modern conflict between hunters and nonhunters? Or the sudden widespread interest in vegetarianism in Western countries? What about animal liberation, or the movement against the use of test animals in the laboratory, or even the growing literature deploring factory farming of chickens, cattle, and pigs? These questions are related to the more basic philosophical issue of the relationship between humans and animals, which is part of a larger issue of the relationship between humans and nature.

In a widely reprinted lecture at the 1966 American Association for the Advancement of Science meeting, Lynn White (1969) blamed the Judeo-Christian tradition of transcendence for the modern ecologic crisis. He stated that since Christianity and the Bible posit a radical dichotomy between God and the world and between humankind and nature, humans are given power over nature, including all animals, to use for their own good and ultimately for the glory of God. Human beings participate in God's power by exercising dominion over nature.

The primary difficulty with the White interpretation is that humans acted the same way toward nature and the animals for many centuries before any specific Christian view was developed, and when theologians did write commentaries on the Bible, they presented many different interpretations, usually influenced by other historical traditions. The most common interpretation until the modern era came from St. Thomas Aquinas (Translat. English Dominicans 1947), who claimed that man "excels" the animals by virtue of his reason and intelligence, not because of his power. Although early Christian interpreters held to the dominion view, their position could have come as readily from pre-Christian Greek philosophers as from biblical or other Christian writings.

Thus the Greek philosophers held to a radical dichotomy between human beings and animals long before any of the Bible was written down or a uniquely Christian approach was accepted. Most of the famous philosophical arguments to prove the existence of God (from which other positions were derived), especially in the Middle Ages, originated in the classic period of Greek philosophy, beginning in the fifth century B.C. with Socrates and Plato and lasting for at least a century. The most famous argument from design—that God has shown

His divine plan in the arrangement of everything on earth (including
the animals) as existing for a purpose—has been utilized by philosophers
and theologians to the present day. As shown in Glacken (1967), Xenephon
in *Memorabilia* put the design argument in the mouth of Socrates.

> Euthydemus: I begin to doubt whether after all the gods are occupied
> in any other work than the service of man. The one difficulty I feel is
> that the lower animals also enjoy these blessings.
>
> Socrates: The animals are produced and nourished for the sake of man,
> who gains more advantages from the animals than animals do from the
> fruits of the earth. All men tame and domesticate the useful kinds of
> animals, and make them their fellow-workers in war and many other
> undertakings. Animals are stronger than man, but man can put them to
> whatever use he chooses. The gods gave man his senses in order that he
> might take advantage of the innumerable beautiful and useful objects in
> the world. (1967:43)

Glacken explained that this argument from design, which implies the
superiority of humans over animals, has become a central theme in the
history of Western culture. Therefore, at least since classical Greek
times, Western culture has at least subconsciously considered animals
inferior beings to be used instrumentally by humans for their own
purposes.

After the classical Greek writers, the Stoics developed the notion of
design and emphasized the idea that humans are the caretakers of the
earth and use human reason to change the world for the better. They
till the soil and tame wild beasts. At the same time the Stoics believed
that humans participated in the reason that guided the whole world,
which lower animals could not. Because of their reason humans could
create a "second nature" within nature, changing the earth and all on
it for their own benefit and perfection. This notion was expressed by
many Christian philosophers and theologians in the Middle Ages. The
inspiration for the thought of St. Thomas Aquinas came primarily from
Aristotle, whose central notions were not significantly dissimilar from
the Stoics. Aquinas considered reason an essentially human quality, one
that placed human beings above the animals and gave them the right
to act as masters over the earth. The monks of the Christian church
had already shown their willingness to tame the forests and build enclaves
of faith in wilderness areas of Europe.

This central cultural assumption of Western society—that human
beings are supreme over the rest of the world—predated and undoubtedly
influenced the later Judeo-Christian idea of stewardship or domination,
which strengthened this cultural stance. A new dimension was added

in the West with the coming of the scientific revolution in Europe. Science came to be equated with the earlier philosophical understanding of reason in the project of controlling nature and the natural world for the benefit of humankind, but without a transcendent power. No longer could philosophers or theologians invoke the mediation of a gentler higher being to mitigate the effects of humanistic science. The new assumption of Western culture did not place reason at the disposal of a higher reason but at the whim of the private person, nationalistic state, or corporate power. Humans were left with the job of discovering the secrets of the machine of nature, which was endowed with no godly powers of its own. Today reason is still in the saddle over nature or nonreason.

Of course, this cultural assumption did not mean that all humans necessarily had the social or legal right to exercise their power over wildlife. One reason that thousands flocked to the shores of the new continent was the freedom to hunt and fish to their hearts' content. Throughout Europe fish and game laws promulgated by the nobility or gentry prohibited peasants from access to game. In the New World game were present in such numbers that no one dreamed that they could ever drop to extinction levels. At the same time the immigrants were too preoccupied with wresting survival from a harsh environment to worry about the extinction of wildlife. The conditions of life in America supported the perennial assumptions of Western culture of humankind's dominance. In truth, human beings needed to dominate the environment to survive.

By the time of the Civil War the situation had begun to change. Gold had been discovered in California, and enormous population pressures began to be felt in the west. The number of buffalo, which had roamed the plains in the millions at the midnineteenth century, fell to a few thousand by the end. In the east, wildlife populations dropped at an alarming rate. During the nineteenth century a movement was started by a few people and organizations that slowly changed the pattern of valuing wildlife.

Wildlife conservation was not a new idea in Europe since the nobility prohibited open access to their forests precisely because they wanted to keep their game for themselves, for sport and for food. But the few American conservationists who spoke out early in the 1800s had to struggle to even get laws passed to observe hunting seasons on endangered game. When sportsmen's clubs managed to have state laws passed, counties were usually permitted to exempt themselves. Game laws were considered an unwarranted infringement of liberty.

The prototype club, the New York Sportsmen's Club, was founded in 1844 to protect and preserve game for purposes of hunting. The club formulated laws for hunting season in the counties and later the state of New York, but much of its work was educational. Henry William Herbert, who drafted the club's petition to the state legislature, wrote articles on the outdoors and was one of the first writers to take up the cause of wildlife depletion in the country. He wrote under the pen name of Frank Forester in *The Spirit of the Times* and *Turf Register,* two well-known sportsmen's magazines. There were no game wardens at the time so members of the New York club sought out and sued poachers who violated county game laws. Herbert wrote to club members in 1847, "I rejoice to hear of your success with the Game-killers; one or two more examples will work wonders" (Trefethen 1975:74).

A second influential writer was George Bird Grinnell, who became an editor of *Forest and Stream* magazine in 1876 and was a founding member of the famous Boone and Crockett Club. His life-long crusade in association with the magazine, in which he became senior editor and publisher in 1880, was a campaign against market hunting and for realistic game laws. He worked with Theodore Roosevelt and others interested in big game hunting in the Boone and Crockett Club for the preservation of big game in North America. Grinnell's investigatory articles on big game poaching in Yellowstone National Park in 1894 led directly to Congress's enactment of the Yellowstone Park Protection Act, a pivotal piece of legislation for the many national parks that followed. He had great influence on later wildlife legislation and in 1886 founded the New York Audubon Society, forerunner of the National Audubon Society.

Forest and Stream magazine contributed another inveterate campaigner for game preservation in John Bird Burnham, its business manager from 1891 to 1897. He later operated a game preserve, became the chief game protector of New York state, and served as the first president of the American Game Protective and Propagation Association in 1911. By that time Theodore Roosevelt's administration had established strong legal foundations for the long-term economic management of land and wildlife for future use of the American people. The central assumption of Western culture—that the right to enjoy animals belongs to all Americans (not only mean-spirited poachers and profiteers)—was not changed significantly in the literature and campaigns of the game preservation and management movement.

The most popular early figure to move away from this position was William Temple Hornaday, who became chief taxidermist for the U.S. National Museum in 1882. He was instrumental in starting the National Zoological Park in Washington, D.C., and later became the first director of the New York Zoological Park. Throughout his career his fame as a zookeeper was equaled by his notoriety as a champion of wildlife protection and as a vicious foe of sport hunting and the manufacturers of sporting arms. He worked tirelessly for laws against the sale of wild game and importation of wild bird plumage. The frontispiece for his immensely popular book, *Our Vanishing Wildlife,* published in 1913, was a cartoon depicting a saloon filled with hundreds of furs and game trophies and with caricatured hunters. He established the Permanent Wild Life Fund in 1913 and wrote about 20 books on wildlife preservation, including *30 Years War for Wildlife* in 1913.

During the same period John Muir was writing on conservation themes for national journals and newspapers as well as his own magazine, *Picturesque California.* He founded the Sierra Club and wrote a dozen books that urged care for the land and the beauty of the forest beyond management notions. Muir is best known for his descriptions of mountain scenery, but included in many of his writings were comments on bears, sheep, deer, squirrels, and even lizards and rattlesnakes. Muir was an early advocate of animal rights, at least in the sense of treating animals as equals. For example, in 1901 in *Our National Parks* Muir wrote:

> Before I learned to respect rattlesnakes I killed two, the first on the San Joaquin plain. He was coiled comfortably around a tuft of bunch-grass, and I discovered him when he was between my feet as I was stepping over him. He held his head down and did not attempt to strike, although in danger of being trampled. At that time, thirty years ago, I imagined that rattlesnakes should be killed wherever found. I had no weapon of any sort, and on the smooth plain there was not a stick or a stone within miles; so I crushed him by jumping on him, as the deer are said to do. Looking me in the face he saw I meant mischief, and quickly cast himself into a coil, ready to strike in defense. I knew he could not strike when traveling, therefore I threw handfuls of dirt and grass sods at him, to tease him out of coil. He held his ground a few minutes, threatening and striking, and then started off to get rid of me. I ran forward and jumbed on him; but he drew back his head so quickly my heel missed, and he also missed his stroke at me. Persecuted, tormented, again and again he tried to get away, bravely striking out to protect himself; but at last my heel came squarely down, sorely wounding him, and a few more brutal stampings crushed him. I felt degraded by the killing business, farther from heaven, and I made up my mind to try to be at least as fair and charitable as the snakes themselves, and to kill no more save in self-defense. (1980:170, 171)

Muir often talked about animals as conscious beings. In *The Story of My Boyhood and Youth* (1912) (Kimes and Kimes 1984) he recounted how as a young man he was impressed by a goose who attacked him to defend another bird he had shot. After this time he rarely took firearms into the wilderness. Muir was different from even a kindred spirit like Hornaday in that he defended the so-called varmints or bad animals like alligators, snakes, and lizards. He wrote benignly about flies and revised his stern criticism of domestic sheep—"hoofed locusts" that destroyed the vegetation of mountain meadows. He deeply loved his dog Stickeen who accompanied him through difficult adventures across an Alaskan glacier, saying "through him as through a window I have ever since been looking with deeper sympathy into all my fellow mortals" (Mighetto 1985:71). At the time of writing *The Story of My Boyhood and Youth,* Muir advocated the rights of animals in and for themselves. He "never happened upon a trace of evidence that seemed to show that any one animal was ever made for another as much as it was for itself" and denounced the notion that "animals have neither mind nor soul, have no rights that we are bound to respect, and were made only for man, to be petted, spoiled, slaughtered, or enslaved" (Mighetto 1985:71). This philosophy represents a clear departure from the assumptions of the superiority of humans over animals in Western culture. Muir's most famous works were *The Mountains of California* (1894), *The Yosemite* (1912), *Our National Parks* (1901) and *Travels in Alaska* (1915).

Aldo Leopold carried on this tradition, but his *Game Management* (1933) was a traditional, though more sophisticated, version of earlier notions of game management. His *Sand County Almanac,* published posthumously in 1949, carried Muir's biocentric appreciation of nature and all its creatures to the young environmentalists of the 1970s. However, even in this famous book, which introduced the notion of a land ethic, Leopold recommended hunting in the wilderness as an excellent form of recreation (Callicott 1980). Leopold's appreciation of wildlife was set in the context of ecological balance and species preservation, as opposed to a biocentric valuing of animals as important in themselves or even the traditional economic considerations of game management. (Petulla 1980*a, b*).

A more recent philosophical development in the history of thought of valuing animals, one completely separate from any kind of "management" thinking and in the biocentric tradition, has been the animal liberation movement in the 1970s. In 1973 Peter Singer wrote a widely reprinted article that attempted to prove on rational and philosophical grounds that animals are an oppressed group. He attempted to illustrate the many ways in which animals are treated as things to be used rather than as beings with a right to live their own lives. In the essay and a book, *Animal Liberation* (1975), he mainly used examples from animal experimentation and factory farming. Another philosopher, Tom Regan, wrote in the mid-1970s on the philosphical and ethical aspects of animal rights, including essays on vegetarianism, animal experimentation, whaling, the need for reform in laws relating to animals, and the possibility of a new environmental ethic. Both Singer and Regan argued for a new ethical status of animals by examining the principle of equality to include nonhuman as well as human animal species. Both were interested in the elimination of individual animal suffering in any form but did not advocate the upgrading of the value humans place on nonhuman species or the importance of wildlife in ecosystems as much as Leopold and his followers did.

The significant aspect of the animal rights movement is that a great deal of legislation has been formulated regarding the treatment of nonhuman animals, but most of it has addressed the protection of animals or mammals whose perceptions of pleasure and pain we assume to be similar to our own. Thus the Federal Laboratory Animal Welfare Act proposed, according to a House committee report, to ensure that animals are "accorded the basic creature comforts of adequate housing, ample food and water, reasonable handling, decent sanitation . . . and adequate veterinary care including the appropriate use of pain-killing drugs" (U.S. House of Representatives 1970).

Beyond new philosophical and legal challenges to the assumptions of Western culture are serious scientific experiments on consciousness in animals. In *Animal Thinking* Donald Griffin (1984) of the Rockefeller University describes dozens of experiments that indicate that primates can lie and even bees can think. Other scientists who have presented evidence that indicates that animals have a degree of consciousness similar to human thinking are James Gould (*Ethology: The Mechanisms and Evolution of Behavior* [1982]) and Alison Jolly (*The Evolution of Primate Behavior* [1985]). Scientific experiments and new research on the activity of the brain are forming the basis for new philosophical assumptions regarding human/animal relationships.

REFERENCES

AQUINAS, T. Translat. English Dominicans. 1947. Summa theologica. Part I, Quest. 3, Art. 1, and Quest. 96, Art. 2. Burns and Oats, London.

CALLICOTT, J. B. 1980. Animal liberation: a triangular affair. Environ. Ethics 2:311–338.

GLACKEN, C. J. 1967. Traces on the Rhodian shore. Univ. Calif. Press, Berkeley. 763pp.

GOULD, J. L. 1982. Ethology: the mechanisms and evolution of behavior. W. W. Norton and Co., New York. 544pp.

GRIFFIN, D. R. 1984. Animal thinking. Harvard Univ. Press, Cambridge, Mass. 256pp.

JOLLY, A. 1985. The evolution of primate behavior. Macmillan Co., New York. 526pp.

KIMES, W. F., AND M. B. KIMES, editors. 1984. The complete John Muir: a reading bibliography. Peregrine Smith, Salt Lake City. 384pp.

LEOPOLD, A. 1933. Game management. Charles Scribner's Sons, New York. 481pp.

———. 1949. A sand county almanac. Oxford Univ. Press, New York. 226pp.

MIGHETTO, L. 1985. Muir among the animals. Sierra, Mar/Apr:71.

MUIR, J. 1980. Wilderness essays. Peregrine Smith, Salt Lake City. 263pp.

PETULLA, J. M. 1980a. American environmentalism: values, tactics, priorities. Texas A&M Univ. Press, College Station. 239pp.

———. 1980b. Historical values affecting wildlife in American society. Pages 23–30 *in* W. W. Shaw and E. H. Zube, eds. Wildlife values. Cent. for Assessment of Noncommodity Nat. Resour. Values, Inst. Ser. Rep. No. 1, Univ. Arizona, Tucson.

SINGER, P. 1973. Animal liberation. New York Rev. of Books, April 5:17–21.

———. 1975. Animal liberation: a new ethics for our treatment of animals. New York Rev., New York. 297pp.

TREFETHEN, J. B. 1975. An American crusade for wildlife. Winchester Press, New York. 409pp.

U.S. HOUSE OF REPRESENTATIVES. 1970. Rep. No. 1651, 91st Congr., 2nd sess. 2.

WHITE, L. 1969. The historical roots of our ecologic crisis. Science 155:1203–1207.

Case Studies and Management Examples: Poster Sessions

Chaired by
Rainer H. Brocke, *Associate Professor of Wildlife Ecology, SUNY–College of Environmental Science and Forestry, Syracuse, New York*

Section B-1

Perceived Value of Woodland Caribou in Establishing a Northwestern Ontario Park

Harold G. Cumming, *School of Forestry, Lakehead University, Thunder Bay, Ontario, Canada, P7B5E1*

This section reports on the results of a study of woodland caribou (*Rangifer tarandus caribou*) that helped to resolve a land use dispute in the Wabakimi Lake area of northwestern Ontario. Since 1900 the southern limit of caribou distribution in wooded northern Ontario has been receding northward (Cringan 1956), and now they are found only in scattered bands (Simkin 1965). In a previous, unpublished study of woodland caribou around Lake Nipigon, Ontario, a winter concentration of about 100 caribou was located south of Wabakimi Lake, approximately 50 km northwest of Armstrong, Ontario, and 350 km north of Thunder Bay on Lake Superior. This number represented half of the caribou in the entire 32,000 sq km study area. Therefore, they seemed worthy of further investigation.

Fieldwork began in 1981, but after only one winter of study, the information became public that logging was planned in the area for the first time. Opposition to the logging resulted in a series of public meetings in which wilderness proponents demanded a park even larger than the one suggested in a Strategic Land Use Plan for Northwestern Ontario (Minist. Nat. Resour. 1980) by the Ontario Ministry of Natural Resources (OMNR). As the controversy grew, groups on both sides became interested in the whereabouts of the caribou. The objective of the study was to identify and delineate those areas used by caribou in the general vicinity of the proposed park.

The study area was approximately 70 km by 110 km, beginning in the south at the transcontinental Canadian National Railway line. The area is typical of the Canadian Shield: cold (mean daily January temperature −20°C) and moderately dry (total annual precipitation 750 mm of water) with rounded rock outcrops covered with lichens (e.g., *Cladonia* spp.) and scattered jack pine (*Pinus banksiana*). Some pockets of deeper soil support good stands of black spruce (*Picea mariana*). Human activities in the area included outfitting for fishermen and hunters, canoe tripping during summer, and traditional trapping.

Transects were flown with a Cessna 185 at 3-km intervals, north-south over the southern half of the study area and east-west over the northern half. Tracks of caribou were recorded on 1:126.720 maps and later transferred to the CARIS Geographic Information System for compilation. No effort was made to look for caribou except during March and April when they sometimes walked or lay on the ice of frozen lakes. A helicopter permitted following tracks in snow for spring movements. During the snow-free period lakes in the area were visited by air and by canoe to look for tracks on sand beaches (as suggested by Bergerud, pers. commun.). Many areas were also searched for caribou pellet groups. Four caribou were collared with radio transmitters.

Aerial transects during the winters of 1981-1983 totaled 7,634 km and provided 557 sightings of caribou tracks. The caribou used approximately the same general portion of the study area each winter, with annual variation around the edges; thus the observations could be combined to show a total range occupied by caribou with an intensive use area that contained the greatest concentration of tracks (Fig. B-1.1). Summer observations fell within this same general area except for one band of about six caribou whose tracks were followed in spring outside the study area to the west.

The Strategic Land Use Plan (Minist. Nat. Resour. 1980) had proposed a park that might have contained the caribou, but its boundaries were purposely vague. Furthermore, at the time it was published the area occupied by caribou was unknown. Thus as each year's caribou data became available they were communicated to all interested parties, including the local office of the OMNR Parks Branch that was charged with investigating the possibility of a new park.

Logging companies were interested mainly in access through the area occupied by caribou to better timber in surrounding areas. However, general development often follows road building, and in previous decades caribou disappeared from developed areas (Cringan 1956). Therefore, a proposal for a new trunk logging road through the middle of the major caribou concentration caused some public concern (Fig. B-1.1).

Wilderness enthusiasts voiced this concern and pressed for a park that would include the caribou range and a large area to the north with several interesting natural features and some attractive canoeing country, including access to the Albany River (Fig. B-1.1). Although the presence of caribou could be used as an argument for stopping construction of the road, it could not be used to support the proposed northern addition to the park requested by wilderness enthusiasts.

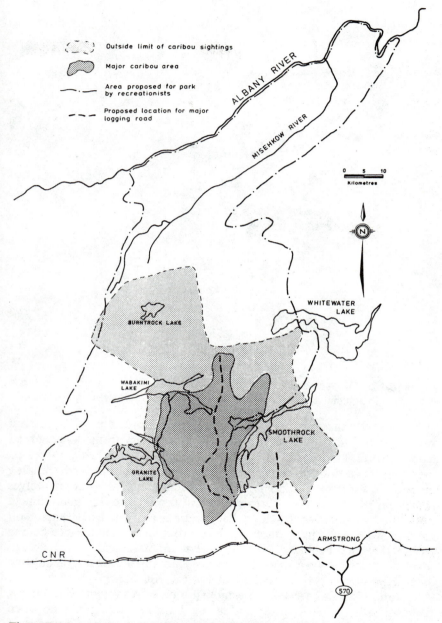

Figure B-1.1 Alternative proposals for use of the Wabakimi area—logging roads and an extended park—showing their relationships to areas occupied by woodland caribou

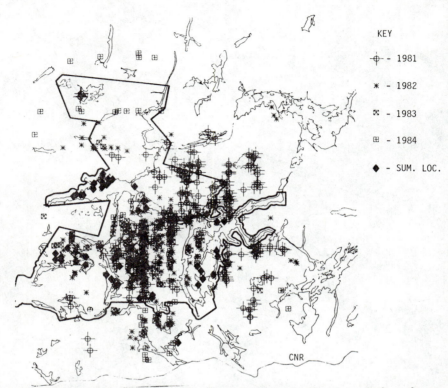

KEY

⊕ - - 1981

✳ - 1982

� - 1983

⊞ - 1984

◆ - SUM. LOC.

Figure B-1.2 GIS-generated map of study area showing boundaries of new Wabakimi Provincial Park and locations of caribou track sightings

Throughout the controversy I maintained a neutral position. A park would prevent any major developments associated with the logging road from harming the caribou. However, it would also bring increased numbers of vacationers who might pose a different threat by camping on islands used by the caribou for protection of calves from wolves (Bergerud et al. 1984). Furthermore, if some kind of management initiative were desired (such as habitat improvement or perhaps wolf control), wilderness park status might prevent such action. Since zoning within the park could be used to deal with these concerns, I argued that if a decision were made to have a park in the area, it should be located in such a way as to protect the caribou herd.

In June 1983 the decision to establish a park was announced, ending the possibility of a logging road being built. However, the northern addition requested by the wilderness proponents was not included in the park; instead, the boundaries generally coincided with the areas occupied by caribou (Fig. B-1.2). Some less used areas around the edges of the major concentration were excluded. These and an incursion in the boundary on the west side of the park probably represented areas where the value of timber was judged to outweigh the value of caribou; elsewhere the paramount value of the caribou was recognized. The conservation of caribou was probably facilitated by their use of areas with many rock outcrops supporting lower volume stands that would be difficult to regenerate. Nevertheless, the logging roads were excluded, the extended canoeing area was not included, and the major caribou range was protected. The conclusion seems justified that the perceived value of the caribou contributed substantially to decisions determining the establishment, final location, and boundaries of the park.

Acknowledgments.—Support for this study was provided by Great Lakes Forest Products, the World Wildlife Fund, the Canadian Forestry Service and the Ontario Ministry of Natural Resources (OMNR). D. B. Beange and other members of the OMNR assisted greatly with the field work. J. S. Kapro of Lakehead University Center for Application of Resource Information Systems (CARIS) helped with computer compilations.

REFERENCES

BERGERUD, A. T., H. E. BUTLER, AND D. R. MILLER. 1984. Antipredator tactics of calving caribou: dispersion in mountains. Can. J. Zool. 62:1566–1575.

CRINGAN, A. T. 1956. Some aspects of the biology of caribou and a study of the woodland caribou of the Slate Islands, Lake Superior, Ontario. M.A. Thesis, Univ. Toronto, Ont. 300pp.

MINISTRY OF NATURAL RESOURCES. 1980. Strategic land use plan. Northwestern Ontario planning region. Ont. Minist. Nat. Resour. 84pp.

SIMKIN, D. W. 1965. A preliminary report of the woodland caribou study in Ontario. Dep. Lands and For. Resour. Rep. (Wildl.) 59. 76pp.

Section B-2

Attitudes Toward Wildlife in West Germany

Wolfgang Schulz, *Wildbiologische Gesellschaft München e.V.,*
Postfach 270, D-8103, Oberammergau, West Germany

In this study W. Schulz measured attitudes toward wildlife in West Germany. Stephen R. Kellert's questionnaire was translated and adapted to German conditions, and Kellert's attitude scales were used (Kellert 1980). Pupils of adult colleges from every part of West Germany responded to the questionnaire. A total of 1,484 questionnaires were evaluated.

The following hierarchy of attitudes toward wildlife were identified: moralistic, humanistic, naturalistic, ecologistic, negativistic, scientistic, utilitarian, and dominionistic. The response scores in these categories are shown in Table B-2.1 under the category "whole sample." According to these data the predominant attitudes are emotional ones, namely moralistic, which represent the "primary concern for the right and wrong treatment of animals" (Kellert 1980:35); humanistic, which reflect the "strong affection for individual animals" (Kellert 1980:35), and naturalistic, which express the affection for the whole nature. The ecologistic attitude, which shows the "primary concern for the environment as a system" (Kellert 1980:34), ranks fourth. The two materialistic attitudes—utilitarian and the dominionistic—subordinate.

The mean values of the attitudes are graphed in Figure B-2.1. They were significantly different for various demographic groups, activity groups, and groups with differing knowledge. The median of knowledge in the whole sample has a value of 57; the minimum is 11; and the maximum is 90 in a potential range from 0 to 99.

Knowledge was the best variable to explain different scores on the attitude scales (Table B-2.1). Respondents with a very high knowledge level have high values on the moralistic, the naturalistic, the ecologistic, and the scientific attitude scales. On the other hand, people with very low knowledge level have high values on the humanistic, negativistic, and utilitarian attitude scales. On the dominionistic attitude scale respondents with intermediate knowledge levels have the highest values (Table B-2.1).

TABLE B-2.1
Attitude Scale Scores by Different Knowledge Classes

| Attitude | Knowledge Class | | | | | Whole |
(Sig. of F-value)	Very low	Low	Middle	High	Very high	sample
Moralistic (0.3314)	0.606	0.629	0.642	0.637	0.643	0.632
Humanistic (0.0000)	0.331	0.328	0.317	0.279	0.282	0.307
Naturalistic (0.0000)	0.224	0.259	0.285	0.317	0.351	0.287
Ecologistic (0.0000)	0.180	0.202	0.222	0.267	0.311	0.236
Negativistic (0.0000)	0.1923	0.1917	0.166	0.144	0.134	0.166
Scientistic (0.0000)	0.1049	0.107	0.1047	0.120	0.158	0.119
Utilitaristic (0.0007)	0.124	0.106	0.098	0.100	0.088	0.103
Dominionistic (0.1380)	0.056	0.052	0.058	0.046	0.044	0.051

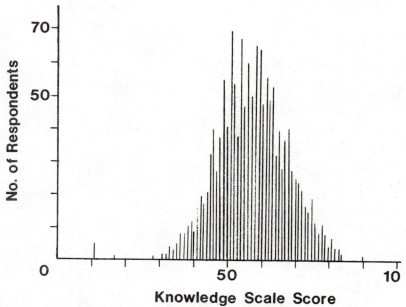

Figure B-2.1 Distribution of knowledge scale scores

Respondents with high knowledge level worry about the right and wrong treatment of animals and oppose the exploitation of and cruelty toward animals (moralistic attitude). The humanistic attitude is expressed by respondents who have a very low knowledge level and appear to demonstrate affection for individual animals. This affection for animals seems to prevent an affection for wildlife and nature, as people with a very low knowledge score also score low on the naturalistic attitude scale. Perhaps people with a very low knowledge level are thinking in terms of simple constructs typified by individual' animals, and though they demonstrate affection for individual animals, they may not be able to see the complexity of nature as a whole and are less concerned about the problems of environmental degradation.

REFERENCES

KELLERT, S. R. 1980. Contemporary values of wildlife in American society. Pages 31–60 *in* W. W. Shaw and E. H. Zube, eds. Wildlife values. Cent. for Assessment of Noncommodity Nat. Resour. Values, Inst. Ser. Rep. No. 1, Univ. Arizona, Tucson.

Wildlife Problems, Human Attitudes, and Response to Wildlife in the Syracuse, New York, Metropolitan Area

Michael A. O'Donnell, *Department of Biology, State University College at Cortland, Cortland, NY 13045*

Larry W. VanDruff, *Faculty of Environmental and Forest Biology, State University of New York, College of Environmental Science and Forestry, Syracuse, NY 13210*

A telephone survey of Syracuse, New York, metropolitan households was conducted over a four-month period. Thirty percent of the contacted households had experienced problems with wildlife during the two years preceding the survey. Those respondents who had had problems with wildlife were asked about the types of problems, their solutions, and their attitudes toward certain local wildlife species.

Those species that caused the most problems in the city were the gray squirrel (*Sciurus carolinesis*) and pigeon (*Columba livia*) (23% and 20% of all problems, respectively), whereas the species that caused most suburban problems were the gray squirrel and cottontail rabbit (*Sylvilagus floridanus*) (23% and 19% of all problems, respectively). The most common type of problem reported in the city was "general nuisance" (39% of all problems), but in the suburbs the most frequently reported problem involved damage in the yard (41% of all problems), usually to the lawn or a vegetable garden. General nuisance accounted for 25% of all suburban problems. The distribution of wildlife-related problems and responses to those problems were independent of measured socio-economic factors. Only half of all respondents attempted to solve their problems. Of those who did try, only 45% were successful.

Measurements of respondents' attitudes showed common songbirds to be the most liked species, followed by squirrels and rabbits. There was a significant correlation between reports of problems with a species and attitudes toward that species. Respondents' species preference strongly correlated with their preferred management goal for that species (gamma

> 0.60 for all species), and the experience of a previous problem made the preference rating an even stronger predictor of the preferred management goal for that species (gamma > 0.70). Respondents with nonrural backgrounds had a stronger correlation between likability of a species and desired management goal for that species than respondents with rural backgrounds (gamma = 0.722 vs. 0.561). Urban residents were more emotionally attached to animals and did not respond to wildlife problems and control in the same manner as rural residents did. The effect of wildlife problems or attitudes is an important consideration in urban wildlife management.

Section B-4

Public Values and White-Tailed Deer Management in New York

Gerri A. Pomerantz, *Department of Natural Resources,*
New York State College of Agriculture and Life Sciences,
Cornell University, Ithaca, NY 14853

Randall Stumvoll, *New York State Department of*
Environmental Conservation, Warrensburg, NY 12885

Daniel J. Decker, *Department of Natural Resources,*
New York State College of Agriculture and Life Sciences,
Cornell University, Ithaca, NY 14853

Biological knowledge is essential to natural resource management, but the ability to apply wildlife management principles is often dependent on social values and political considerations. A state natural resource agency cannot effectively manage deer if its management authority has been limited by legislative action. Understanding the public's needs and concerns and communicating the rationale for agency programs back to the public are necessary steps to achieving management objectives.

In New York, it was recognized that incorporating public values into the formation of management objectives was a prerequisite to a successful deer management program. Historically, deer management programs in northern New York (NNY) have been seriously curtailed by negative public sentiment (Fig. B-4.1). The antlerless deer hunting authority exercised during the 1960s in NNY ended in 1970 because of legislative mandate. The Human Dimensions Research Unit at Cornell University, under contract by the New York State Department of Environmental Conservation (DEC) conducted a series of studies from the mid1970s to 1980s to identify the underlying reasons for the controversy over DEC deer management programs (Table B-4.1). It was determined that many NNY residents were unaware of deer management programs in the area. People claimed that the agency did not communicate with its constituents and that there was a lack of "responsiveness" from DEC representatives (Brown and Decker 1976, Decker et al. 1980).

Figure B-4.1 Evolution of Northern New York Strategic
Plan for Deer Management

The DEC recognized that public understanding and support were paramount if initiation of any major management modification was to occur. Without this support only minor changes in recreational opportunity and no control of ecological or economic impacts by deer could be expected. Consequently, a team of managers developed the Northern New York Strategic Plan for Deer Management. The plan considered both the biological and the social factors necessary for deer management in the northern zone (NZ) (Fig. B-4.2).

The highest priority of the DEC deer management plan was to gather information to develop and implement an effective communications program. A basic understanding of how the public perceives the DEC deer management program, the methods of communicating their concerns, and the ways in which they learn about deer management programs was needed. To fulfill this need, a series of four studies was contracted with Cornell University.

In the first study (Decker et al. 1983, Smolka et al. 1983) the degree of support among NNY hunters for DEC's suggested deer management alternatives in the region was determined. The second study (Smolka et al. 1985, Smolka and Decker 1985) provided information on the attitudes toward deer and deer management held by leaders or officials of organizations representing a broad spectrum of interest in NNY deer

TABLE B-4.1
Studies of Public Concerns About Deer Management in Northern New York
Conducted Between 1975-1981

Objectives	Audience	Findings
Study I[a] 1975-76 Determine causes of communications barriers between DEC and northern zone (NZ) residents	NZ residents	•General lack of knowledge about existing deer management programs •Hunters were more negative about DEC than were non-hunters •Agency personnel viewed favorably but DEC communications rated poorly •People perceived lack of responsiveness to their problems
Study II[b] 1976 Identify communications problems within DEC	Environmental conservation officers (ECOs) Forest Rangers Bureau of Wildlife	•Communications problems existed between the Bureau of Wildlife and the ECOs and Forest Rangers
Study III[c] 1977-78 Determine if illegal deer killing is socially acceptable	Landowners Local Magistrates Environmental Conservation Officers (ECOs)	•Recognized illegal deer killing occurred •Not generally acceptable •Compared with downstate regions: -more ECOs and magistrates believed arrest and prosecution of violators were extremely important to protect deer -arrest and prosecution rates were similar to those throughout the state

[a]Source: Brown and Decker 1976.
[b]Source: Decker 1976.
[c]Source: Decker et al. 1980, 1981.

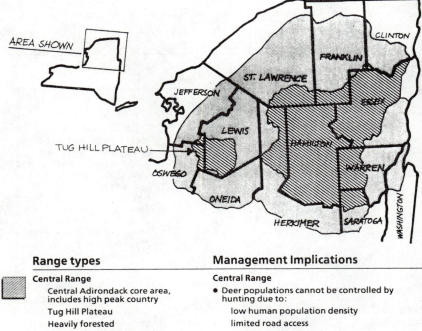

Range types

Central Range
Central Adirondack core area,
includes high peak country
Tug Hill Plateau
Heavily forested
Predominantly state-owned land
Mostly inaccessible

Transition Range
Surrounds the "core area"
Heavily forested
Predominantly privately owned land
Fairly accessible

Agricultural Range
Borders Lake Champlain, St. Lawrence
River, Lake Ontario, and Black River
Rolling farmland

Management Implications

Central Range
● Deer populations cannot be controlled by
hunting due to:
  low human population density
  limited road access
  high winter mortality
● Area is well-suited for recreational hunting

Transition Range
● Deer could be controlled by hunting:
  meeting recreational needs of people
  meeting biological needs of deer
  preventing undue damage to private
  property by deer

Agricultural Range
● Deer populations could be allowed to grow in
some areas:
  antlerless harvests could be used if necessary
  for control later

Figure B-4.2 Biological factors and management implications for deer management in the northern zone of New York

management. The purpose of the third study was to determine the
importance of the deer resource to nonconsumptive recreationists in
NNY. Two surveys were conducted, one of nonresident recreationists
and one of resident (landowner) recreationists. The fourth and final
study in the NNY plan concerned the role of teachers in integrating

wildlife management principles and concepts into curricula of NNY public schools.

As a result of the first two studies, four general attitude orientations toward granting DEC deer management authority were identified (Fig. B-4.3). The four management acceptance typology groups were (1) the "full support" type, which granted DEC unequivocal deer management authority in the NZ, (2) the "conditional support" type, which favored antlerless deer harvests in the NZ only under certain conditions, (3) the "qualified opposition" type, which either opposed extending general DEC deer management authority in the NZ or opposed the use of antlerless deer harvests in the NZ, (4) and the "full opposition" type, which opposed both the expansion of DEC deer management authority in the NZ and the use of antlerless deer harvests in the NZ.

The "conditional support" and "qualified opposition" groups represent the people most likely to be influenced by personal communication from DEC. However, though the respondents to the hunter and organizational leader surveys gave fair to good marks for agency management of white-tailed deer, they rated DEC's public communications behavior poorly. It became clear that there was a need to open channels of communication to influence management issue beliefs and to enhance DEC's image.

To aid development of a two-way communications program, a wildlife management communication planning model was formulated (Fig. B-4.4). This model represents the process by which public opinions about a management program are determined. It is designed to guide situation analysis research needed to develop a communication strategy for generating public support for the agency's proposed management program. A management program specific for each deer range should identify communication objectives, considerations for developing communication messages, and suggestions for message content.

Although the major management program emphasis is placed on consumptive use of the NZ deer resource, it is acknowledged that nonconsumptive deer use must also be considered to ensure that the interests of all recreationists are represented. For this reason, NZ residents and visitors from the southern zone (SZ) were surveyed via mail questionnaire in spring 1985 to (1) determine the importance of the wildlife resource and deer to nonconsumptive recreationists, (2) describe the role that nonconsumptive use plays in the overall NZ recreational experience, and (3) identify preferences for increasing the nonconsumptive use of deer.

Three-quarters of the residents and one-half of the visitors felt that seeing or hearing wildlife was moderately or extremely important to their recreation experiences and listed deer as a preferred wildlife species.

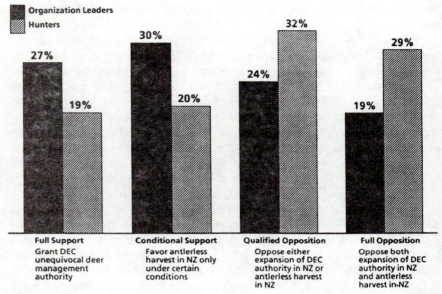

Figure B-4.3   Management acceptance typology groups of hunters and organization leaders

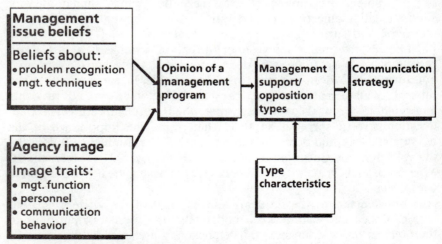

Figure B-4.4   Wildlife management communication planning model

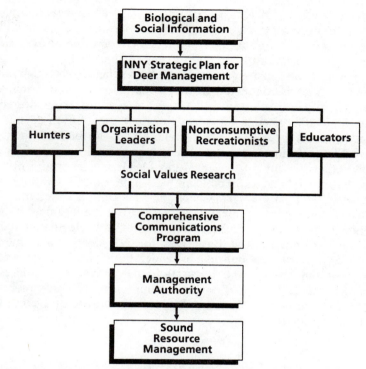

Figure B-4.5   Use of human dimensions information to facilitate
sound resource management

The majority of respondents favored an increase in opportunities to
observe and/or learn more about deer in the NZ.

One of the ways that New York residents can learn about wildlife is
through the public school system. There is concern, however, that teachers'
attitudes about wildlife management may be affecting what and how
they are teaching youngsters. If teachers have a negative attitude toward
wildlife management, particularly deer management practices that DEC
deems necessary to manage deer effectively in the NNY area, they may
be transmitting or reinforcing this attitude or may simply be excluding
discussion of resource management practices from the classroom.

Wildlife education has not traditionally been treated as a basic
component of the school curriculum. In New York, however, the state
education department is implementing an ecologically oriented science
curriculum for grades kindergarten through six. The implementation of
the new elementary science syllabus provides an opportunity to incorporate wildlife education into the public school system. DEC is currently

considering a variety of approaches, including teacher evaluation, participation in in-service teacher training, provision and evaluation of curriculum materials, and interdepartmental cooperation on educational programming to facilitate the achievement of this goal.

The biological and social values information generated through human dimensions research conducted in the 1970s helped resource managers at DEC identify the questions that most needed to be answered for DEC to understand better the social barriers that prevented effective deer management in the NZ (Fig. B-4.5). DEC formulated the NNY Strategic Plan to address communications problems perceived by four different audiences: hunters, organizational leaders, nonconsumptive recreationists, and educators. The plan was a landmark for human dimensions research in New York. For the first time a series of human dimensions studies was an integral part of the deer management program development effort. The results of the studies indicate that it may be possible to implement new initiatives for NZ deer management, if preceded by communications that consider the characteristics and experiences of the public. The integration of the results of these four studies will enable DEC to develop a comprehensive communications program that has as its objective the reestablishment of agency management authority in the NZ.

REFERENCES

BROWN, T. L., AND D. J. DECKER. 1976. Identification of the image of the Bureau of Wildlife (N.Y.S.D.E.C.) held by residents in the peripheral Adirondack area of New York. Pittman-Robertson Proj. W-145-R-1, Dep. Nat. Resour., N.Y.S. Coll. Agric. and Life Sci., Cornell Univ., Ithaca, N.Y. 239pp.

DECKER, D. J. 1976. The influence of internal communications on the development of the Bureau of Wildlife's public image in relation to deer management in the peripheral Adirondack region of New York State. M.S. Thesis, Cornell Univ., Ithaca, N.Y. 184pp. (Unpubl.)

———, T. L. BROWN, AND C. P. DAWSON. 1980. Deer hunting violations and law enforcement in New York. Trans. Northeast Sec. Wildl. Soc. 37:113–128.

———, ———, AND W. SARBELLO. 1981. Attitudes of residents in the peripheral Adirondacks toward illegally killing deer. N.Y. Fish and Game J. 28:73–80.

———, R. A. SMOLKA, JR., N. SANYAL, AND T. L. BROWN. 1983. Hunter reaction to a proposed deer management initiative in Northern New York: antecedents to support or opposition. Trans. Northeast Sect. Wildl. Soc. 40:76–93.

SMOLKA, R. A., JR., AND D. J. DECKER. 1985. Identifying interest groups' issue positions and designing communication strategies for deer management in Northern New York. Trans. Northeast Fish and Wildl. Conf. 41:(in press).

———, ———, AND T. L. BROWN. 1985. Implementation of a survey of attitudes of key public leadership toward deer management alternatives for Northern

New York. N.Y. Fed. Aid in Wildl. Restoration Proj. W-146-R-10, Study VIII-6.

———, ———, N. SANYAL, AND T. L. BROWN. 1983. Northern New York deer management: hunters' opinions and preferences. Fed. Aid in Wildl. Restoration Proj. W-146-R-8, Study VIII-3. 278pp.

Section B-5

White-Tailed Deer in a Suburban Environment: Reconciling Wildlife Management and Human Perceptions

Thomas S. Litwin, *Seatuck Research Program, Cornell Laboratory of Ornithology, Islip, NY 11751*

Thomas A. Gavin, *Department of Natural Resources, New York State College of Agriculture and Life Sciences, Cornell University, Ithaca, NY 14853*

Mary C. Capkanis, *Seatuck Research Program, Cornell Laboratory of Ornithology, Islip, NY 11751*

The character of the landscape used by wildlife is rapidly changing in many areas of the U.S. A primary factor contributing to this phenomenon is the urbanization of rural environments. As of 1980, 167 million people (74% of the total U.S. population) lived in suburban or urban areas concentrated in the coastal U.S. (U.S. Bur. Census 1984). In addition, approximately 1.0 million ha of rural land per year is being developed for residential and commercial purposes (Counc. on Environ. Quality 1981). These developments have contributed to increased non-traditional interactions between suburban human populations and a growing number of wildlife species, including the turkey (*Meleagris gallopavo*) (A. D. Geis, pers. commun.), raccoon (*Procyon lotor*) (Manski and Hadidian 1985), coyote (*Canis latrans*) (Leach and Hunt 1974), Canada goose (*Branta canadensis*), and white-tailed deer (*Odocoileus virginianus*) (Flyger et al. 1983). Although a significant portion of these interactions are "positive" (U.S. Fish and Wildl. and U.S. Bur. Census 1982), the wildlife manager is faced with the challenge of reconciling these benefits with a growing number of "negative" interactions (San Julian 1983).

These factors are particularly important to managers of wildlife refuges in areas undergoing suburbanization. A multidisciplinary study focusing on the growth and expansion of a white-tailed deer population in suburban Long Island illustrates this phenomenon. The study area, the 80-ha Seatuck National Wildlife Refuge in Islip, Suffolk County (population 1.2 million), New York, is 60 km east of New York City (Fig. B-5.1). Residents living adjacent to the refuge typically are middle aged and college educated and live in houses valued between $100,000 and $250,000.

Using radio telemetry, 15 different deer were monitored from 1 June 1984 to 31 May 1985, resulting in 518 ratio locations distributed over a 24-hour daily period. Preliminary results indicate that deer were located off the refuge 106 (20%) times, with off-refuge movement slightly higher in summer and winter compared to spring and fall (Table B-5.1). Movement into the surrounding neighborhoods generally occurred at night. Eleven of the 15 deer traveled off the refuge more than once, with 3 animals spending more than 50% of their time off the refuge. The results indicate that deer often used a neighborhood habitat that was highly fragmented and developed, in which they became accustomed to the sights and sounds of human activity, vehicular traffic, and domestic animals.

Both positive and negative interactions between human populations and refuge deer resulted from their ranging behavior. Deer movement into a human-dominated environment enabled them to be perceived simultaneously as a source of enjoyment, property damage, personal injury, and disease. Concern by residents about ornamental shrub damage and Lyme disease prompted further examination of interactions between deer and humans. Lyme disease is caused by a spirochete transmitted by the deer tick (*Ixodes dammini*), which uses the white-tailed deer as a host (Spielman et al. 1985). A minimum of 252 cases of Lyme disease occurred in Suffolk County in 1983–1984 (E. M. Bosler, pers. commun.) with 4 in the vicinity of the refuge. Media coverage sensitized the public to the issue. The analysis of the blood samples from 22 deer revealed that at least 27% of the sampled refuge deer tested positive for the spirochete that causes the disease.

A survey of homeowners in the vicinity of the refuge was conducted, allowing quantification of public attitudes about deer (Decker and Gavin 1985). Preliminary concerns of the respondents (N=300) were Lyme disease (50%), deer-car collisions (41%), damage to ornamental plantings (5%), and personal injury (4%). Forty-nine percent of the respondents had seen either deer on their property or evidence of their feeding during the preceding year; respondents also reported damage to 132 fruit trees and 3,512 ornamental shrubs with a total replacement cost of $28,000. Although deer-car collisions were a major concern of the respondents, only four such accidents were documented in the previous year.

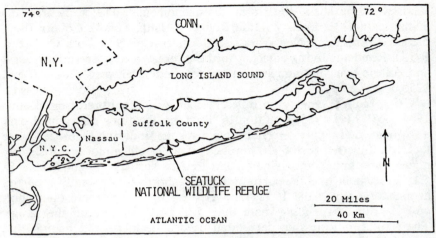

Figure B-5.1   Seatuck National Wildlife Refuge on Long Island, N.Y.

TABLE B-5.1
Systematic Observations of 15 White-tailed Deer on the
Seatuck National Wildlife Refuge Obtained by Radio
Telemetry During 1 June 1984-31 May 1985

| | No. of observations | | % Off- |
Season	Off-refuge	On-refuge	refuge
June–August	56	203	22
September–November	26	118	18
December–February	19	60	24
March–May	5	31	14
	106	412	20

Although one might predict that the respondents' summary attitude
toward deer would be negative, this was not the case. Despite concerns,
72% of the respondents wanted the deer population to remain the same
or increase, which indicated a greater emphasis on some positive ascribed
value of deer, in contrast to the strictly negative economic value (i.e.,
property damage). In addition, respondents had a generally negative
view toward recreational hunting.

The fragmentation of wildlife habitat and subsequent interspersion of suburban development and wildlife populations result in increased and varied interactions between humans and wildlife. It can be predicted that public attitudes toward wildlife will change as demographic and land use patterns shift. In the terms of Kellert (1980), land use changes from a rural to suburban environment may be paralleled by a shift from utilitarian/dominionistic to aesthetic/moralistic wildlife values. The survey of wildlife values held by Islip residents suggests that this shift has already occurred. It is clear that the off-refuge movement of deer has resulted in *specific* negative interactions with the public, yet the *general* attitude toward deer was positive.

Because a wildlife refuge is often a permanent community resource, the manager is faced with the difficult challenge of solving resource-related problems while not undermining the broader goals of the suburban refuge. Wildlife management practices derived solely from a rural heritage and practicality (Schole 1973, Flyger et al. 1983, O'Donnell and VanDruff 1983) may promote confusion in a community in which attitudes are shaped more strongly by the mass media (Langenau et al. 1984), literature (More 1977), and anthropomorphic interpretations. In the development of management strategies for suburban refuges, the inclusion of public attitudes and values, public and media relations, and education may be as important to the success of the plan as are the biological concepts of carrying capacity and species diversity.

REFERENCES

COUNCIL ON ENVIRONMENTAL QUALITY. 1981. National agricultural lands study: final report. U.S. Gov. Print. Off., Washington, D.C. 108pp.

DECKER, D. J., AND T. A. GAVIN. 1985. Human dimensions of managing a suburban deer herd: situation analysis for decision making by the Seatuck National Wildlife Refuge, Islip, N.Y. Outdoor Recreation Res. Unit Publ. No. 85-3, N.Y.S. Coll. Agric. and Life Sci., Cornell Univ., Ithaca, N.Y. 43pp.

FLYGER, V., D. L. LEEDY, AND T. M. FRANKLIN. 1983. Wildlife damage control in eastern cities and suburbs. Pages 27–32 *in* D. J. Decker, ed. Proc. 1st East. Wildl. Damage Control Conf. N.Y.S. Coll. Agric. and Life Sci., Cornell Univ., Ithaca, N.Y.

KELLERT, S. R. 1980. Public attitudes toward critical wildlife and natural habitat issues. Phase I. Doc. No. 024-010-00-623-4, U.S. Gov. Print. Off., Washington, D.C. 148pp.

LANGENAU, E. E., JR., S. R. KELLERT, AND J. E. APPLEGATE. 1984. Values in management. Pages 699–720 *in* L. K. Halls, ed. White-tailed deer: ecology and management. Stackpole Books, Harrisburg, Pa.

LEACH, H. R., AND E. G. HUNT. 1974. Coyotes and people. Pages 117–119 *in* J. H. Noyes and D. R. Progulske, eds. Wildlife in an urbanizing environment. Planning and Resour. Dev. Ser. No. 28, Mass. Coop. Ext. Serv.

MANSKI, D., AND J. HADIDIAN. 1985. Rock Creek raccoons: movements and resource utilization in an urban environment. Prog. Rep. Nat. Park Serv., Cent. for Urban Ecol., Washington, D.C. 40pp.

MORE, T. A. 1977. An analysis of wildlife in children's stories. Pages 84–92 *in* D. Linton, ed. Children, nature, and the urban environment. U.S. Dep. Agric. For. Serv. Tech. Rep. NE-30, Northeast For. Exp. Stn., Broomall, Pa.

O'DONNELL, M. A., AND L. W. VANDRUFF. 1983. Wildlife conflicts in an urban area: occurrence of problems and human attitudes toward wildlife. Pages 315–323 *in* D. J. Decker, ed. Proc. 1st East. Wildl. Damage Control Conf. N.Y.S. Coll. Agric. and Life Sci., Cornell Univ., Ithaca, N.Y.

SAN JULIAN, G. J. 1983. The need for urban animal control. Pages 313–314 *in* D. J. Decker, ed. Proc. 1st East. Wildl. Damage Control Conf. N.Y.S. Coll. Agric. and Life Sci., Cornell Univ., Ithaca, N.Y.

SCHOLE, B. J. 1973. A literature review on characteristics of hunters. Colo. Div. Wildl. Publ. GFP-R-S-33, Fort Collins. 15pp.

SPIELMAN, A., M. L. WILSON, J. F. LEVINE, AND J. PIESMAN. 1985. Ecology of *Ixodes dammini*-borne human babesiosis and Lyme disease. Annu. Rev. Entomol. 30:439–460.

U.S. BUREAU OF THE CENSUS. 1984. Statistical abstract of the United States: 1985. U.S. Dep. Commer., Washington, D.C. 991pp.

U.S. FISH AND WILDLIFE SERVICE AND U.S. BUREAU OF THE CENSUS. 1982. 1980 national survey of fishing, hunting, and wildlife-associated recreation. U.S. Dep. Inter. and U.S. Dep. Commer. U.S. Gov. Print. Off., Washington, D.C. 156pp.

Section B-6

Landowners' Willingness to Tolerate White-Tailed Deer Damage in New York: An Overview of Research and Management Response

Ken G. Purdy, *Department of Natural Resources,*
New York State College of Agriculture and Life Sciences,
Cornell University, Ithaca, NY 14853

During the past decade, increasing attention has been given to incorporating socioeconomic considerations into wildlife management plans. Seldom has this been more important than for managing population levels of white-tailed deer (*Odocoileus virginianus*) in agricultural areas where deer damage to crops is a primary concern. In such areas, farmers' attitudes about deer and deer damage are important inputs to decision making. Establishing management policy on the basis of unsolicited farmer complaints, however, may assume that (1) complaints about deer indicate a desire for decreased deer populations and (2) that farmers voicing complaints represent the opinions of other farmers. These assumptions may result in management objectives that unduly deprive many wildlife enthusiasts of potential benefits from the deer resource. Instead, a systematic and scientific process of inquiry is needed to obtain accurate information about farmers' perceptions of optimum deer population densities. Through such inquiry, management may respond by regulating deer levels to avoid excessive agricultural impacts while simultaneously meeting the demands of deer enthusiasts. Over time, these tests of treatment efficacy and assessments of public response provide important feedback into a cyclic process of program development (Fig. B-6.1).

The New York State Department of Environmental Conservation (DEC) has sponsored a series of studies of New York farmers' attitudes toward deer and deer damage. Conducted by the Human Dimensions Research Unit, Department of Natural Resources, New York State College of Agriculture and Life Sciences, Cornell University, these studies have been designed to give DEC the ability to evaluate deer depredation

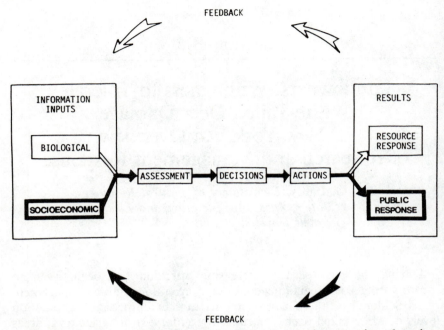

Figure B-6.1 The cyclic process of incorporating socioeconomic values into wildlife management programs

problems beyond the individual, unsolicited complaint level and help managers make decisions regarding damage mitigation and herd management in various areas of the state. The initial study, conducted in three phases (1976, 1978, and 1979), helped define the relationships between farmer tolerance, attitudes about deer, and attitudes and perceptions of deer damage and deer population levels (Brown et al. 1977, 1978, 1980, Decker et al. 1981). Mail questionnaire responses from 9,543 farmers indicated that deer populations in most areas were below levels at which crop damage became intolerable to farmers. Even though relationships were observed between increasing economic loss and decreasing tolerance of deer, with few exceptions farmers were willing to tolerate considerable amounts of damage in return for the presence of deer. Farmers' responses indicated a custodial attitude toward deer and appreciation of deer for aesthetic as well as hunting purposes. Overall, the relationship between farmers' deer preferences and DEC indices of deer numbers indicated that for the deer population levels in the study areas at that time, most farmers desired deer population increases.

With the information obtained from this study, managers decided to allow controlled deer population increases in many deer management

TABLE B-6.1
Comparisons of Farmers' Estimated Amounts of Deer
Damage and Preferences for Deer Populations

Dollars-of-damage	Percent of farmers	
	Original study[a] (N=2,189)	Resurvey[b] (N=620)
$0	72.6	72.1
$1-$99	9.3	5.2
$100-$499	11.8	12.5
$500-$999	2.7	3.7
$1000-$2999	2.1	4.2
$3000-$4999	0.1	1.0
$5000+	1.4	1.3
	100.0	100.0

Deer population trend desired	Original study[a] (N=2,122)	Resurvey[b] (N=1,860)
Increase	45.0	25.8
No change	48.1	57.4
Decrease	6.9	16.8
	100.0	100.0

[a]Source: Brown et al. 1980.
[b]Source: Decker et al. 1983.

units. Deer populations responded providing increased opportunities to
observe and hunt deer. Monitoring the degree to which farmers were
affected by these changes and the effects of increased deer levels on
their preferences, attitudes, and perceptions was important for providing
continued input into deer management.

Response to the new deer population levels was evaluated by a
resurvey of 2,650 farmers in 1982 (Decker et al. 1983). As expected,
farmers' estimates of the costs of deer damage increased, and in most
areas respondents' attitudes suggested that a "sociological" carrying
capacity had been reached as evidenced by diminished tolerance
for increasing populations and greater acceptance of 1982 deer levels

(Table B-6.1). Unexpectedly, however, the percentage of farmers reporting damage remained virtually unchanged. The findings implied that individuals incurring deer damage suffered greater monetary losses as a result of increased numbers of deer. The level of loss from deer damage at which farmers' threshold of tolerance was exceeded appeared to be at or above $500–$999.

From a management perspective, the results of the resurvey indicated that farmers in different areas reacted differently to various levels of deer damage or perceptions of population levels and that deer management should continue to be prescribed at the individual management unit basis. Broader, regional applications of deer management programs assume that farmers in different areas react similarly to deer population densities or have similar levels of acceptance of crop damage. Such management assumptions, however, are likely to discriminate against farmers in some areas and may impede meeting deer management objectives.

The cyclic development of deer management programs in New York has provided deer managers with new understanding of the socioeconomic dimensions of deer management in agricultural areas. Current DEC deer management objectives have incorporated the results of these studies, and the DEC is striving to maintain deer population levels in management units that are both biologically and sociologically optimal. A continuing farmer preference monitoring effort is scheduled to assist in further program assessment and planning. Continuing considerations for biological feasibility and social acceptability are expected to enhance DEC deer managers' ability to serve their constituencies by providing management programs responsive to the needs and desires of the public.

Acknowledgments.—The author extends appreciation to Daniel J. Decker for his helpful review of this manuscript.

REFERENCES

BROWN, T. L., D. J. DECKER, AND C. P. DAWSON. 1977. Farmer willingness to tolerate deer damage in Erie-Ontario Lake Plain. Dep. Nat. Resour. Res. and Ext. Ser. 8, Cornell Univ., Ithaca, N.Y. 33pp.

———, ———, AND ———. 1978. Willingness of New York farmers to incur white-tailed deer damage. Wildl. Soc. Bull. 6:235–239.

———, ———, AND D. L. HUSTIN. 1980. Farmers' tolerance of white-tailed deer in central and western New York. Search: Agriculture. Cornell Univ. Agric. Exp. Stn. No. 7, Ithaca, N.Y. 16pp.

DECKER, D. J., T. L. BROWN, AND D. L. HUSTIN. 1981. Comparison of farmers' attitudes toward deer abundance in two regions of New York having different agricultural and deer population characteristics. N.Y. Fish and Game J. 28:202–207.

————, N. Sanyal, T. L. Brown, R. A. Smolka, Jr., and N. A. Connelly. 1983. Reanalysis of farmer willingness to tolerate deer damage in western New York. Pages 37–45 *in* D. J. Decker, ed. Proc. 1st East. Wildl. Damage Control Conf. Cornell Coop. Ext., Ithaca, N.Y. 379pp.

Wildlife Utilization on Private Land in South Africa with Implications for the United States

Delwin E. Benson, *Extension Wildlife Specialist, Colorado State University, Fort Collins, CO 80523*

Wildlife is estimated to contribute from 64 to 75 million rands (R) (US$32 to US$37 million) toward the agricultural income of 8,200 farmers in the Republic of South Africa. Between June and September 1985, 2,207 persons were sent a survey booklet with 47 questions and 222 variables about their beliefs, values, management practices, and economic returns from game animals on their lands. Seventy percent of the survey forms were accounted for, and 69% of the sample was used for calculation of results.

SURVEY RESULTS

Of all respondents, 752 persons (52%) were seeking income from game, 471 persons (32%) did not seek income, and 230 persons (16%) returned the form unanswered as the directions indicated if they were not using game on their property. The average game farmers were 48 years old, had farmed for 24 years, and had been game farming on 2,500 ha for 15 years. They made 14% of their gross income from game (R14929.60), spent 12% of their time on the enterprise, and had good feelings about the enterprise (94%). Game farmers believed or strongly believed that the neighbors approved of what they did (75%) and that clients were happy (90%). Farmers ranked six categories of game farming as they contributed toward net income in the following order of priority: (1) and (2) game meat sales and recreational hunting for meat, (3) trophy hunting, (4) live animal sales, (5) game viewing, and (6) camping. In Table B-7.1 the number of animals removed from private lands between 1982 and 1984 is shown by categories of cropped, hunted, and sold live. Meat sold from properties represented in the survey totaled 913,768 kg in 1982, 738,908 kg in 1983, and 872,851 kg in 1984, for a total of 2,525,527 kg.

TABLE B-7.1
Numbers of Animals Removed from Private Lands Between
1982 and 1984 by Category of Cropped, Hunted, and Sold
Live

	1982	1983	1984	Total
Number cropped	45,530	37,005	38,934	121,469
Number hunted	30,374	33,386	37,284	101,044
Number sold live	10,397	10,818	10,669	31,884
Total	86,301	81,209	86,887	254,397

IMPLICATIONS FOR THE UNITED STATES

The following implications are listed as food for thought on the basis of knowledge gained in the U.S. and information presented in this section:

1. Opportunities to provide quality recreational experiences for hunting on private land in the U.S. are already taking place and can be expanded.
2. Management of habitats, wildlife, and recreational clients needs improvement.
3. The sale of wild game meats could be developed (on a controlled basis) to benefit herd management, to diversify consumer use of red meats, and as income for landowners in the U.S. Special consideration should be given to white-tailed deer in the south and east, and perhaps pronghorn and larger ungulates in the west.
4. Controlled live sales of animals between farms may enable landowners to increase production and use of wildlife.
5. Current need and interest to diversify returns from agricultural lands provides increased opportunities for enhancing wildlife.
6. Wildlife managers could devote more energy toward working with wildlife producers on private lands to enhance recreation, habitat and wildlife management, and overall values of wildlife on rural agricultural environments.

Economic Values of White-Tailed Deer Hunting in an Eastern Wilderness Setting

Richard W. Sage, Jr., and William F. Porter, *Faculty of Environmental and Forest Biology, State University of New York, College of Environmental Science and Forestry, Syracuse, NY 13210*

U.S. hunting has evolved under a tradition that permits "free access to hunt." This tradition is gradually being changed as private landowners recognize the value of the wildlife resource on their lands and as public lands are called upon to serve a wider variety of conflicting interests.

Two basic approaches have been employed by private landowners to generate income through hunting: land lease hunting and fee hunting. In the Adirondack region of New York private landowners have capitalized upon the recreational potentials of their lands through the land lease system for many years. In contrast, fee hunting, although widely practiced throughout the southeast and south-central United States, is relatively uncommon in the northeast and particularly in the Adirondack region.

In this study we compare the economic returns associated with a fee hunting program with those of land lease hunting as currently practiced throughout the Adirondack region.

METHODS

A fee hunting program, limited to archery and muzzleloader hunters, was initiated on the northern 2,106 ha of the Huntington Wilderness Forest, a research station of the State University of New York, College of Environmental Science and Forestry. The program was begun in 1978 and continued through 1984. All hunting was conducted during the regular big game seasons established for the northern zone of New York. All regulations, including those pertaining to bag limits, weapons, and hunting participants, were those prescribed by law. The number of participants, fee schedules, number of days open to hunting, and reservation procedures varied during the seven years of hunting. Participants camped in designated camp sites in the hunting area during their stay. Each hunter was provided a map of the hunting area. All animals taken (deer or bear) were required to be checked by staff prior to removal from the property. All participants were asked to complete a questionnaire and return it before checking out of the hunt area. Comparative information relating to lease hunting was obtained from three large private landowners in the region through telephone interviews and from written materials provided by landowners.

RESULTS

Land Lease System

The survey of private landowners employing a land lease hunting system revealed that 80% of their combined 255,173 ha was under lease to recreationists in 1982. Current incomes generated under the land lease system in the central Adirondack area ranged from $1.85 to $9.88/ha/year, depending primarily on the resources available on the lease area and the uses permitted by the landowner. The average income generated from the land lease system, exclusive of added charges for special uses (e.g., club houses, camps) was $5.55/ha/year. Administrative costs associated with the operation of the leases were approximately 10% of gross income. Thus, net income derived from the land lease system in the central Adirondack region was determined to be $4.99/ha/year. This figure is related to year-round use of the land for a wide variety of recreational activities, including big game hunting.

Originally, big game hunting was the primary recreational pursuit associated with the land lease system. In more recent years a greater diversity of recreational activities characterize the use of these private lands. Based on data available from one of the private landowners surveyed, user days associated with big game hunting activities accounted for an average of 22.5% of the total number of user days reported during 1978–1982. From this figure, the net income that can be attributed to big game hunting under the average land lease is $1.11/ha/year.

Fee Hunting Program

The first four years of the fee hunting program served as a testing period: Several fee schedules were tried, hunter quotas varied, season lengths were changed, and a hunter clientele was being established. In contrast, no major changes were instituted the following three years.

As a result, the data from these three years (1982–1984) best represent the economic returns associated with this program.

During this period of the program between 200 and 225 hunters participated each year. A fee of $50 for a season pass was charged each hunter, and the average season length was 21 days. Gross income generated as a result of the 1982–1984 fee hunts at the Huntington Wildlife Forest ranged from $3.64 to $5.09/ha/year. Administrative and operational costs averaged 19.6% of gross income during this same period. Net income ranged from $2.15 to $4.07/ha/year.

A sealed bid survey involving both hunters who had participated previously and newcomers to the program was conducted in 1983. Each hunter was asked to submit a bid indicating the amount he or she was willing to pay to participate in the 1983 fall hunting program. Of the 1985 bids distributed to hunting party leaders, 60 bids (32.4%) were returned, representing a total of 243 hunters. Responses from new hunters accounted for 36.5% of the bids returned with past participants providing the remainder (63.5%). The bids ranged from $7 to $101. There were no significant differences between the mean bids of archery hunters and muzzleloader hunters or between new hunters and past participants. The mean bid for a season pass, based on all respondents, was $47.82/hunter.

Questionnaire Survey

Based upon responses to the questionnaire survey and informal interviews with hunters in the field, five major factors were identified as the primary reasons that attracted these hunters to the fee hunting program:

1. The wilderness character of the hunting area and the quality of the hunting experience.
2. The ability to camp on the hunting area and the available road and trail access.
3. The opportunity to shoot a trophy buck or black bear.
4. Hunting in an area where only "primitive weapons" were permitted.
5. The forest management activities (logging) on the hunting area were associated with "good" deer habitat management and "higher" deer populations than unmanaged lands in the region.

CONCLUSIONS

The results of this study suggest that big game hunting can provide significant income to private landowners in the Adirondack region. Both land lease and fee hunting systems appear to be attractive to the hunting public. The wilderness setting, together with a quality hunting experience, is the primary component of a wilderness hunting program. When these factors are combined with the provision of adequate access and on-site camping privileges, a successful wilderness hunting program is likely to result.

Florida Alligators: Economics, Harvest, and Conservation

Tommy C. Hines, *Wildlife Research Laboratory,
Florida Game and Fresh Water Fish Commission,
Gainesville, FL 32611*

H. Franklin Percival, *U.S. Fish and Wildlife Service,
Florida Cooperative Fish and Wildlife Research Unit,
University of Florida, Gainesville, FL 32611*

Clarence L. Abercrombie and Allan R. Woodward,
*Wildlife Research Laboratory, Florida Game
and Fresh Water Fish Commission,
Gainesville, FL 32611*

Over the past two decades conservationists worldwide have become increasingly concerned about declining crocodilian populations. Legal protection from direct exploitation, the conventional solution, has been difficult to enforce in many parts of the world, and in any case it largely neglects the major threat of habitat destruction. A recent, more innovative response has been the attempt to conserve crocodilians by cropping them on a sustained-yield basis. The rationale is that limited commercialization can add value to the resource and thereby provide obvious incentive against wanton destruction of the animals or their habitat.

This section summarizes Florida's approach to alligator management. It highlights present management strategies and research efforts.

PRESENT PROGRAMS

In Florida, we have investigated the effects of exploiting a wild alligator population. Economic and biological facts have emerged that have enabled an experimental management program to be implemented. But very important data needs still must be met before an intensive approach to alligator management is possible.

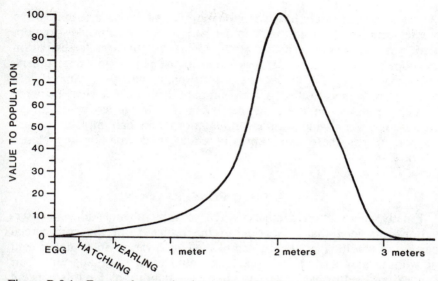

Figure B-9.1 Expected reproductive value (scaled to 100) of all alligator size classes to the population (C. L. Abercrombie, T. C. Hines, A. Woodward, and H. F. Percival, Florida alligator: economics, harvest, and conservation, presented 7th working meet., Crocodile Specialist Group, 1986; reprinted by permission)

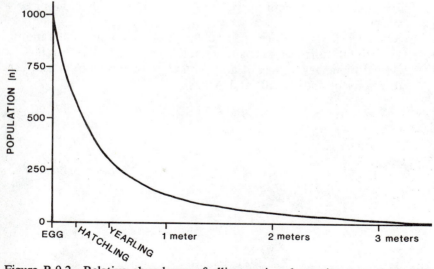

Figure B-9.2 Relative abundance of alligator size classes in a population (C. L. Abercrombie, T. C. Hines, A. Woodward, and H. F. Percival, Florida alligator: economics, harvest, and conservation, presented 7th working meet., Crocodile Specialist Group, 1986; reprinted by permission)

The effects of adult harvest upon population levels are difficult to predict because the role that compensatory mechanisms play in population response is unclear. However, some size and age classes within the population are clearly of less value to the population than others, providing a basis for management strategies (Figs. B-9.1 and B-9.2). The data presented can be used to compare demographic costs incurred by the population to the economic value of a harvested wild animal. These costs vary widely among populations and habitat, but the underlying trends these data represent could hold true for any classic crocodilian.

VALUE-ADDED CONSERVATION

Finally, this section emphasizes the concept of value-added conservation—the idea that a portion of the return from the commercial harvest of wildlife can be returned to the conservation and management of wildlife and its habitat. The high value of crocodilians and their tropical and subtropical habitats satisfy the conditions for this concept to work. Several obvious mechanisms can be used in value-added conservation.

1. Benefactors of exploitation have vested interests in alligator conservation, thus becoming political advocates for habitat preservation.
2. Revenues from licenses, tags, taxes, and so on provide funding for habitat enhancement, species management, and research.
3. Added monetary values of alligators in wetlands modify land use decisions by individual landowners.

Workshop Summaries

Chaired by
Robert E. Henshaw, *Environmental Management Specialist, New York State Department of Environmental Conservation, Albany, New York*

Larry W. VanDruff, *Professor of Wildlife Biology, SUNY–College of Environmental Science and Forestry, Syracuse, New York*

Section C-1

Participation in Administrative Hearings and Other Forums for Effecting Wildlife Decisions

Summary prepared by Robert E. Henshaw

Workshop Participants

William J. Dickerson, *Administrative Law Judge, NYS Dept. of Environmental Conservation, Albany, NY*

Carl G. Dworkin, Esq., *Natural Resources Councel, NYS Dept. of Environmental Conservation, Albany, NY*

Arthur Johnsen, *Wetland Habitat Specialist, NYS Dept. of Environmental Conservation, Wildlife Resources Center, Delmar, NY*

Sidney Manes, Esq., *of Manes, Rifken, Frankel and Greenman, P.C., Syracuse, NY*

David Palmer, *Professor, SUNY–College of Environmental Science and Forestry, Syracuse, NY*

The most common forum for wildlife professionals to effect policy change is the public hearing. Two types of hearings are conducted: administrative or adjudicatory hearings, which are somewhat like a civil court proceeding, and enforcement hearings, which are similar to a criminal court proceeding.

The hearing is usually the last stage in the lengthy process of obtaining a permit for a proposed action (e.g., construction or development). A hearing is used to resolve contested points or to determine a course of action when problems arise. The hearing provides a stylized forum for conflict resolution, which follows very strict rules of procedure. The parties and the issues that may arise are identified. Each party speaks in sequence a specific number of times, including for appeals. Ultimately, a recommended decision is prepared by the administrative law judge for the agency head who may be guided but is not bound by it.

In preparing to go to hearing, parties first prepare their case for direct testimony ordinarily delivered by one or more expert witnesses. Usually the case is prefiled in the form of a statement, papers, and documents or in written question and answer format. Parties may make inquiries about any points in the other parties' testimony by filing interrogatories with the judge who transmits them to all parties. Interrogatories should seek to clarify issues and facts and to narrow the number of items in contention. When parties find they can agree on issues, a stipulation may be placed on record. If all issues are resolved by agreement, the hearing may be concluded if the agreements to not infract laws and regulations.

In the hearing room, essentially six key players participated in a real-time drama. The administrative law judge is responsible for conducting the hearing according to law. He or she enforces all rules and procedures, rules of evidence or discussion, and other procedural issues. Impartial to the issues under debate, the judge stands between the parties to ensure that a complete and fair record is developed. The applicant is represented by an expert witness who is protected by the applicant's attorney. The regulatory agency likewise is represented by an expert witness who is protected by the agency's attorney. The court stenographer transcribes every word that is to be a part of the record. The typescript becomes the official record of the hearing. In large cases, every one of these responsibilities may require several people, and many parties may participate.

Although hearings vary among administrative units and agencies, most provide the applicant first opportunity to present his or her case. The hearing may be used to supplement prefiled testimony as desired. The applicant's expert witness takes the stand and is sworn to tell the truth. The opposing parties cross-examine the witness to bring out underdeveloped information, test the witness's veracity and credibility, test the accuracy of the witness's perception of observed events, and test the basis of the expert opinion. Questions from the cross-examining party's expert are asked by that party's attorney. The defending attorney listens to the form of the questions as well as the factual content. If the interrogating attorney articulates the question appropriately and survives objections by the defending attorney, the defending witness answers on the record. Once the applicant's case has been presented and cross-examined, each party in turn presents its case and sustains cross-examination from any other party. At no time do the experts speak directly on the record, even though by doing so accord might be reached much more expeditiously.

Each stage of the hearing is critical to the process. The interrogatory process may be a "fishing trip" trying to discern weakness, errors, and distortions or to find useful facts. Cross-examination should not be a fishing trip. A well-prepared expert for the cross-examining party should provide his or her attorney with a complete list of questions together with the expected answers. These should be sequenced into a strategy to most effectively nullify the witness in the "hot seat." Cross-examination may weaken the opposing case, but a position is made in the direct testimony. All statements on the record are made to influence the decision of the judge; therefore, the witnesses must be credible, correct, and impressive, their attorney clever, smooth, and incisive. No one profits by belligerency or smugness. Complete answers are expected. Judges, attorneys, and recorders are well trained professionally to participate in a hearing. The wildlife professional who would enter this arena has much to learn and would do well to master the art of witnessing.

Much has been written on how to be an effective witness. The following incomplete list is extracted from several sources:

1. Understand the differences among facts, suppositions, and opinions. The expert may testify to each but must phrase answers appropriately. Otherwise, he or she may never understand why an objection was sustained.
2. Present a neat professional appearance. Seem calm and confident. Speak clearly, decisively, and authoritatively. Use appropriate terminology but do not overwhelm the judge. Interpret and explain as needed.
3. Never hesitate to state that the testimony that you are sponsoring was prepared with the help of others, consultants, supervisors, and lawyers. Never be afraid to admit that your testimony has a limited (finite) scope.
4. Never hesitate to state your lack of knowledge on a particular point. You can confer with other witnesses or staff counsel, call the office during recess, and supply the answer later in writing.
5. Never guess.
6. Never be led away from the scope of your testimony.
7. Never hesitate to say that you do not understand the question. Have it repeated or rephrased.
8. Never offer collateral comments in response to a question. Answer only the specific question asked of you.
9. Never try to outsmart or be clever with the intervenor's lawyer. He or she can cut you to ribbons. The lawyer is a professional at this.
10. Never whisper helpful suggestions to a witness who is testifying.
11. Never discuss the case with anyone but your own staff members during recess.

12. Never fraternize with the other parties during recess.

These points were demonstrated and discussed during the workshop. The five participants conducted a mock hearing on a fictionalized case concerning a peat bog mining permit that turned on wildlife issues. An excellent booklet enlarging on the above information *DEC Guide to Public Hearings* may be obtained from Bureau of Hearings, New York State Department of Environmental Conservation, 50 Wolf Road, Albany, NY 12233-0001.

The hearing process is useful as an ultimate device for conflict resolution when other avenues fail, but it is fraught with inherent problems. "What the adversary system does is pit two sides against one another, with self-interest motivating their lawyers less toward the pursuit of truth and justice than toward the pursuit of victory. Between the lawyers stands a judge, who in the dominant tradition of American law is not a seeker after truth, or justice either, but rather a neutral referee seeking only to ensure that the combatants obey the rules of fair play" (*Washington Monthly,* November 1975, p. 43).

A growing trend toward early negotiation among all would-be parties may reduce automatic dependence on hearings. Citizens and wildlife professionals should hone their negotiating skills, prepare themselves on issues, and then sit down with developers before proposals are "cast in concrete." Often public interests can be accommodated without resorting to a hearing, which is expensive to all parties. At this writing a wholly new field of environmental mediation is being pioneered. Trained mediators help parties negotiate. No record is maintained, but the accords become binding. Even extended mediation efforts are much less expensive than hearings. The wildlife profession today faces a period of changing roles as the environmental movement, now matured in a body of law, settles down for the long period of protecting public interests. There is a role for the well-prepared professional. There is little mercy for the unprepared.

Section C-2

Communication of Values of Wildlife

Summary prepared by Robert E. Henshaw,
Workshop Moderator

Workshop Participants

James Ehmann, *Science Feature Writer, the Syracuse Post Standard Newspaper, Syracuse, NY*

Melodee James, *Naturalist and Outdoor Educator, Project OWL (Outdoor World of Learning), Ravena, NY*

William Mason, *Cinematographer, Old Chelsea, Quebec (formerly with the National Film Board of Canada)*

H. Wayne Trimm, *Artist, Art Director, and Editor, The Conservationist Magazine, NYS Department of Environmental Conservation, Albany, NY*

Values of wildlife exist in the mind of the beholder. Each individual brings to the moment unique experiences, perceptions, and prejudices formed in their individual settings. With each passing decade, the environmental apathy of the increasingly urbanized voters is demonstrated more frequently in the voting booth. This inaction is derived from environmental naïveté rather than an antiwildlife attitude. With ever increasing isolation from natural ecosystems, urbanites little appreciate the subtle interdependencies among species.

How can this broad and disparate public be sensitized and better informed on wildlife matters? Wildlife scientists communicate through a robust and respected professional literature. Wildlife managers exchange information through journals and periodic reports, although the latter "gray literature" is less accessible. No route, however, is used for effective communication with the public; that job falls to professional communicators.

Communicators (who are seldom wildlife professionals), as interpreters of wildlife values, must use all avenues and work in all media. Many people can be reached rationally through lectures and classes, books, magazines and newspapers, exhibits and museum displays, and radio and television discussions. Others are better reached emotionally through stories and demonstrations, models, nature trails and sponsored outdoor experiences, photography, television, and art. These latter are more experiential than factual; they speak more to the receiver's right lobe than the left. The communicator provides meaning but may only connote value. Wildlife values then and the communication of value may be felt even when little expressed.

It is said, "In nature there are no generalities, only moments in real time." The communicator must view the specific event, interpret its meaning, extract its essence, and transpose it to a universal. By compressing a lifetime of experiences into one, the interpreter must freeze a moment, telescope eons, discern the critical thread, and elucidate the phenomenon. A painting thus is equivalent to the statistical generalization in a research paper.

The interpreter is the natural historian of yesteryear viewing the world through new insights of functional anatomy, biochemical physiology, and behavioral ecology. Information must be assembled from bits and pieces and often from indirect evidence. He or she must think, like the animal, like the research biologist, and also like the kid next door. The audience may be as unselected as unseen movie or television viewers or as precisely known as a class of schoolchildren.

Although appealing to the emotions of their audience, communicators make unarticulated rational decisions on how best to portray a subject. For instance, a vertical orientation to a picture evokes energy whereas a horizontal orientation pacifies the viewer. Incorporation of the cinematographer's experiences in seeking an animal involves the audience vicariously. A newspaper feature that develops the significance of an obscure endangered species engenders public cooperation.

The communicator must possess the integrity of the scientist. With the rare exception of direct sightings on camera, usually the portrayed event is composed at the easel or word processor, in the darkroom or class discussion. True-to-nature accuracy cannot be sacrificed for artistic generalization. Live animals must be portrayed from nature because there is a tension and alertness that disappears in captivity and cannot be recreated from stuffed skins. A century after their creation, John J. Audubon's fanciful paintings continue to distort accurate understanding of behavior and ecological setting while inspiring keen interest in the animal.

The interpreter coexists symbiotically with wildlife scientists and managers. Without the latter, the interpreter has no grist; without the former, the biologist may have no job. But the reader is cautioned not to repeat the inaccurate story, accept the distorted painting or film, believe the erroneous teacher, or countenance the boorish or uninformed reporter.

Communicators have the responsibility to be correct, informed, incisive, and lucid. When they are successful, the audience finds new insight into

> The silence of the owl in flight—
>
> Survival in the southfacing glade—
>
> The protective flow of warm blood
> in the ears of a winter rabbit—
>
> The supportive recycling of the decomposer fungi—
>
> Celestial cues to an instinctive migration route.

They may forget the facts but be forever moved by the experience. They will give subliminal agreement to the value of wildlife, the value of nature.

Section C-3

Strategies for Generating and Maintaining Support for Wildlife

Summary prepared by Larry W. VanDruff,
Workshop Moderator

Workshop Participants

Jack W. Gramlich, *Director, Centers for Nature Education, Inc., Marcellus, NY*

Herbert E. Doig, *Assistant Commissioner for Fish, Wildlife and Marine Resources, NYS Department of Environmental Conservation, Albany, NY*

Wallace John, *Legislative Associate for Environmental Conservation, NYS Assembly, Albany, NY*

Wildlife professionals can develop top-notch programs, but without support from lay citizens, public interest groups, scientists, state and federal officials, legislatures, and executives, such efforts may be for naught. The field of wildlife science has access to an extensive body of scientific knowledge on the biology and ecology of organisms, populations, and ecosystems. Assuming that the structure and objectives of programs (research, management, or education) are based on sound biological science, as well as social and managerial sciences, how is support for programs developed? What constituencies should be courted? What base of fiscal and political support can be garnered for wildlife programs? How do wildlife professionals maintain and expand a base of support for evolving and dynamic programs?

This workshop reviewed the programs of a local, private, nonprofit environmental education center, a state natural resources agency, and a state legislative committee.

PRIVATE NONPROFIT ORGANIZATIONS

At the local level, environmental or wildlife programs may compete with free city, county, and state programs and area attractions such as parks, zoos, and museums. The burden of financial obligations to the private organization's payroll, property maintenance, and programmatic costs may quickly lead to debts that demoralize the staff and doom the program. Seeking sources of financial and moral support may require diligent efforts by all staff members.

Three strategies have been successful in overcoming a debilitating debt and increasing revenues for Centers for Nature Education (CNE). First, aggressively building membership and volunteer numbers has paid off for the program. Second, allowing volunteer members to become involved in development and maintenance of the 65-ha Baltimore Woods natural area and offering quality on-site and in-school programs have generated more interest in and stronger support for CNE's efforts. Third, the sale of 10,000 calendars, 6.3 t of birdseed, and wildlife habitat seedlings has supplemented revenues generated by presenting contracted environmental education programs for public schools. The CNE public school environmental programs, presented through a two-county Board of Cooperative Educational Services agency, reach 150 students per day for 150 days annually. Such contact with children has yielded very positive publicity for the CNE program and subsequently has increased support arising from family awareness. These three strategies (cultivating membership, developing Baltimore Woods and quality programs, and holding annual fund-raisers for active support) have worked in concert to make a debt-ridden operation solvent with a revitalized staff keen on the future. The 20-year anniversary theme—"Look at what we've done, think of what we can do"—reflects this optimism.

PUBLIC AGENCIES

State natural resource agencies must promote their programs and engender support from many sources to accomplish mandated wildlife-related missions. These sources include fiscal support, public support, governmental support, legal and legislative authority, staff and administrative support, research and professional support, and philosophical support. Key elements in gathering support include gaining the confidence of supporters, having credibility, informing and being informed, knowing audiences and seeking their participation, maintaining a positive perspective while downplaying conflicts, remaining flexible, and not overselling an approach that may need to be changed in the future. Obviously these elements are interrelated and must be carefully orchestrated by the successful program leader of a public wildlife agency.

Techniques that may lead to successfully generating and maintaining support vary with the issue, program, agency's philosophy, and administrator's personal style. Effective techniques usually include personal diplomacy, identification of key leaders, timely flow of information, controlled information release, audience or constituency involvement, recruitment of known supporters, and avoidance of flaunting successes, which denigrate others or belittle opponents.

Corporate support, given certain legal, political, and ethical limitations, may be on the horizon as an untapped source for state wildlife programs.

GOVERNMENTAL LEGISLATIVE BODIES

At the legislative level, programmatic support develops in an arena foreign to most wildlife professionals. It is absolutely necessary for anyone interested in wildlife to also become interested in politics because the very basis for management of wildlife is established in law. Because of disparate views and political affiliations and constituencies, the political process dealing with wildlife must be built around coalitions.

Individuals can act most effectively by keeping in close contact with local legislators and state committee chairpersons. The most effective contact is established by a sequence of telephone calls, followed by a letter, followed by a personal visit including an offer to supply additional information if requested. Communications should be kept simple and limited in length—a five-minute verbal contact and a two- to three-page letter with an offer of more should be sufficient.

To increase awareness and concern for fish and wildlife issues among elected officials, wildlife professionals and their supportive environmentalists must be organized; they must know what is happening at the legislative level, including bills in committee, read and comment on proposed bills, and then completely back the resultant bill. Proper information, correct timing, perseverance, accountability, credit, and recognition seem to be key elements in getting legislative and executive support for statutes, budgets, and new programs.

CONCLUSION

Gaining support for local private nonprofit organizations, public natural-resource agencies, or legislative efforts is a continuing task for wildlife professionals. The three panelists emphasized the value of commitment, credibility, contact, and continuity in all efforts. Another common thread is flexibility: flexibility in response to public needs, interests, even whims, and priorities as well as flexibility by the managing agency to creatively explore new approaches, liaisons, and program marketing.

Strategies and Techniques for Generating Support for Minnesota's Nongame Wildlife Checkoff

Carrol L. Henderson

In 1980 the Minnesota legislature established a nongame wildlife checkoff that allowed taxpayers to donate $1 or more to the Nongame Wildlife Fund on their state income tax and property tax forms. This technique is now the major source for funding state nongame wildlife programs. In tax year 1984, a nationwide total of $8.96 million was donated to this cause in 33 states.

The intensity and ingenuity necessary for successful checkoff promotion have generated some important peripheral benefits that can help natural resource and wildlife agencies. The primary benefit is learning how to generate and maintain support for wildlife conservation programs. Unfortunately, an inadequate amount of attention has been given to generating support by publics associated with fish and wildlife resources. This inattention can lead to an agency credibility gap and a lack of support for agency programs.

INTERELATIONS ESSENTIAL TO PROGRAM IMPLEMENTATION

The following nine-part sequence of interactions has been essential in the development and implementation of Minnesota's nongame wildlife program. It can readily be adapted to similar programs in other states.

1. Clearly State Goals and Objectives

The first step is to state program goals and objectives succinctly so that both the agency and its publics have a clear idea of where programs are going, why the publics should be concerned, and how success is to be measured. As an example, an agency might establish a goal, "to preserve the diversity and abundance of a state's nongame wildlife resource," and an objective, "to raise $500,000 per year to fund a state nongame wildlife program."

2. *Identify and Target the Publics*

There is no such thing as the general public, rather, many specific publics exist, each with its own special needs and interests, which need to be reached by different techniques. Examples of publics for a state nongame program include birdwatchers, media personnel, sportsmen, teachers, urban home owners, college professors, librarians, state revenue department personnel, youth groups, county extension agents, and civic groups.

3. *Understand the Learning Process Necessary to Achieve Desired Actions for Programs*

People can pass through six developmental steps on the way to commitment and action: (1) no awareness or concern, (2) awareness of a program/problem, (3) appreciation, (4) understanding, (5) concern, and (6) action. Although most people remain in the very early stages of commitment to programs, that situation can be improved by carrying out an active education program that presents a message to targeted publics and by working with the media—radio and television personnel—to achieve continuing positive program exposure.

4. *Identify Your Messages*

The next step is to develop brief and catchy messages to inform the public. These should be short messages that can be presented in a 30-second public service announcement or a seven-word billboard message, for example, "Help wildlife. Don't mow roadsides until August 1."

5. *Select the Proper Publicity Techniques*

Television. The most important form of advertising has been 30-second public service advertisements (psas) featuring well-known species that are benefiting from the checkoff (bald eagle, peregrine falcon, common loon). Television news coverage can be obtained by calling the news assignment desk whenever a special event or project activity is scheduled or by holding special media days to publicize major nongame projects like peregrine falcon releases.

Radio. Two important types of radio publicity have been used: (1) 30-second public service ads featuring wildlife species and their calls and (2) weekly interview programs on wildlife ecology and phenology.

Newspapers, Magazines, and Newsletters. Several other media techniques have been utilized, including a post-Christmas news release package, a camera-ready public service ad, photo news releases with attached cutlines (scripts), and news release feature stories and general program accomplishments.

Posters. Posters are a surprisingly important type of publicity. Each year 43 cm by 56 cm wildlife posters publicizing the checkoff have been distributed free of charge to tax preparers, libraries, banks, county courthouses, newspapers, and radio stations and to a mailing list of friends of the nongame program.

6. Rely on the Multiplier Effect

Welfare professionals should rely heavily on the multiplier effect by utilizing teachers and the media—primarily radio and television. The traditional approach of giving slide-talks to 20 people at a time will not generate adequate support for a statewide wildlife program.

7. Allow for Public Input

Effective communication is a two-way process. Public meetings that allow members of the public to express their opinions on program priorities and direction are essential.

8. Promote Citizen Volunteer Participation in Selected Program Activities

Support for state nongame programs can be significantly increased by providing opportunities for personal involvement by volunteer citizens. The key is to select volunteer activities that can be easily coordinated by mail or phone from a central office. When they regard nongame programs as their programs, citizens will fight and lobby for the programs when the legislative chips are down.

9. Provide Recognition and Feedback to Citizens

It is necessary to provide recognition to volunteers and information on program accomplishments and budgets to the public. This element is one of the most critical in the whole process and helps ensure long-term support and involvement.

SUMMARY

In summary, public support for a wildlife program can be established and maintained by developing a warm, continuing, open relationship with target publics. Let the program be their program. Let them know that the agency cares about their opinion and their support, and let them know where the agency is going. Using the general guidelines outlined in this paper, Minnesota's Nongame Wildlife Program has grown twenty-two-fold since 1977.

Section C-4

Using Habitat Evaluation Procedures to Establish Wildlife Values

Summary prepared by Robert T. Brooks,
Workshop Moderator, and Larry W. VanDruff

Workshop Participants

J. Hugh Palmer, *Game Biologist, Pennsylvania Game Commission, Millville, PA*

David L. Urich, *Wildlife Liaison Coordinator, Missouri Department of Conservation, Jefferson City, MO*

L. Jean O'Neil, *Waterways Experiment Station, U.S. Army Corps of Engineers, Vicksburg, MS*

Impact assessment, mitigation, land use planning, and wildlife management necessitate habitat evaluation. The need for a structured framework for quantifying the value of fish and wildlife resources, including habitats, became more obvious with the National Environmental Policy Act (NEPA) and subsequent state laws requiring a balancing of biotic values with economic interests. State and federal agencies have labored over a decade to develop evaluative procedures and models applicable to numerous locations and at various scales, from a local habitat to an ecosystem to an entire region. Three approaches to determining numerical assessments of wildlife values or assessing habitat replacement costs were reviewed in this workshop.

THE PENNSYLVANIA EXPERIENCE

Pennsylvania Modified 1980 Habitat Evaluation Procedure (PAM HEP) is an outgrowth of the U.S. Fish and Wildlife Service's 1980 HEP. The 1980 methodology was modified because it (1) was time demanding, (2) required complex data analysis, and (3) failed to address certain areas of concern significant to Pennsylvania conditions. PAM HEP is concerned with a biological assessment of habitat resources, and it does not address social or economic values. It was felt that working with economic assessments was outside the scope of most biological investigations.

The majority of PAM HEP methodologies parallel those of traditional HEP. Habitat evaluation employs a team approach. In Pennsylvania the team consists of selected members of the U.S. Fish and Wildlife Service, Pennsylvania Fish Commission, Pennsylvania Game Commission, and the applicant/action agency. Data are recorded and analyzed on a series of forms that may serve as a significant part of the final evaluation report. The methodology follows the habitat evaluation of specific wildlife species for representative habitats of the impact area. Habitat suitability index (HSI) selection and model development are probably the most critical steps in the overall procedure. Field data collection is based on habitat compartment examination rather than on sample point measurements. Evaluations are made in reference to three target years: the present one, that for the end of construction, and that for the end of mitigation. Mitigation plans are developed in part from habitat deficiencies noted during data collection and analysis. The PAM HEP procedure requires 50% to 75% less time yet yields results comparable to those from 1980 HEP.

THE MISSOURI EXPERIENCE

In Missouri, natural resource agencies have jointly developed and validated species models for use with the HEP system, which has led to a variety of HEP applications. Missouri uses HEP in four major natural resource arenas: (1) public land management planning, (2) assessment of farming and forage production assistance on private farmland, (3) supplements to attitude surveys, and (4) economic value determination. On public lands, 14 indicator species are used for simultaneous habitat assessment. With information, a manager can establish objectives, do simulation analyses of management alternatives, investigate trade-offs, and track costs of management chores. On private farmland, for example, trained Soil Conservation Service and Missouri Department of Conservation personnel assess the effects of technical assistance on bobwhite quail habitat. The process for this assessment has been formalized in the Wildlife Habitat Appraisal Guide (WHAG), an offshoot of the HEP system. By using WHAG, management recommendations for up to 12 species can be derived from evaluation of low-scoring habitat components. HEP has been used to supplement landowner attitude surveys of habitat quantity and quality. This information lends support to, or detracts from, subjective observations collected in attitude surveys. Landowners' perceptions of private land habitat quality differed from the actual values determined by HEP.

Finally, the HEP-HUEE (Human Use and Economic Evaluation) methodology has been used to investigate benefits of management actions for game species. Derived numbers can then be compared to costs to evaluate program efficiency. HEP applications provide only information. Cooperative efforts among concerned agencies are critical for the proper use of this information.

THE U.S. ARMY CORPS OF ENGINEERS EXPERIENCE

The U.S. Army Corps of Engineers is involved with many applications of habitat-based assessments. As noted, HEP, one of several available technologies, is the most developed and functions as an accounting system for tracking habitat units. Four major uses are suggested for habitat-based evaluations: impact assessment, land use planning, management, and information. Within each major use class, specific examples were discussed in the workshop. It was noted that in any single application, several uses can be made of the assessment results.

Finally, the advantages and disadvantages of habitat-based assessment were noted. On the plus side, quantification leads to increased objectivity; the methodology is practical and amenable to many varied uses; the system is computerized, contributing to ease of use; and the final product is well documented, which enhances its use. On the negative side, it is possible to bias the process, but the team approach generally guards against this happening. Many basic assumptions are involved in the evaluation process, especialiy in model construction and prediction of future conditions; however, good documentation lessens this concern. Also the quality of each habitat assessment varies but is improving because of continued training and expertise gained from each application.

CONCLUSION

Selection of the evaluation method to use should be based on the composition and resources of the agency or interagency team, study objectives, accuracy and the amount of detail desired, regional or local application, and products needed or expectations within the agency or beyond. Current systems of habitat and ecosystem evaluation in the U.S. are strongly influenced by the Fish and Wildlife Service's HEP model and its HSI elements. Characterizing and evaluating social and economic values of wildlife resources continue to present challenges—and more work is needed. But clearly, the utility and applicability of habitat evaluation procedures and models will increase as we refine commonly practiced methods to establish values of the wildlife resource.

List of Authors

James E. Applegate is a Professor of Wildlife Biology in the Department of Horticulture and Forestry, Cook College, Rutgers University, New Brunswick, NJ.

Joseph P. Bachant is an Environmental Coordinator with the Missouri Department of Conservation, Jefferson City, MO.

Jack H. Berryman is Executive Vice-President of the International Association of Fish and Wildlife Agencies, Washington, DC.

Richard C. Bishop is a Professor of Resource Economics in the Department of Agricultural Economics, University of Wisconsin, Madison, WI.

Robert T. Brooks is a Wildlife Biologist with the USDA Forest Service, Amherst, MA.

Perry J. Brown is a Professor of Outdoor Recreation and Head of the Department of Resource Recreation Management, Oregon State University, Corvallis, OR.

Tommy L. Brown is a Senior Research Associate in the Department of Natural Resources, Cornell University, Ithaca, NY.

Carlo R. Brunori is Chief of Wildlife Technical Services, Maryland Forest Park and Wildlife Service, Annapolis, MD.

J. Baird Callicott is a Professor of Philosophy and Natural Resources in the Department of Philosophy, University of Wisconsin, Stevens Point, WI.

Robert E. Chambers is a Professor of Wildlife Management, SUNY–College of Environmental Science and Forestry, Syracuse, NY, and Past-President of the New York Chapter—The Wildlife Society.

J. John Charbonneau is Project Manager for Budget Execution, Division of Program Analysis, Fish and Wildlife Service, U.S. Department of the Interior, Washington, DC.

Gary T. Christoff is an Environmental Coordinator with the Missouri Department of Conservation, Jefferson City, MO.

Donald J. Cocheba is Professor and Chairman of the Department of Economics, Central Washington University, Ellensburg, WA.

Robert K. Davis is an Economist with the Division of Wildlife, Bureau of Land Management, U.S. Department of the Interior, Washington, DC.

Daniel J. Decker is a Senior Extension Associate with the Department of Natural Resources, Cornell University, Ithaca, NY.

William H. Dieffenbach is an Environmental Services Supervisor with the Missouri Department of Conservation, Jefferson City, MO.

Herbert E. Doig is Assistant Commissioner for Fish, Wildlife and Marine Resources with the New York State Department of Environmental Conservation, Albany, NY.

B. L. Driver is a Research Forester with the Rocky Mountain Forestland Range Experiment Station, USDA Forest Service, Fort Collins, CO.

James R. Fazio is Associate Dean of the College of Forestry, Wildlife and Range Sciences, University of Idaho, Moscow, ID.

Gary R. Goff is an Extension Associate in the Department of Natural Resources, Cornell University, Ithaca, NY.

Dwight E. Guynn is a Wildlife Specialist with the Texas Agricultural Extension Service of the Texas A&M University System, Uvalde, TX.

Jay D. Hair is Executive Vice-President of The Wildlife Federation, Washington, DC.

John C. Hendee is Professor and Dean of the College of Forestry, Wildlife and Range Sciences, University of Idaho, Moscow, ID, and Director of the Idaho Forest Wildlife Range Experiment Station, Moscow, ID.

Carrol L. Henderson is a Nongame Wildlife Supervisor in the Department of Natural Resources, St. Paul, MN.

Robert E. Henshaw is an Environmental Management Specialist with the New York State Department of Environmental Conservation, Albany, NY.

Tommy C. Hines is Supervisor of the Wildlife Research Laboratory, Florida Game and Fresh Water Fish Commission, Gainesville, FL.

Stephen R. Kellert is an Associate Professor of Forestry and Environmental Studies at the Yale School of Forestry and Environmental Studies, Yale University, New Haven, CT.

Edward E. Langenau, Jr., is Big Game Supervisor in the Wildlife Division of the Michigan Department of Natural Resources, Lansing, MI.

Diane Lim is a Research Assistant in the Department of Economics, University of Virginia, Charlottesville, VA.

Lynn G. Llewellyn is Assistant Division Chief of Program Plans, Fish and Wildlife Service, U.S. Department of the Interior, Washington, DC.

James R. Lyons is Director of Resource Policy, Society of American Foresters, Bethesda, MD.

Michael J. Manfredo is an Assistant Professor in the Department of Resource Recreation Management, Oregon State University, Corvallis, OR.

William R. Mangun is Project Manager for Policy Analysis and National Surveys, Division of Program Plans, Fish and Wildlife Service, U.S. Department of the Interior, Washington, DC.

James H. McDivitt is an Economist on the Policy Analysis Staff of the USDA Forest Service, Washington, DC.

James E. Miller is Program Leader of the Natural Resources and Rural Development Unit, USDA–Extension Service, Washington, DC.

H. Franklin Percival is Assistant Leader (Wildlife) with the Florida Cooperative Fish and Wildlife Research Unit, University of Florida, Gainesville, FL.

Tony J. Peterle is a Professor of Zoology in the Department of Zoology, Ohio State University, Columbus, OH.

Joseph M. Petulla is Director of the Environmental Management Program, University of San Francisco, CA.

R. Ben Peyton is an Associate Professor of Human Dimensions in the Department of Fisheries and Wildlife, Michigan State University, East Lansing, MI.

Gerri A. Pomerantz is a Research Associate in the Department of Natural Resources, Cornell University, Ithaca, NY.

Holmes Rolston III is a Professor of Philosophy in the Department of Philosophy, Colorado State University, Fort Collins, CO.

William W. Shaw is an Associate Professor of Wildlife Ecology and Chairman of the Wildlife Department, School of Renewable Natural Resources, University of Arizona, Tucson, AZ.

Ross "Skip" Shelton is Director of the W. E. Walker Wildlife Conservation Foundation, Starkville, MS.

Steven L. Sheriff is a Wildlife Biometrician with the Missouri Department of Conservation, Columbia, MO.

Don W. Steinbach is Project Group Supervisor for Wildlife and Fisheries with the Texas Agricultural Extension Service of the Texas A&M University System, College Station, TX.

Harold W. Steinhoff is Professor Emeritus of Wildlife Biology, Colorado State University, Fort Collins, CO, and President of the Four Corners Research Institute, Durango, CO.

Norman P. Stucky is an Environmental Coordinator with the Missouri Department of Conservation, Jefferson City, MO.

Lee M. Talbot is a Fellow of the East-West–Environmental Policy Institute, East-West Center, Honolulu, HI, and Fellow of the World Resources Institute, Washington, DC.

Larry W. VanDruff is a Professor of Wildlife Biology at SUNY–College of Environmental Science and Forestry, Syracuse, NY.

Edwin A. Verburg is Assistant Director, Office of Planning and Budget, Fish and Wildlife Service, U.S. Department of the Interior, Washington, DC.

Dale A. Wade is an Extension Wildlife Specialist with the Texas Agricultural Extension Service of the Texas A&M University System, San Angelo, TX.

Richard G. Walsh is a Professor in the Department of Agricultural and Resource Economics, Colorado State University, Fort Collins, CO.

David E. Wesley is Director MARSH Programs at Ducks Unlimited, Inc., Long Grove, IL.

Daniel J. Witter is a Resources Planner with the Missouri Department of Conservation, Jefferson City, MO.

Michael D. Zagata is Director–Environmental and Safety at Tenneco Oil, Houston, TX.

Index